I0729657

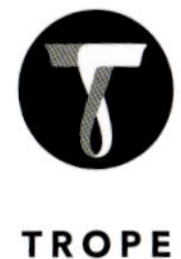

TROPE

ABOVE & ACROSS

CHICAGO

EDITED BY

SAM LANDERS

MICHELLE FITZGERALD

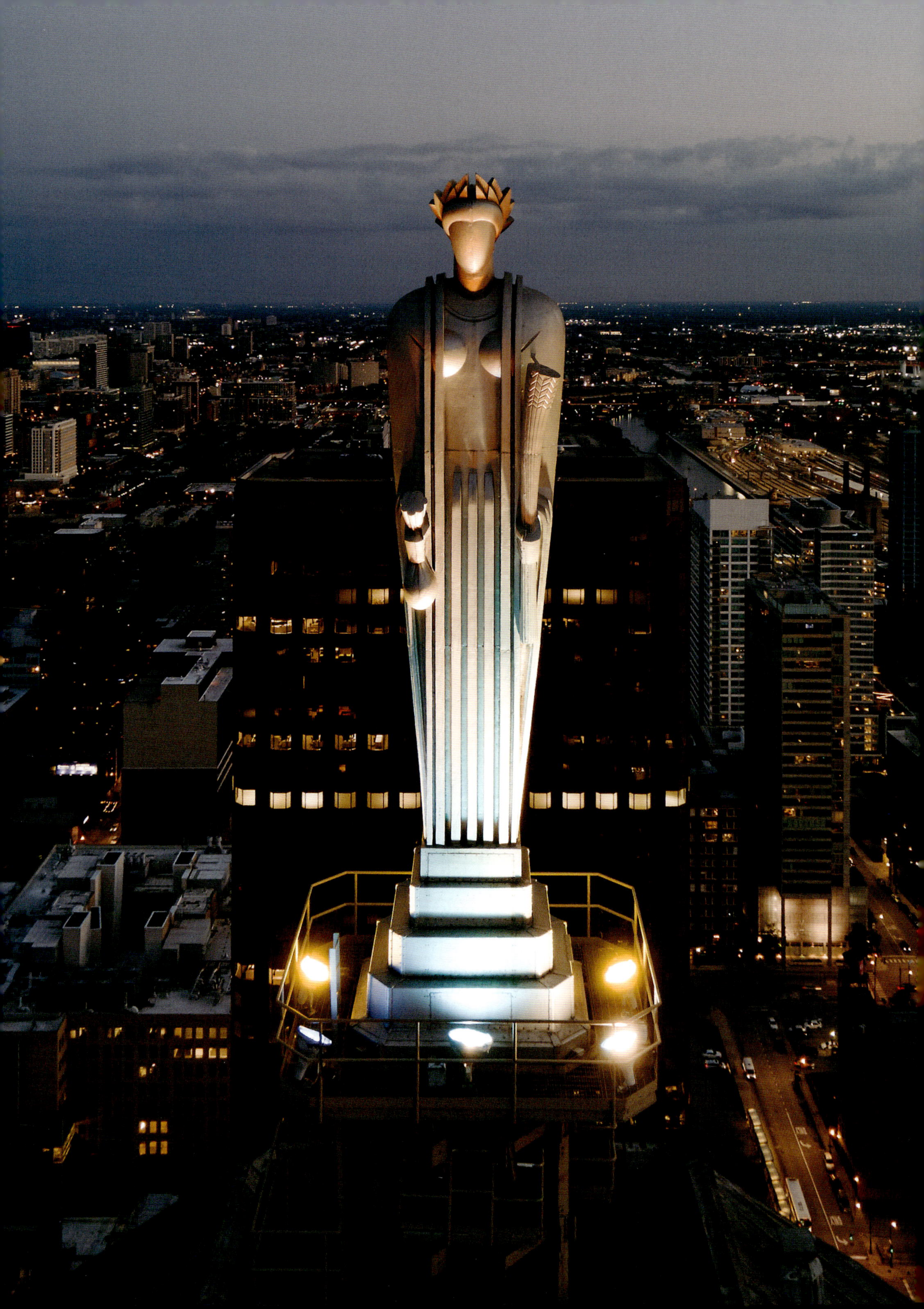

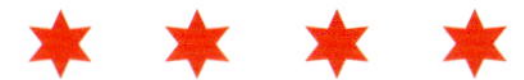

PHOTOGRAPHS BY

ADAM PEARSON
ALBERTO SANTIAGO
ALEX SHEYN
COCU LIU
DANIEL MORENO
DANIEL SCHINDLER
DAVID SOWA
DOMINIKA BRZYKCY
JASON LUMSDEN
KWE BENTUM
LICHAO LIU
MAX LEITNER
NICK CRAWFORD
SONJA WEISS
TERRY MADAY

FOREWORD BY

ADAM RUBIN

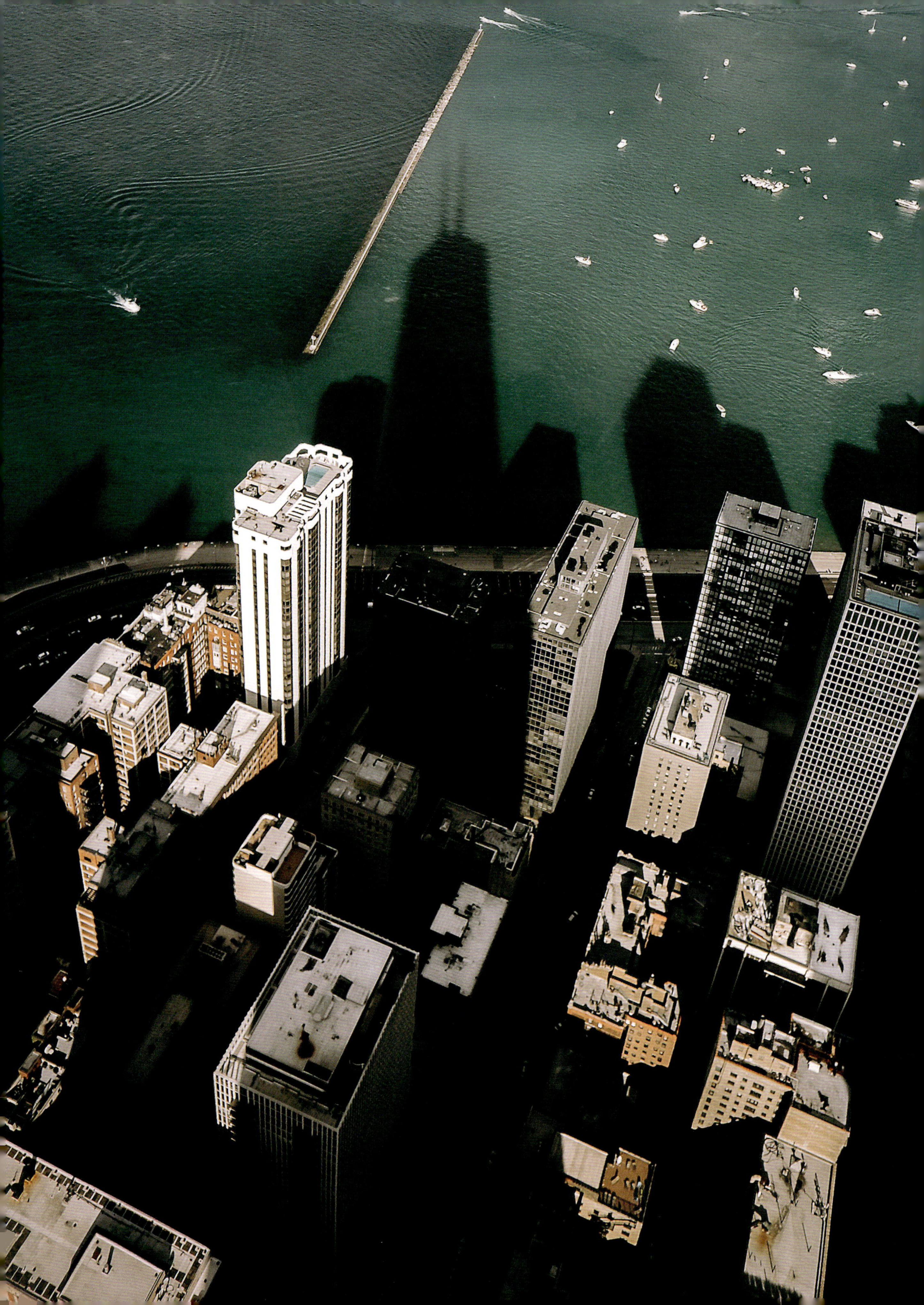

"Eventually, I think Chicago will be the most beautiful great city left in the world."
—Frank Lloyd Wright

Above & Across Chicago is a curated collection of aerial photographs of Chicago from 15 independent photographers.

The birthplace of the modern skyscraper, Chicago is known for its innovative and diverse architecture, iconic shoreline, unpredictable weather, and natural scenery. The images featured in *Above & Across Chicago* represent a contemporary view of the city. Photographed in all weather conditions, from the summer concerts in Grant Park to the serene winter of ice-clad Lake Michigan, each image captures a snapshot of the city's multifaceted character.

Chicago is a city rooted in history, yet constantly progressing. The photographs in this collection, taken from helicopters, from observation decks and atop buildings, and with the use of drones, capture the juxtaposition of time — presenting Chicago from fresh perspectives. From Lincoln Park and Buckingham Fountain to Willis Tower and the St. Regis, Chicago's skyline is both iconic and ever-changing, creating an emblem of Chicago's identity that mirrors the city's ceaseless evolution.

Let *Above & Across Chicago* transport you to our city and experience the breathtaking beauty of Chicago — from above & across.

Sam Landers & Michelle Fitzgerald
Editors

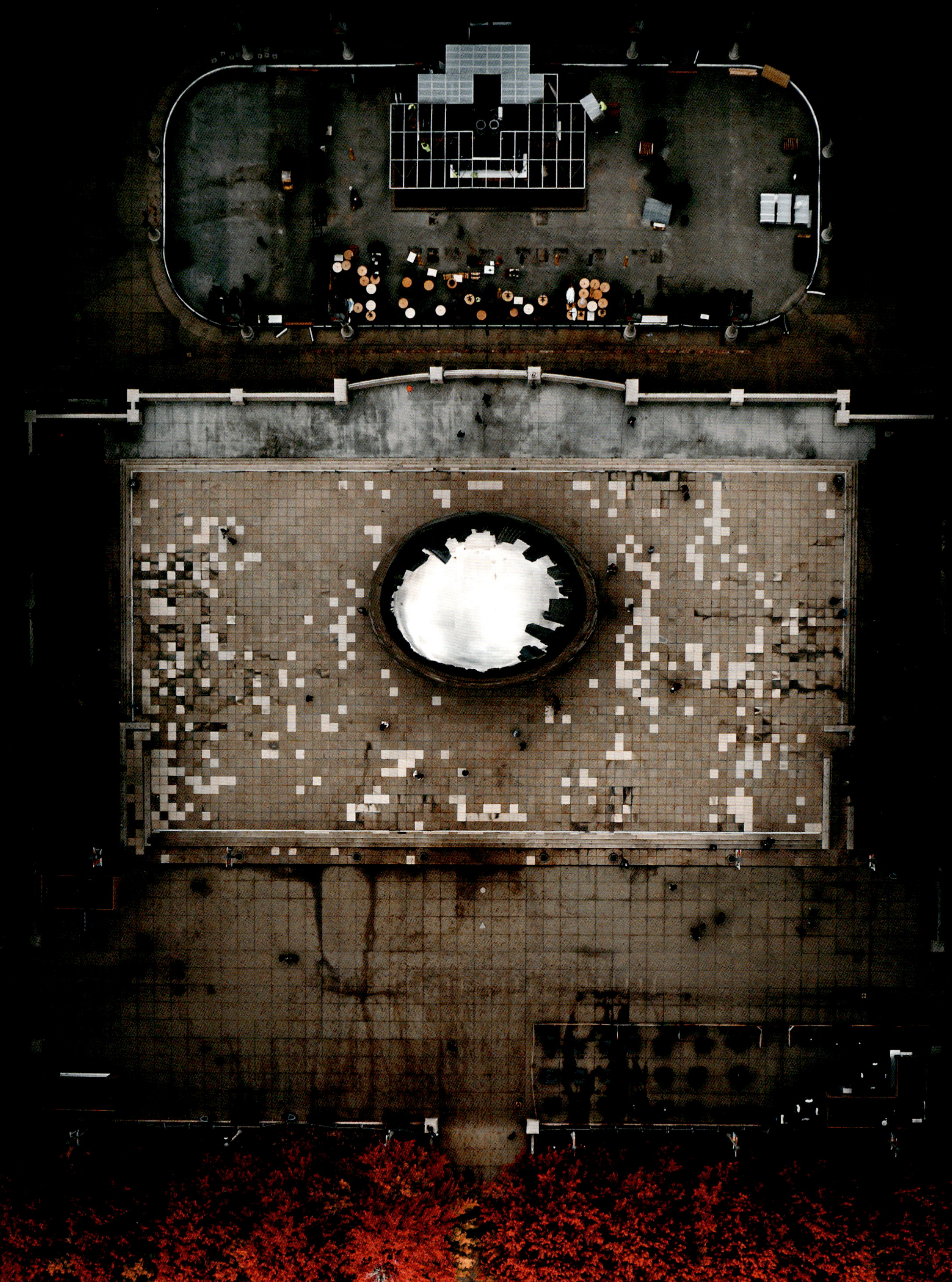

"I warn you, Jedediah, you're not gonna like it in Chicago. The wind comes howling in off the lake and gosh only knows if they ever heard of Lobster Newburg."
—Charles Foster Kane to Jedediah Leland, Citizen Kane (1941)

I didn't start out as a Chicagoan. My first glimpse of the city wasn't through one of the oval windows of old Prentice Hospital's maternity ward, and I harbor no childhood memories sitting in the upper deck at Wrigley Field, staring out at the skyline just beyond the Friendly Confines. Nor did I grow up in one of those sprawling suburbs, gazing from dad's station wagon at that distant cluster of skyscrapers down the highway, like some craggy range thrust up through the flats by a clash of tectonic plates.

Nothing so romantic. I first saw Chicago in my early 20s, my nose pressed against the window of a 737 circling over Lake Michigan on our descent to the tarmac. And like many travelers to Chicago, I carried some baggage with me. Two large bags, in fact: the first from Los Angeles, my hometown; and the second from New York, where I'd recently lived as a college student. I didn't arrive with any particular bias toward the place, but I was undoubtedly an outsider, looking in on a storied midwestern city I'd heard plenty about but had never before visited. True, this downtown wasn't set against the picturesque backdrop of the purple and green San Gabriel Mountains. And the arrangement of the Loop's high-rises was considerably more mannered than the chaotic shock-and-awe of Manhattan's financial district. However, there was something about the gestalt of it all that made it clear the "City of Architecture" moniker was both true and well-earned amidst heavy competition.

Before that first trip, my image of the town had largely been based on what I'd seen in movies.

Chicago on film is always coded as "Real," earthier than the anxious, affected East Coast, more grounded than the ecstatic, eclectic West. In one of my favorite exchanges from *Citizen Kane* (not a proper Chicago flick but try and follow me here), Orson Welles as the eponymous newspaper tycoon begrudgingly accepts that his business partner, Joseph Cotton as Jedediah, is leaving the Big Apple for a new gig in the Second City. Kane, in turn, reduces Chicago to nothing more than an icy tundra populated by Philistines oblivious to the pleasures of haute cuisine. The insult lands, but Kane's contempt unintentionally plays as a back-handed compliment. Instead, Chicago comes across as hardy and unpretentious—in many ways, a healthier alternative to New York—and no one would argue that Cotton doesn't make the right call to get out of town. It would be a lie to say that this was the cinematic moment that inspired my own move to the Midwest, but I did come to appreciate the joke more after a couple rounds of Chicago winters.

Of course, by the time I relocated here, Chicago looked a bit different than when Kane was in wide release. That first generation of late 19th century commercial skyscrapers had changed the form and function of the American downtown but no longer defined urban verticality in a new century where 100-story-plus towers proliferate. Those ancient totems with bold and exotic names like Monadnock, Marquette, Reliance, even Manhattan (cheeky) still contribute to the city's historic character, but only up to about 200 feet above the sidewalk. As subsequent waves of development overtook the downtown in the second half of the 20th century, increasingly taller buildings began to break through the cloud cover, erected by visionary architects, clever structural engineers, and countless other laborers whose names never made the history books. According to its official motto, Chicago was an *urbs in horto*, but it was equally a city in the heavens – a vertical metropolis that begged to be experienced from the vantage of an observation deck.

Like Welles's visionary film, the contemporary Chicago-built environment is both artistically and technically astonishing, full of dramatic narratives told from divergent perspectives and never relayed in linear order. Mid-century monoliths like the Hancock Center and Sears Tower (Willis Tower, if you must) command our highest attention, but share a crowded stage with Mies Van der Rohe's carefully proportioned International Style boxes, breezy 1980s icons like the Smurfit-Stone Building, and Bertrand Goldberg's scalloped concrete Marina City. More recent developments have added new elements and color to the story, most noticeably the St. Regis Chicago by Studio Gang – the tallest structure in the world (thus far) designed by a woman-led firm.

But what good is a tower when you're just looking up from the ground floor? It's much more exciting to take to the skies to see just how all these disparate pieces of the city fit together. It's a marvelous thing to cruise down the Chicago River on a warm summer day, surrounded by a canyon of prestige buildings carefully sited along the banks like an oversized sculpture garden. But it's equally exciting to look down those long expanses of Chicago avenues like Archer, Milwaukee, Ogden and Lincoln, all diagonal slices against the street grid, forcing developers of yore to construct flatiron buildings to accommodate their narrow corner lots. One can begin to appreciate such grandeur from street level, but from a slightly higher elevation, these streets reveal themselves as what they originally were: indigenous footpaths crisscrossing the region.

To the photographers who piloted drones, co-opted helicopters, and scaled the city's tallest structures to capture the breathtaking images you find in this book: your patience, fortitude, and apparent lack of vertigo are an inspiration. Chicago is one of those cities that cleans up well when it's time to strike a pose, regardless of whatever weather pattern happens to be enveloping us on any particular day. But no matter how photogenic the city is, the talent required to not only capture a strong image but to imbue that image with meaning and gravitas is substantial. This collection is Chicago as it begs to be seen: powerful, confident, and loved by its denizens.

I'm glad to have adopted Chicago as my own, and in turn, I'm thankful that the city has welcomed me into its embrace, which is warm despite the lake effect. It's a fascinating place from the inside, but there's nothing quite like that first look down into the great urban fish tank.

Just don't go asking for Lobster Newburg – you aren't going to find it here.

Adam Rubin
Sr. Director of Content & Interpretation,
Chicago Architecture Center
Commissioner on Chicago Landmarks

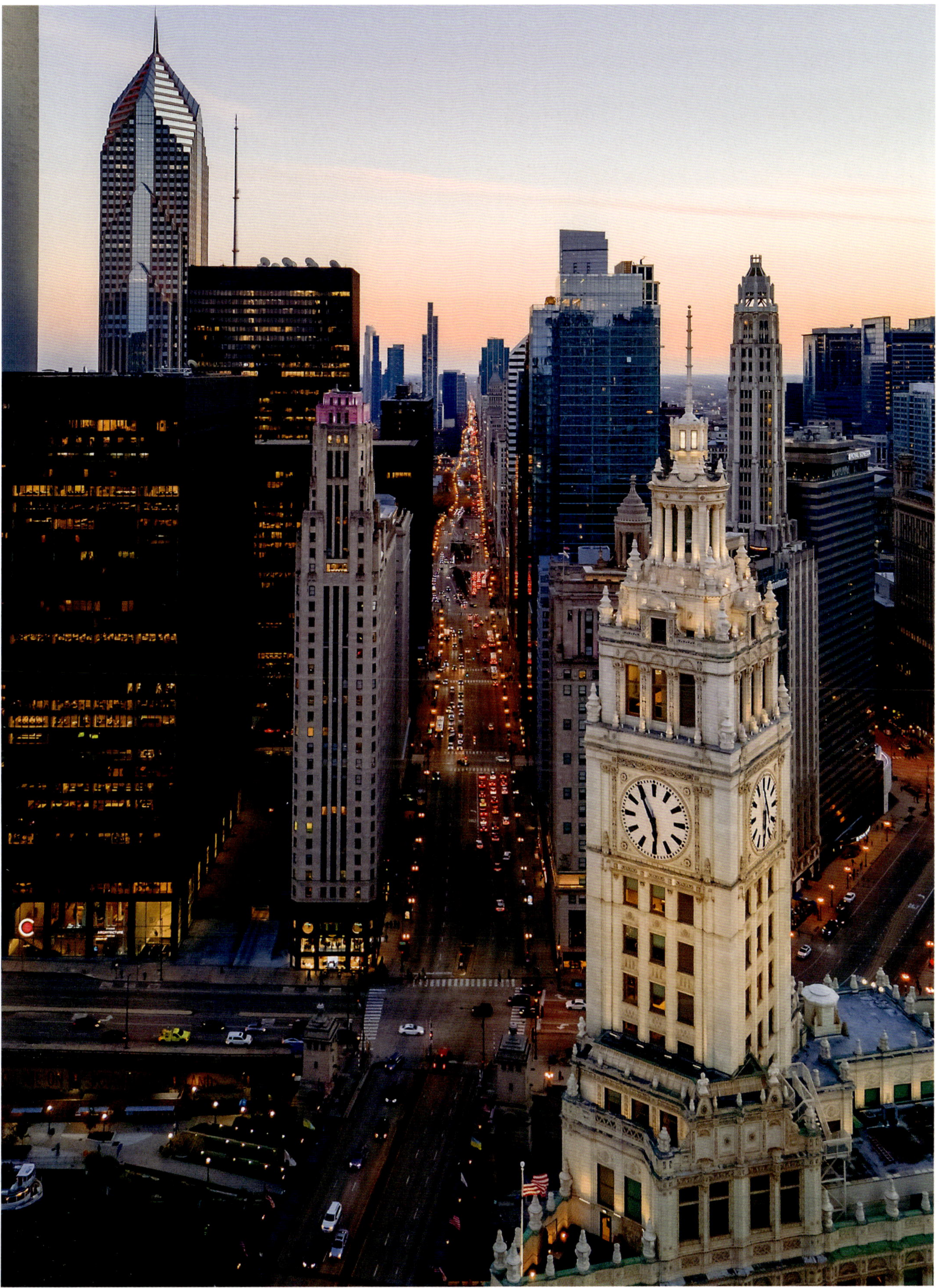

Birth of the Skyscraper ★ In the tumultuous aftermath of the Great Chicago Fire of 1871, a city lay in ruins. One of the most catastrophic events in American history, it destroyed 17,450 buildings covering almost 3.5 square miles. Roughly one-third of the city was destroyed, but from the ashes emerged a profound opportunity for transformation. Devastating as it was, this historic fire became the catalyst that propelled Chicago into a new era of architectural innovation. ★ Amidst the rubble, architects and city planners seized the opportunity to reimagine Chicago. Using modern materials and construction techniques, the skyscraper was born as architects sought to maximize space and create more efficient and taller structures. ★ Chicago's Home Insurance Building, with its innovative use of a steel frame, is often regarded as the world's first skyscraper, completed in 1885. This revolutionary approach incorporated a metal skeleton that bore the weight of the building, allowing for the construction of taller and more robust structures, and paved the way for other architects to experiment with height and design. ★ Louis Sullivan, a visionary of his time, embraced the skyscraper as a canvas for artistic expression. His mantra, "form follows function," became the guiding principle for architects looking to marry practicality with aesthetics. Sullivan's masterpiece, the Carson, Pirie, Scott and Company Building at 1 South State Street, showcased the artistic potential of skyscraper design, emphasizing both functionality and elegance. ★ Although the Home Insurance Building was demolished in 1931, its legacy endures in Chicago's ever-evolving skyline. Modern giants like Willis Tower, John Hancock Center, Aqua, and Aon Center stand tall, reshaping the city's profile from every vantage point. Each architectural wonder pays homage to Chicago's culture of innovation, a testament to how a city can rise, quite literally, from the ashes of adversity.

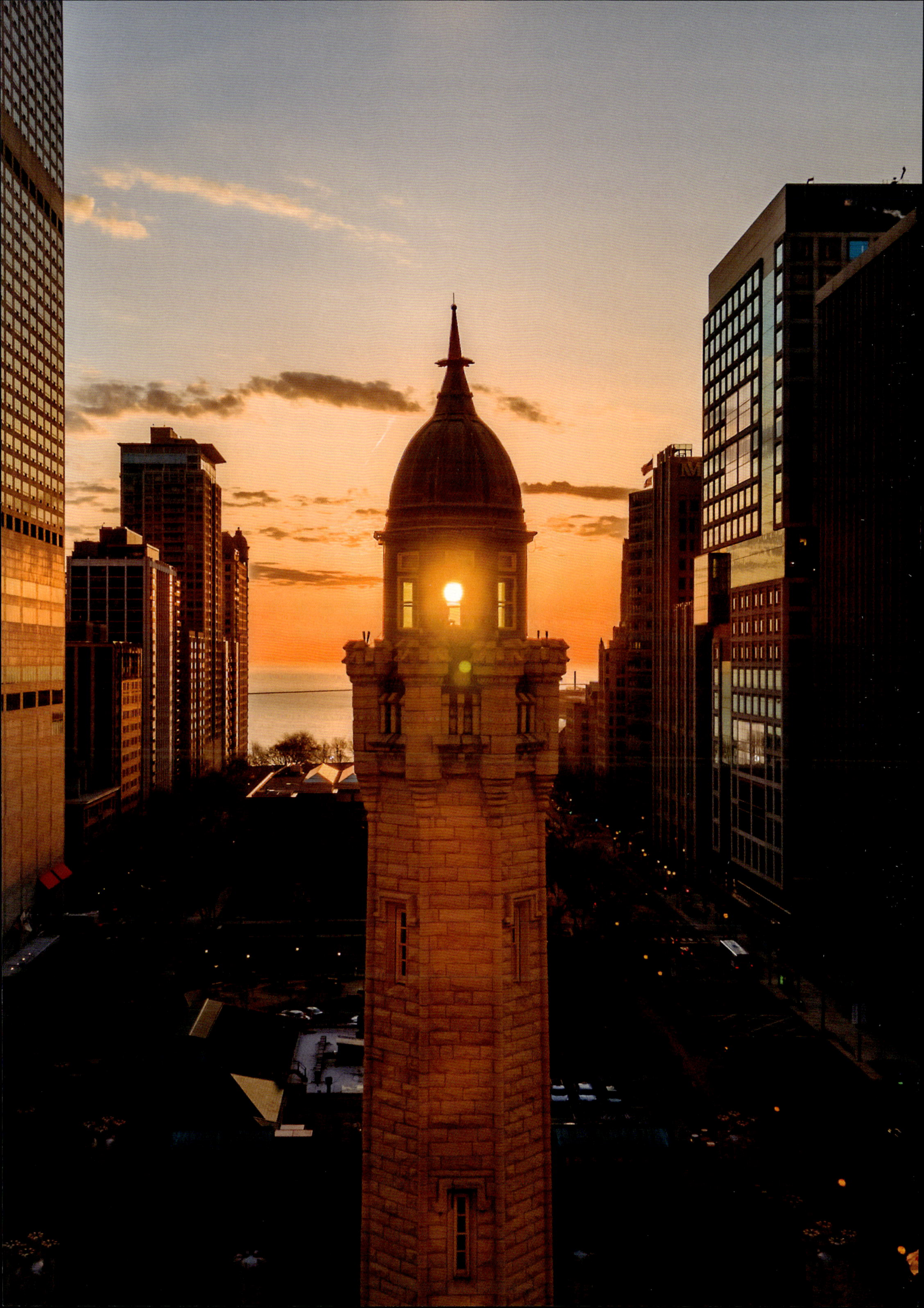

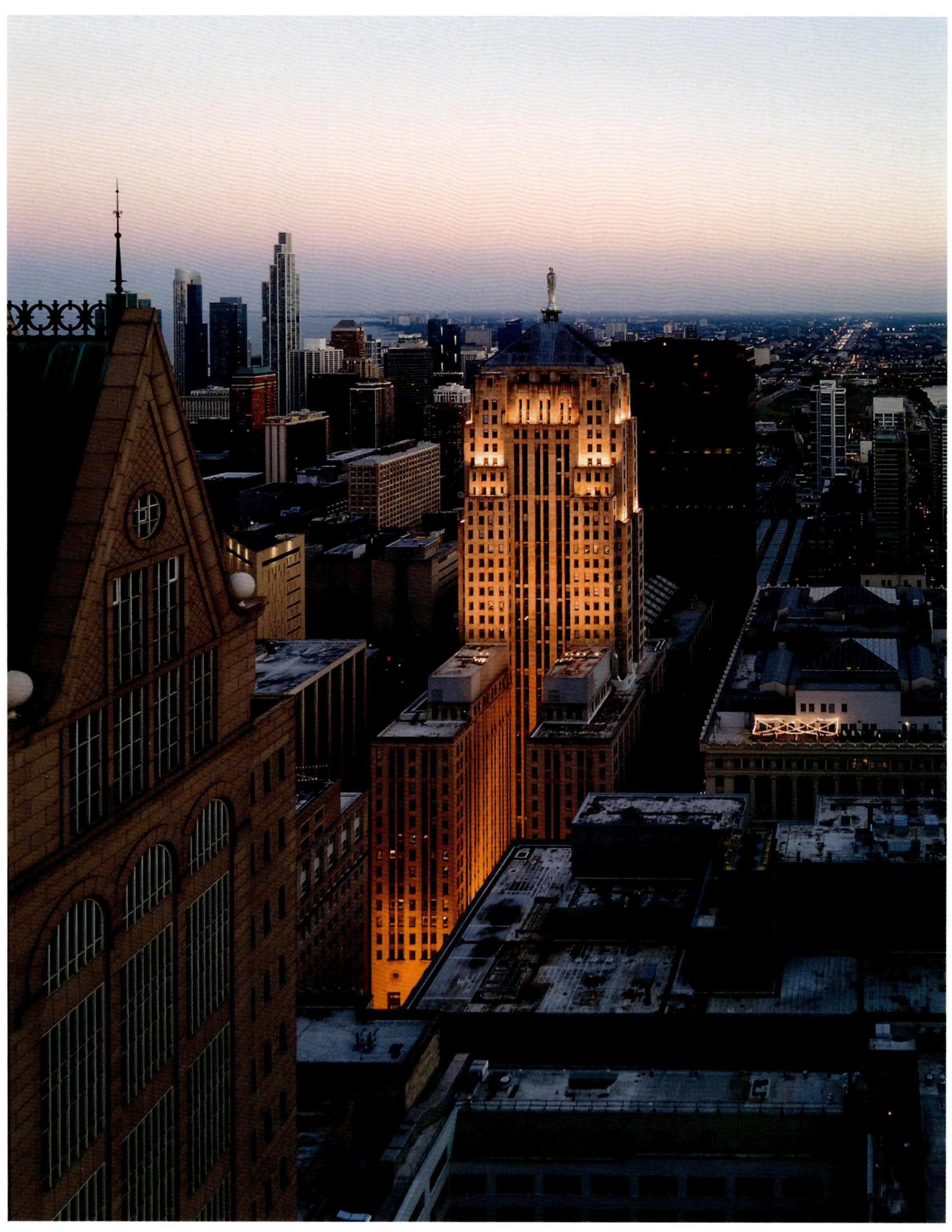

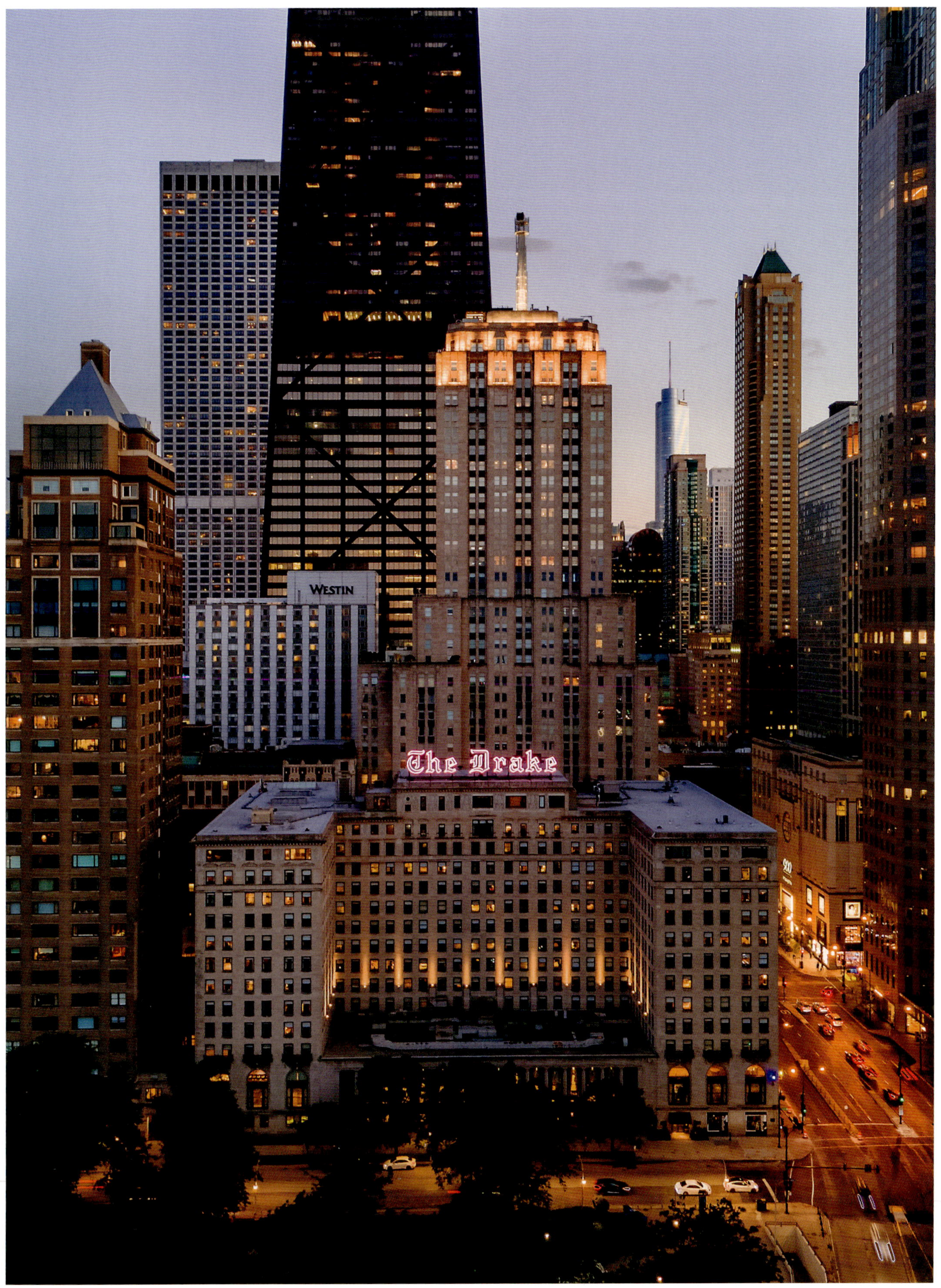
WESTIN
The Drake

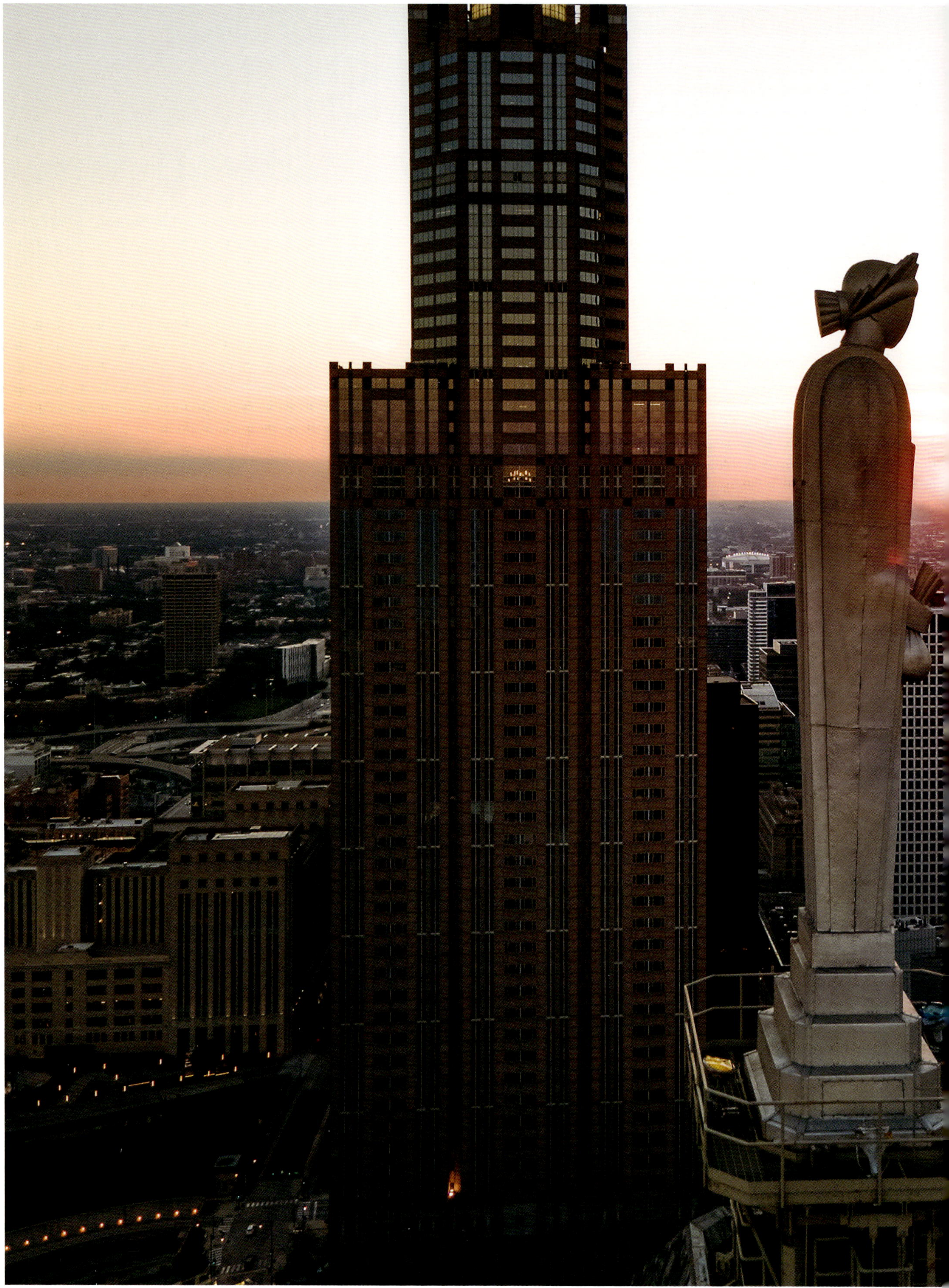

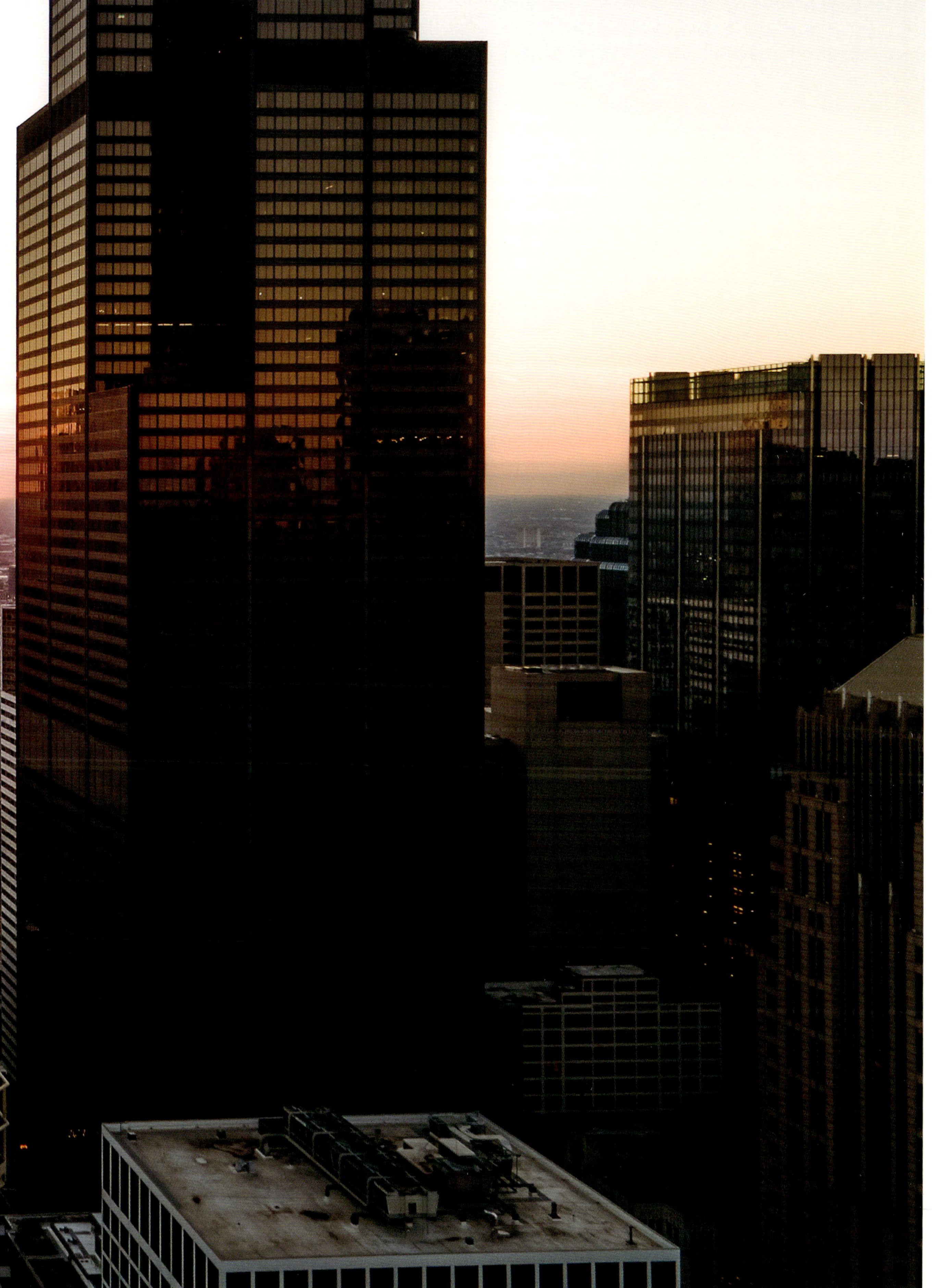

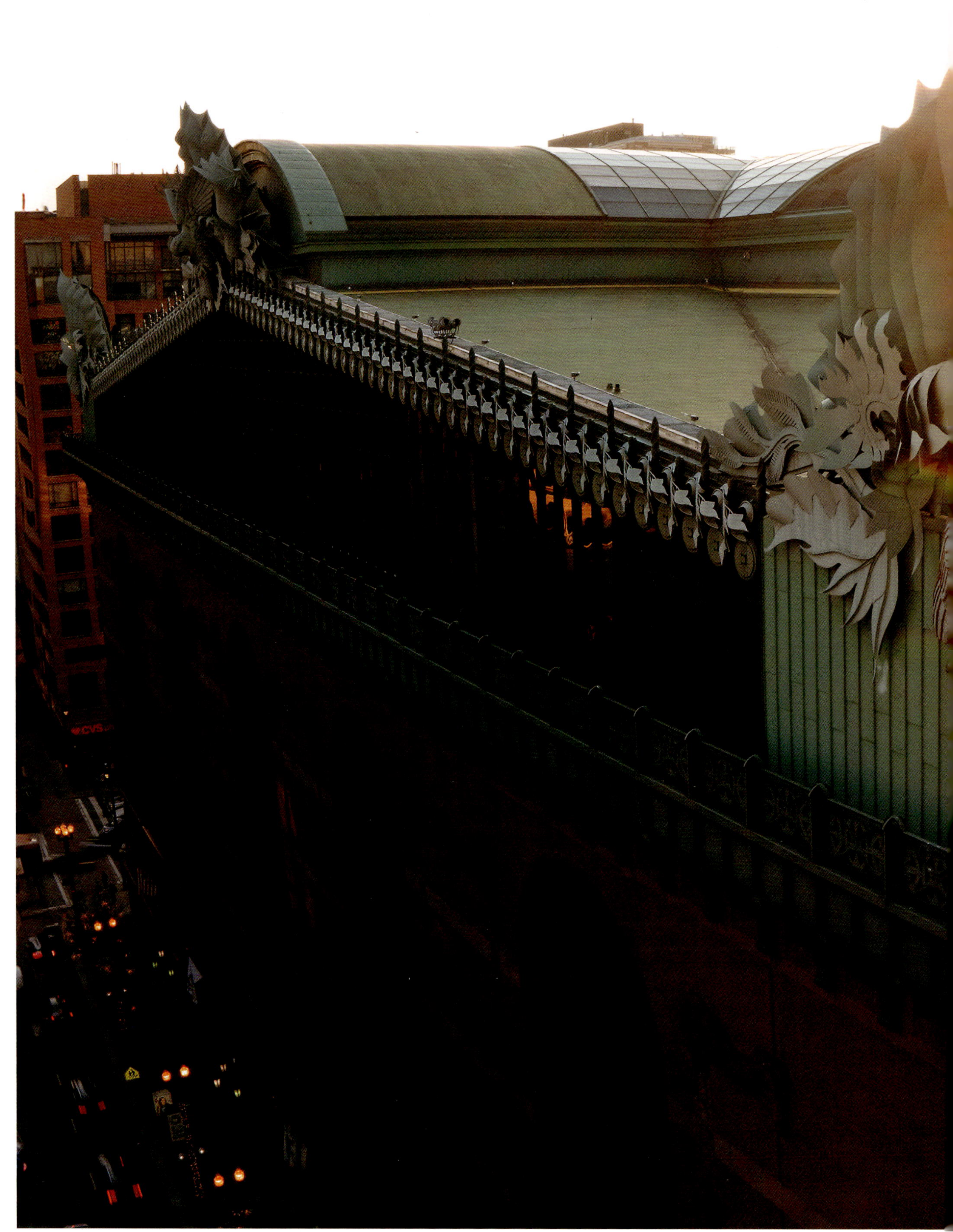

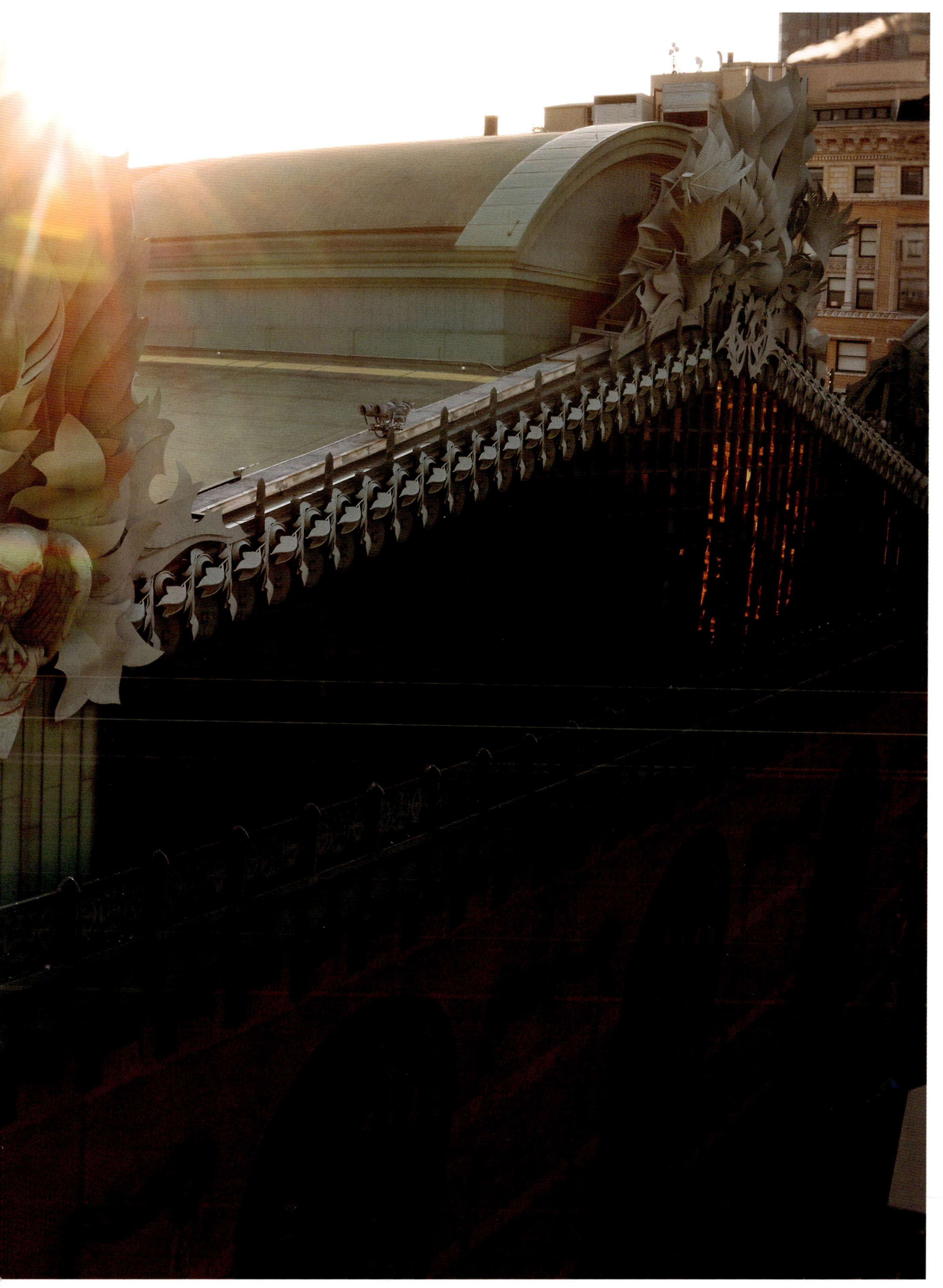

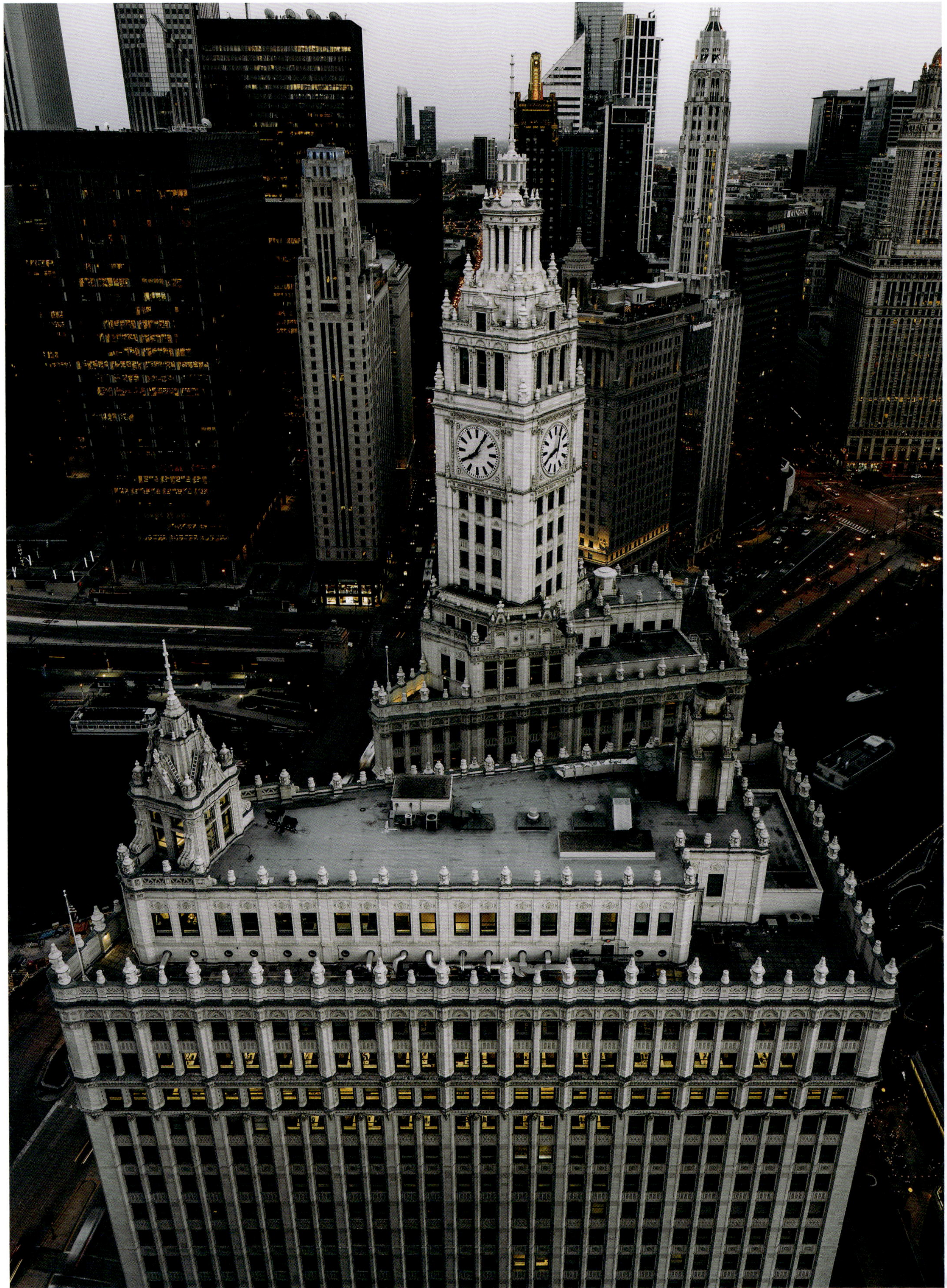

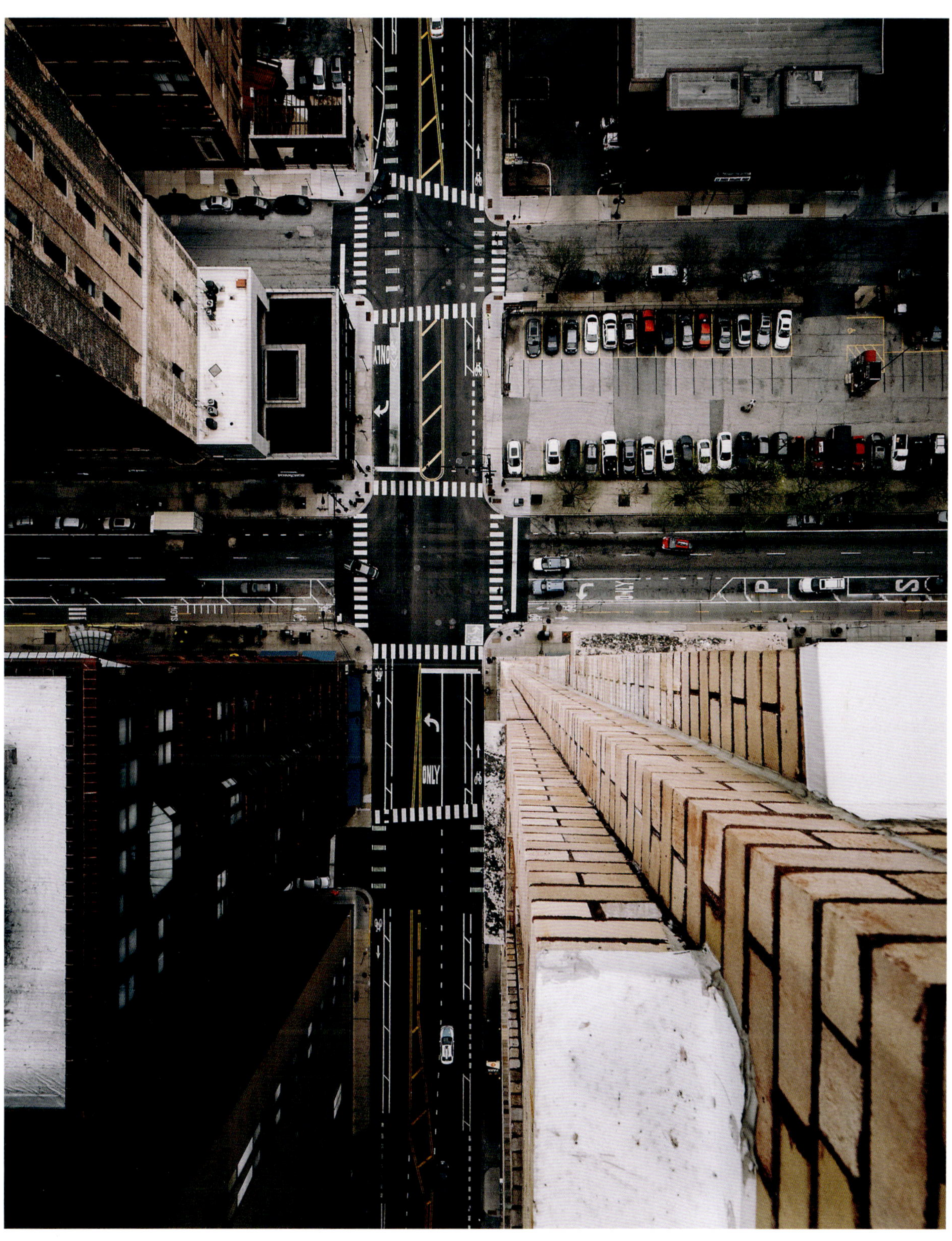

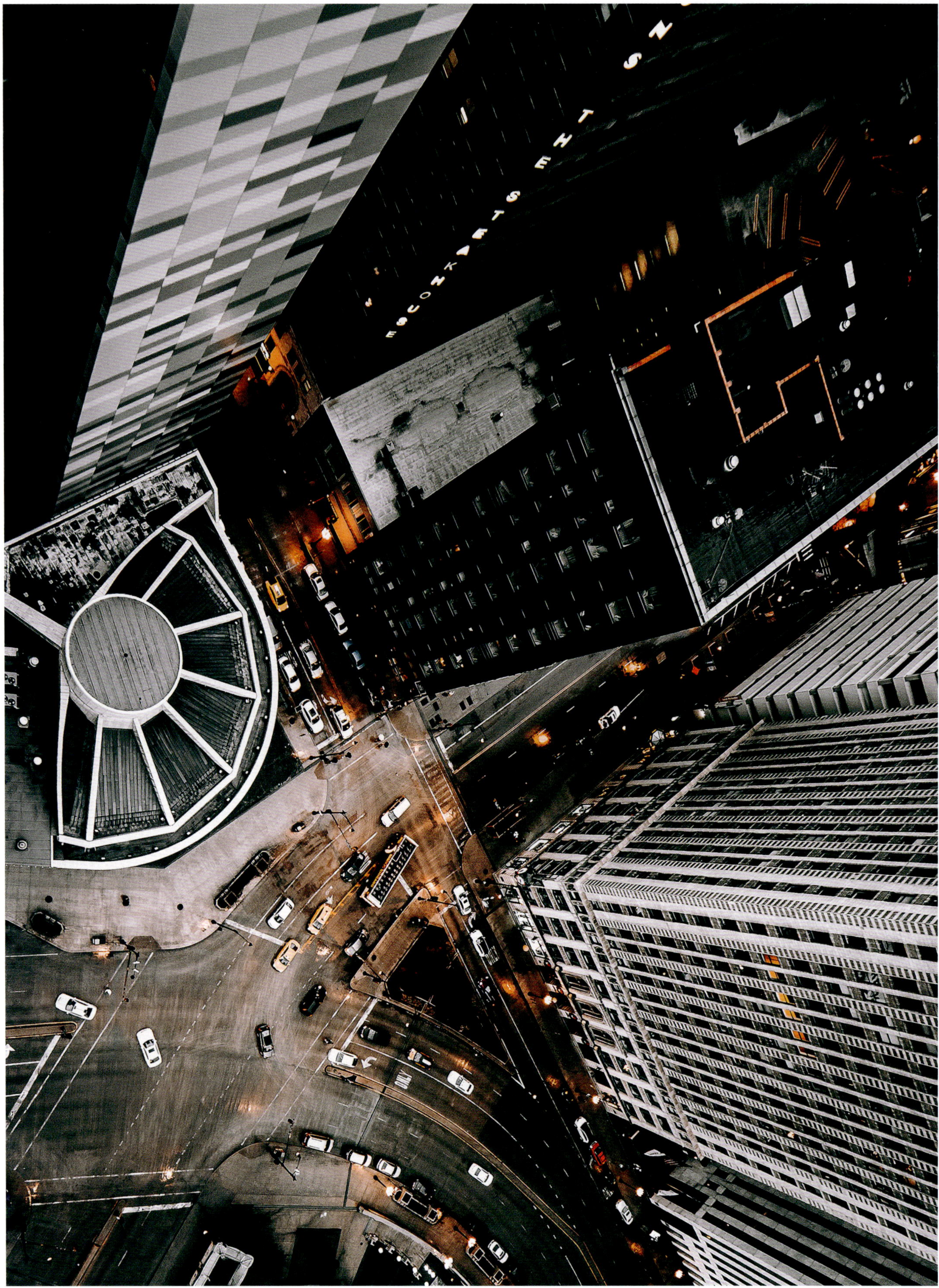

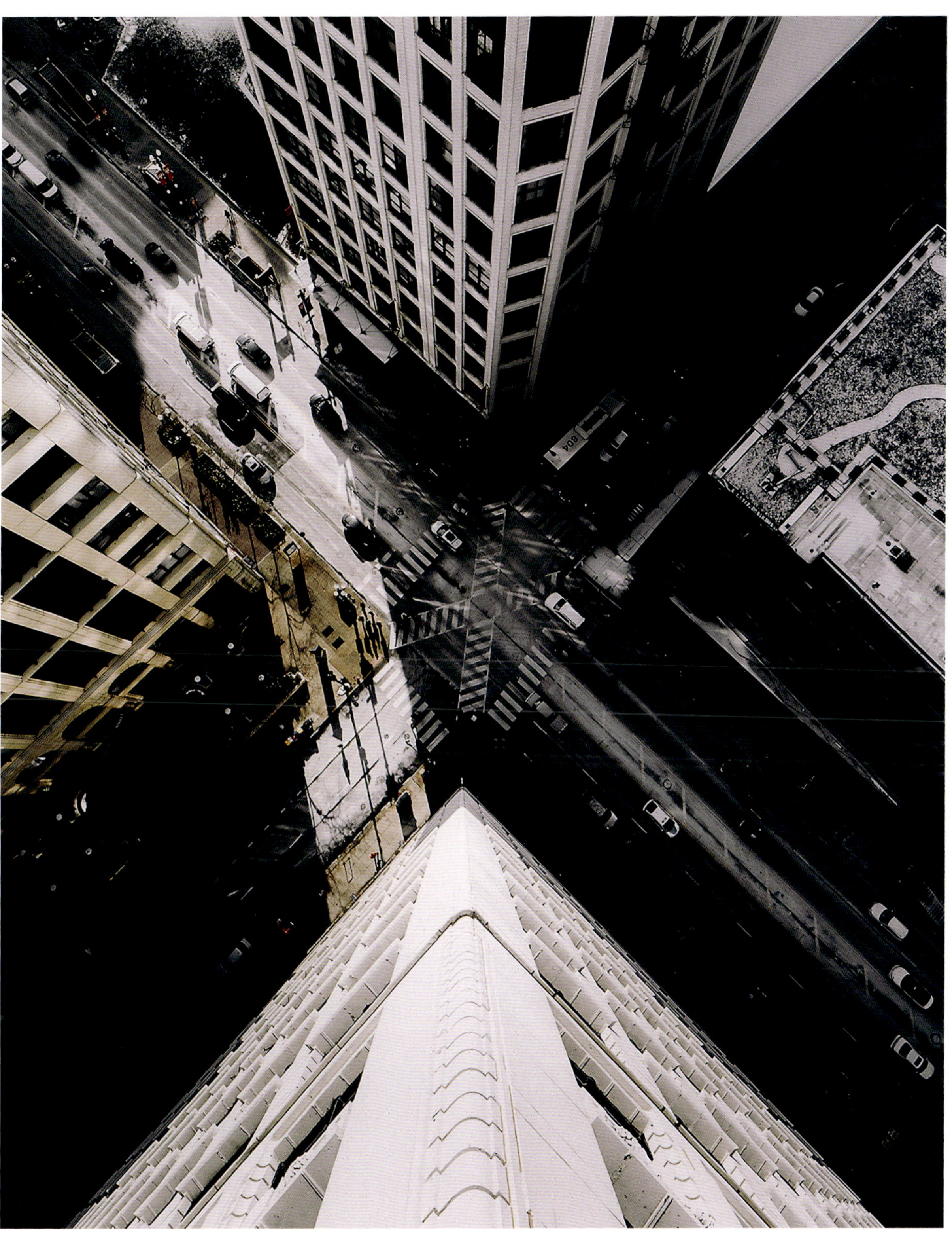

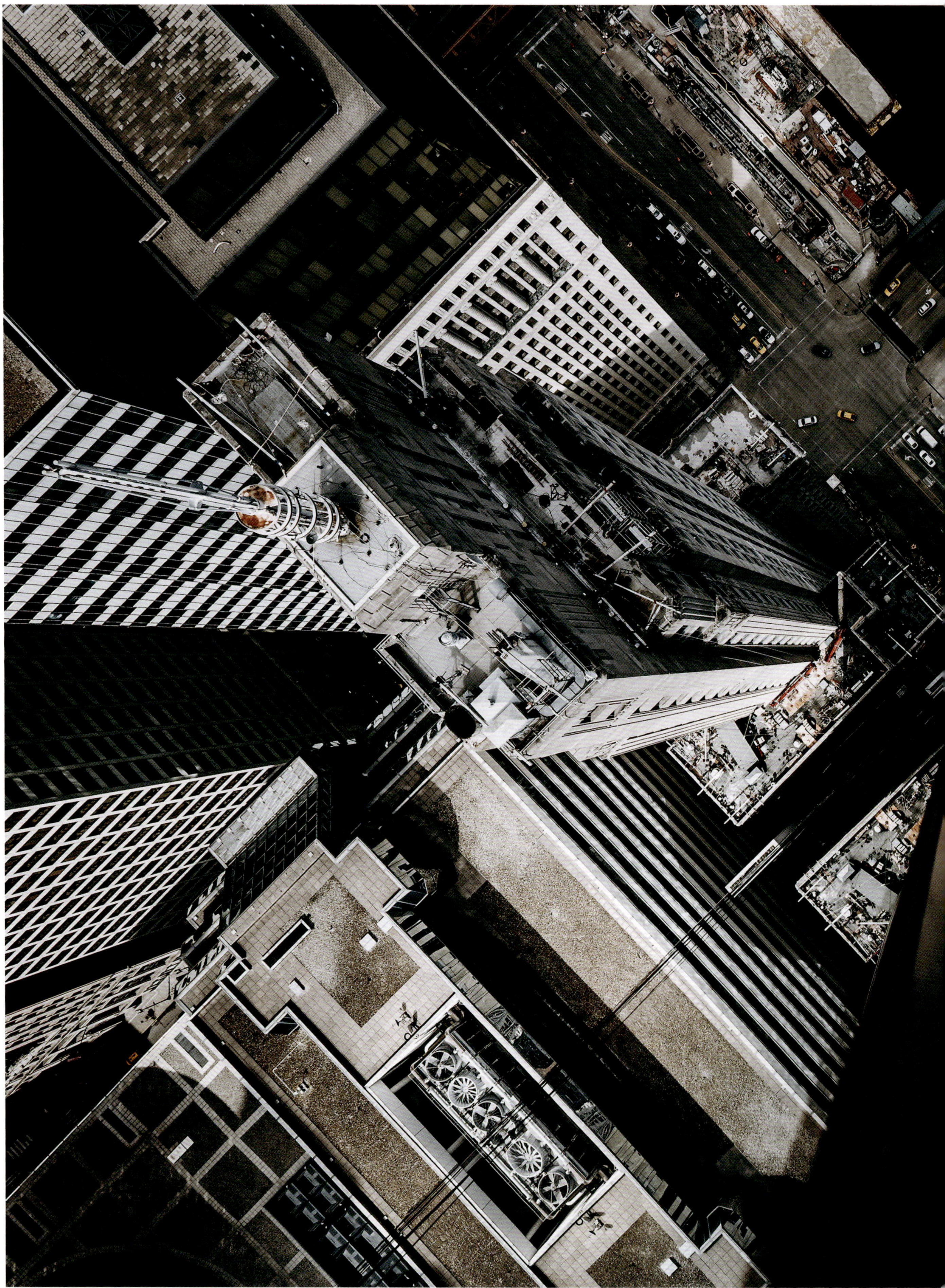

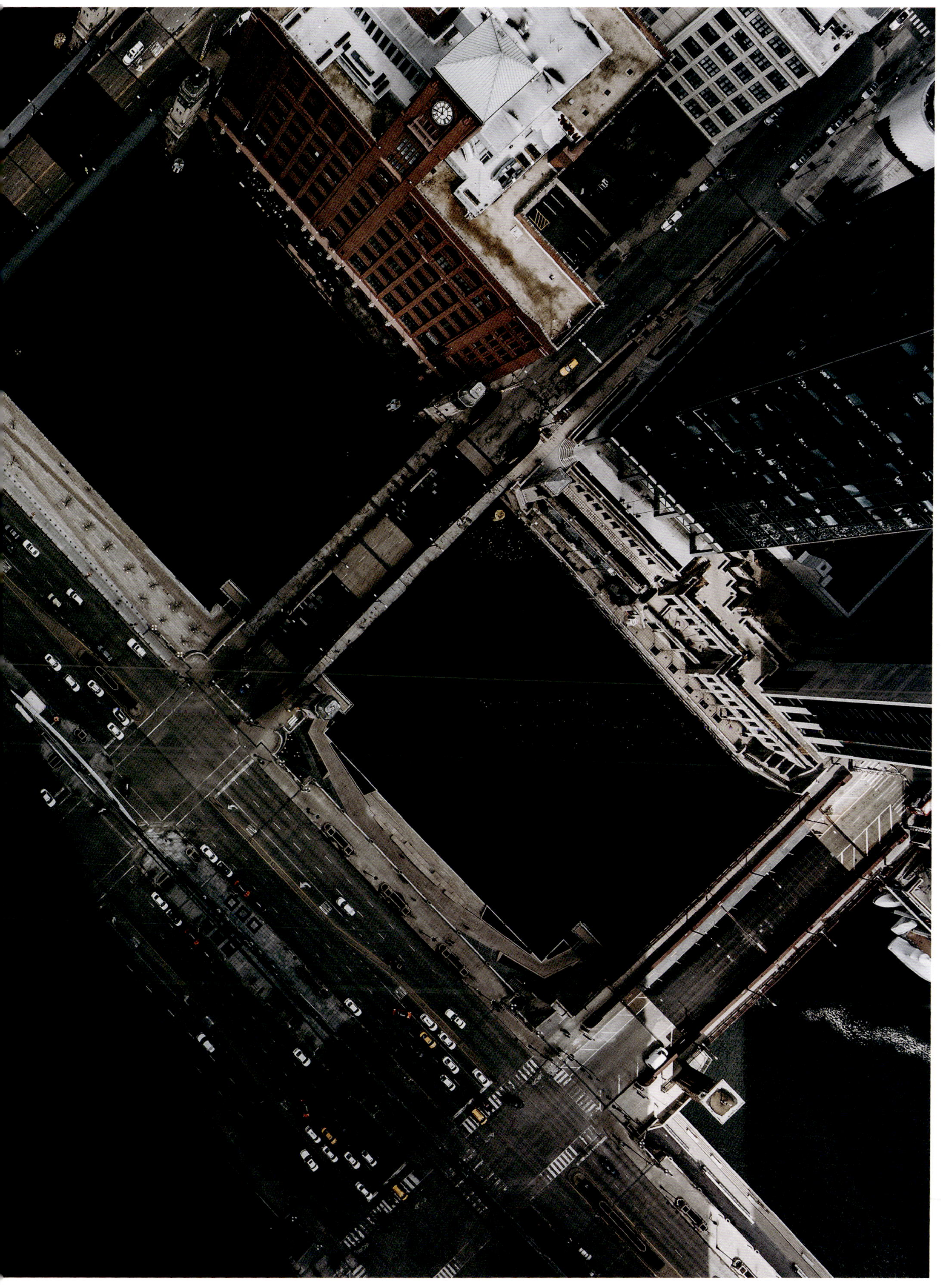

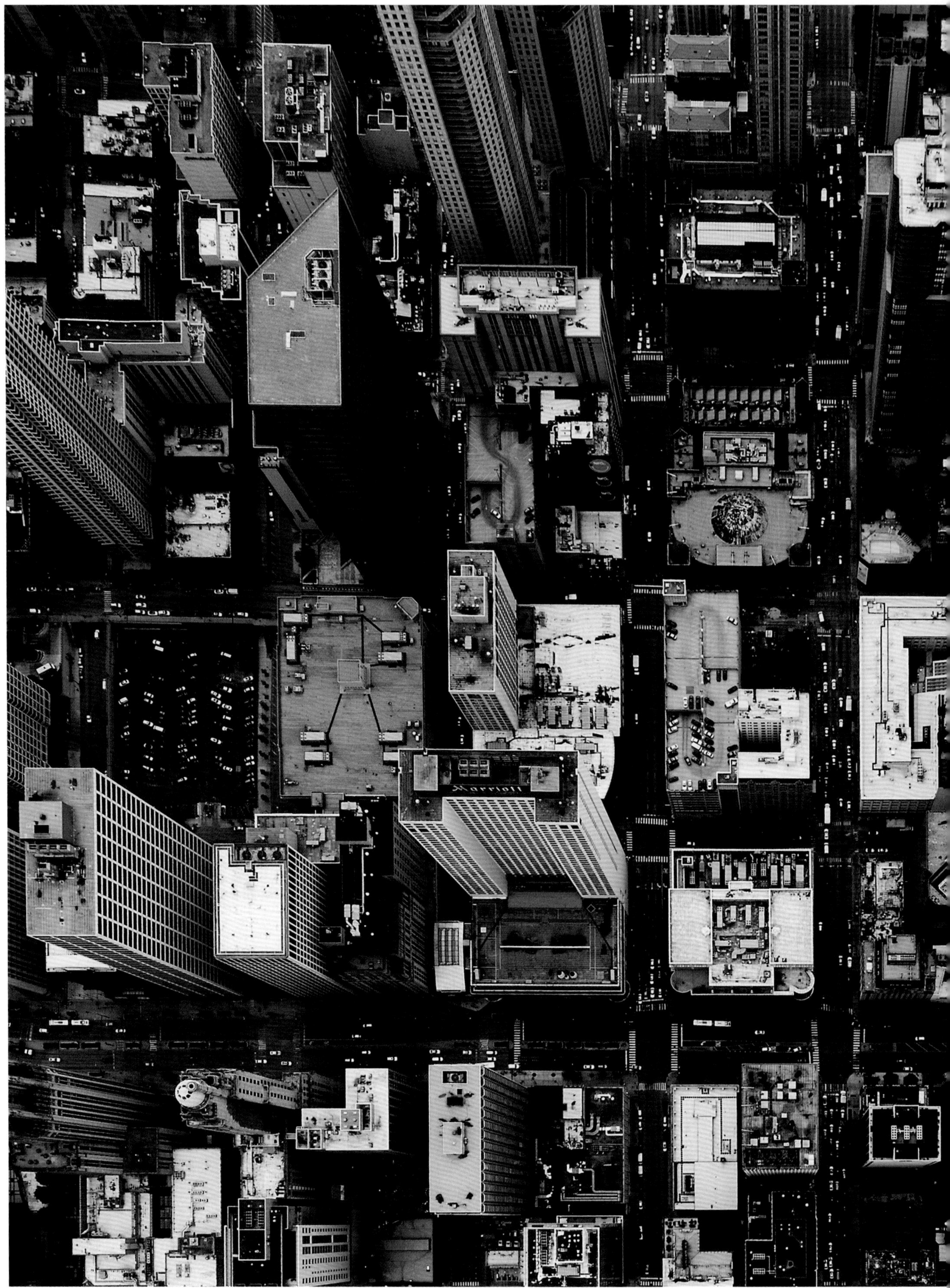
Marriott

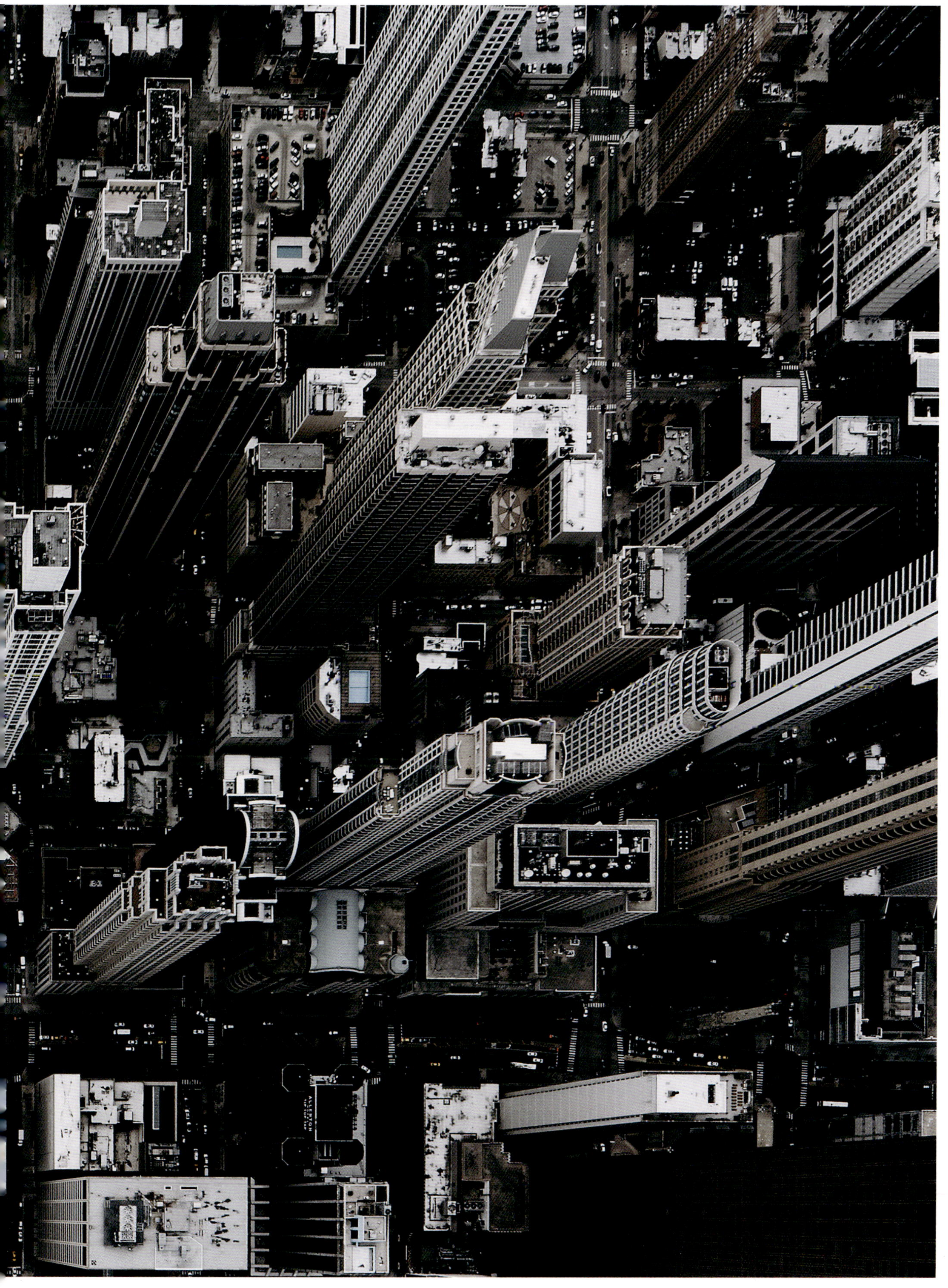

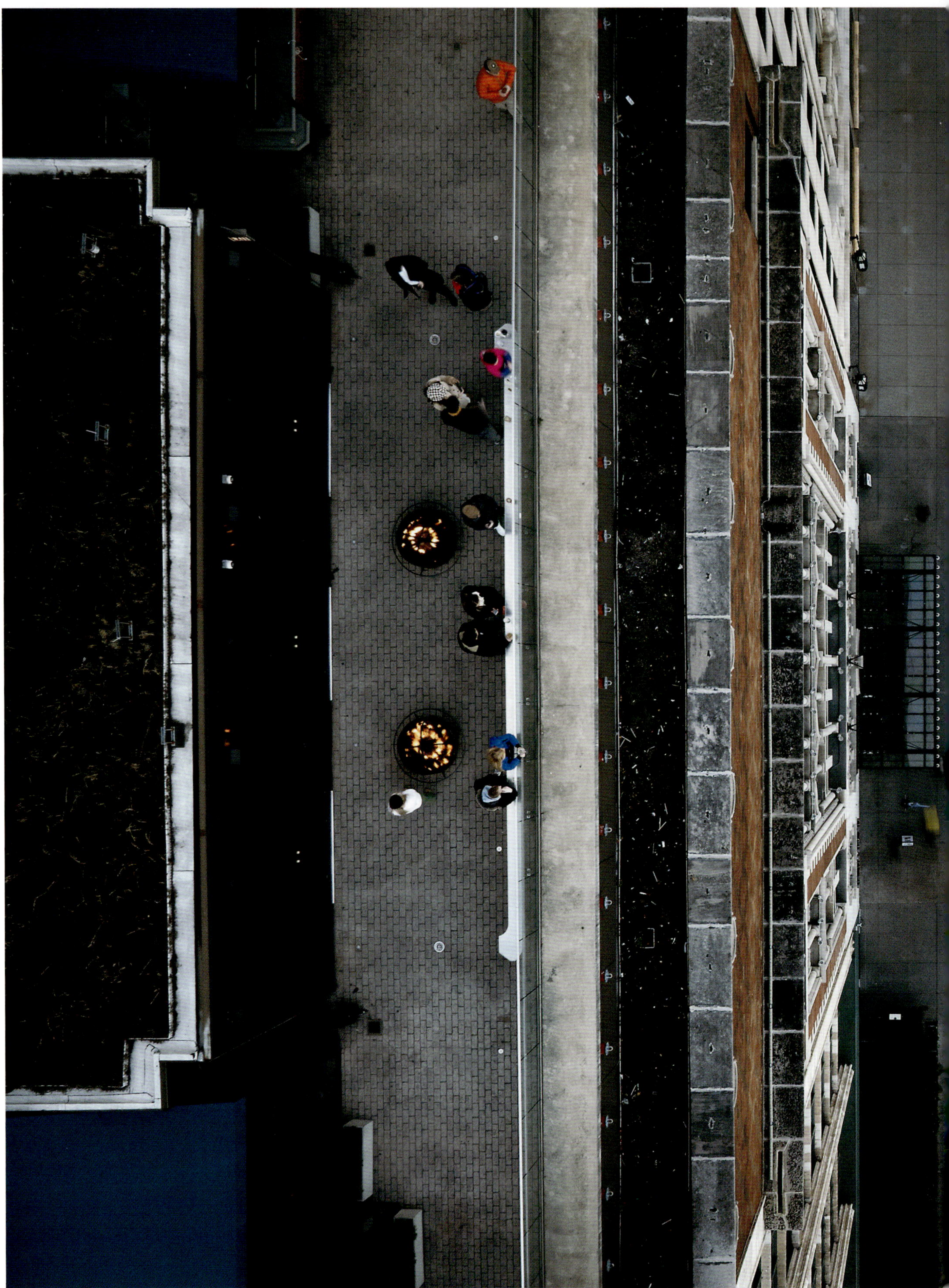

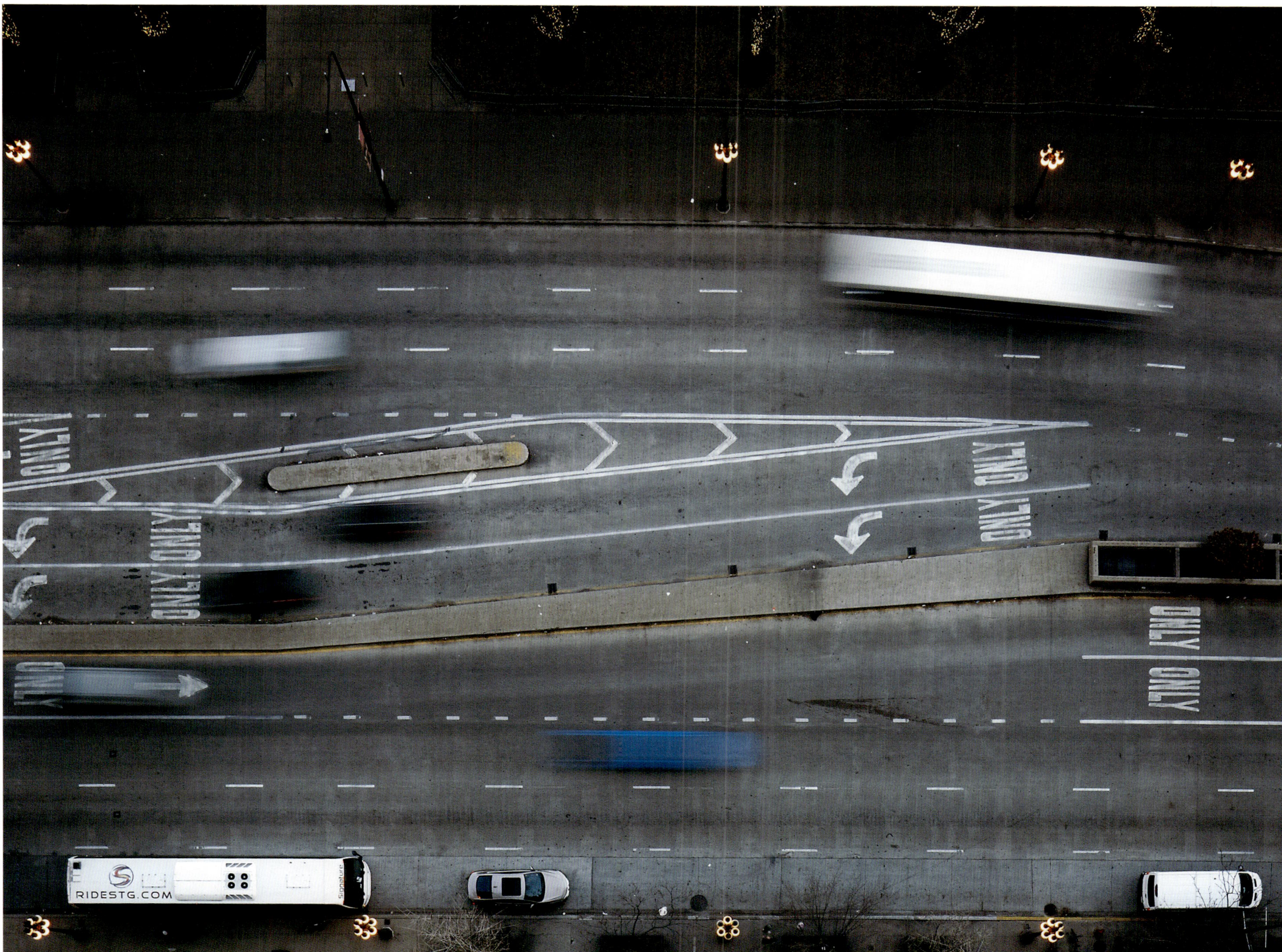

RIDESTG.COM
Signature
ONLY ONLY
ONLY ONLY
ONLY ONLY
ONLY ONLY
ONLY

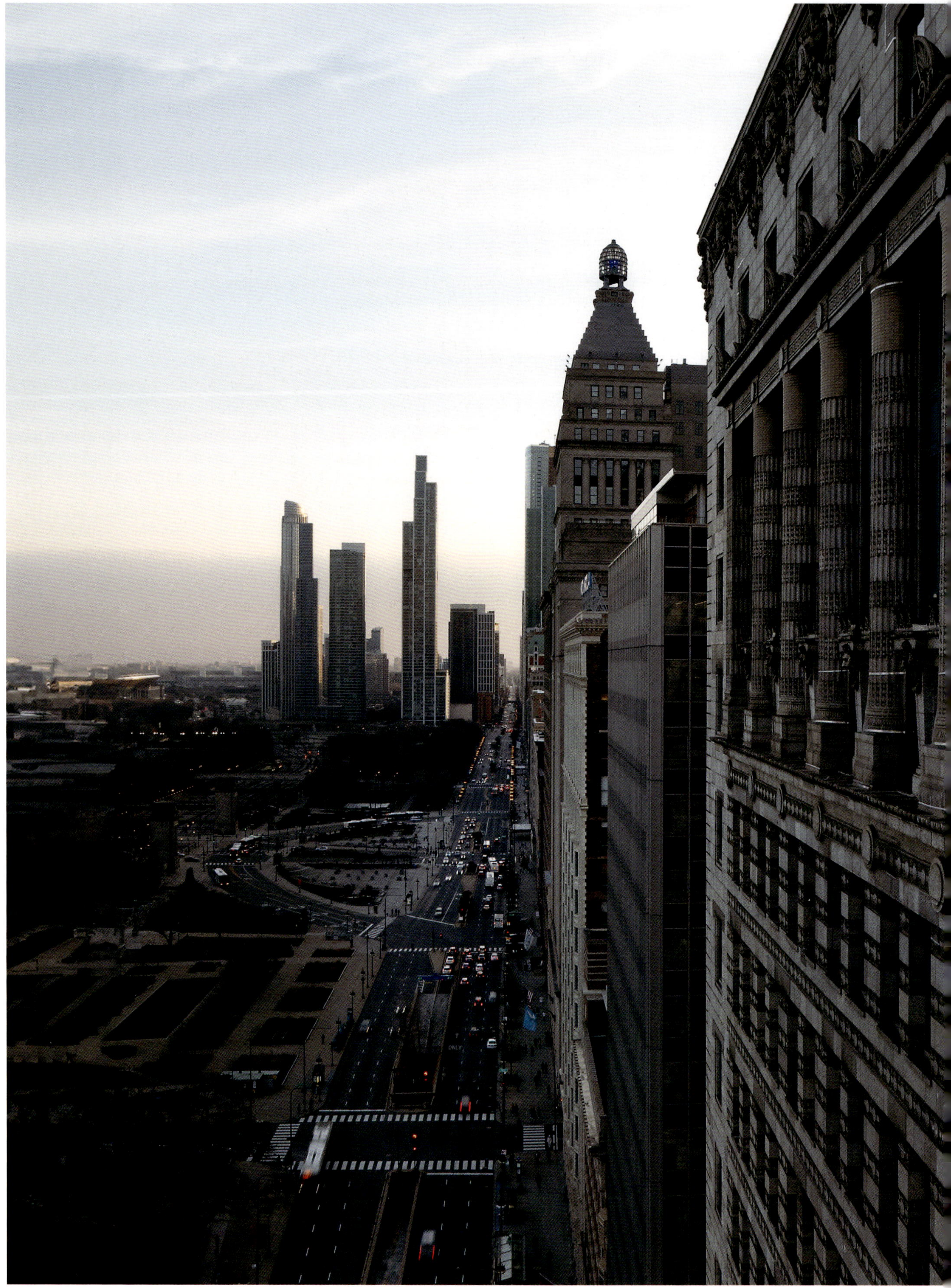

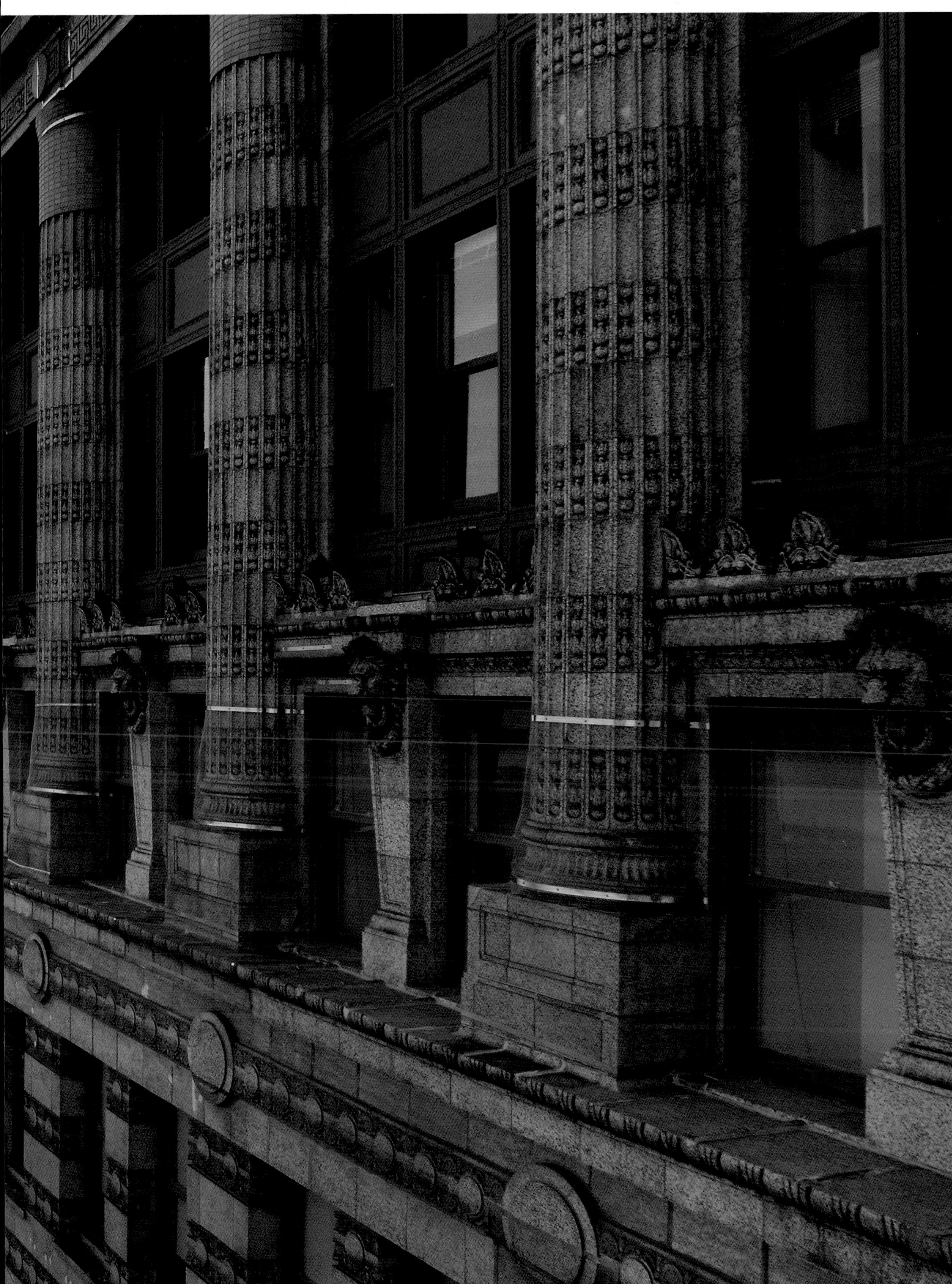

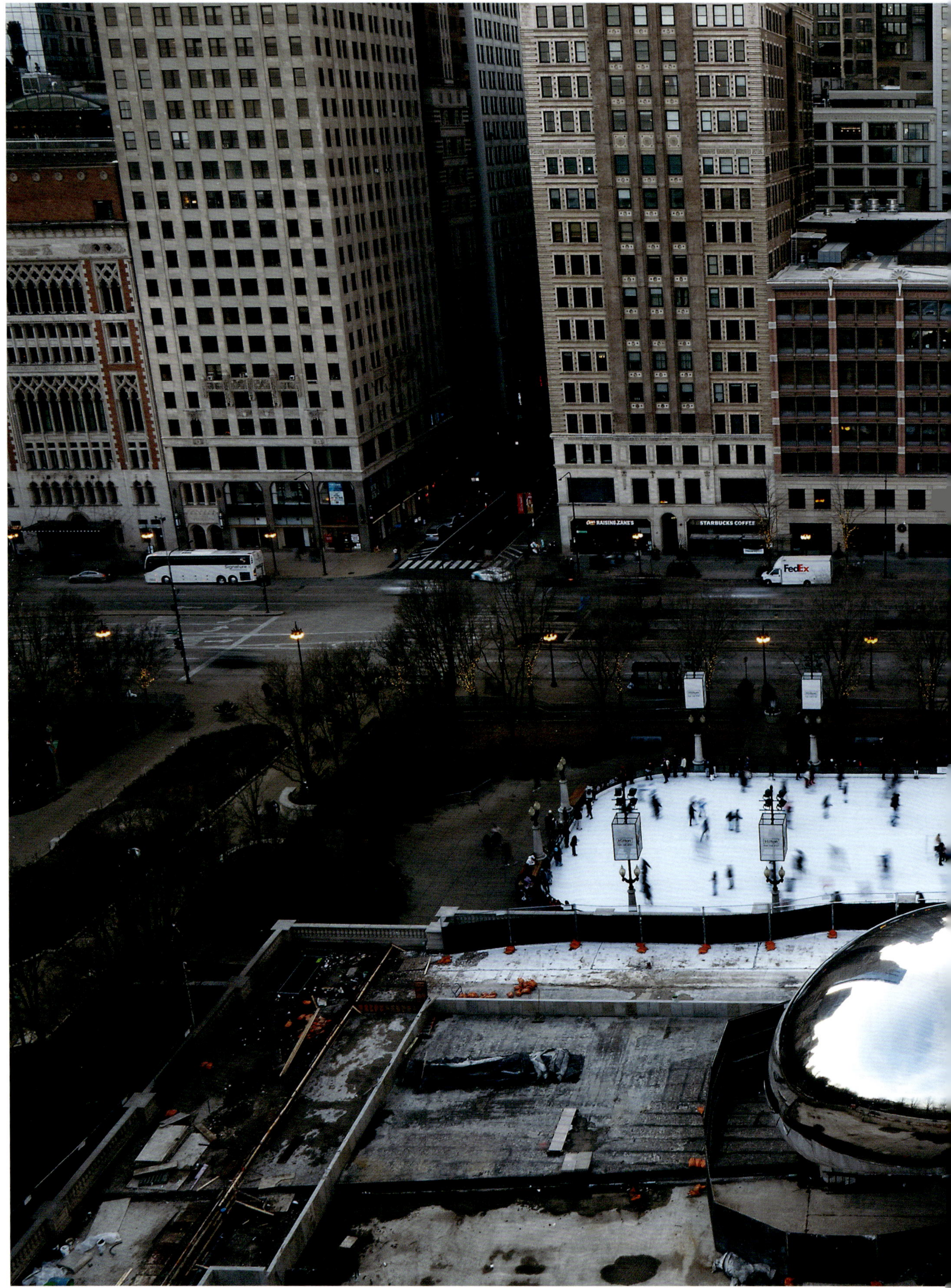

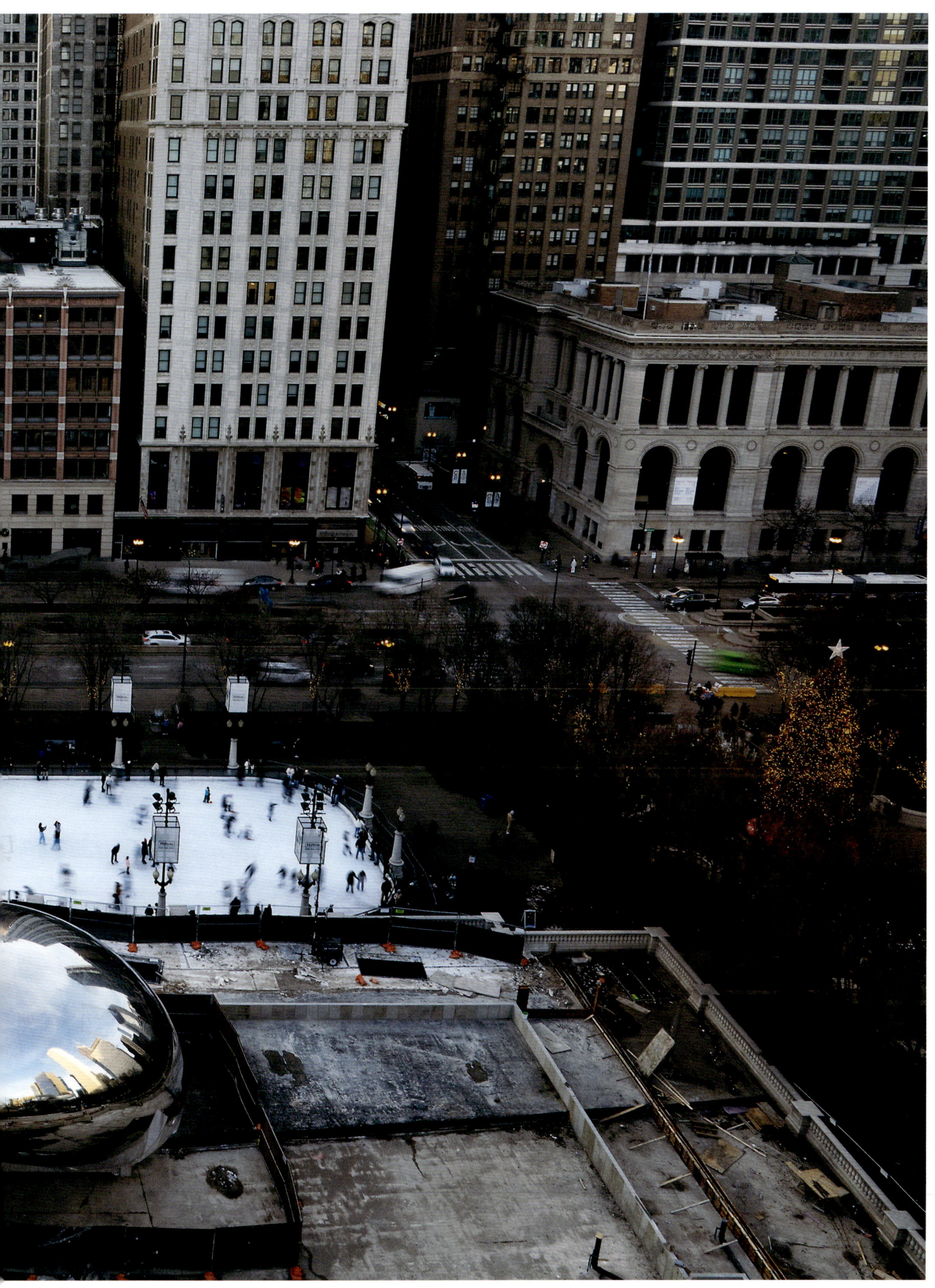

The City of the Future ★ The 1909 "Plan of Chicago" was a visionary urban planning document for shaping the future of the city. Architects Daniel Burnham and Edward H. Bennett worked together to address Chicago's rapid growth, recommending an integrated series of projects including new and widened streets, the addition and expansion of parks, new railroad and harbor facilities, and civic buildings. Their goal? To make Chicago a more livable, efficient, and beautiful city. ★ One of the major focuses of the plan was the development of Chicago's lakefront along Lake Michigan, the world's largest lake not bordering another country. Burnham and Bennett aimed to blend the city with its natural surroundings. In turn, new buildings were strategically placed to take advantage of the amazing lake views. The plan also proposed creating a continuous system of parks, boulevards, and recreational spaces along the lakefront, free and open to the public, granting everyone access to the waterfront. ★ The Plan of Chicago also advocated for the creation of large public parks that all Chicagoans could enjoy, including what later became Grant Park, home to iconic landmarks such as Millennium Park and Buckingham Fountain. ★ While not everything from the original vision was realized, the Plan of Chicago set the stage for how future cities would develop, highlighting how buildings, streets, and public spaces should be interconnected. It's a legacy that can still be felt as you walk the streets of Chicago today, whether along the lakefront, down a boulevard, or in one of the city's magnificent parks.

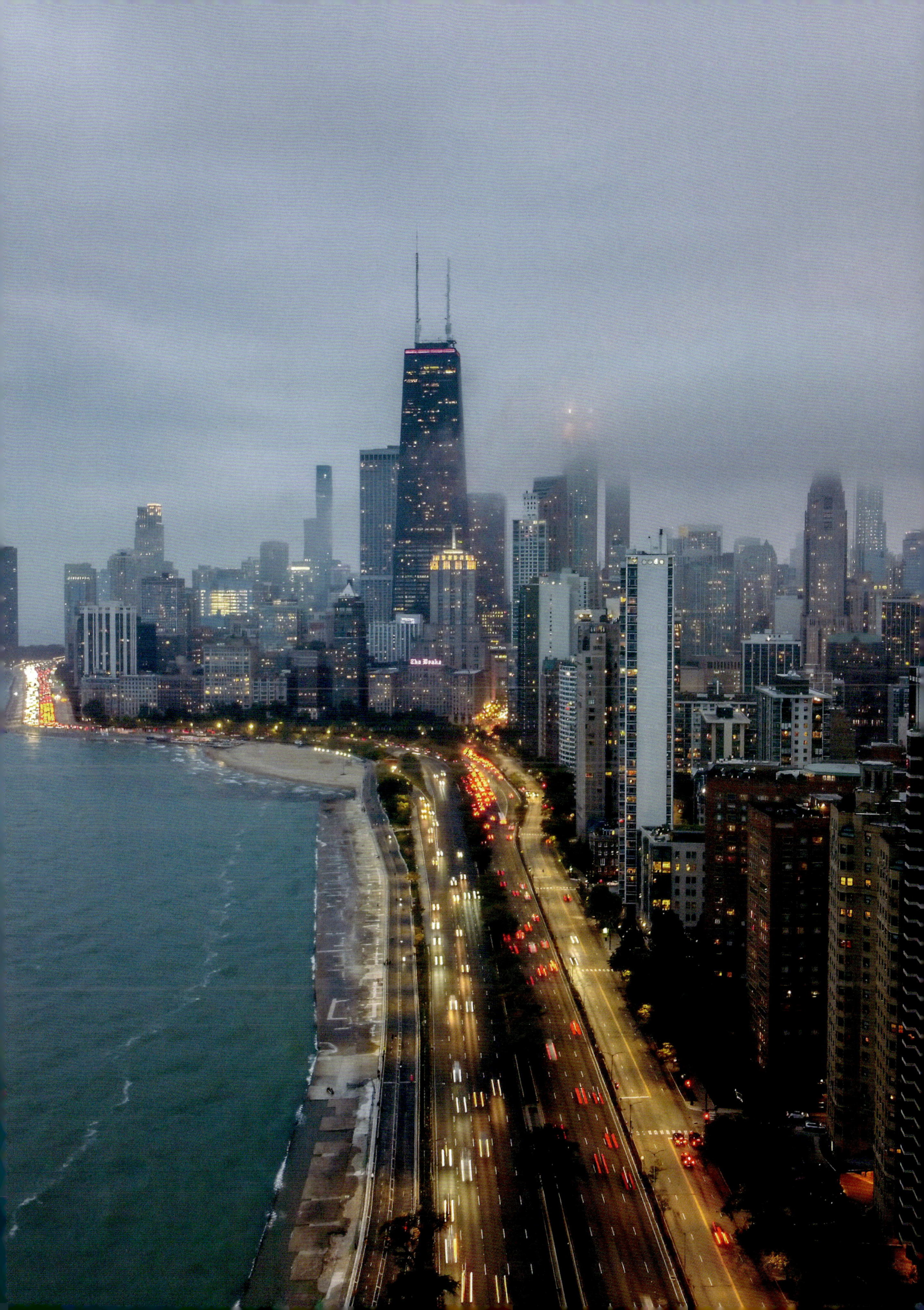

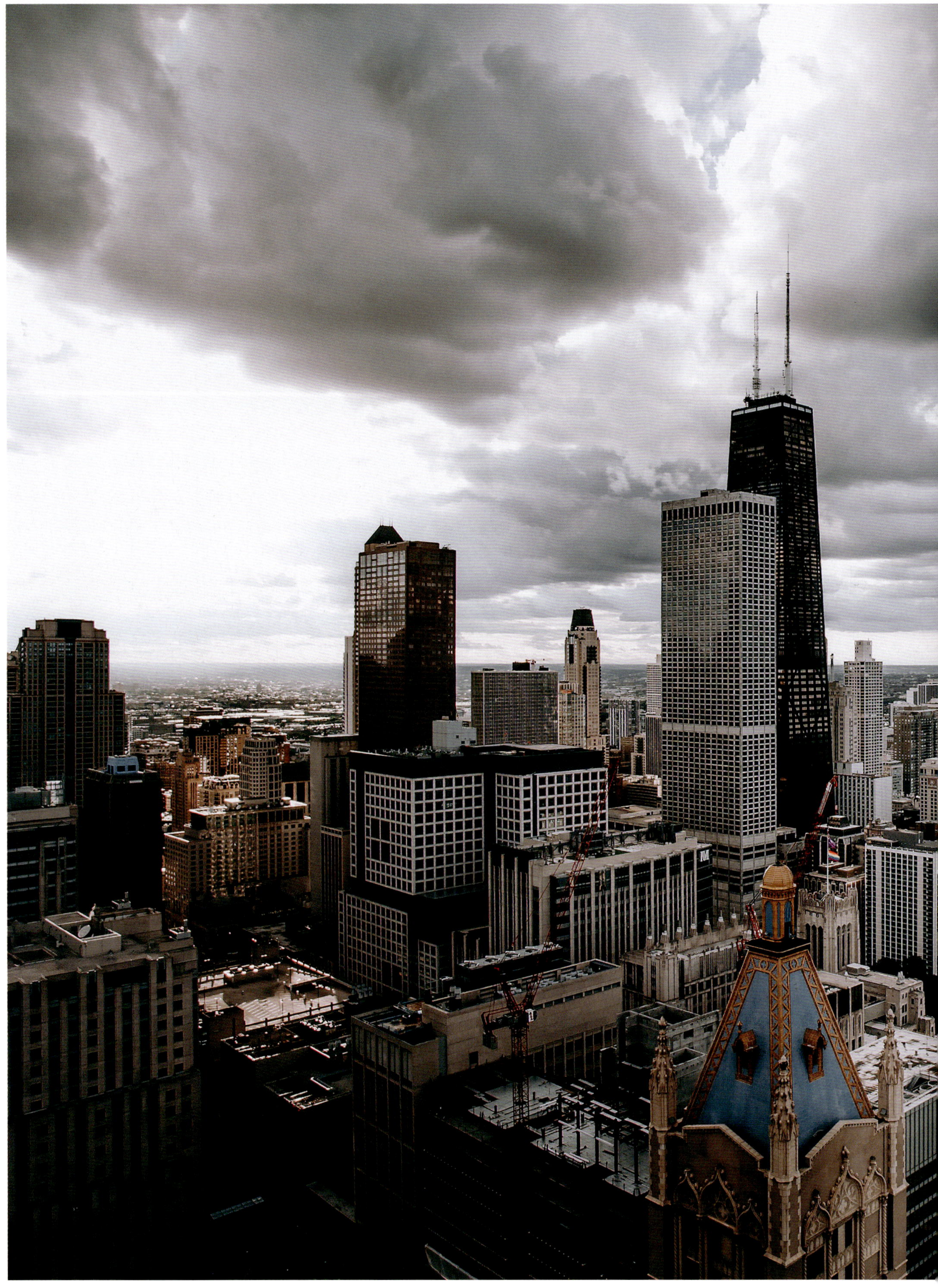

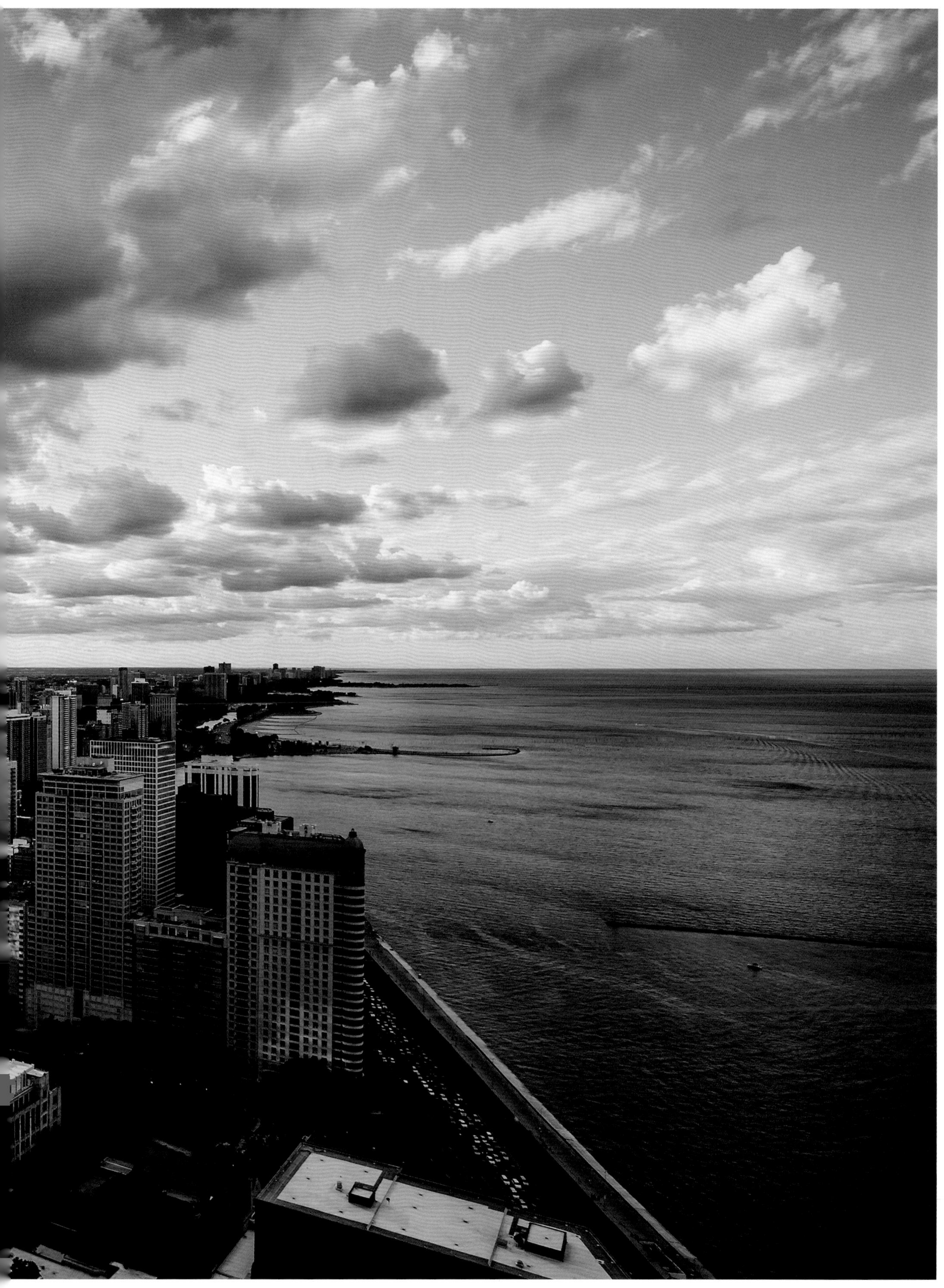

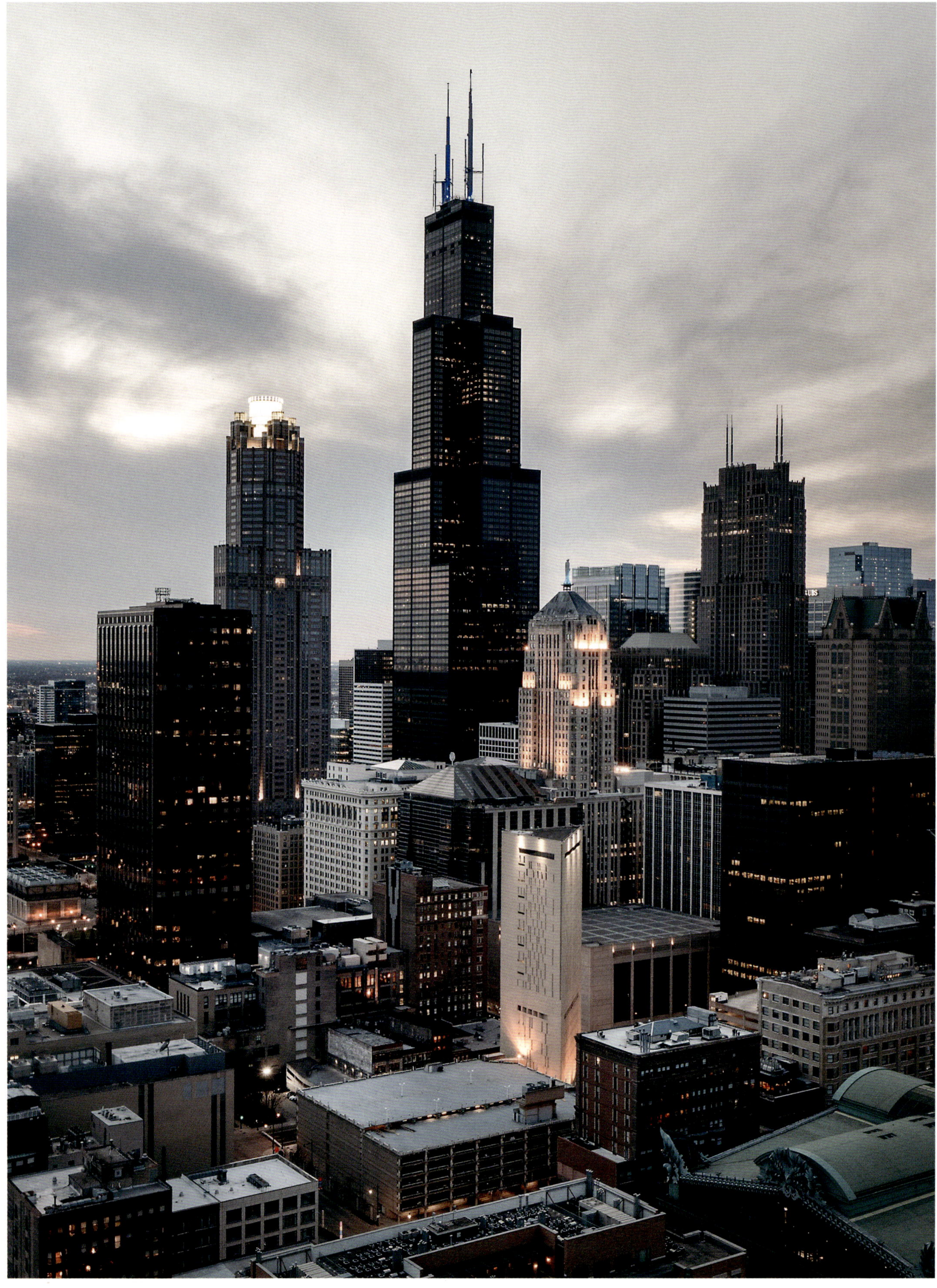

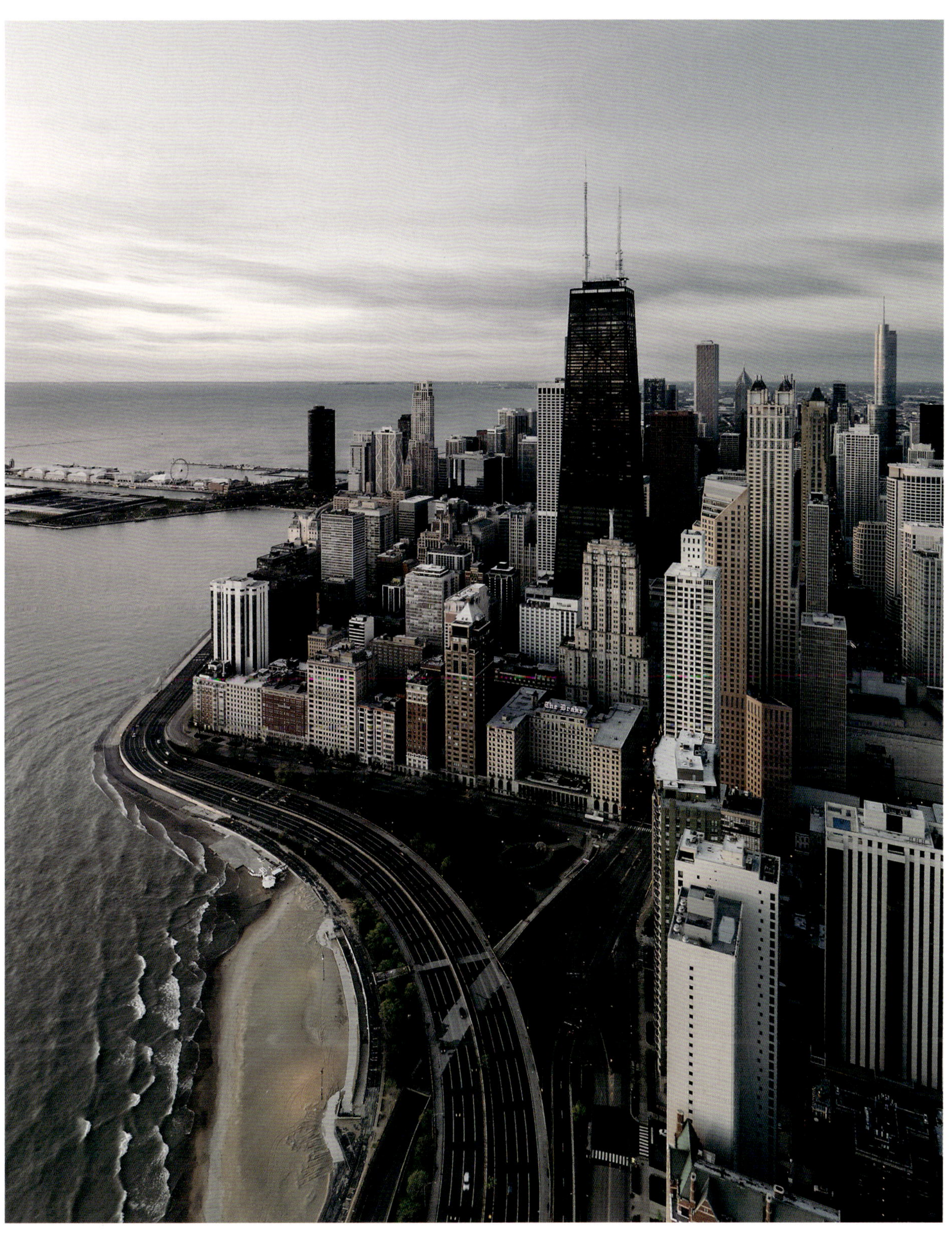

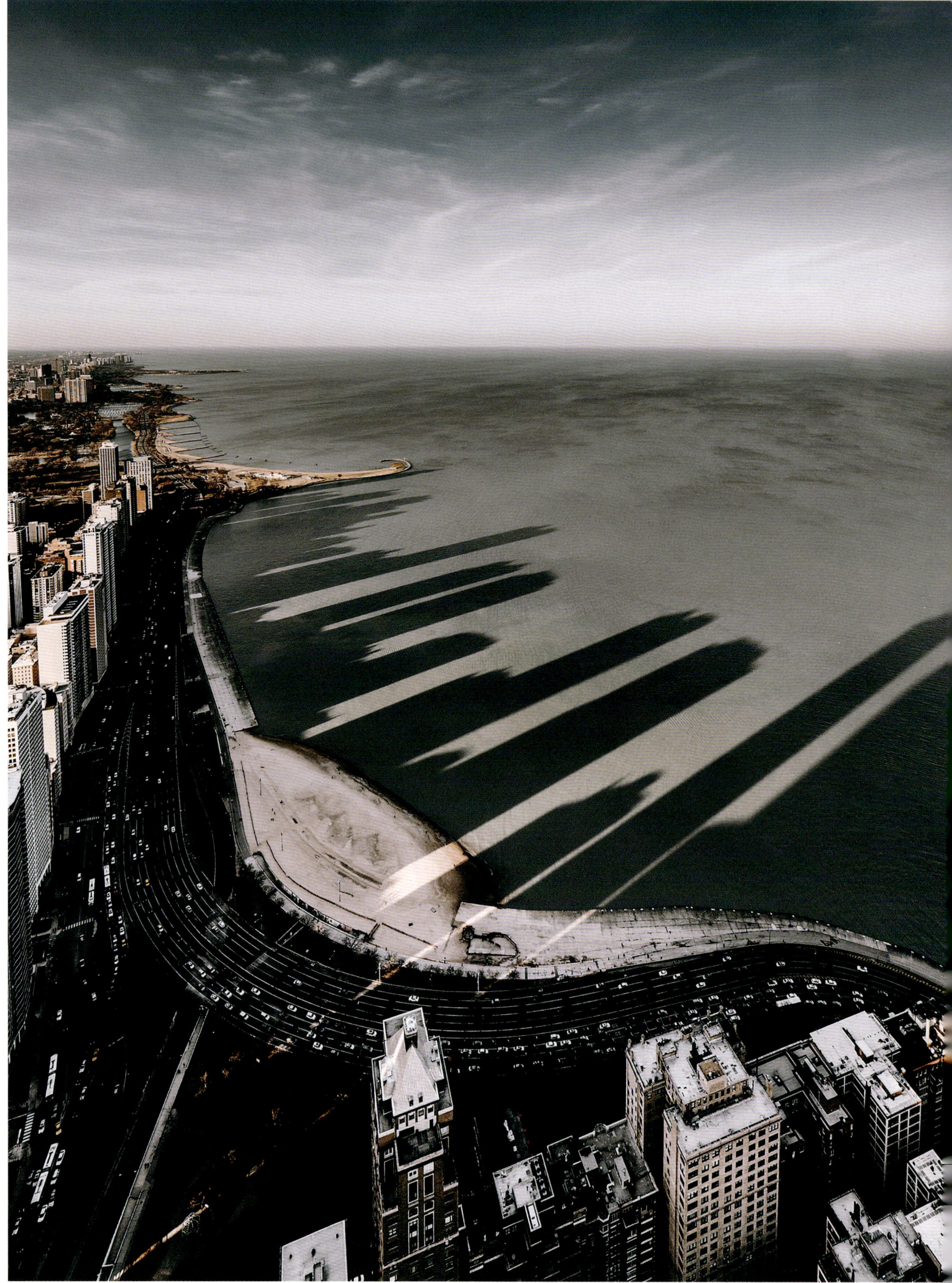

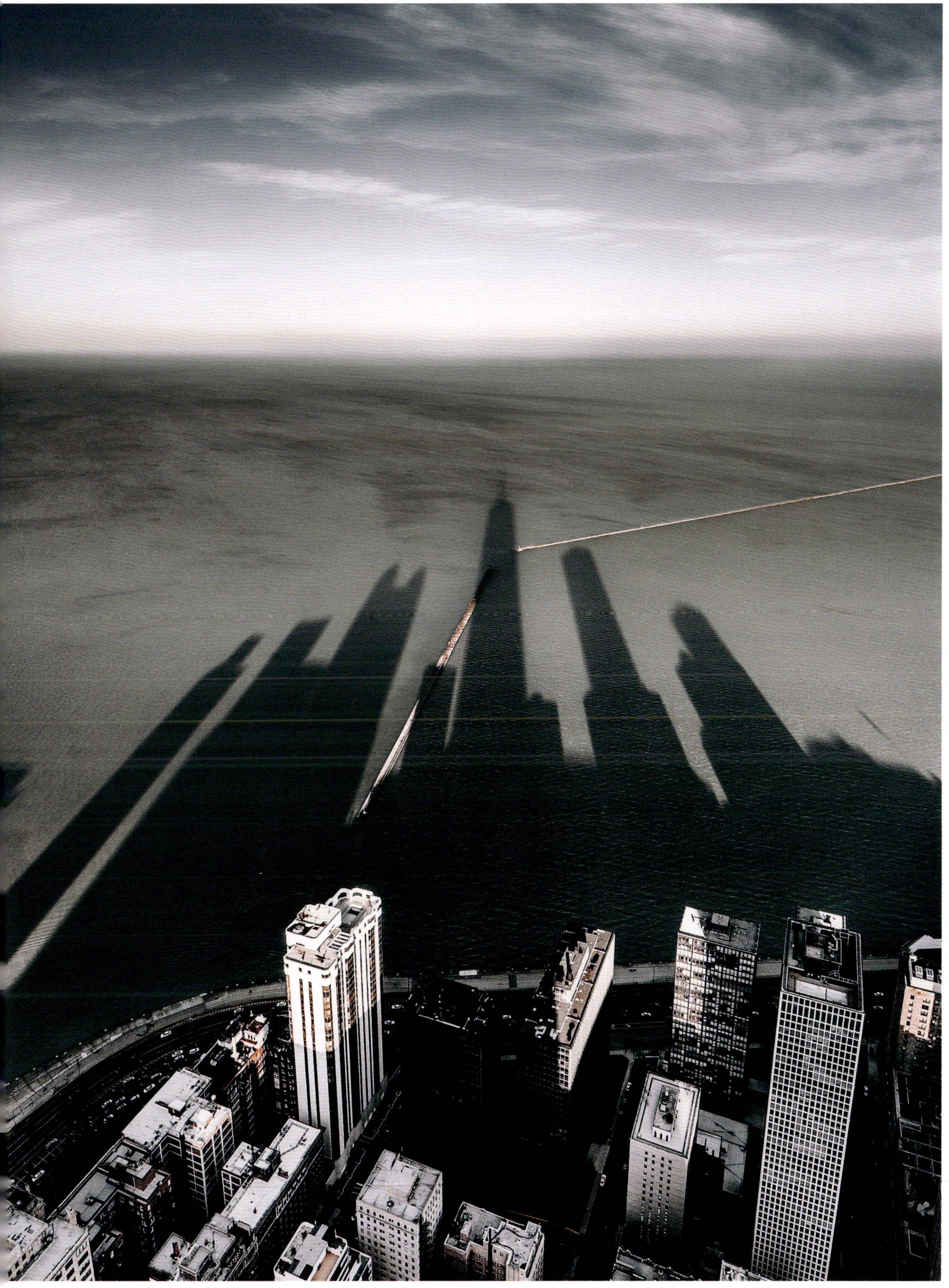

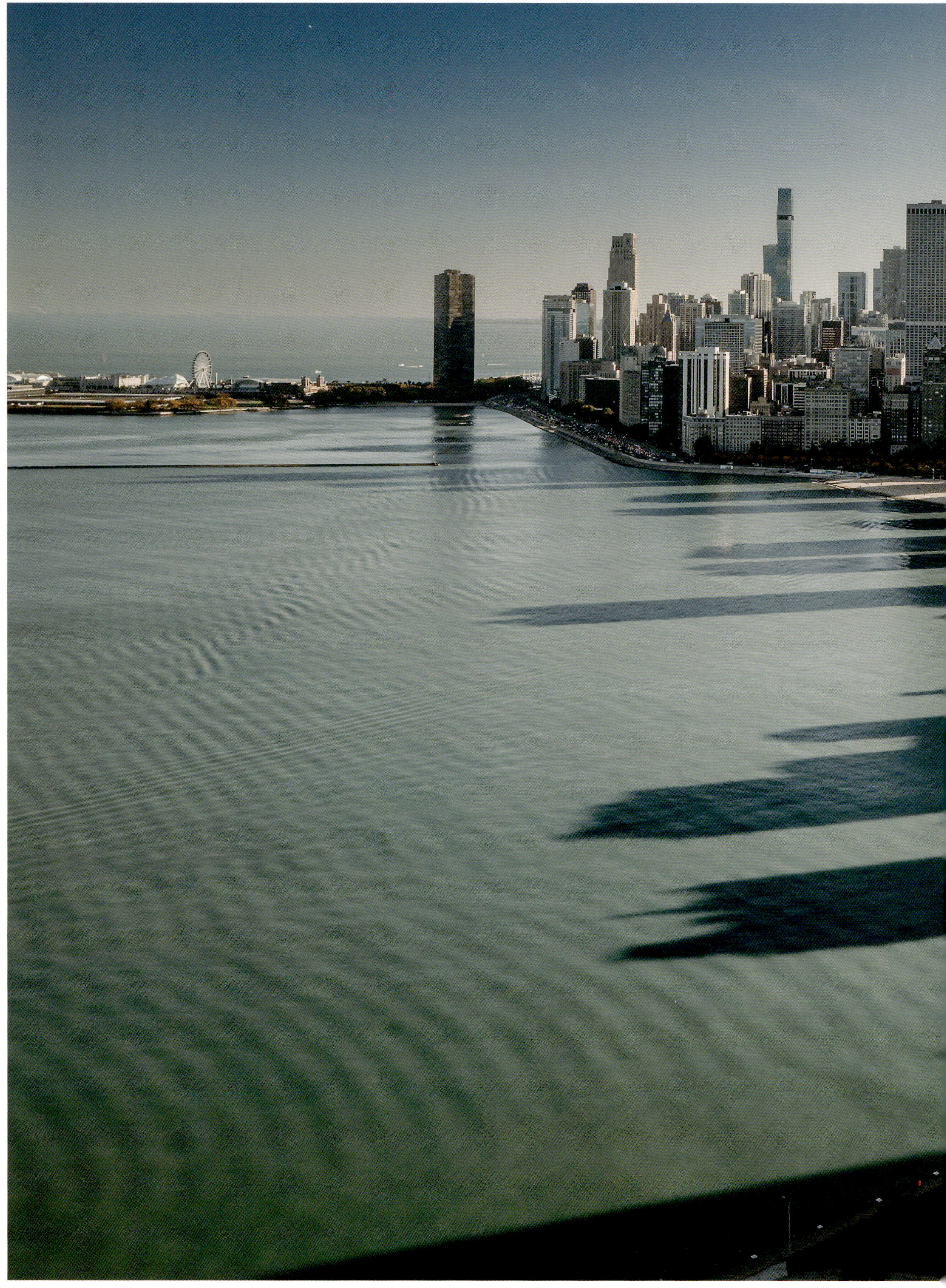

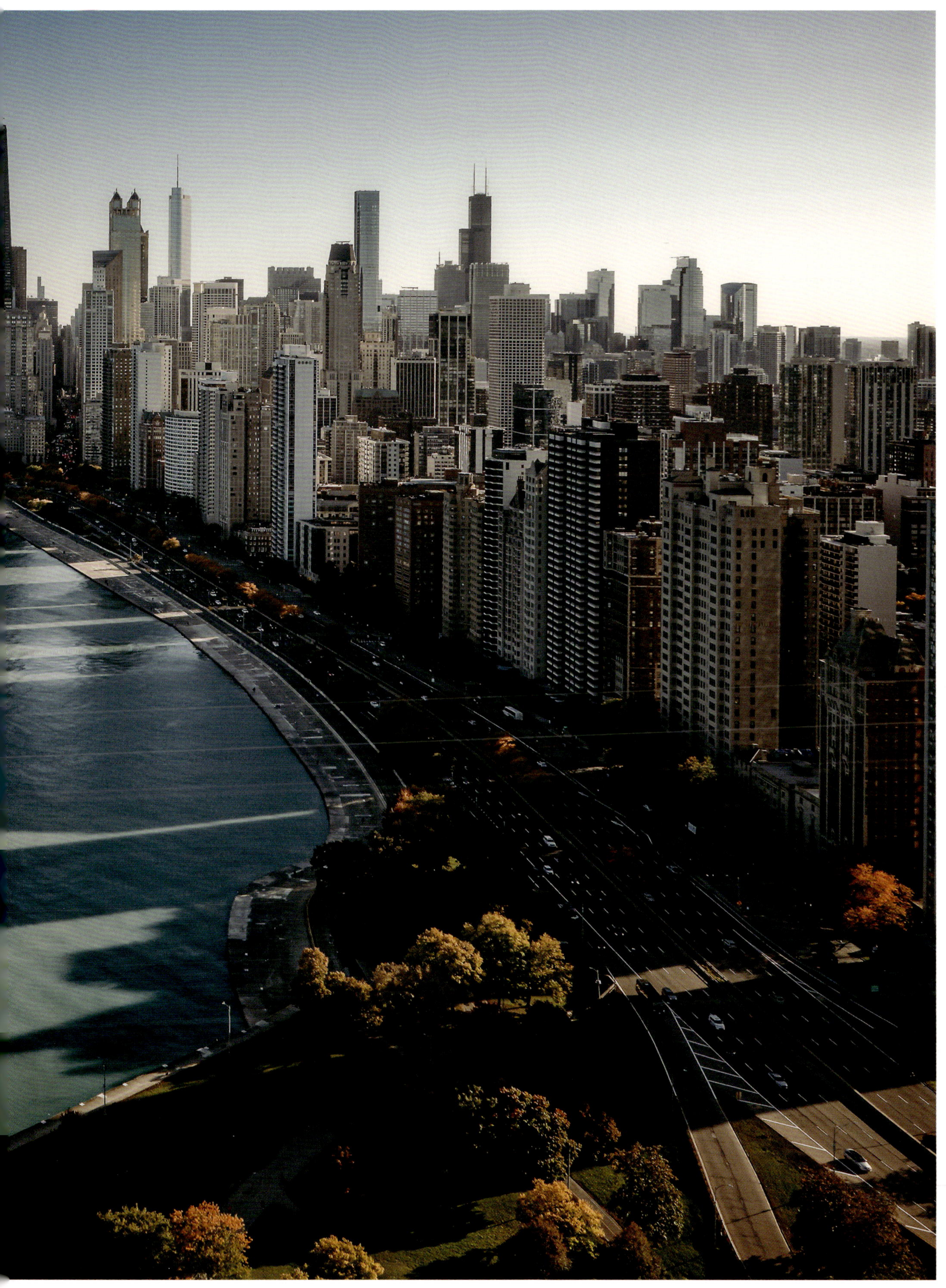

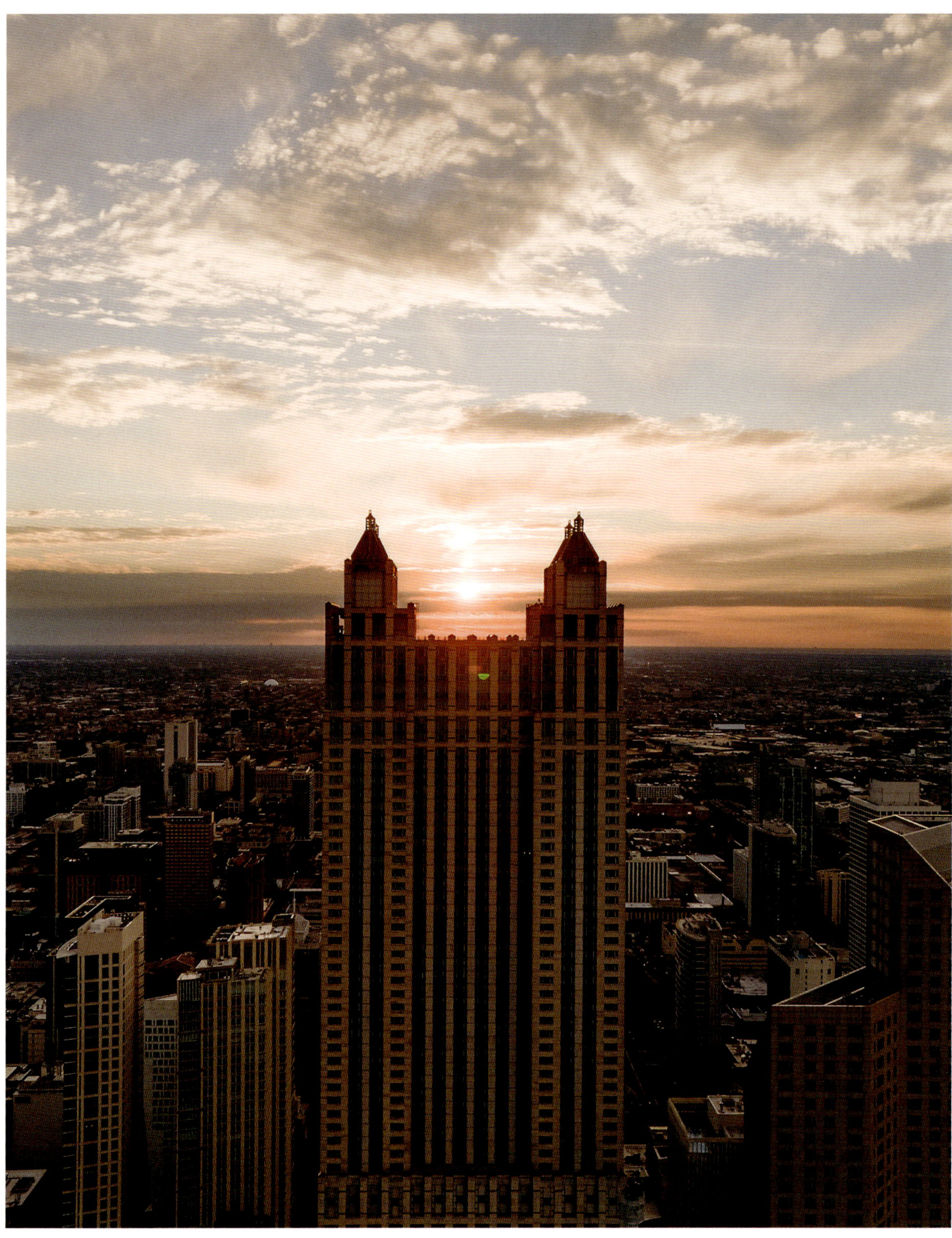

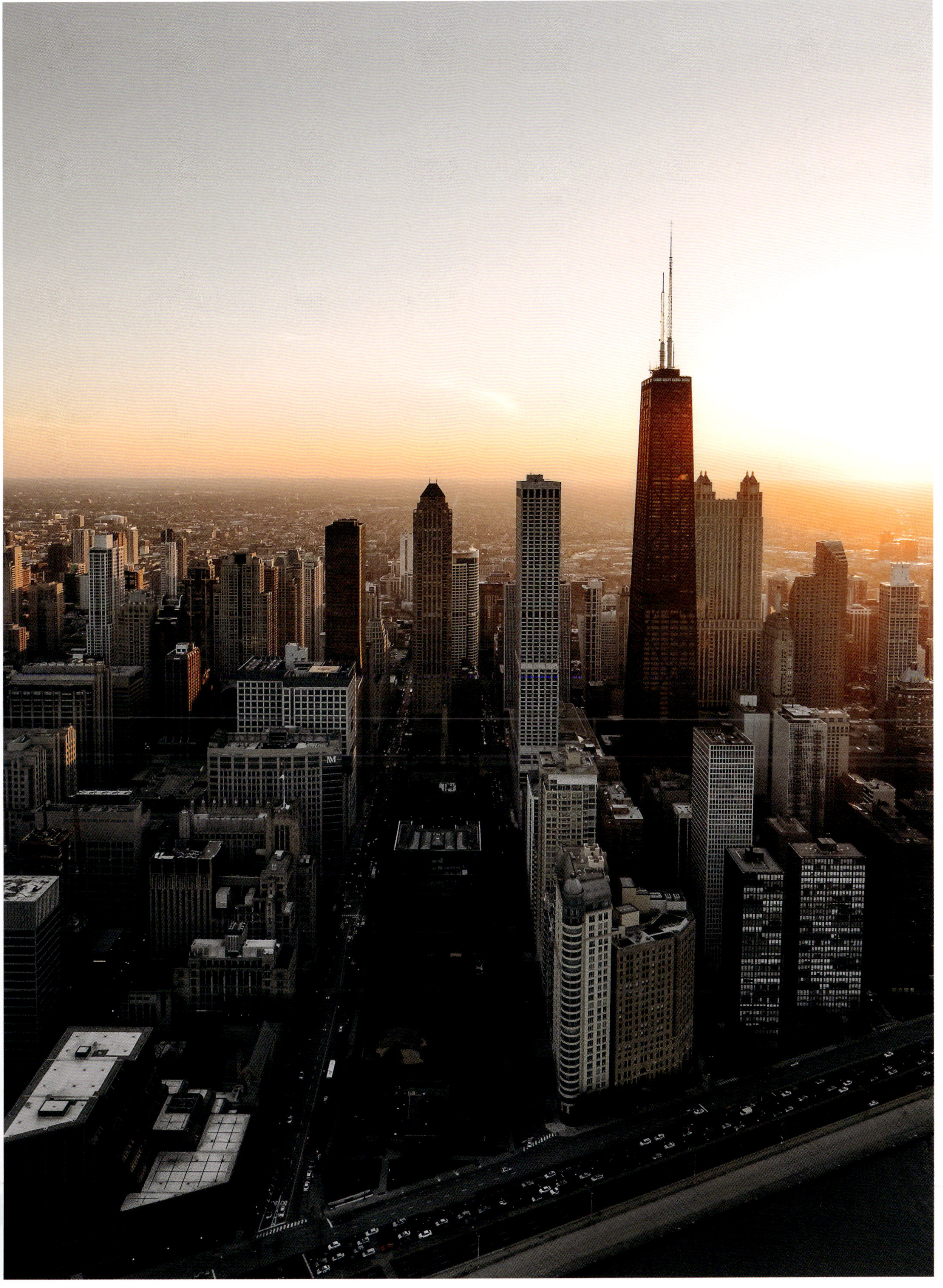

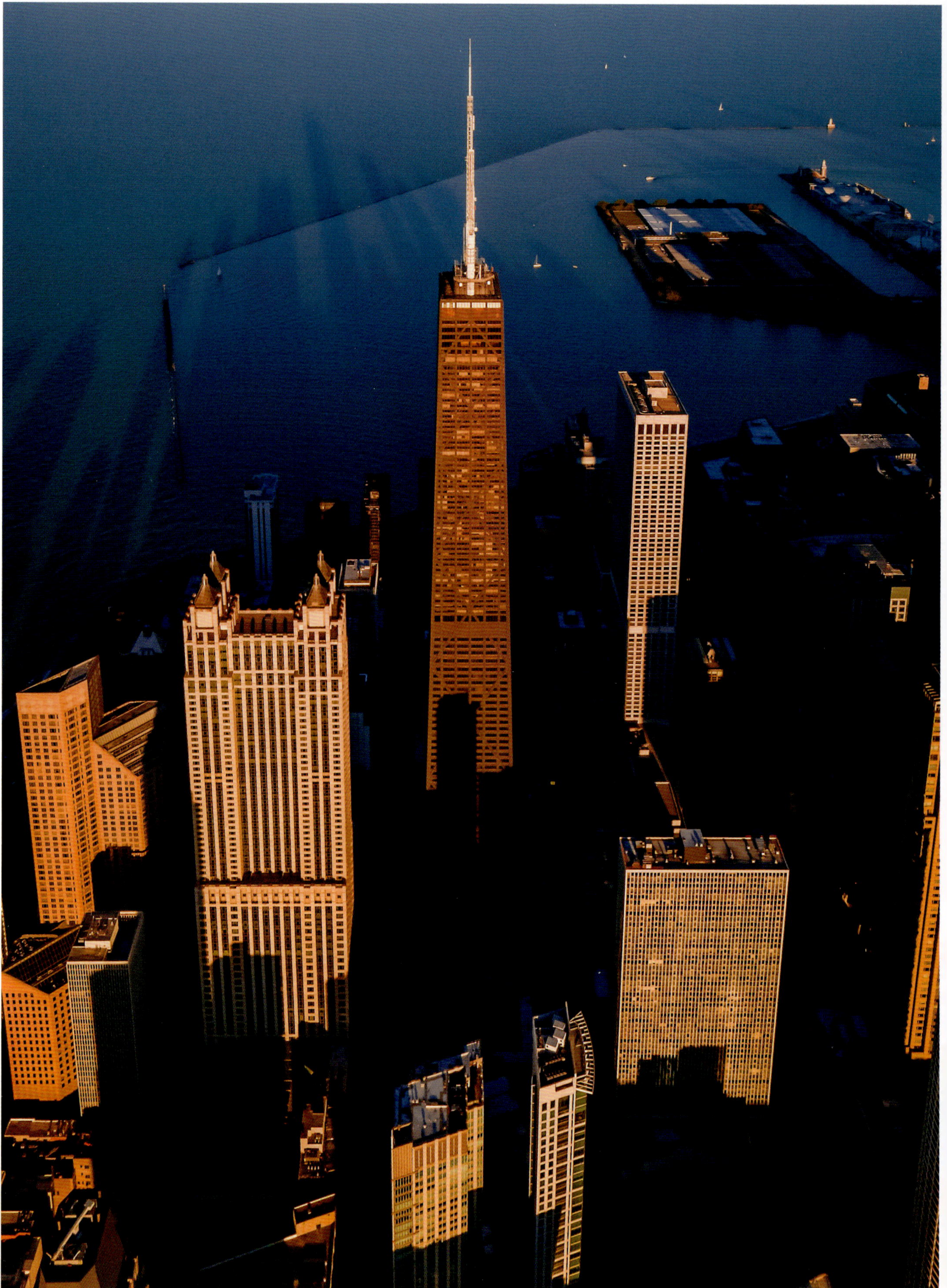

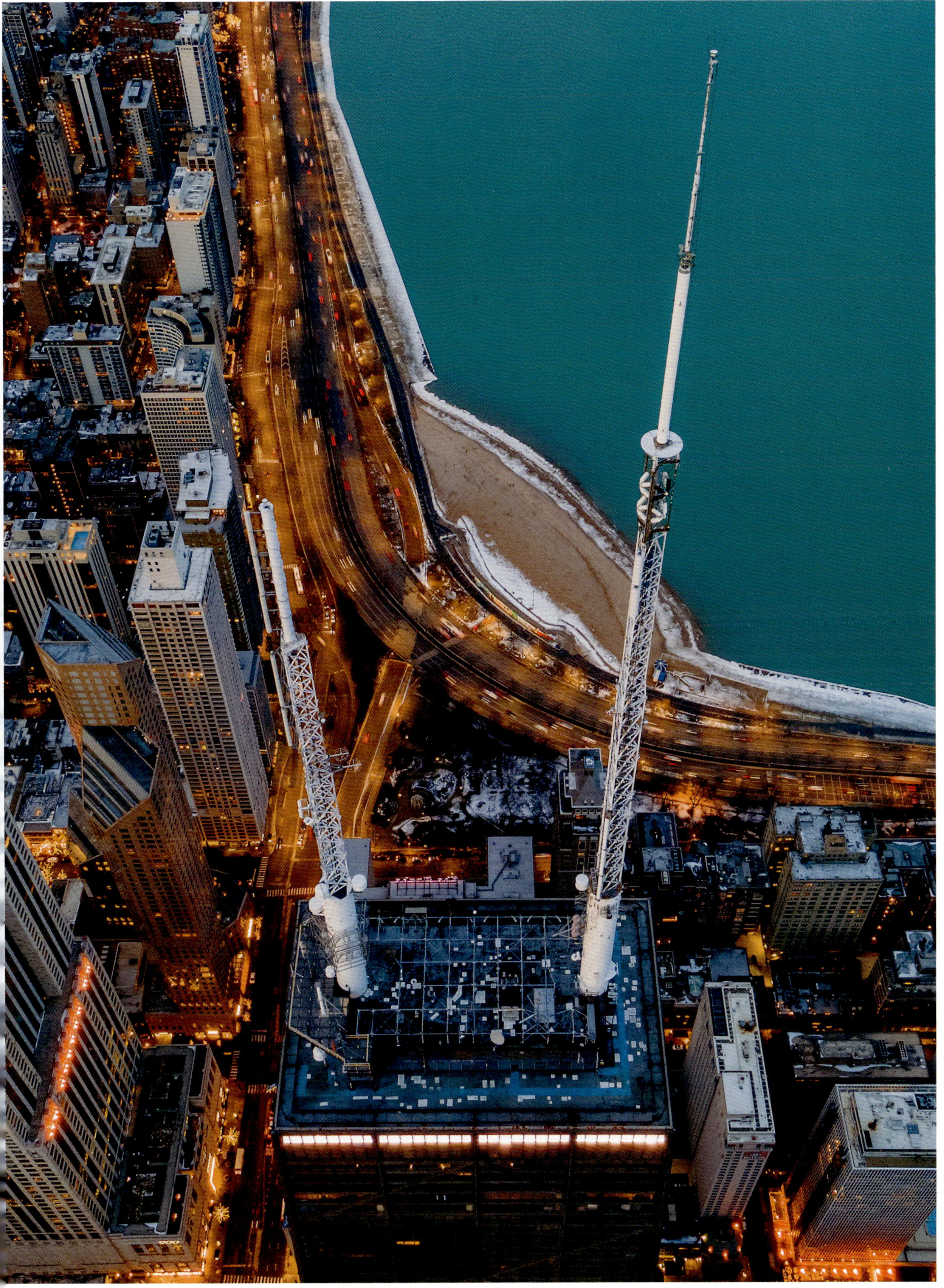

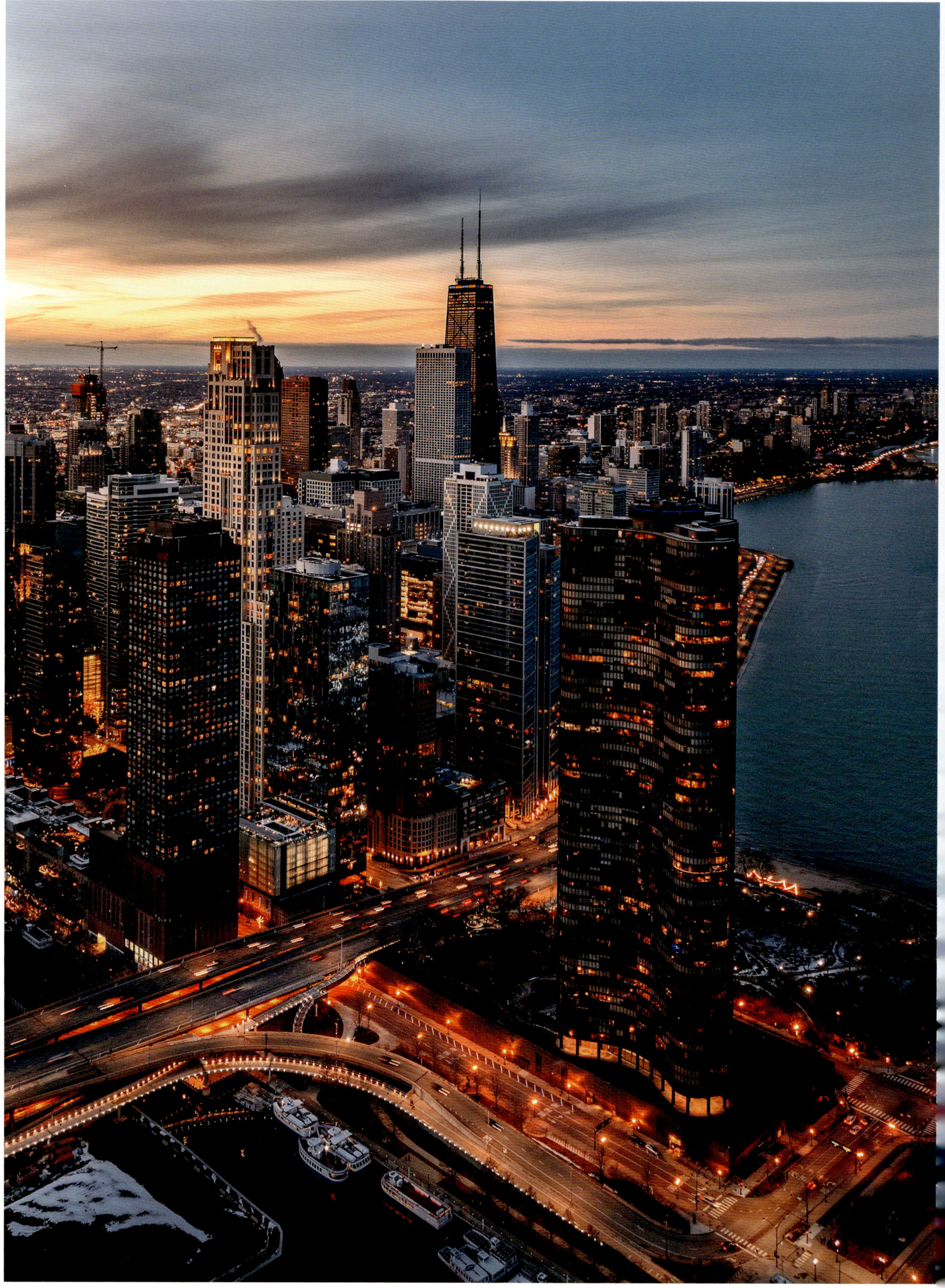

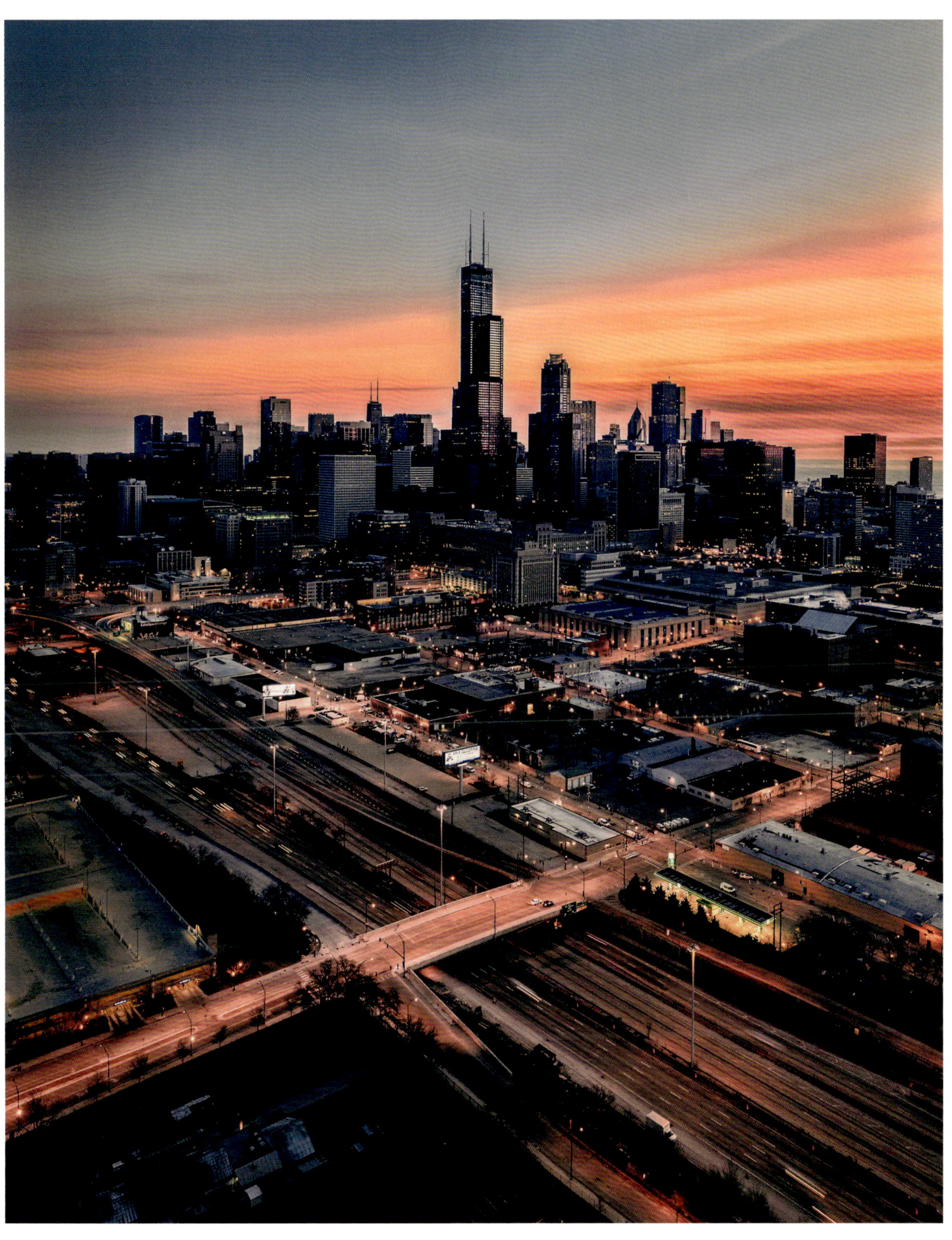

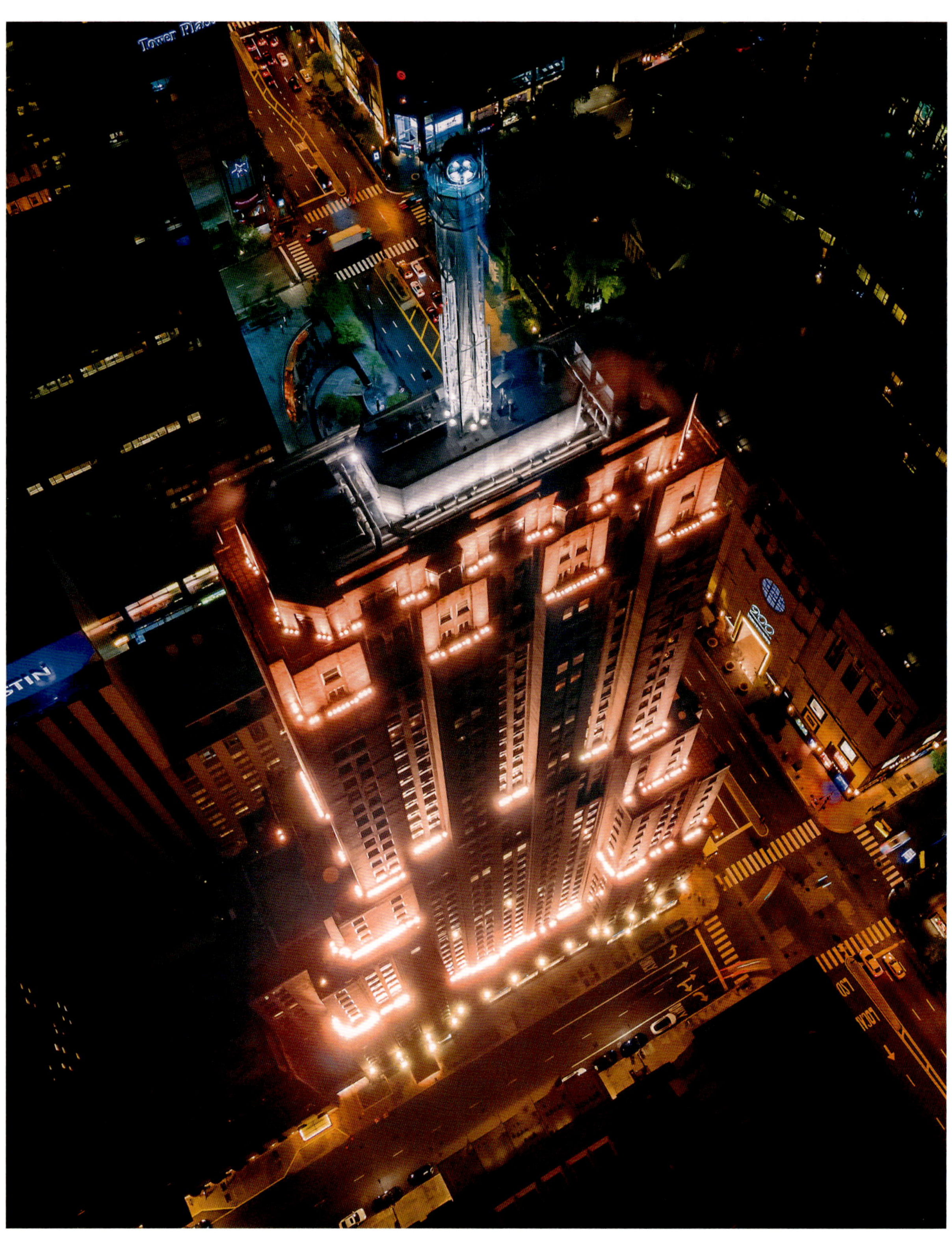

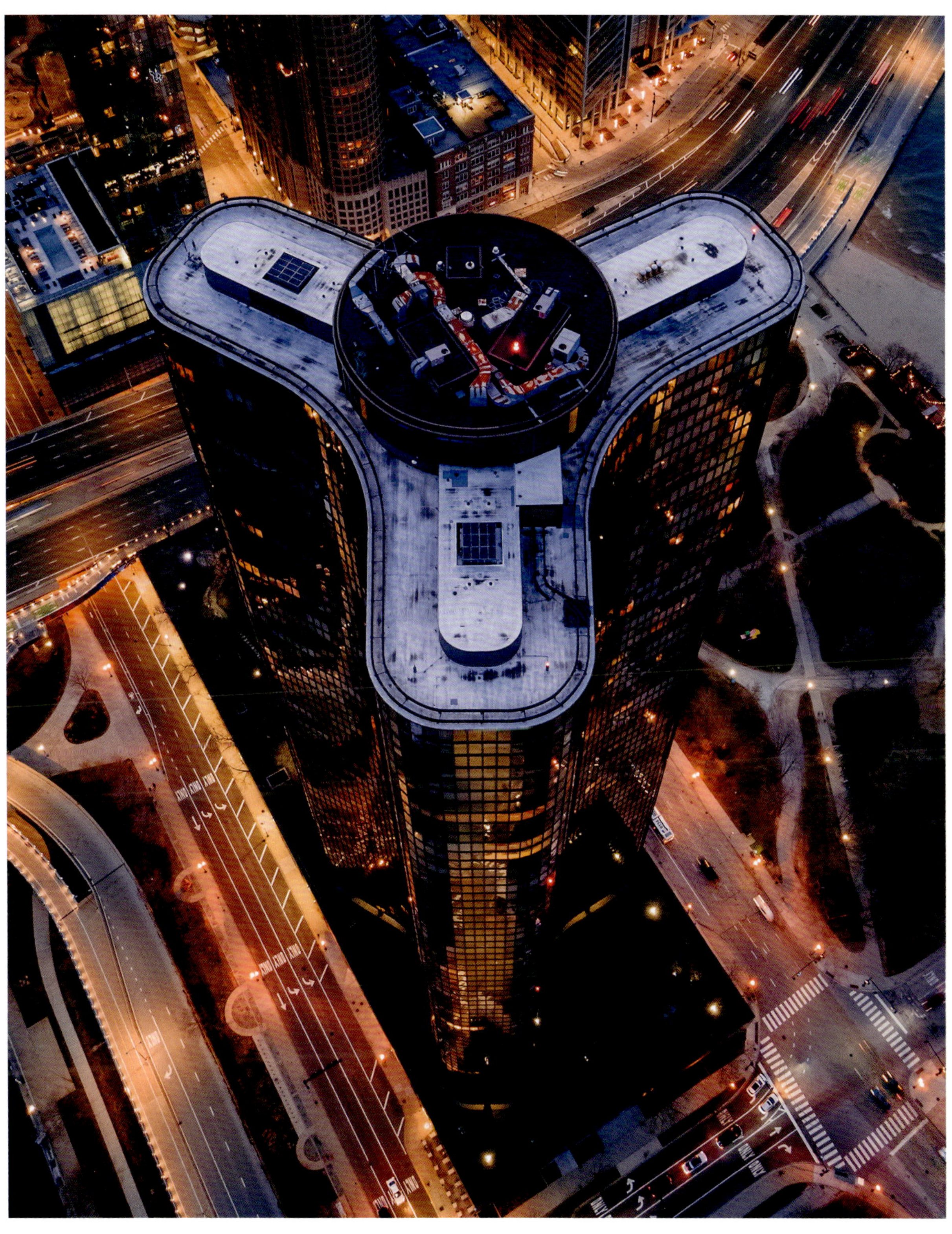

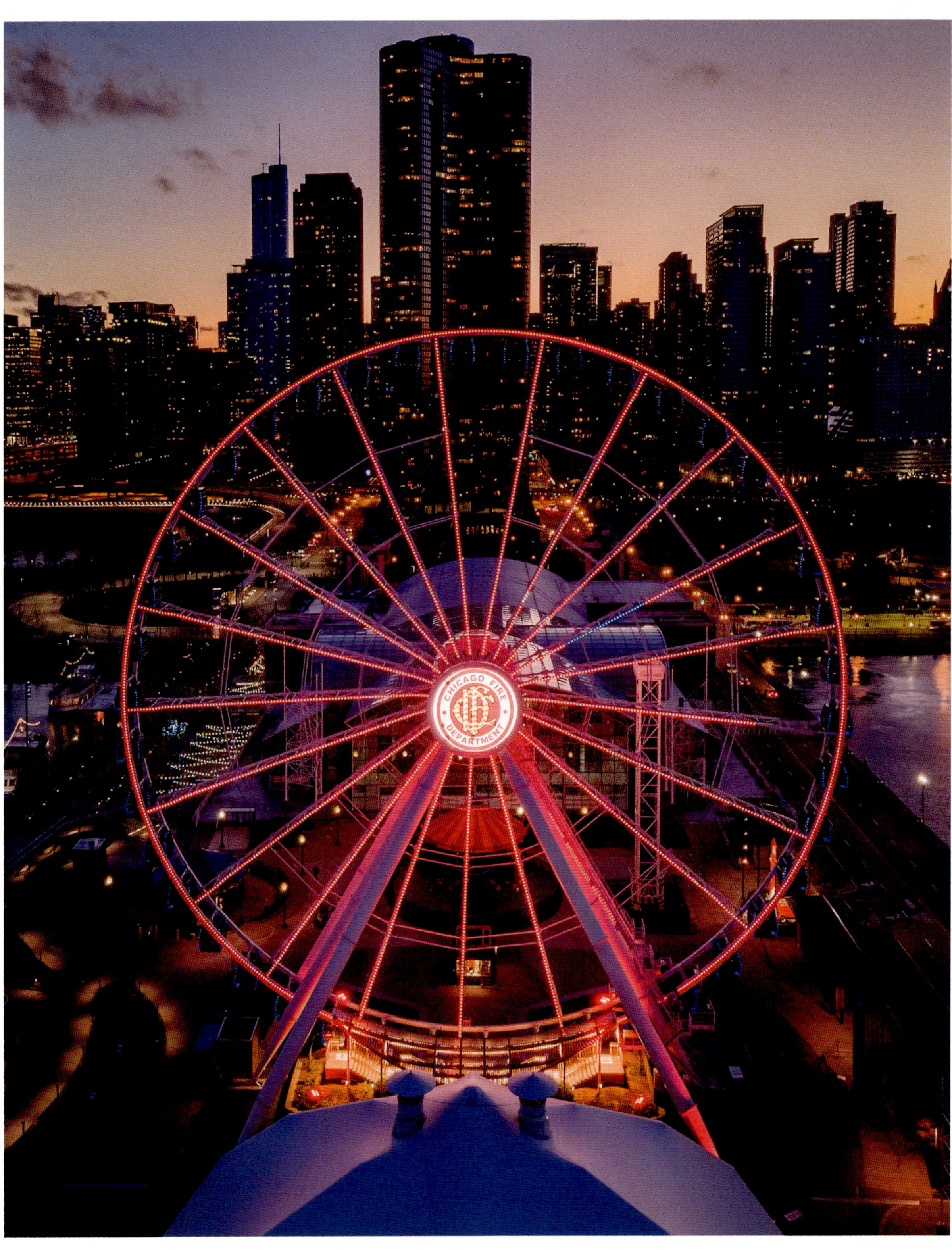

CHICAGO FIRE
DEPARTMENT

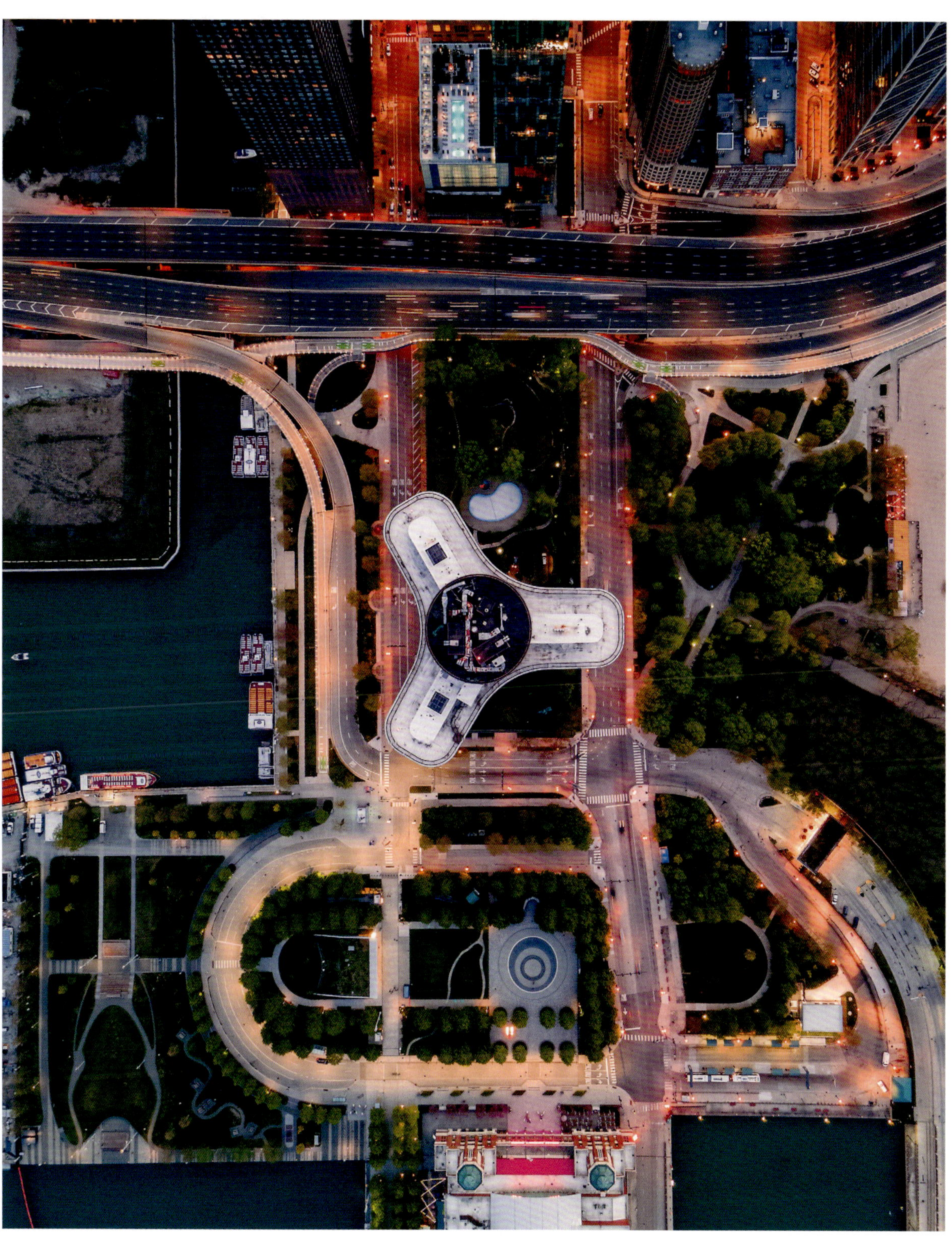

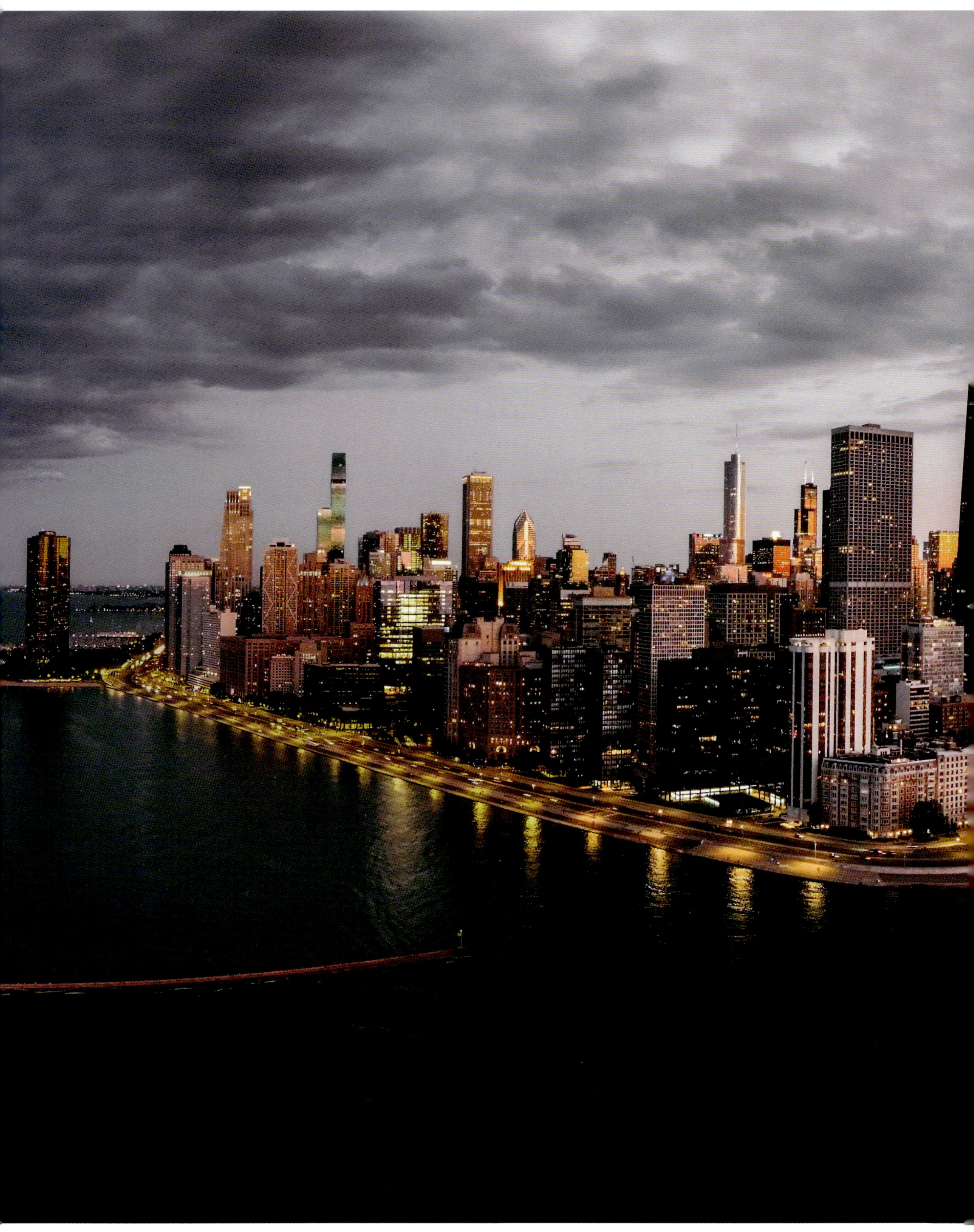

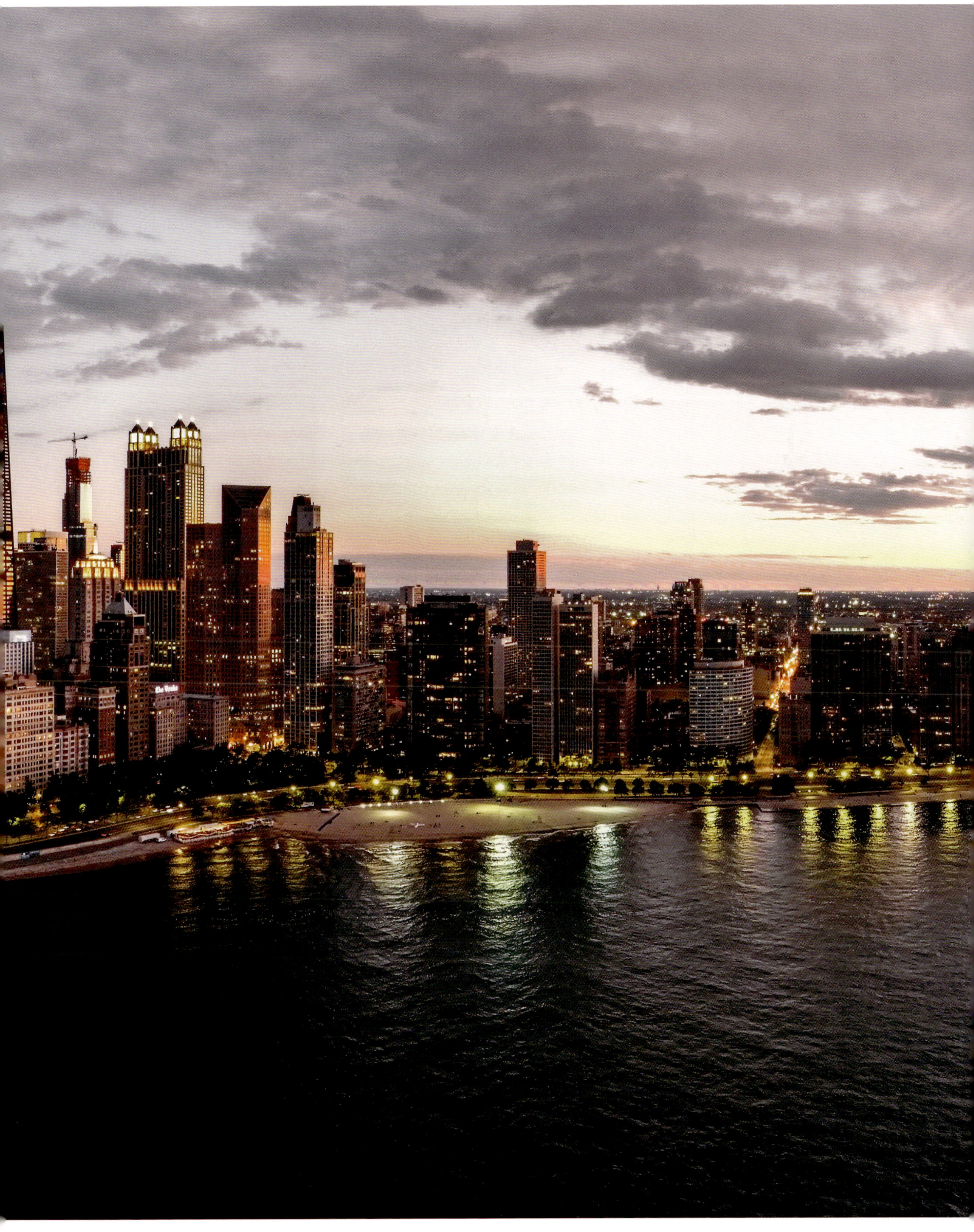

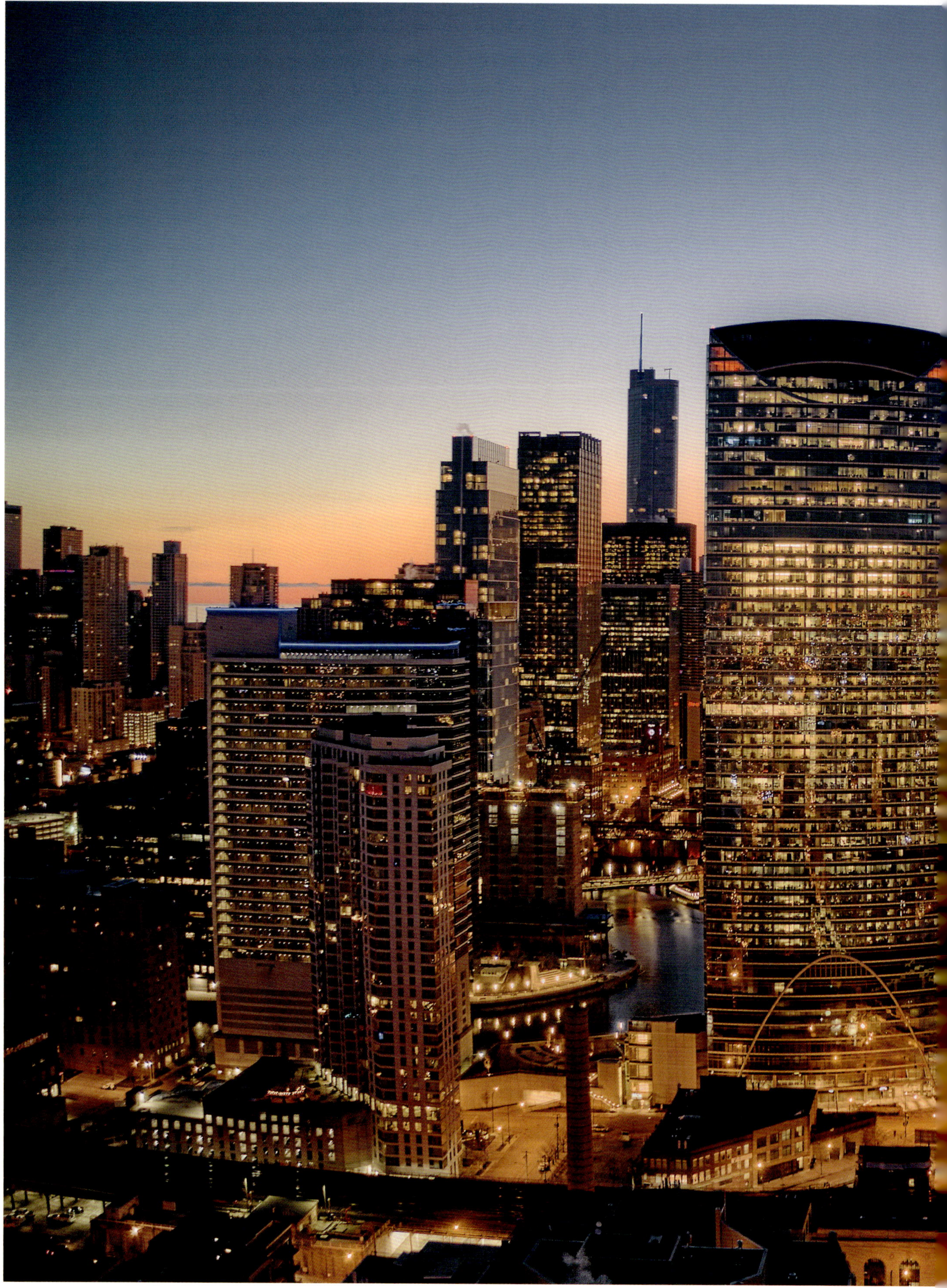

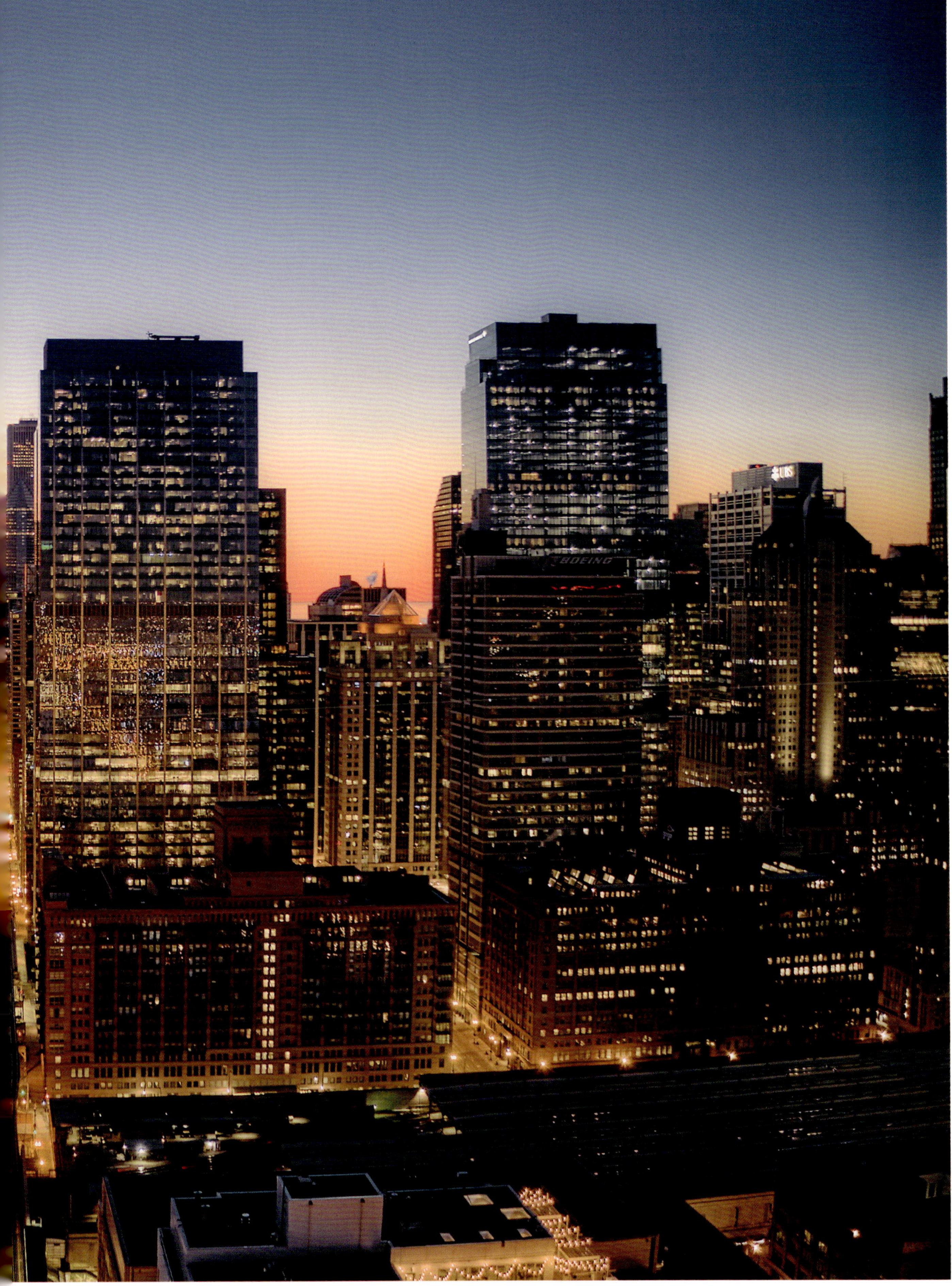

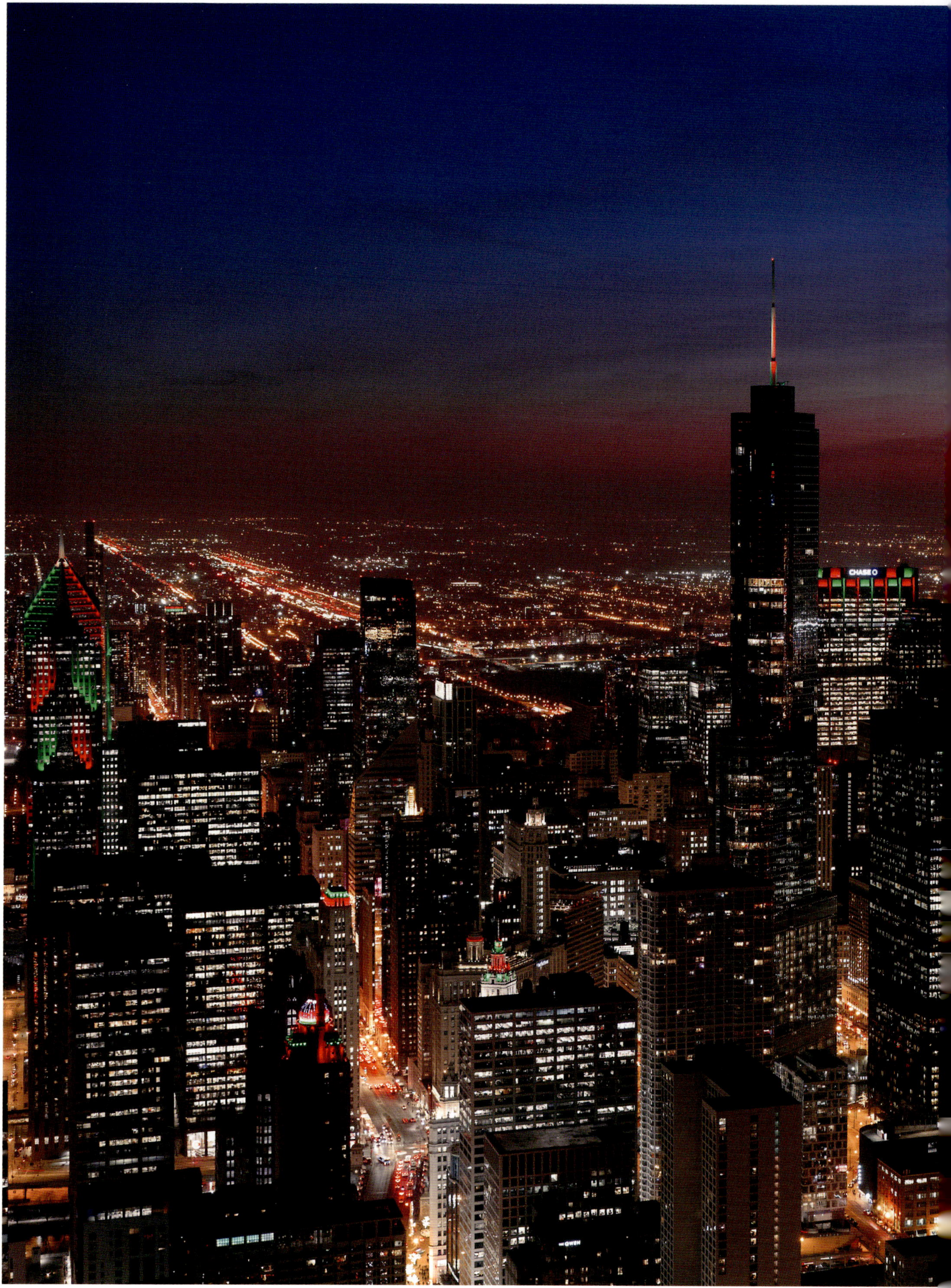

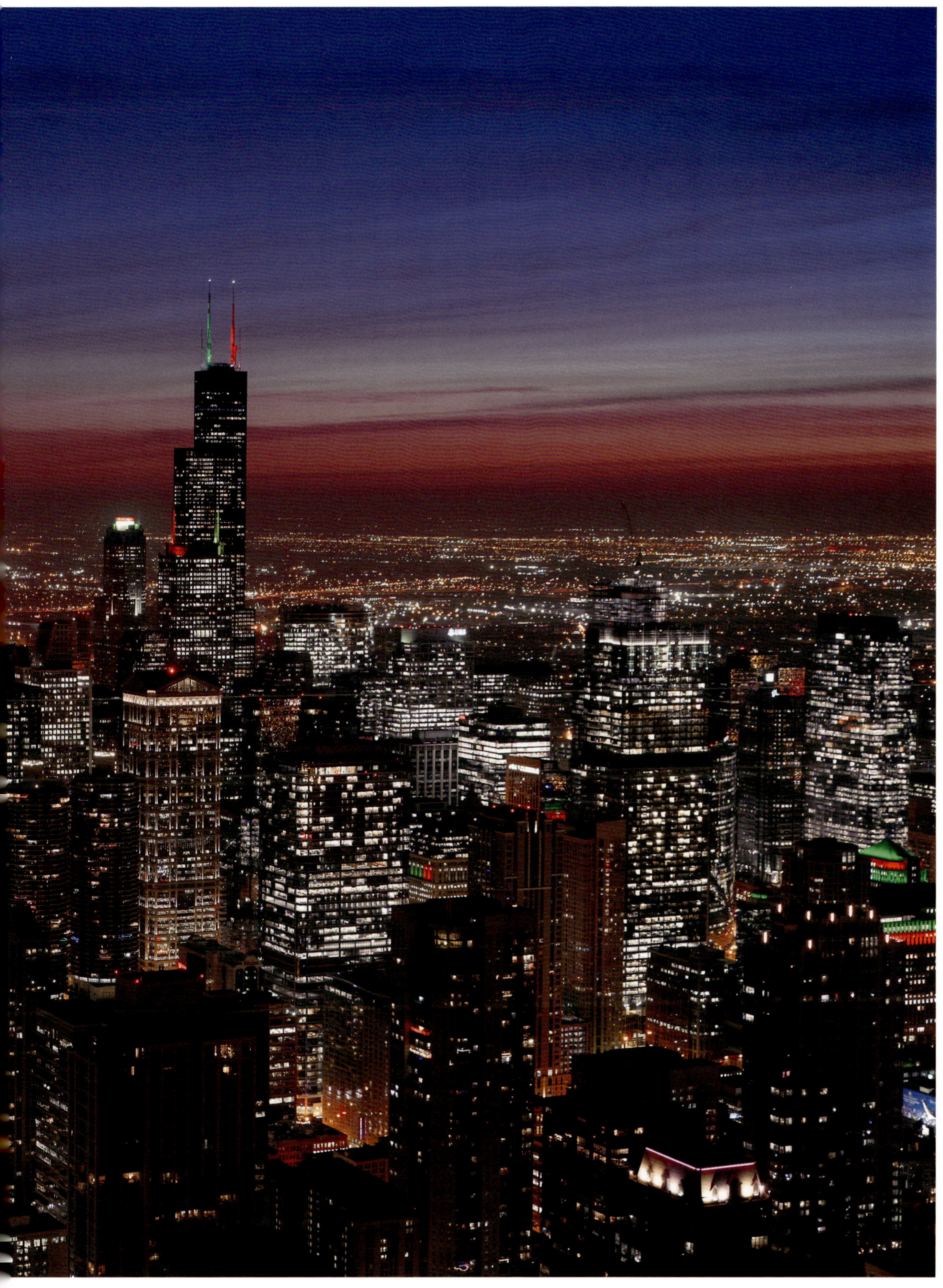

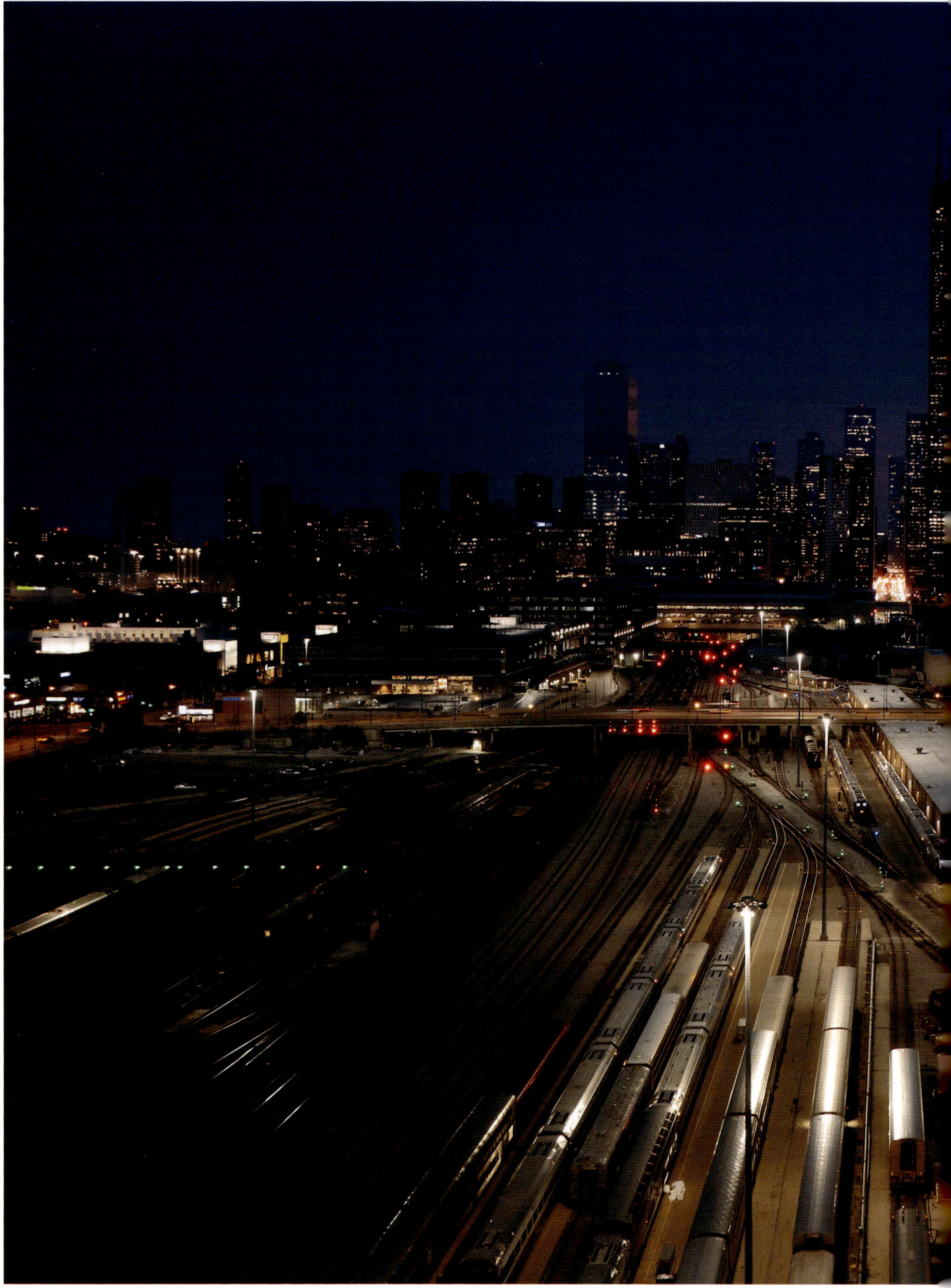

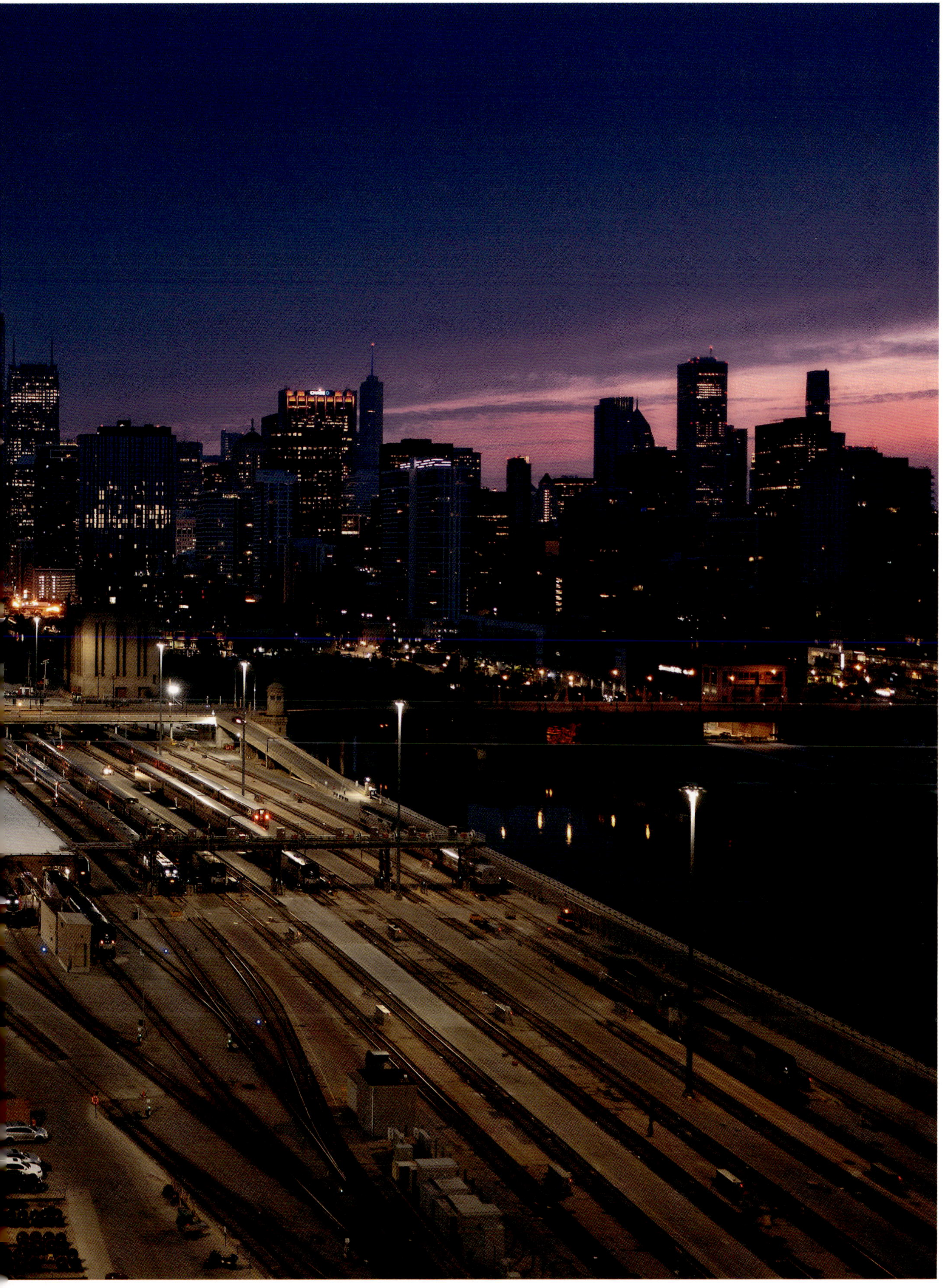

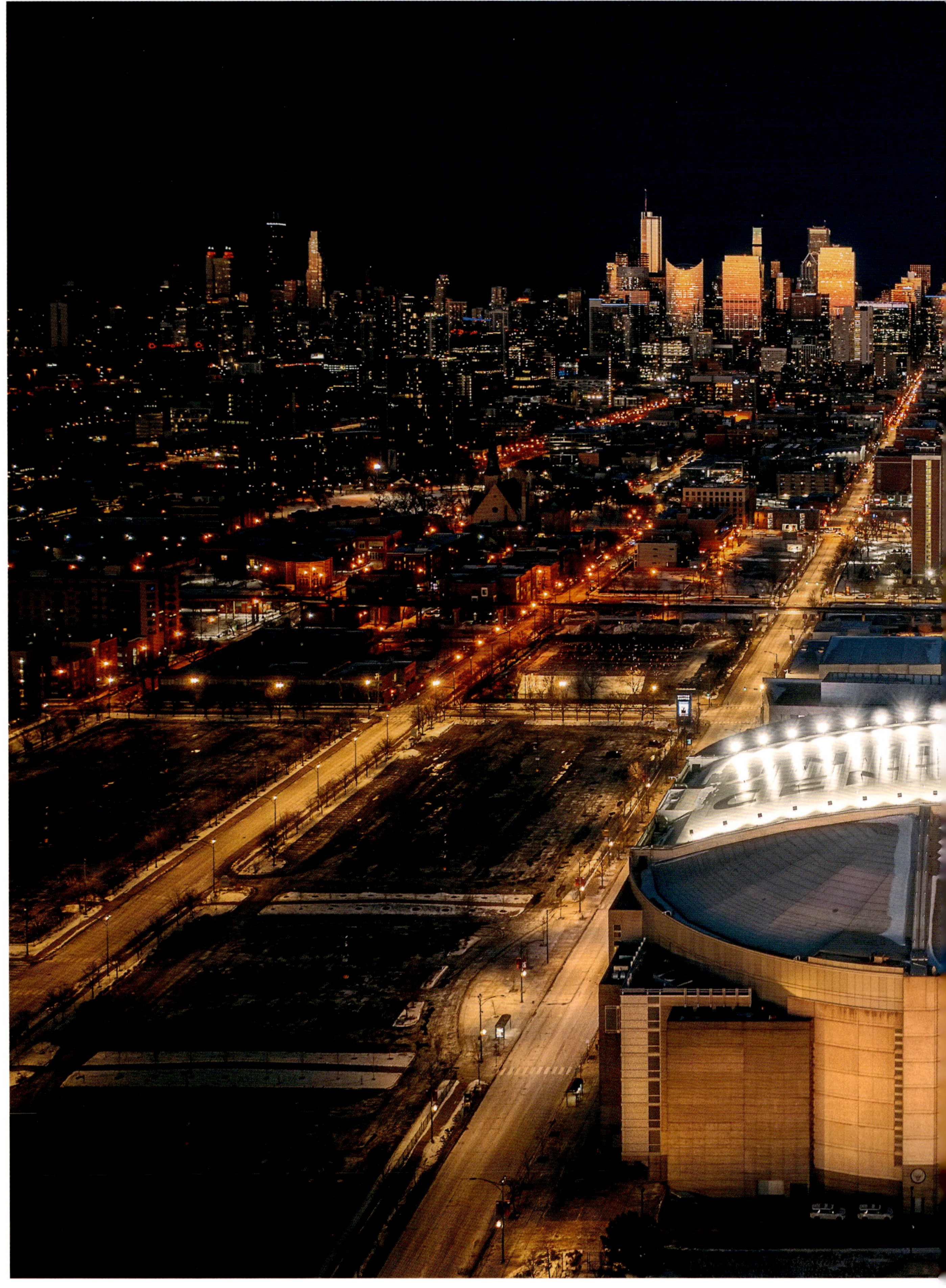

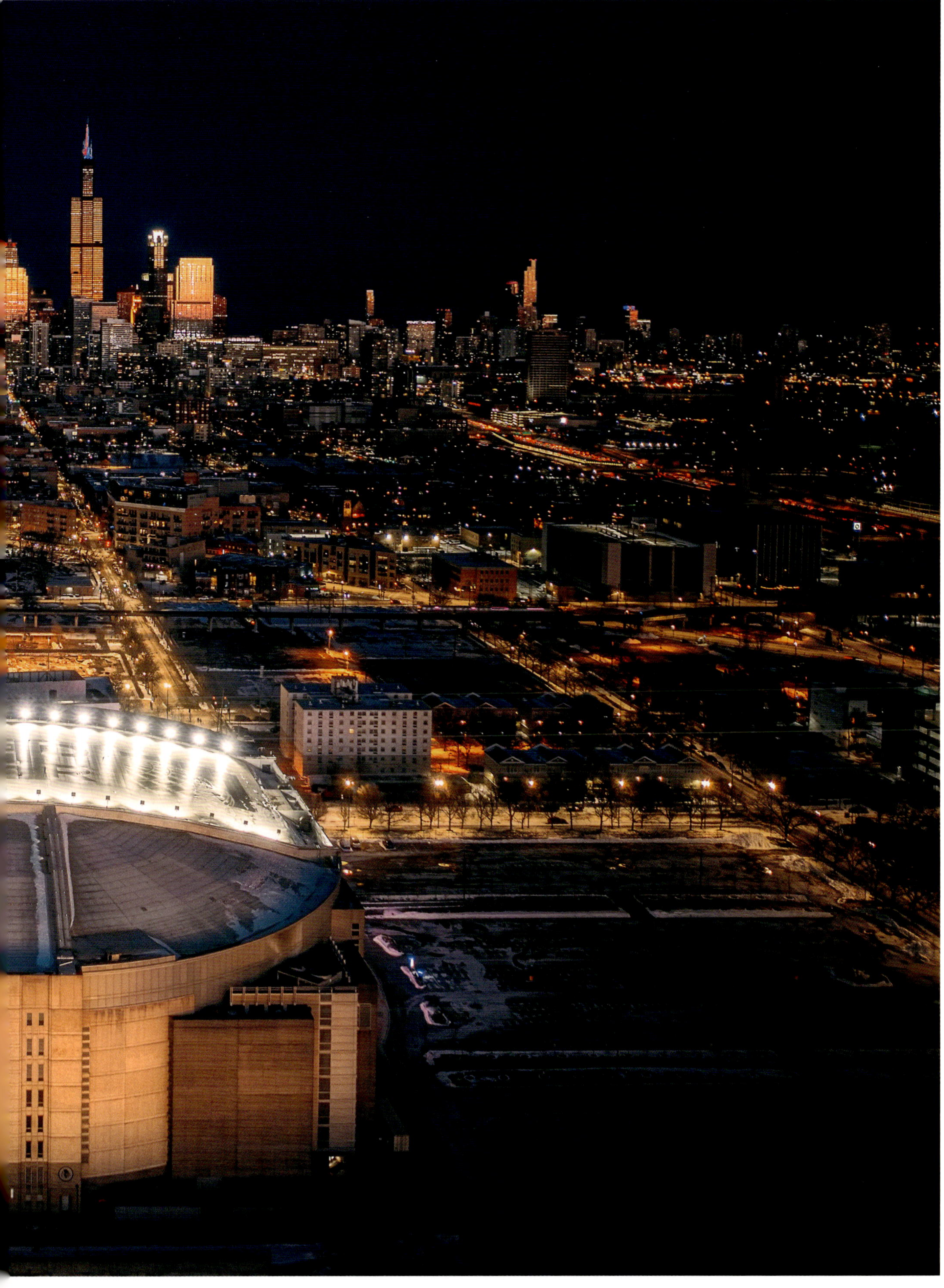

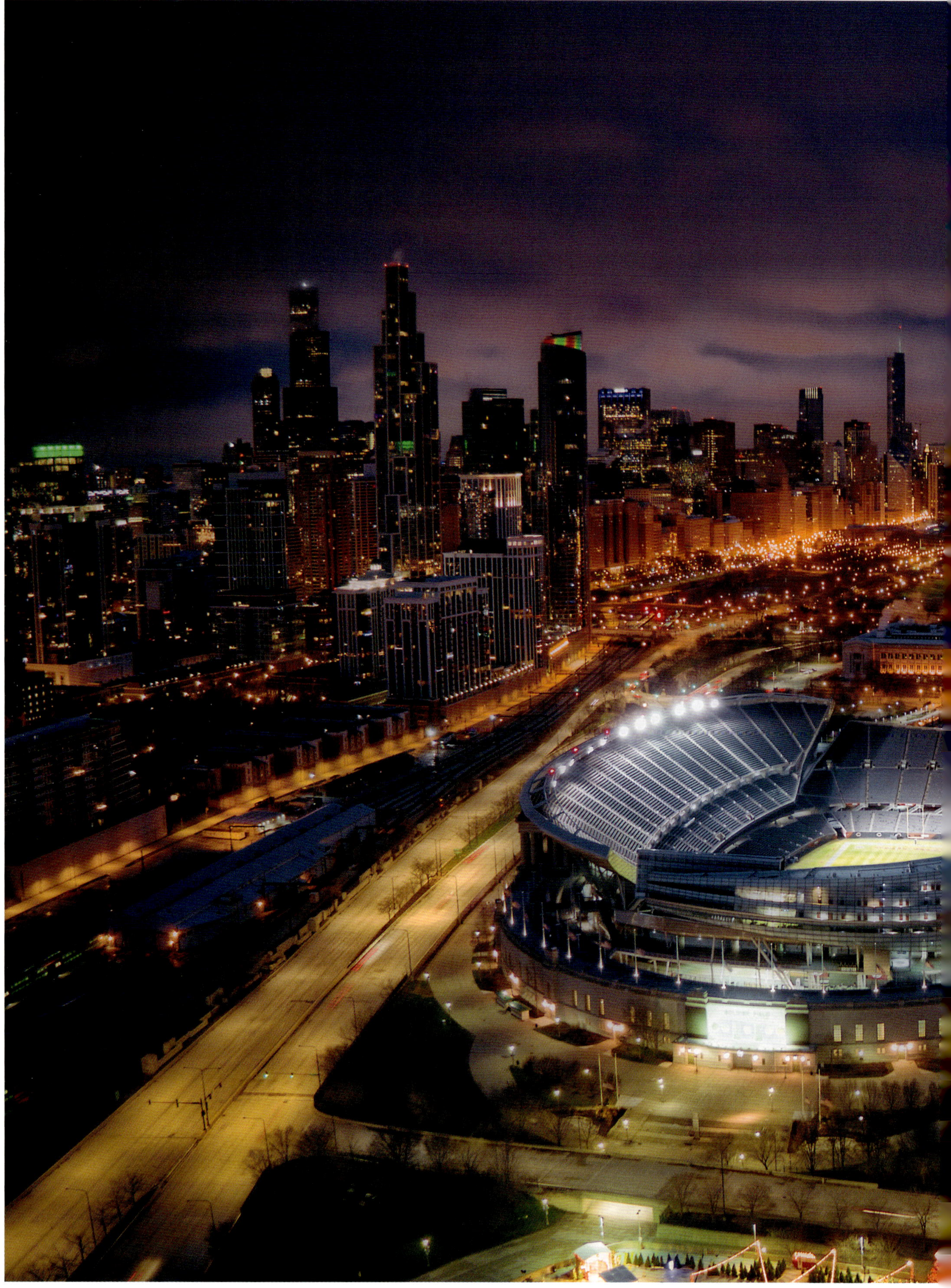

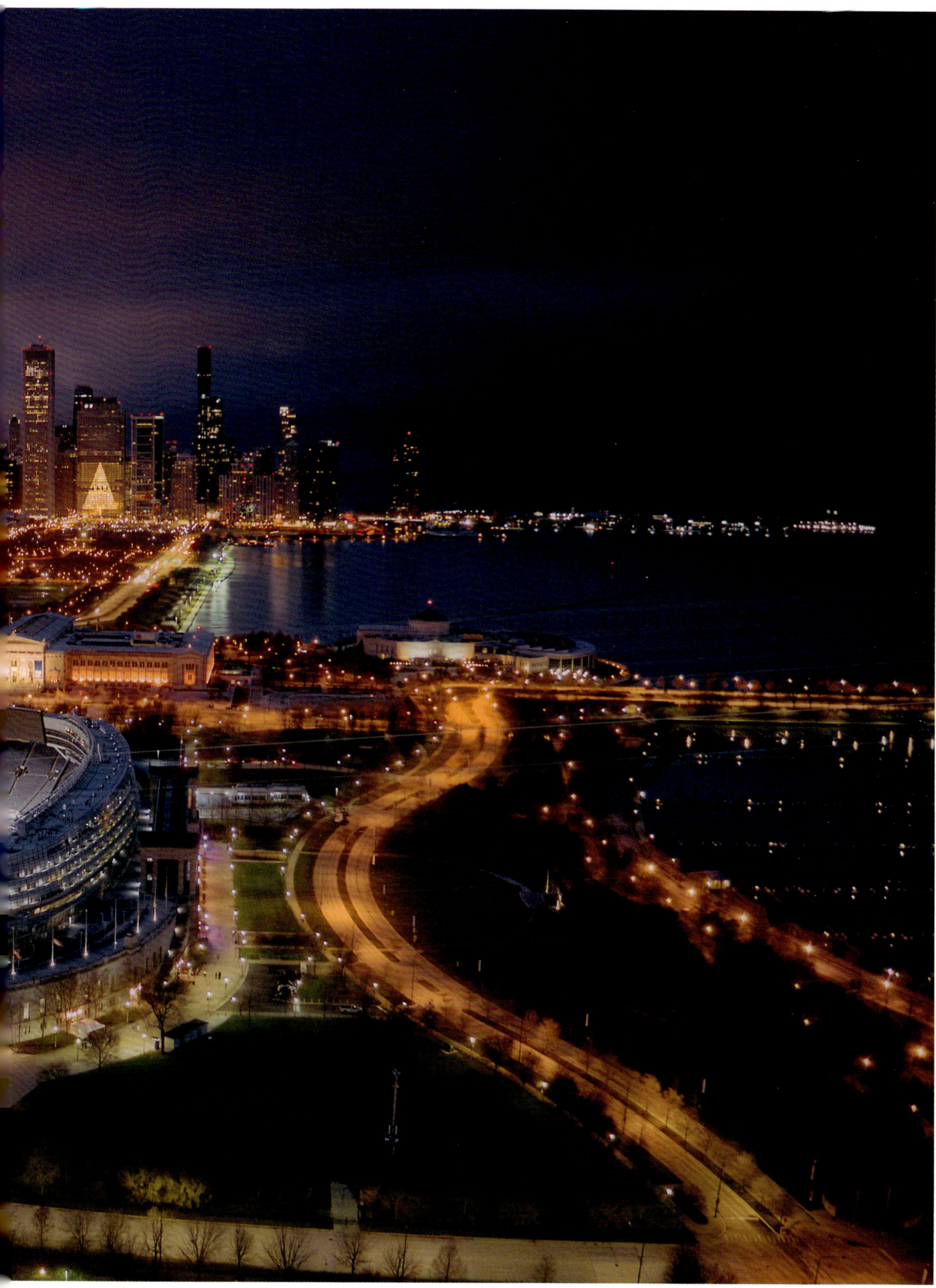

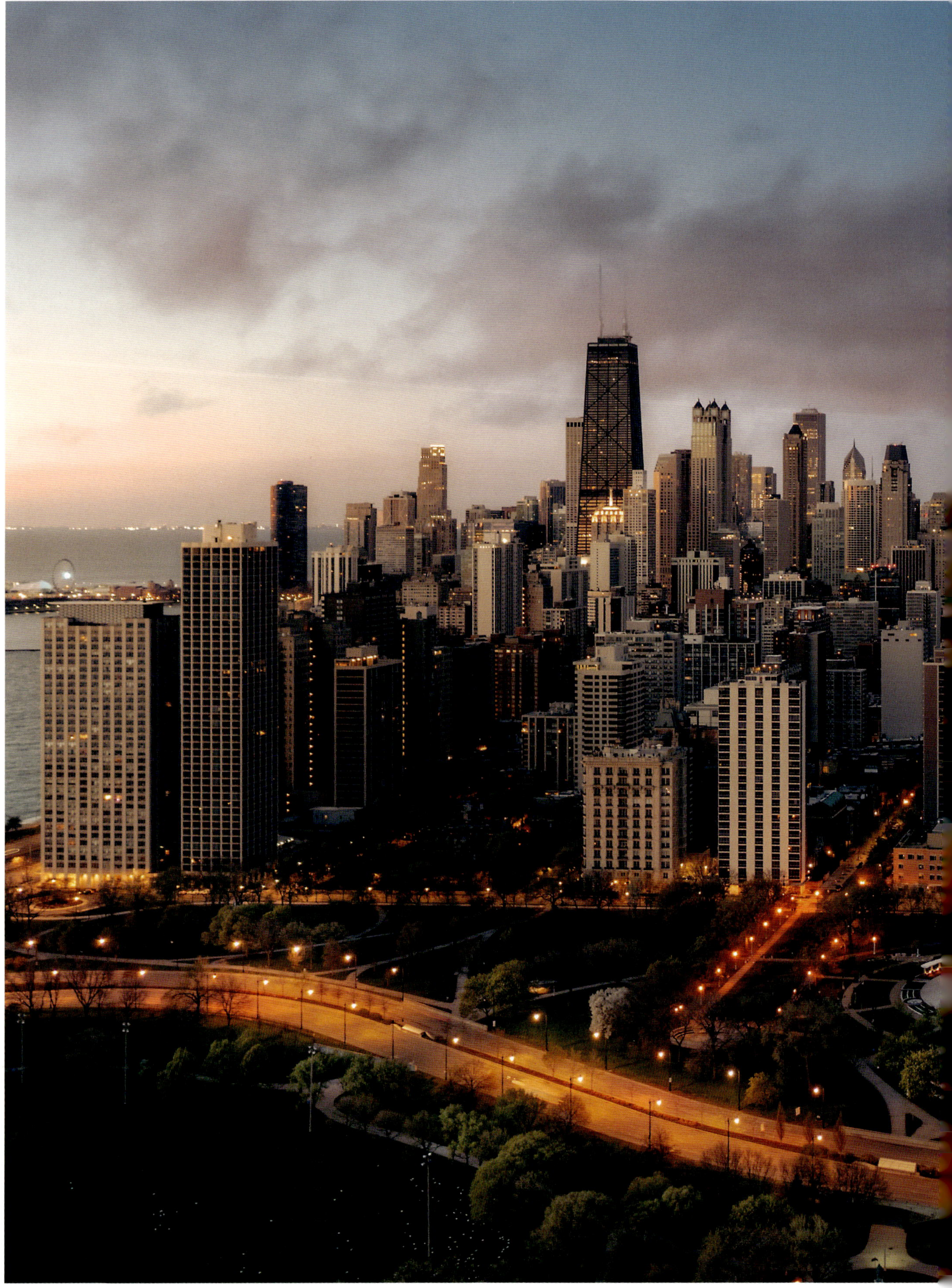

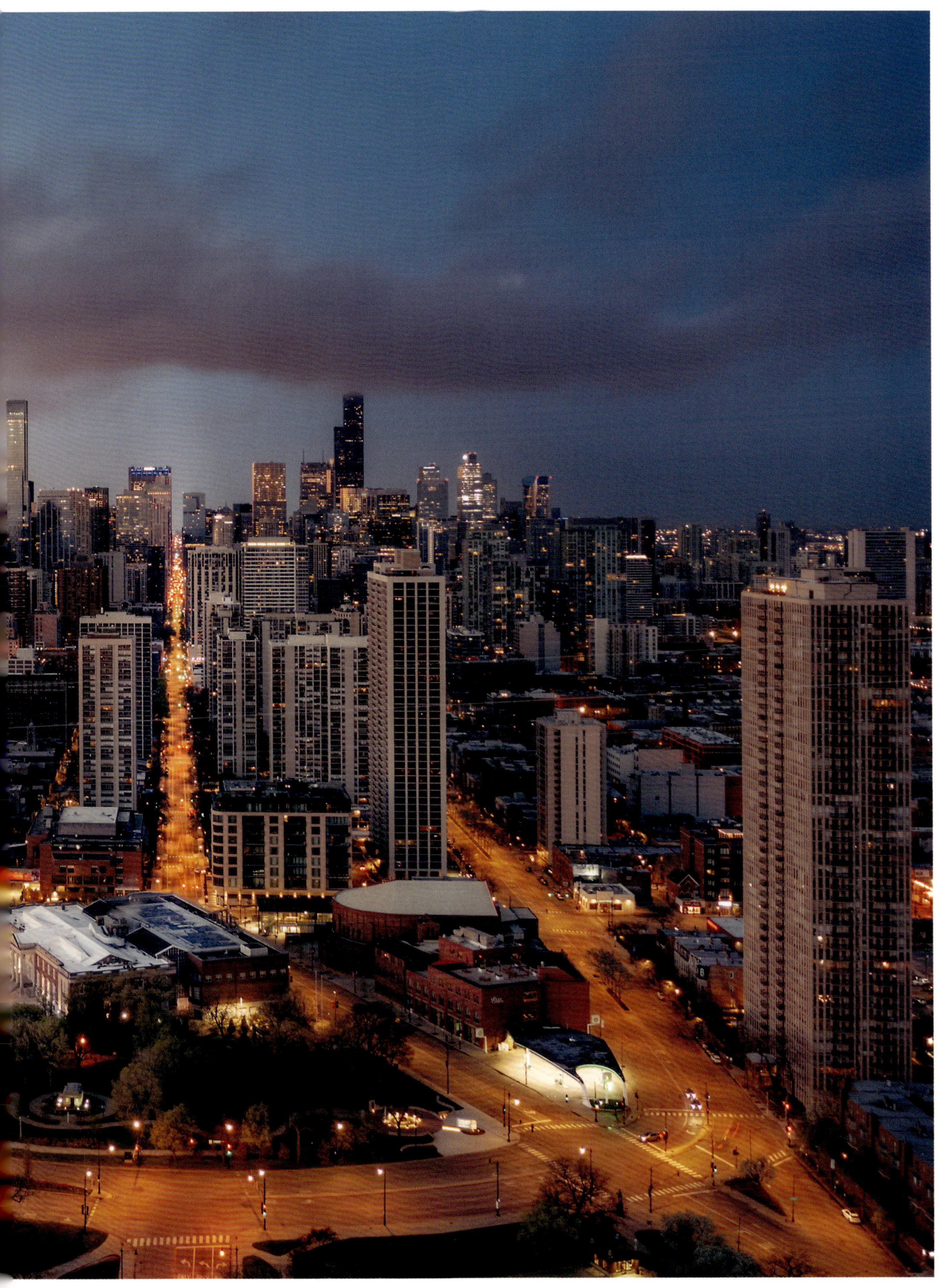

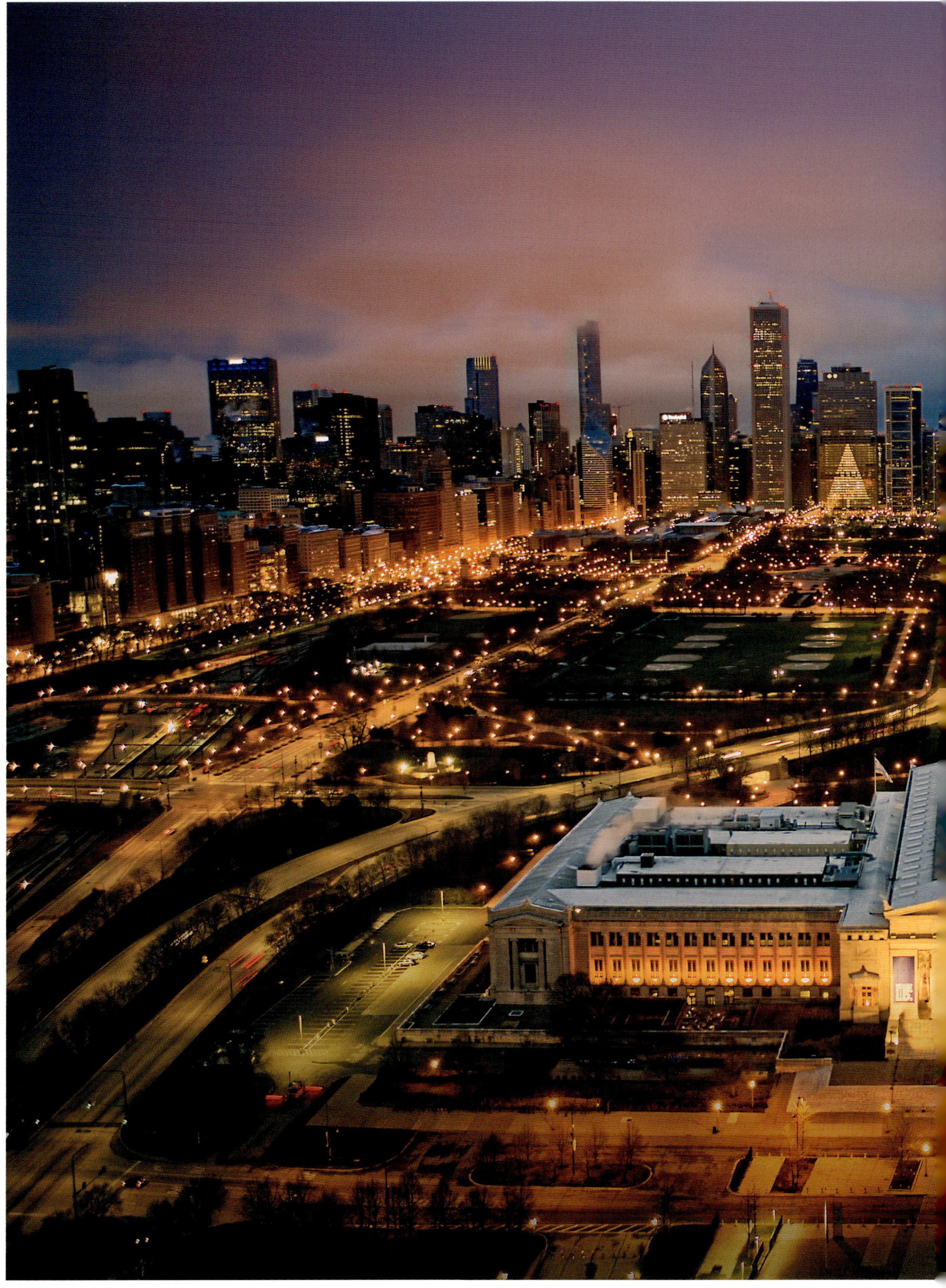

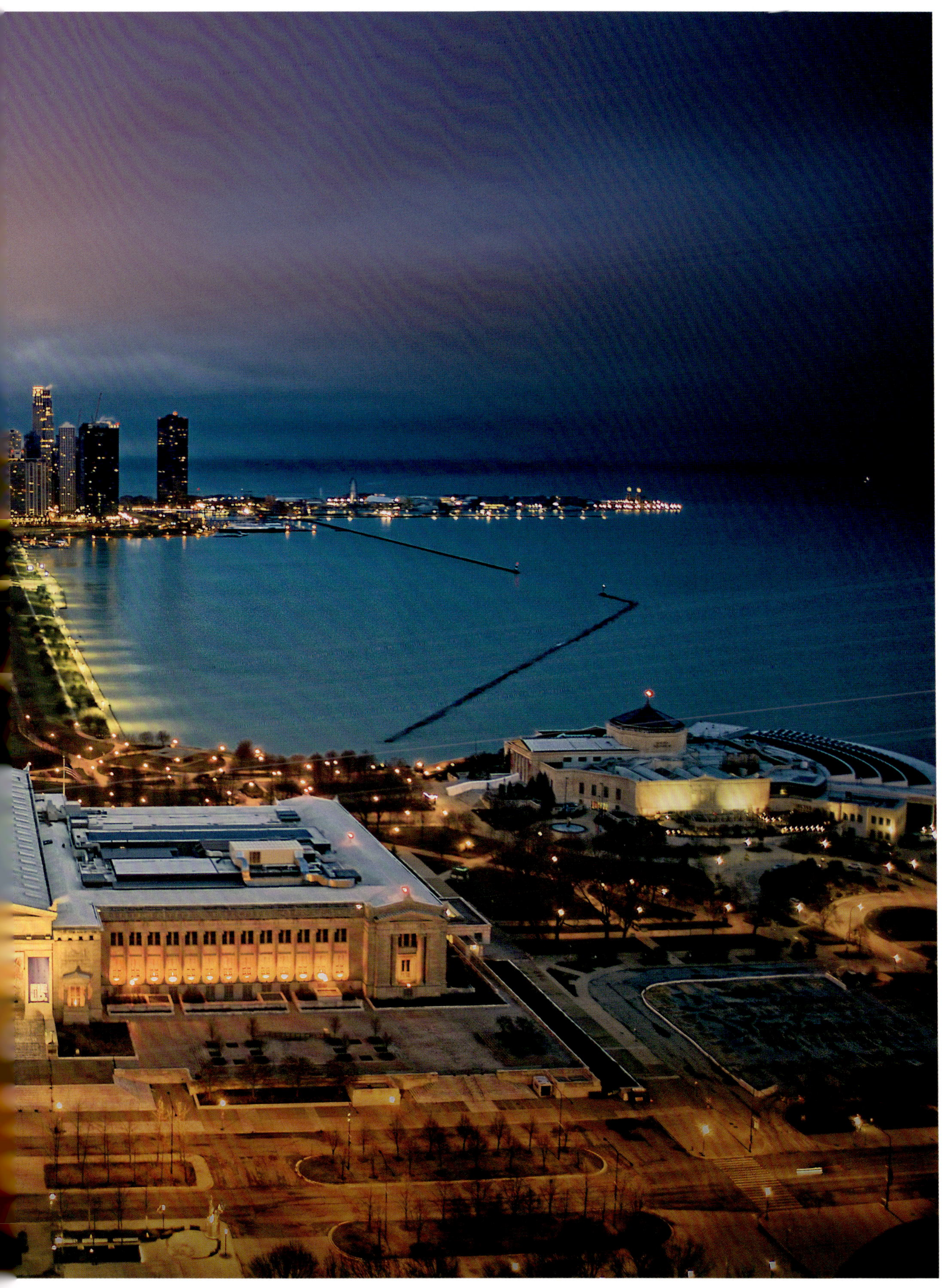

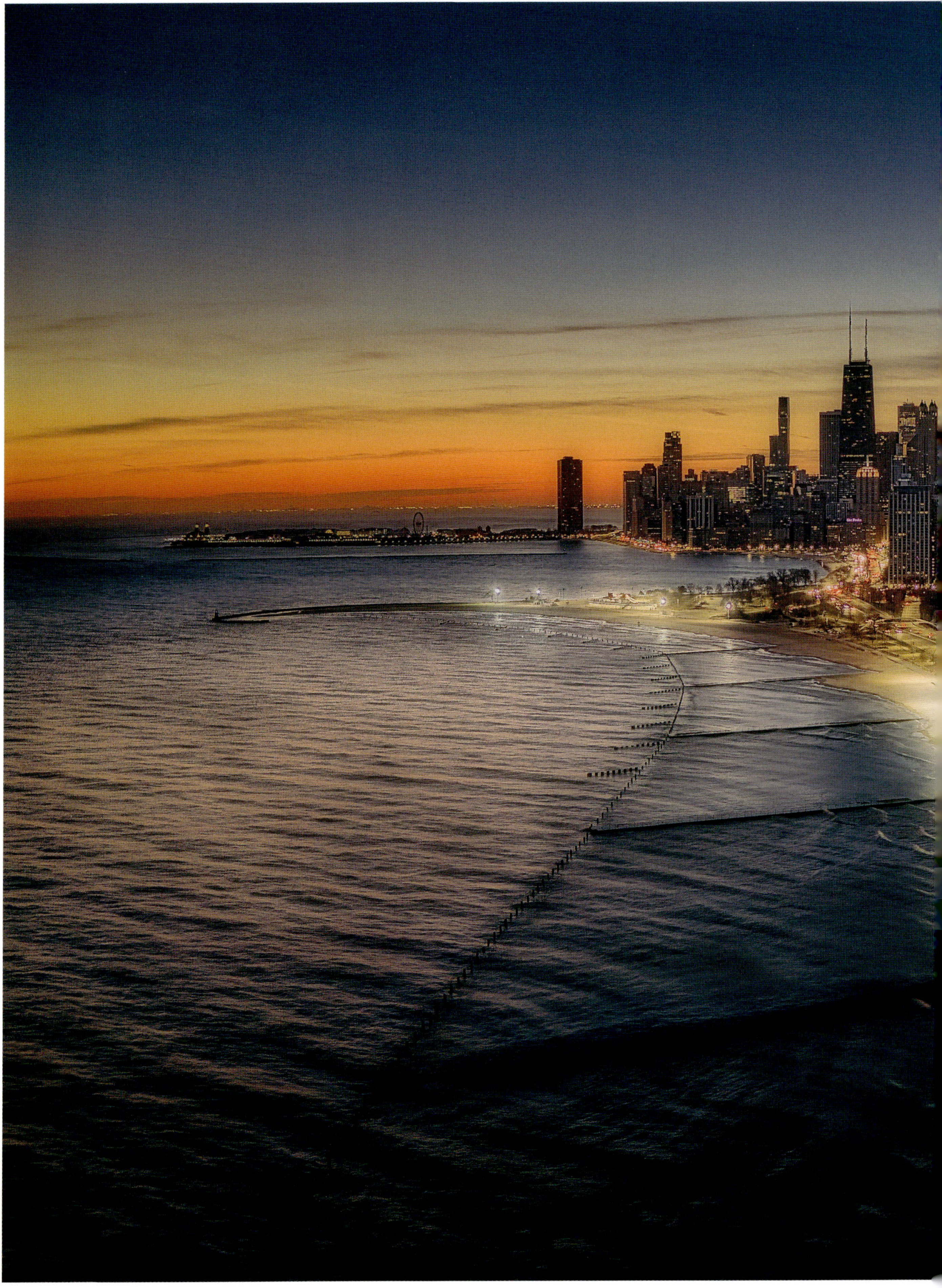

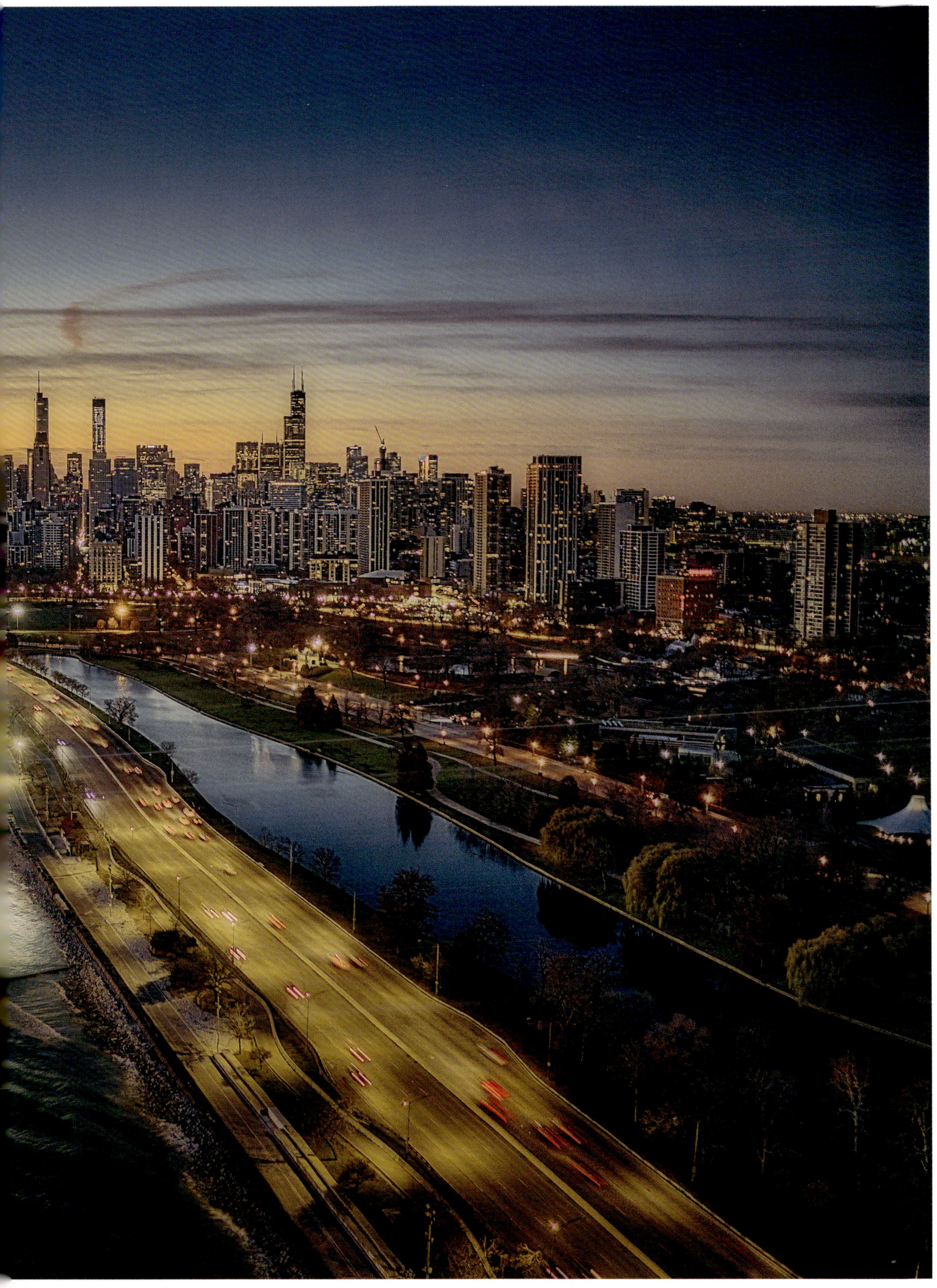

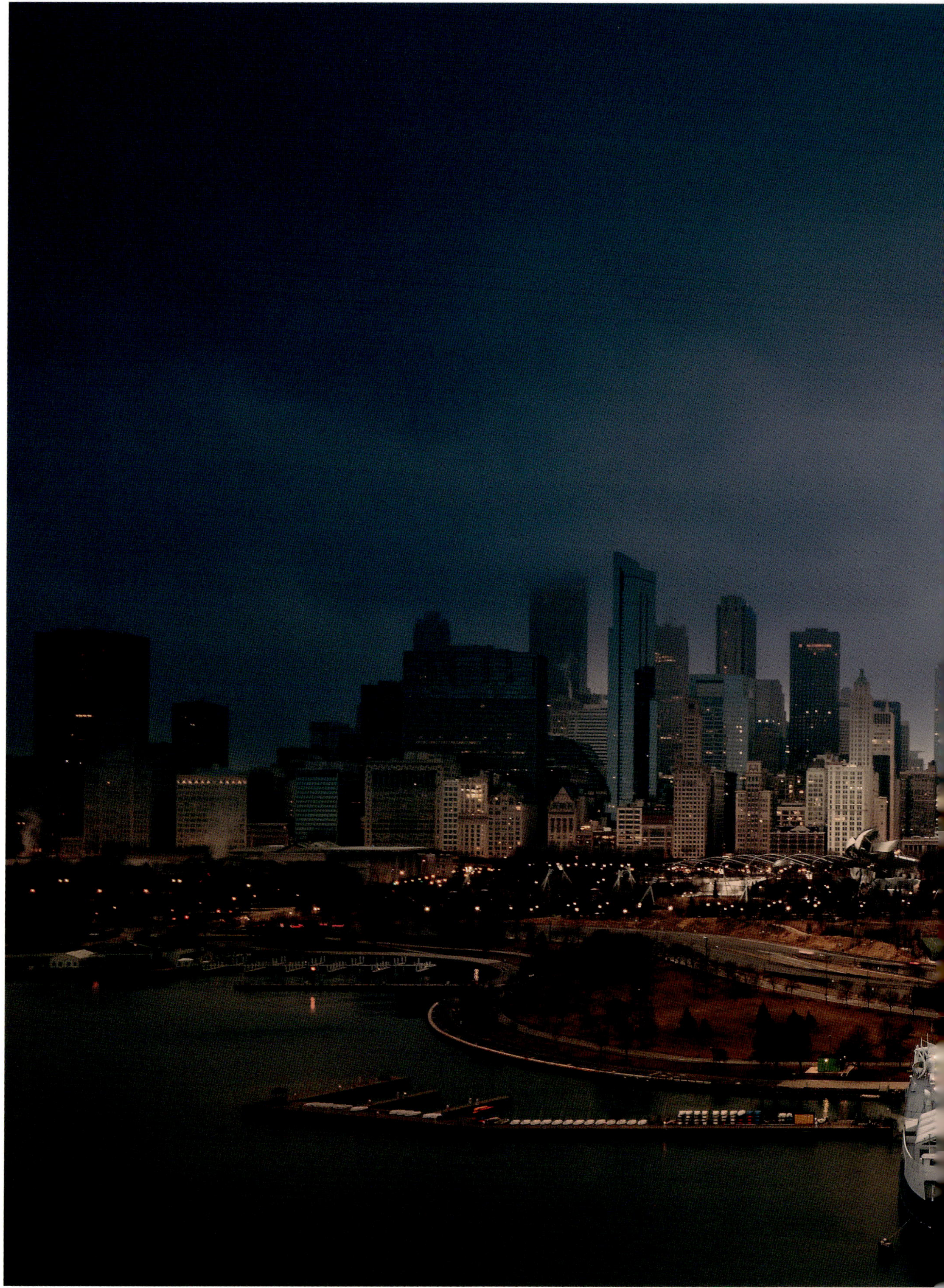

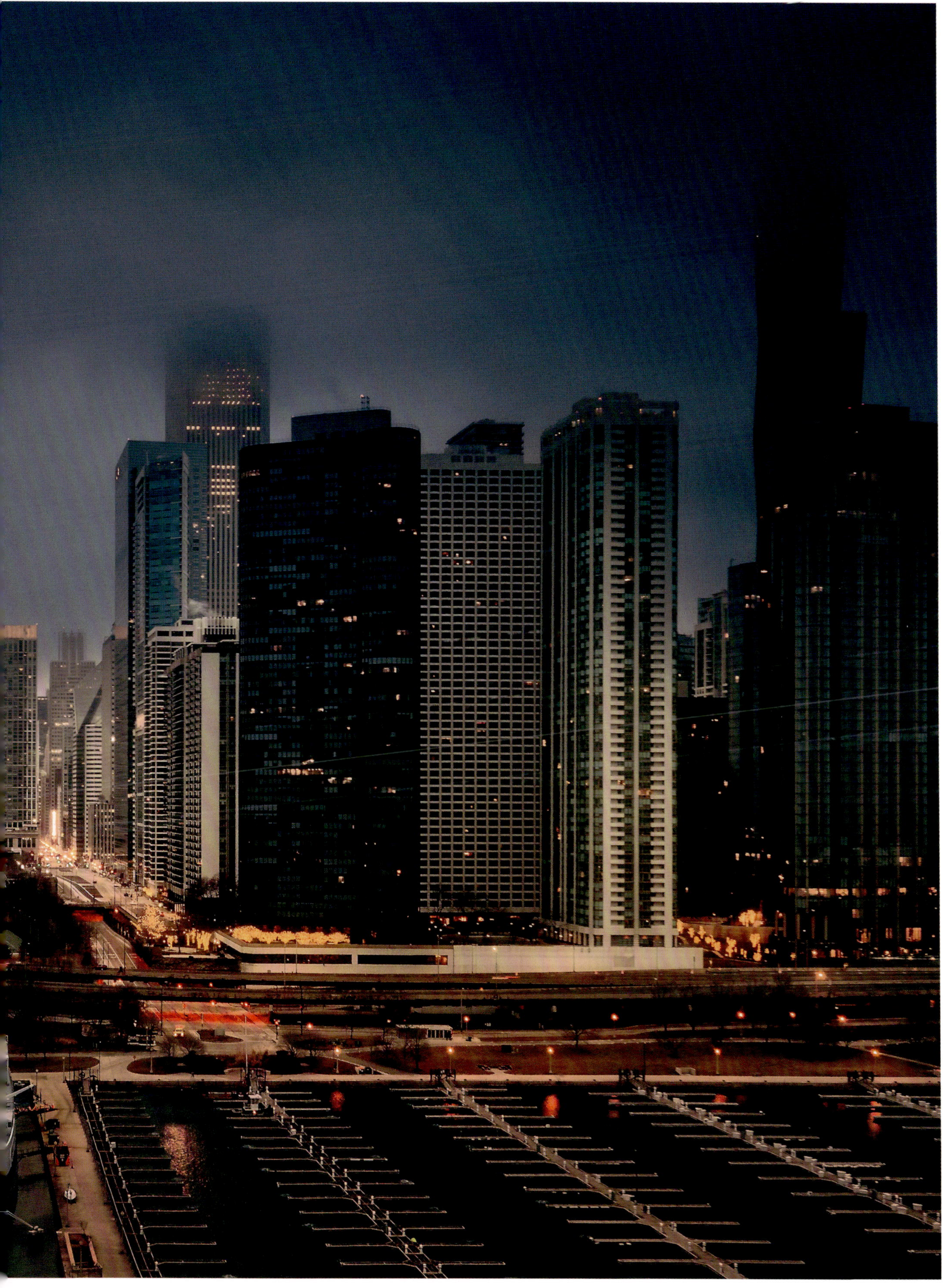

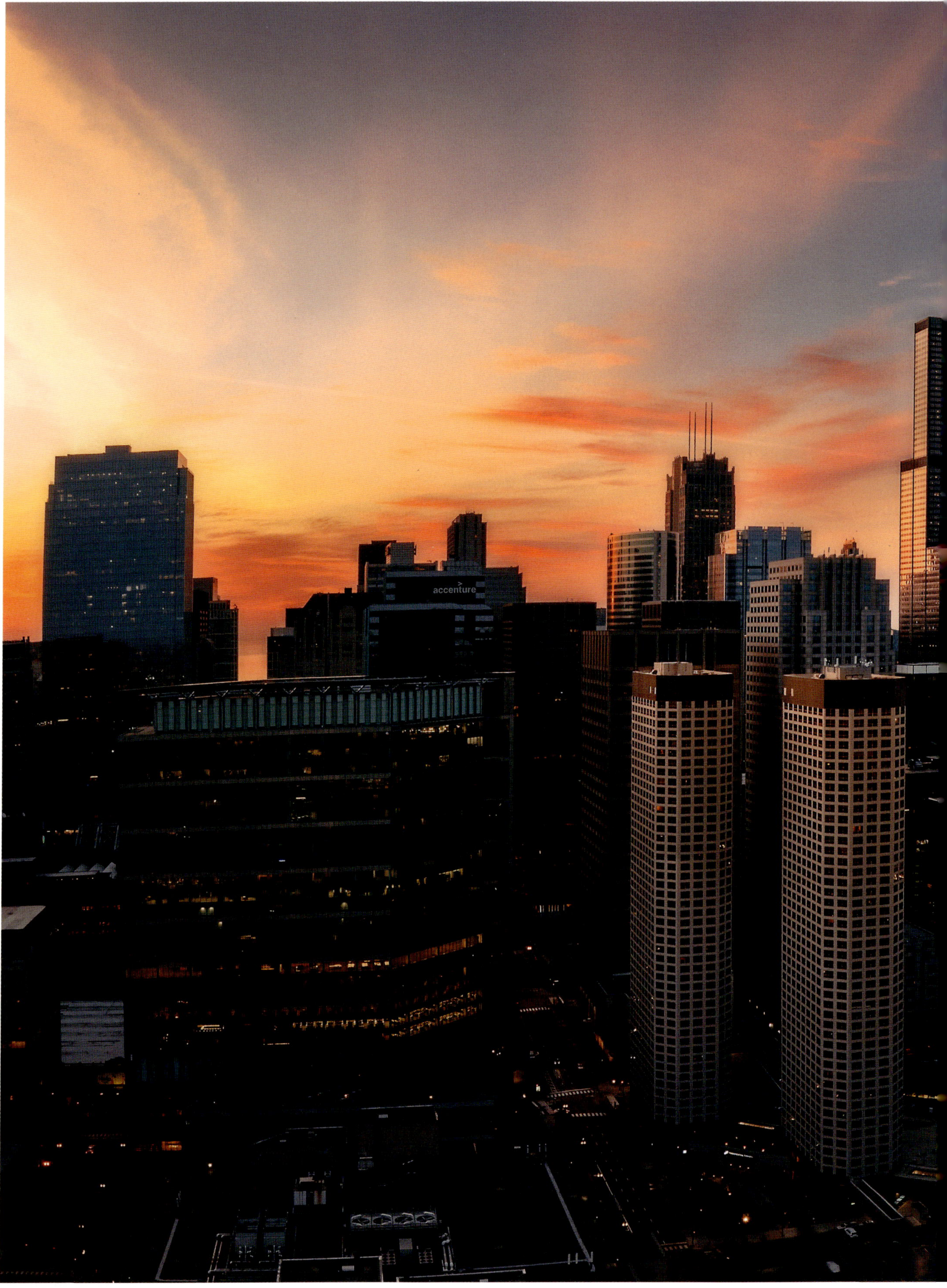

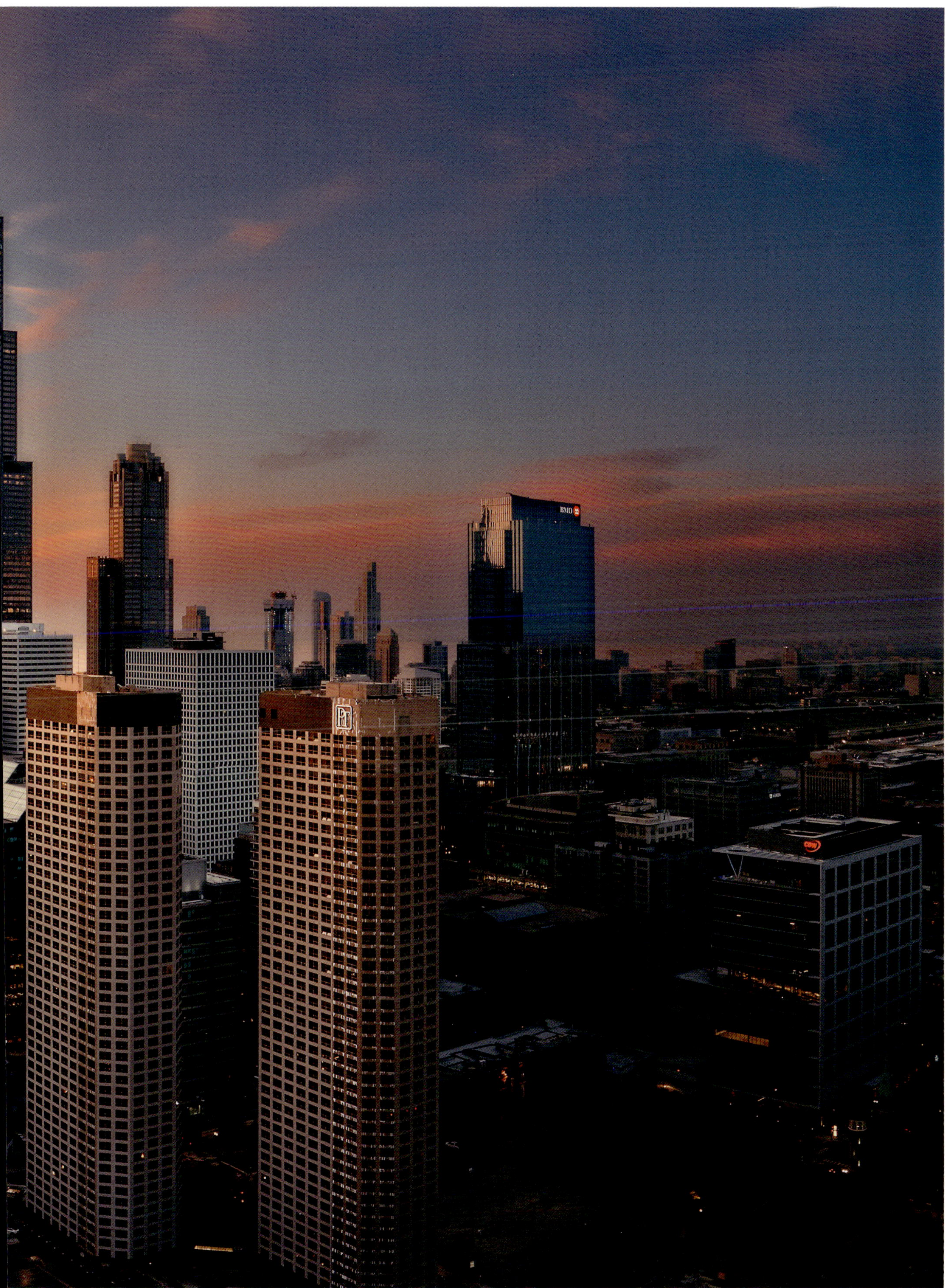

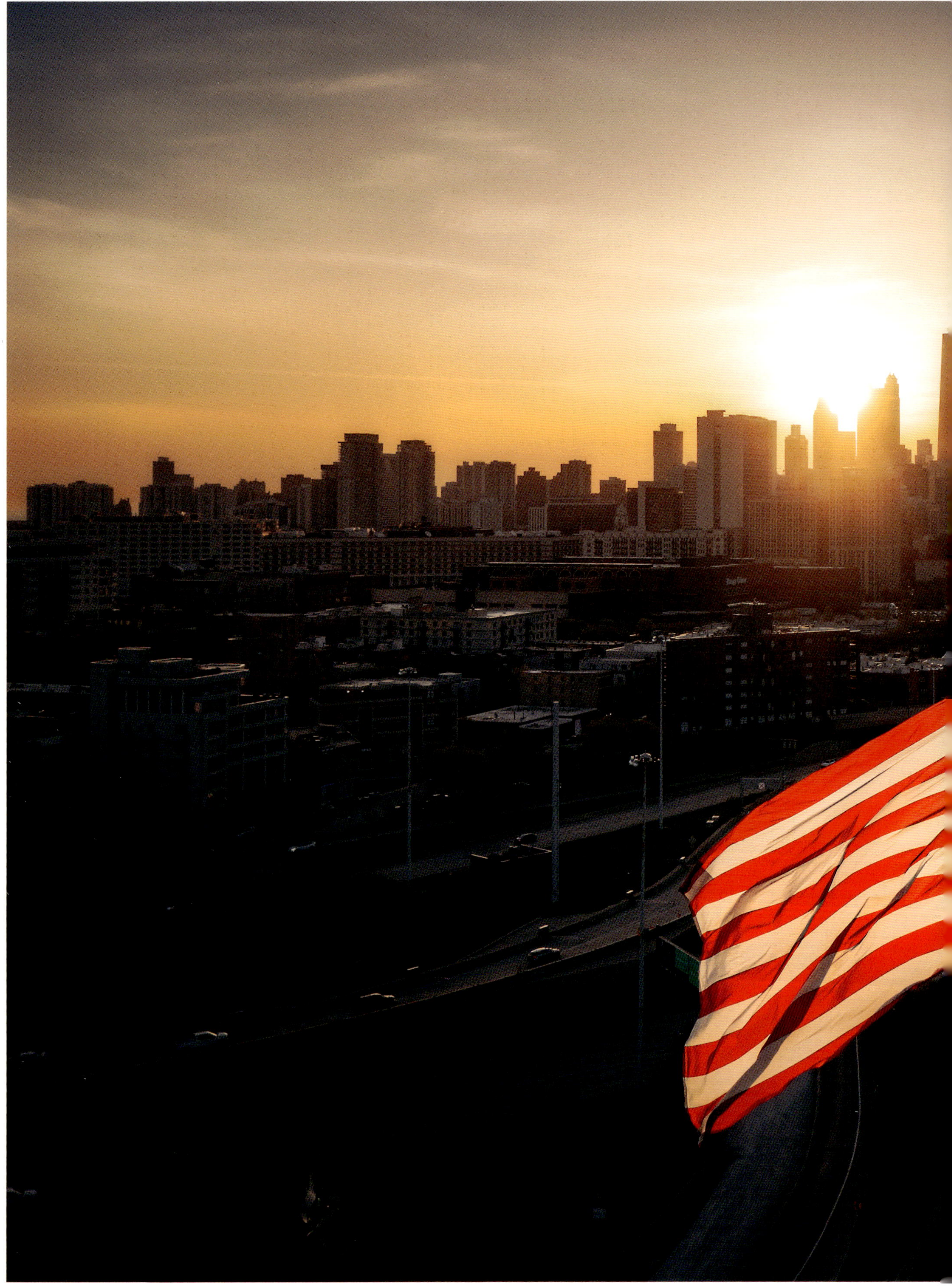

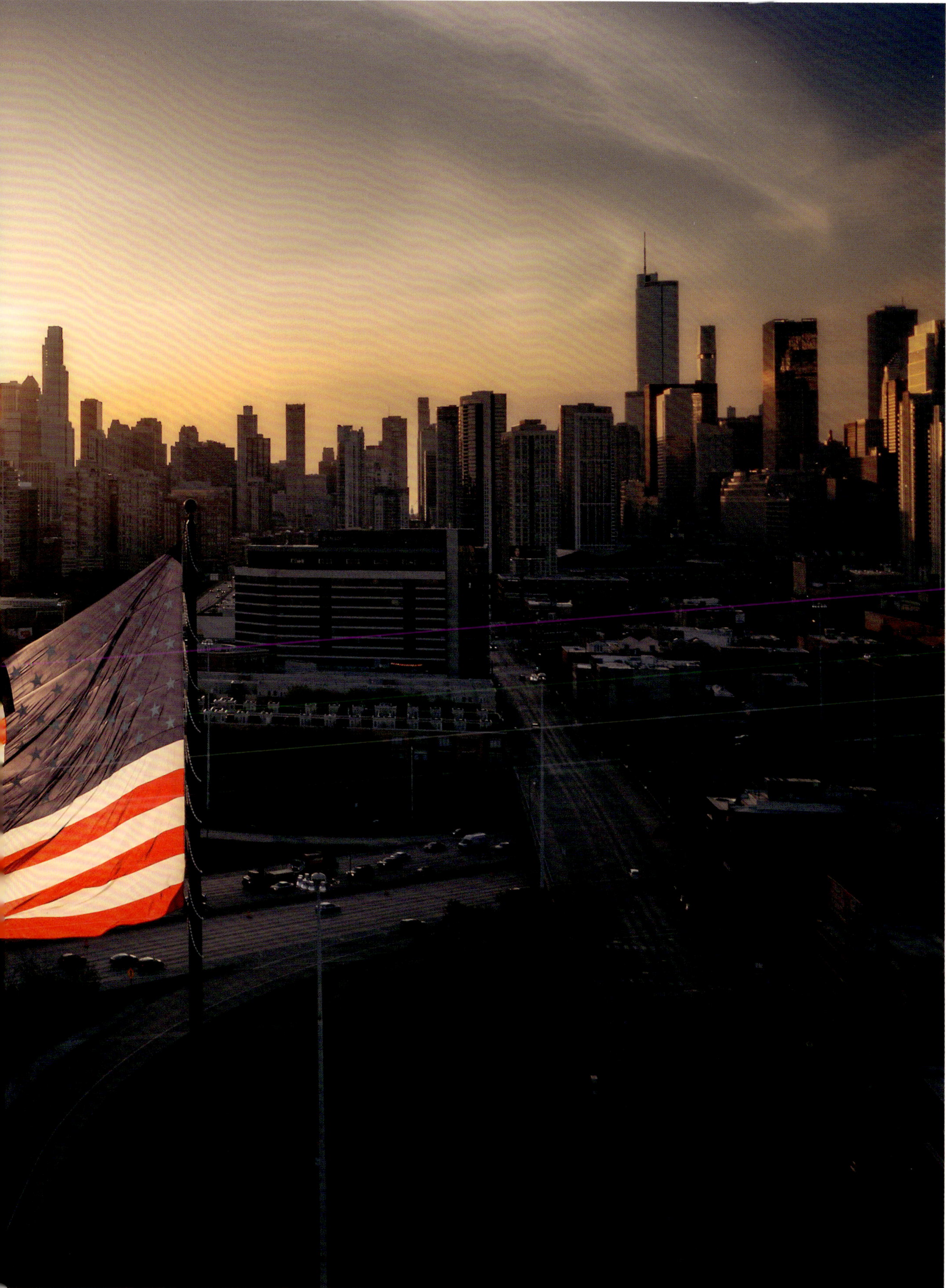

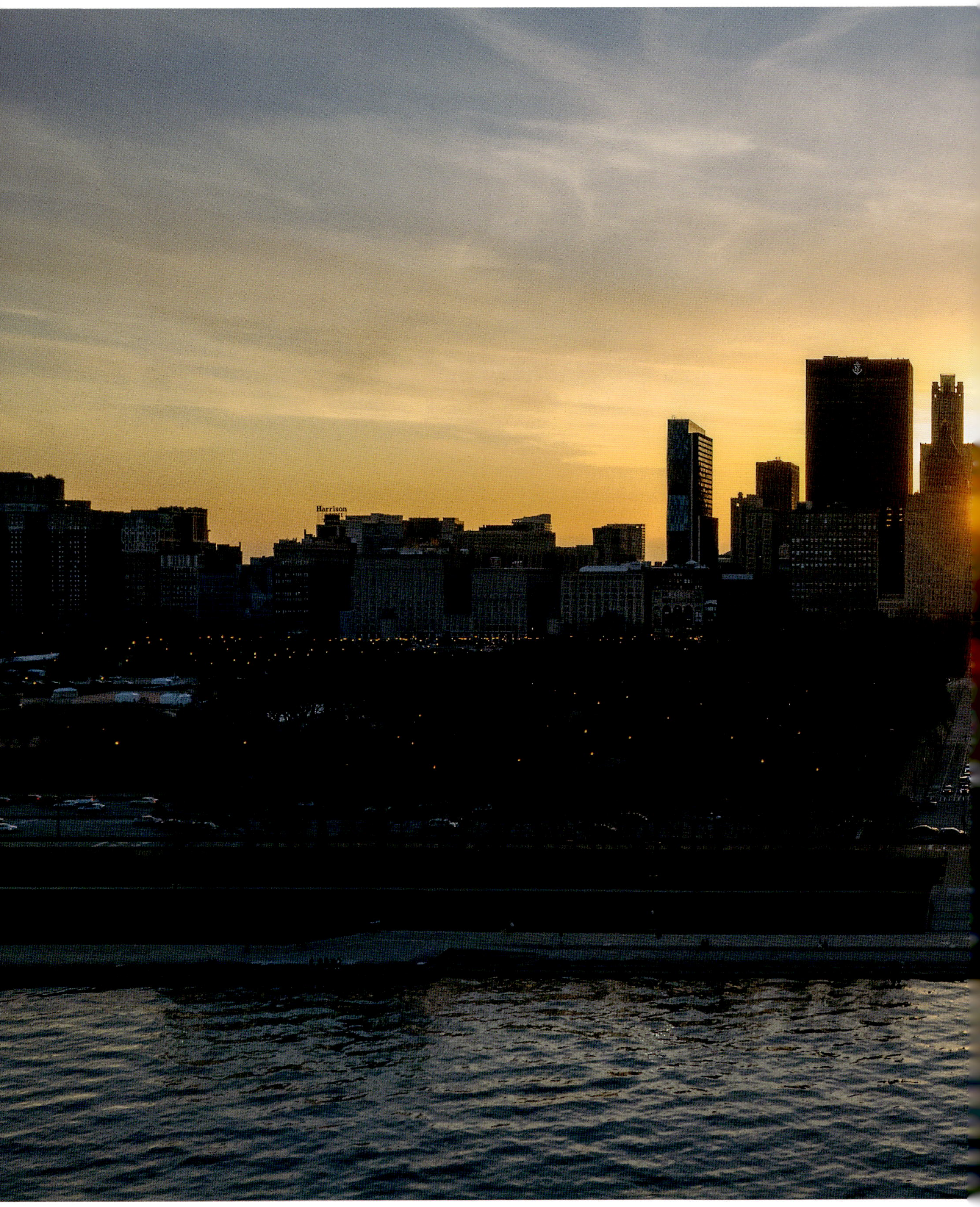

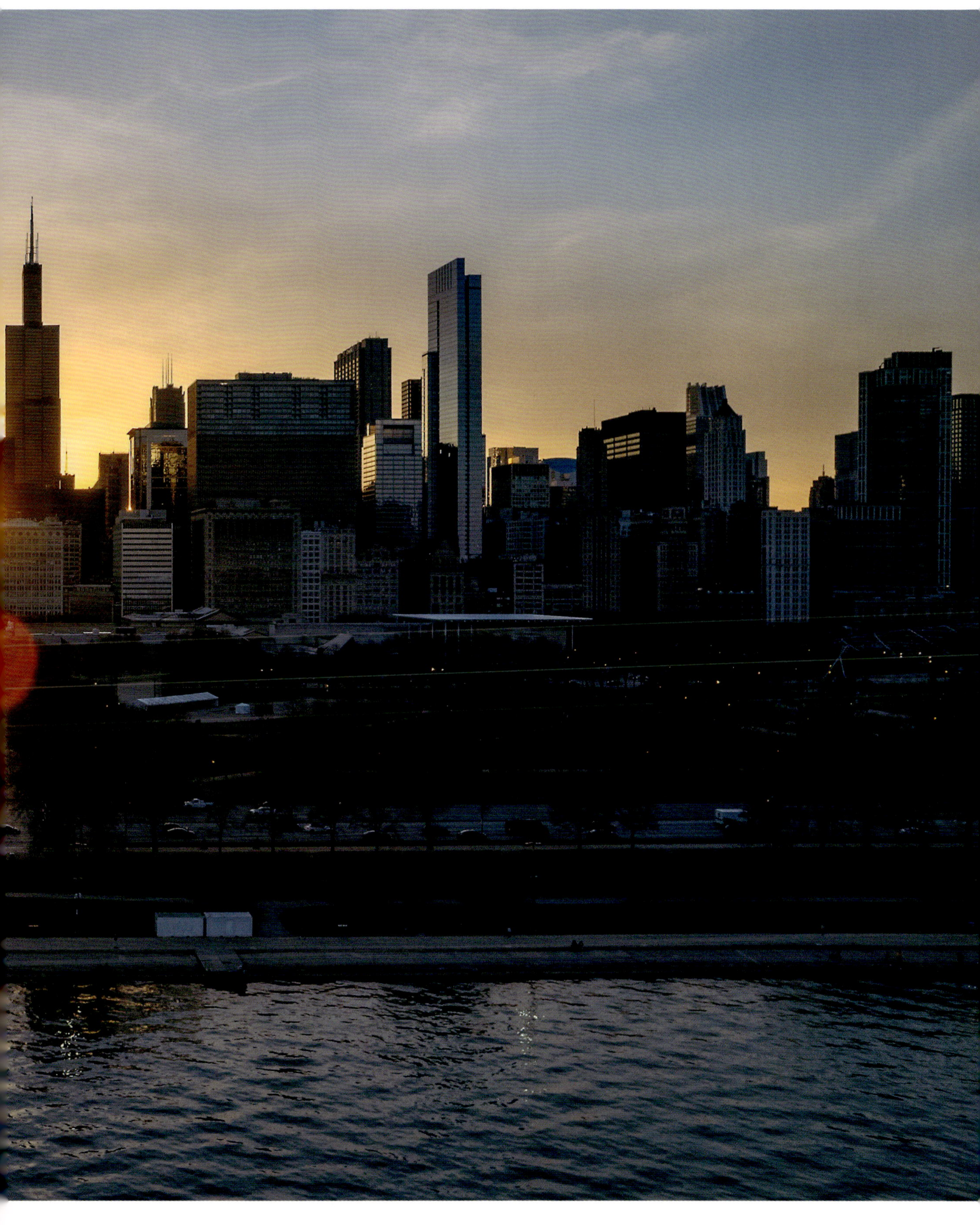

The River ★ A meandering waterway that winds through the heart of the city, the Chicago River stands as a symbol of the city's resilience, adaptability, and ingenuity. During the city's formative years, the Chicago River served as a vital transportation artery, providing a crucial link between the Great Lakes and the Mississippi River system and turning Chicago into a bustling trade and transportation hub. ★ However, as the city burgeoned, the river faced a dark chapter. Used as an open sewer, it became a conduit for pollutants, threatening the purity of Chicago's drinking water. Faced with a growing urban landscape and the specter of disease, city officials took an audacious step — they decided to reverse the river's flow permanently. ★ Enter a groundbreaking engineering feat: a 28-mile-long canal connecting the Chicago River to rivers feeding into the Mississippi. Completed in 1900, this engineering marvel reversed the flow of the Chicago River, sending its once-polluted waters away from Lake Michigan, towards St. Louis and into the Mississippi River. ★ Today, the Chicago River remains an iconic part of the city. The bridges crossing the river, such as the Michigan Avenue Bridge and the DuSable Bridge, remain functional structures in addition to architectural landmarks that add to the city's aesthetic allure. The recent addition of the Riverwalk, a 1.25-mile-long walkway featuring cafes, public art and recreation along the river's south bank, also provides visitors an up-close view of the architectural wonders along the river. ★ And then there's the quirky yet beloved St. Patrick's Day tradition — dyeing the river green. A practice as peculiar as it is uniquely Chicago, this annual event, begun in 1962, has residents and tourists alike eagerly awaiting the river's emerald transformation, adding a splash of color to the city's already rich narrative.

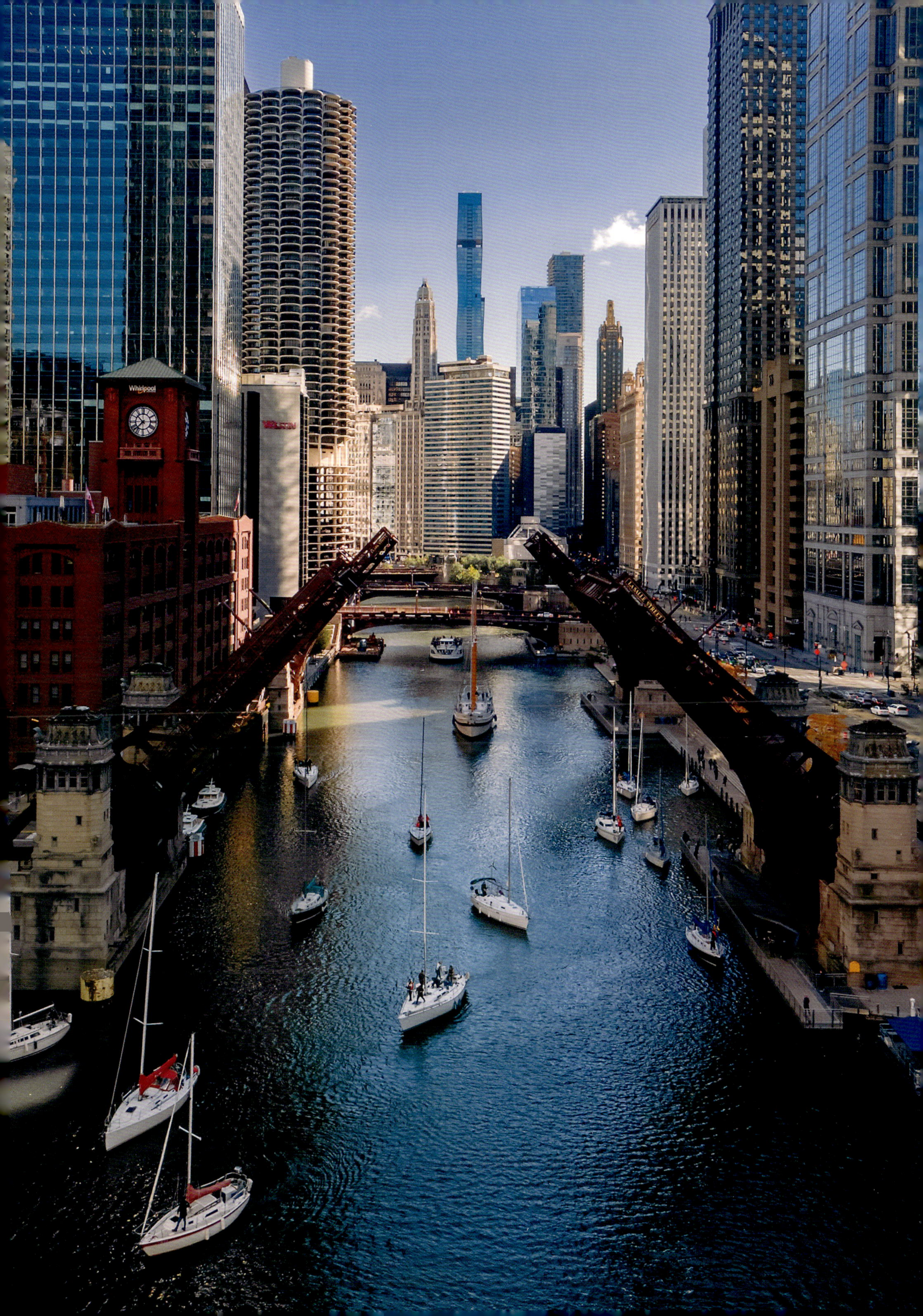

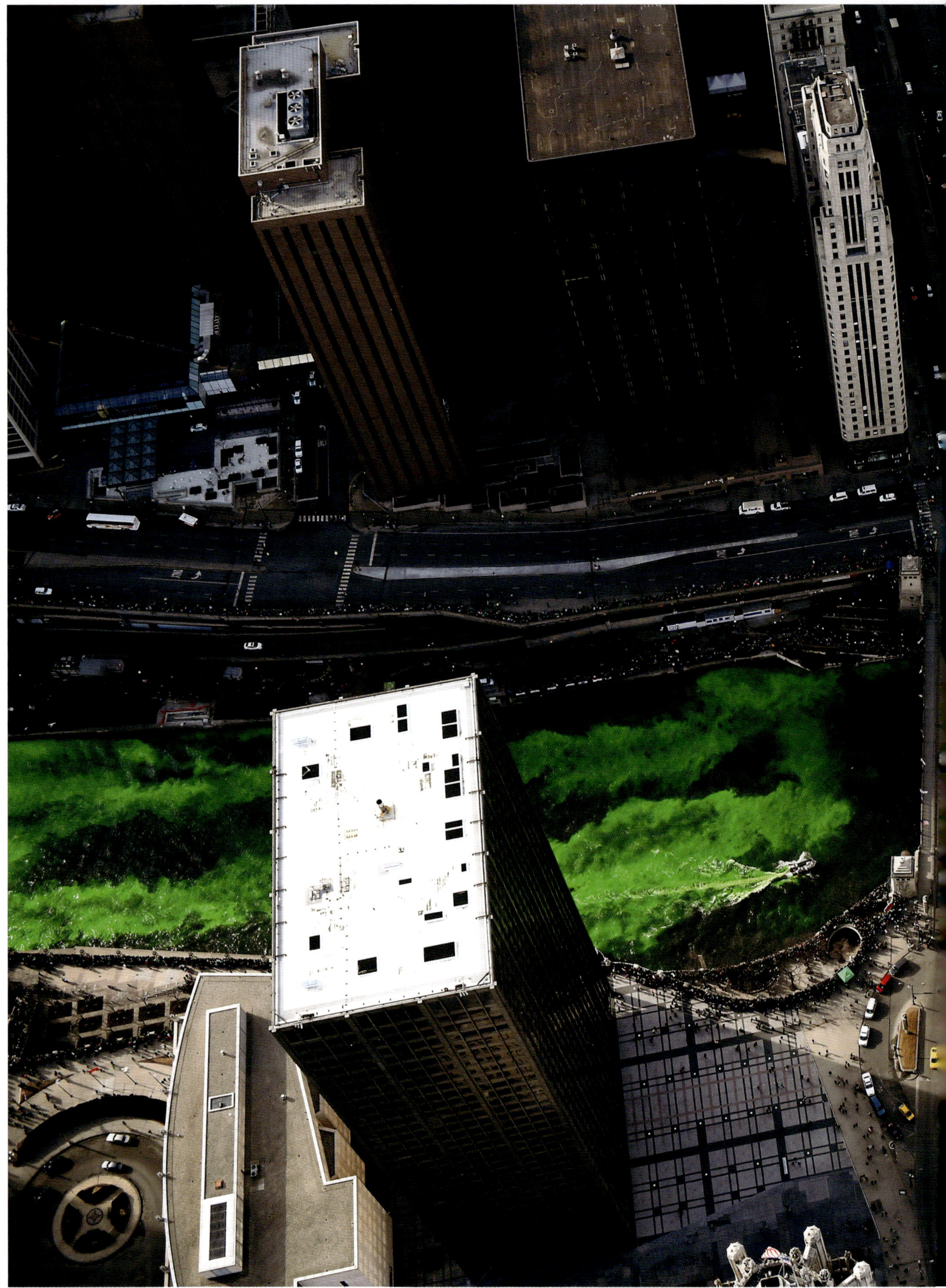

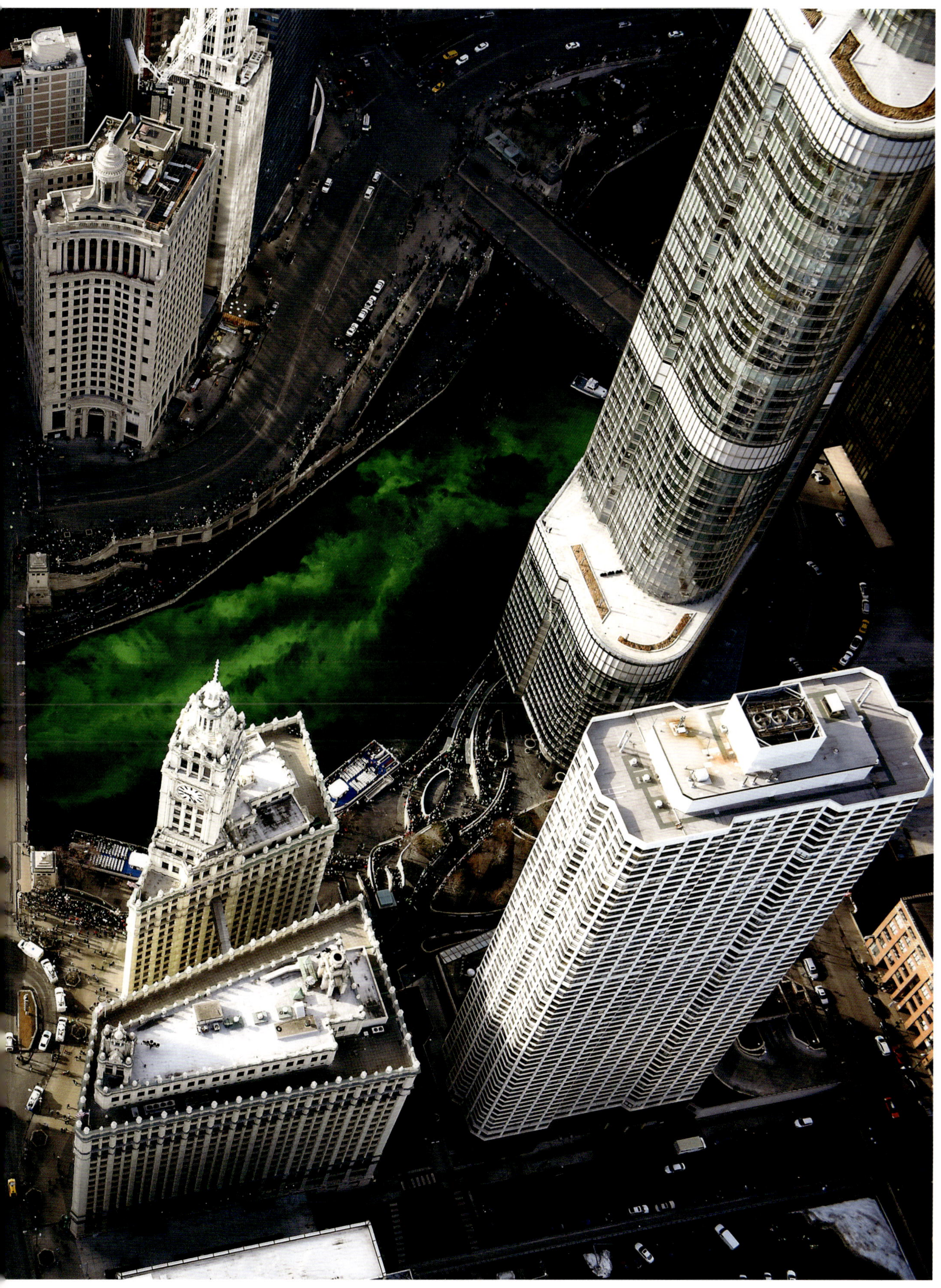

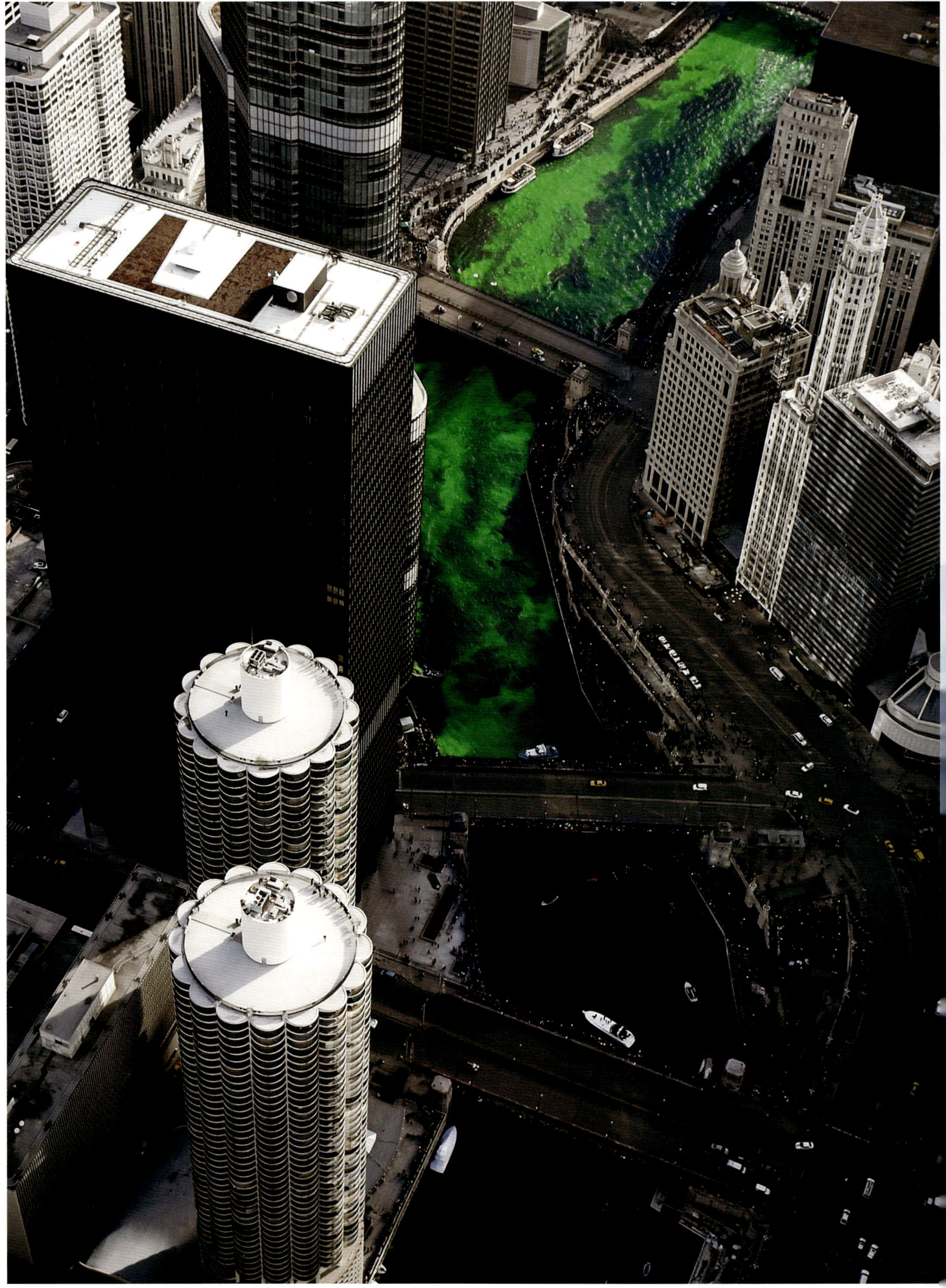

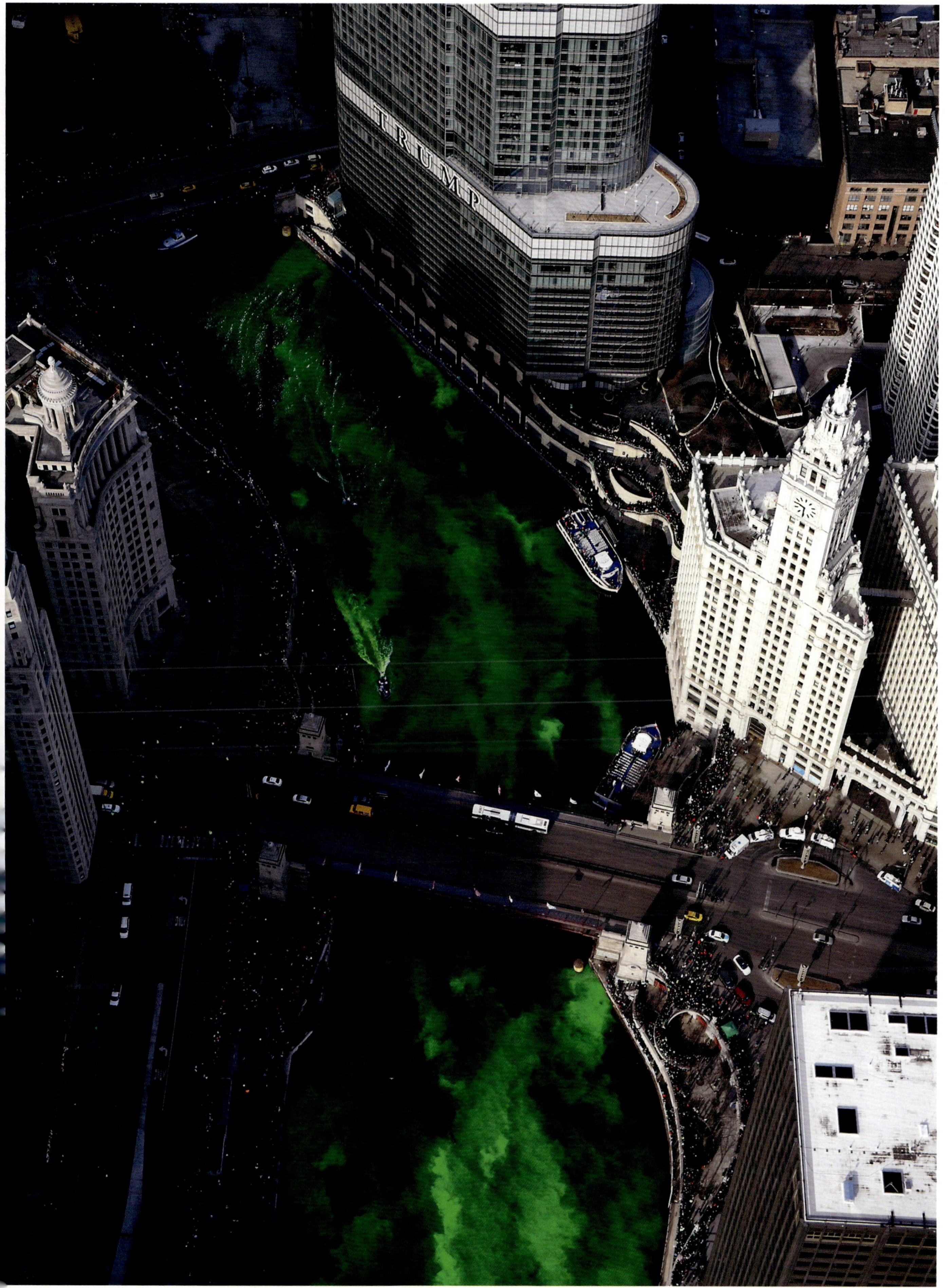

TRUMP

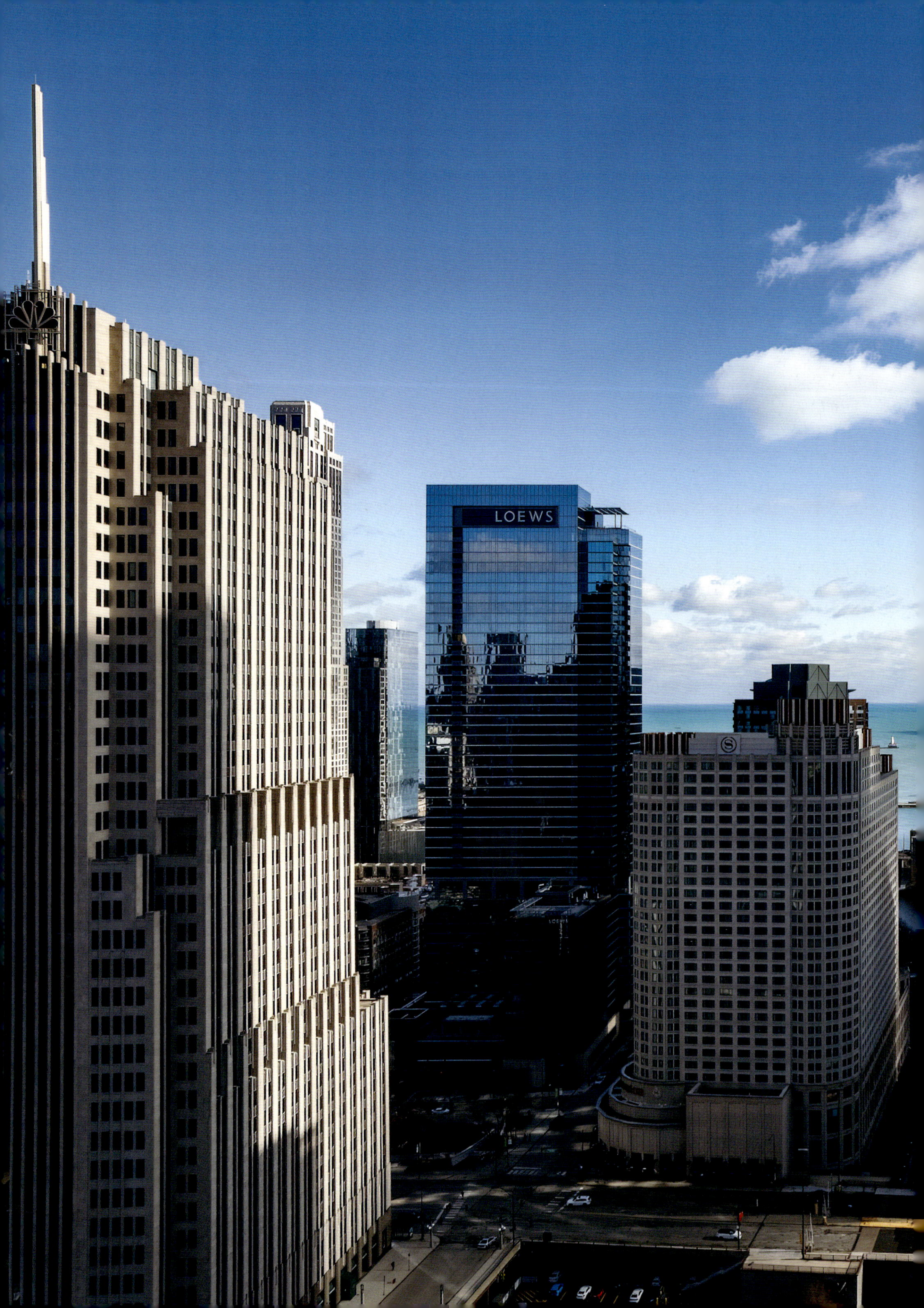

LOEWS

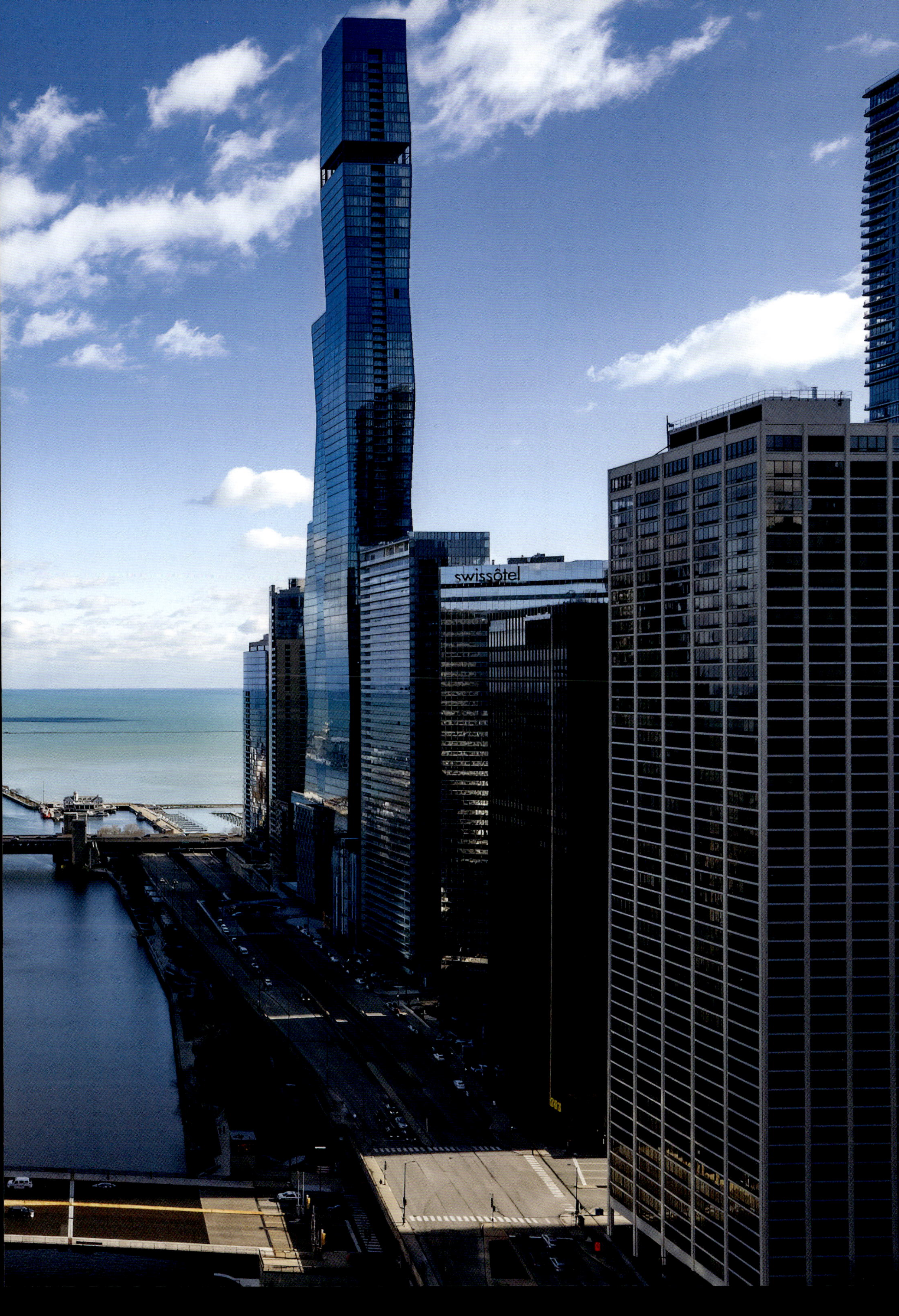

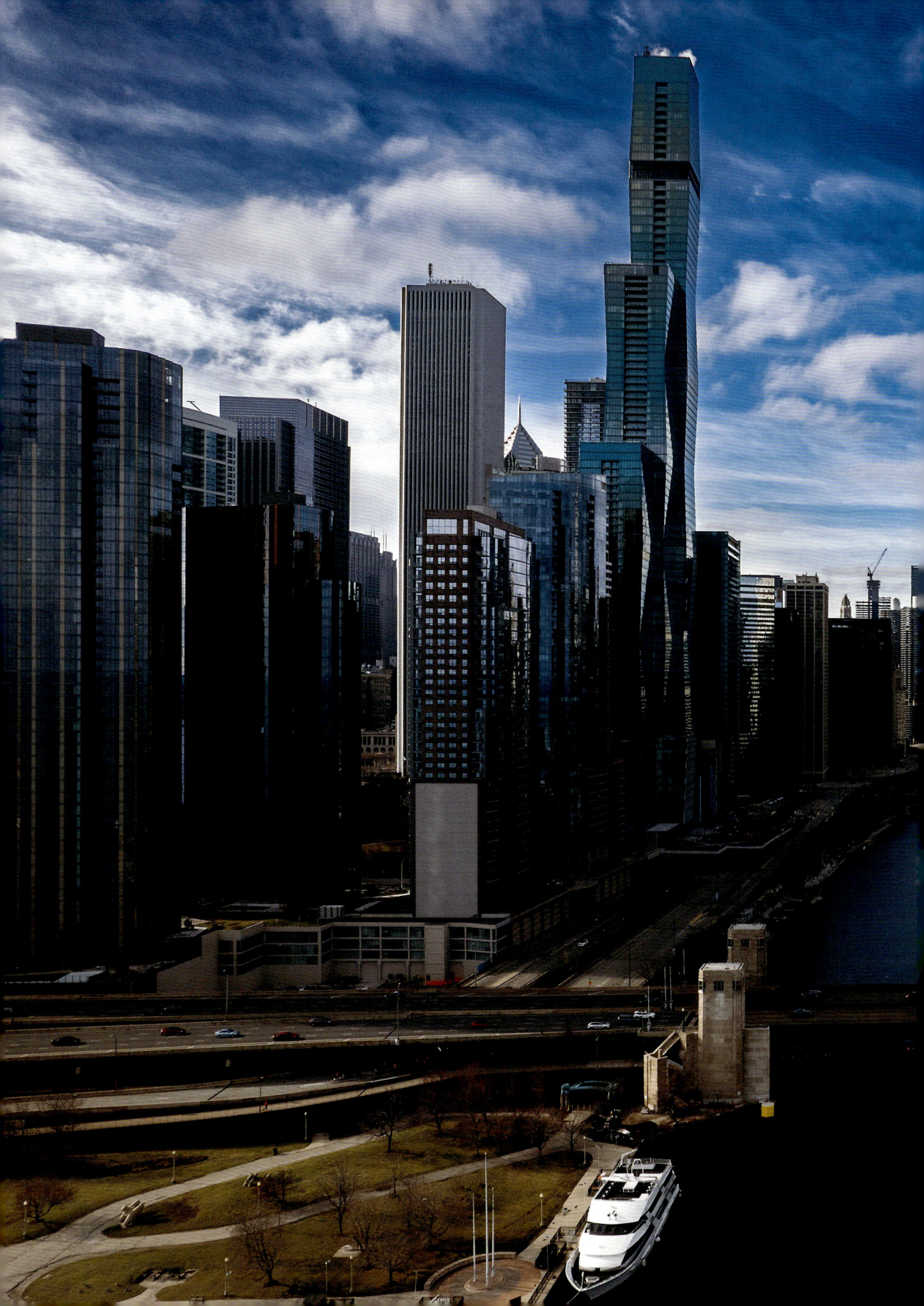

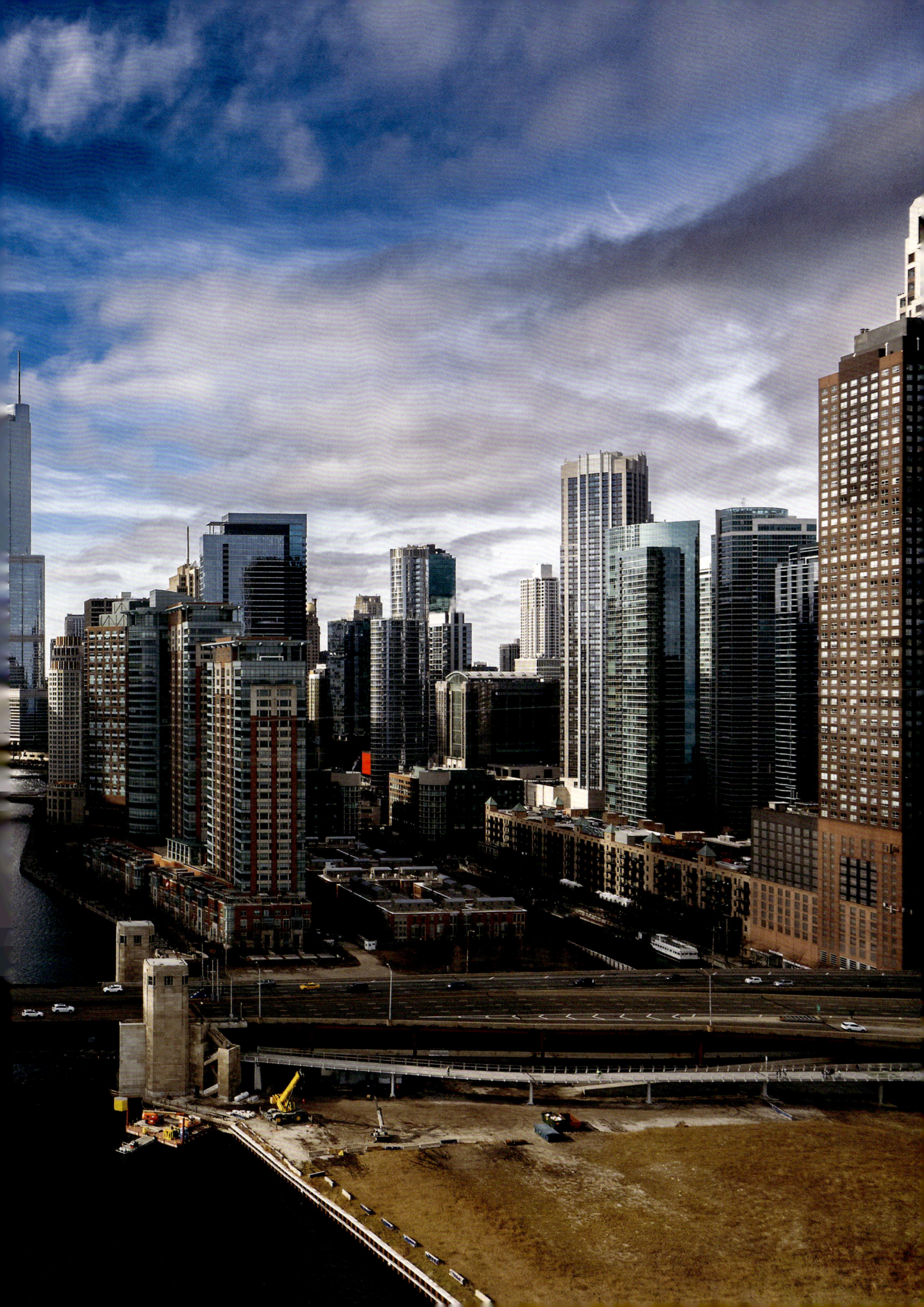

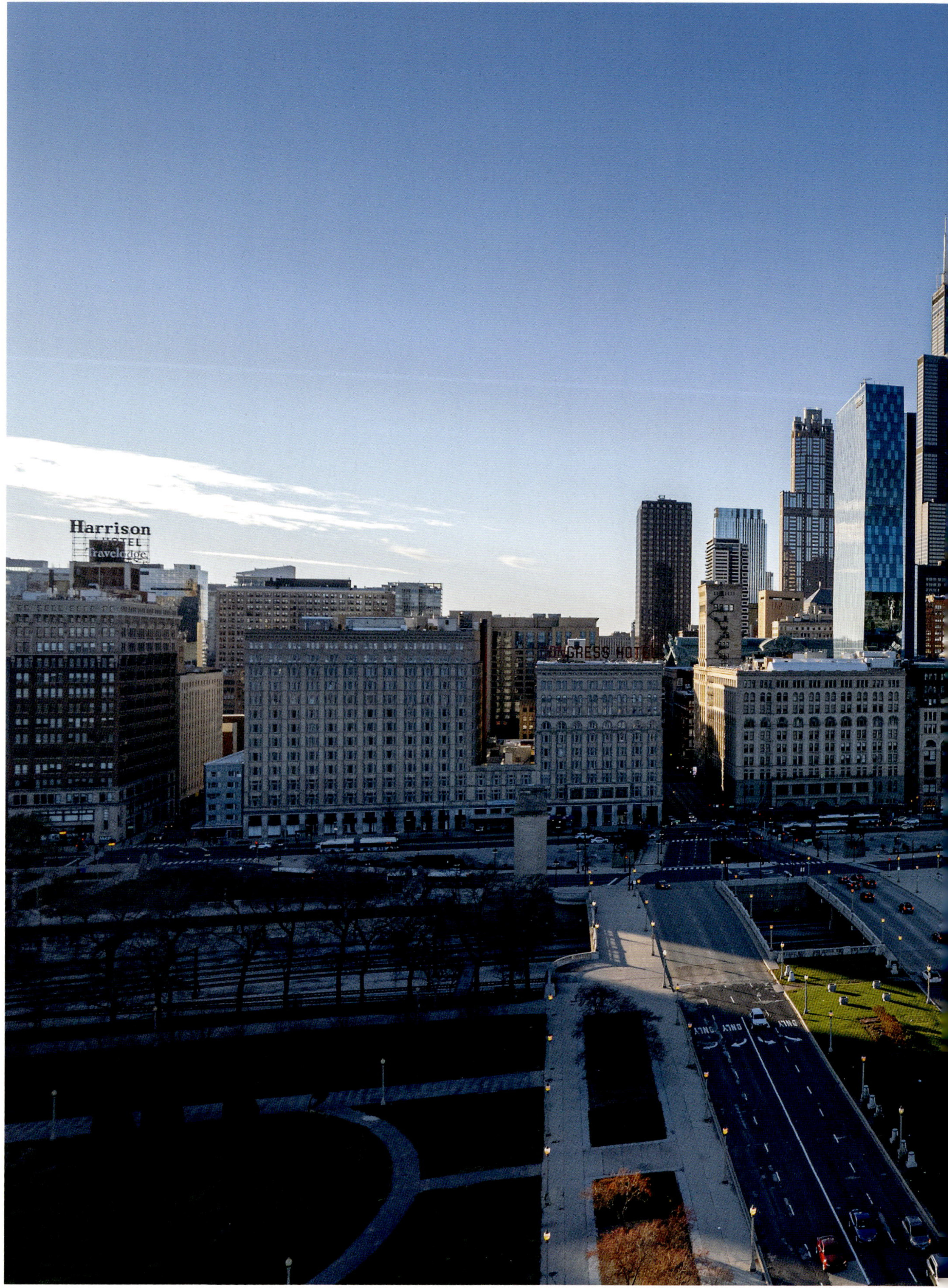
Harrison
HOTEL
Travelodge
CONGRESS HOTEL
ONLY ONLY ONLY

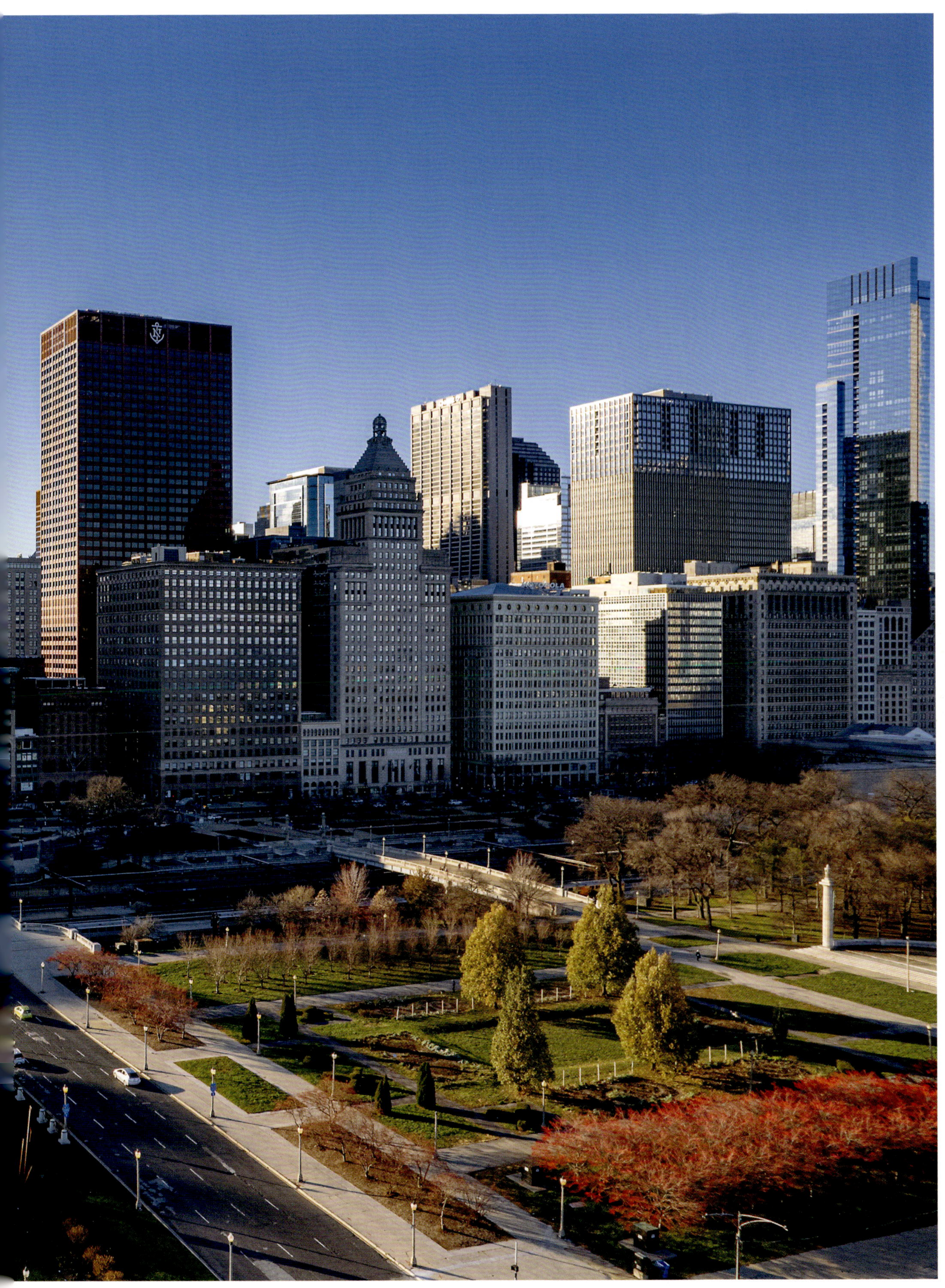

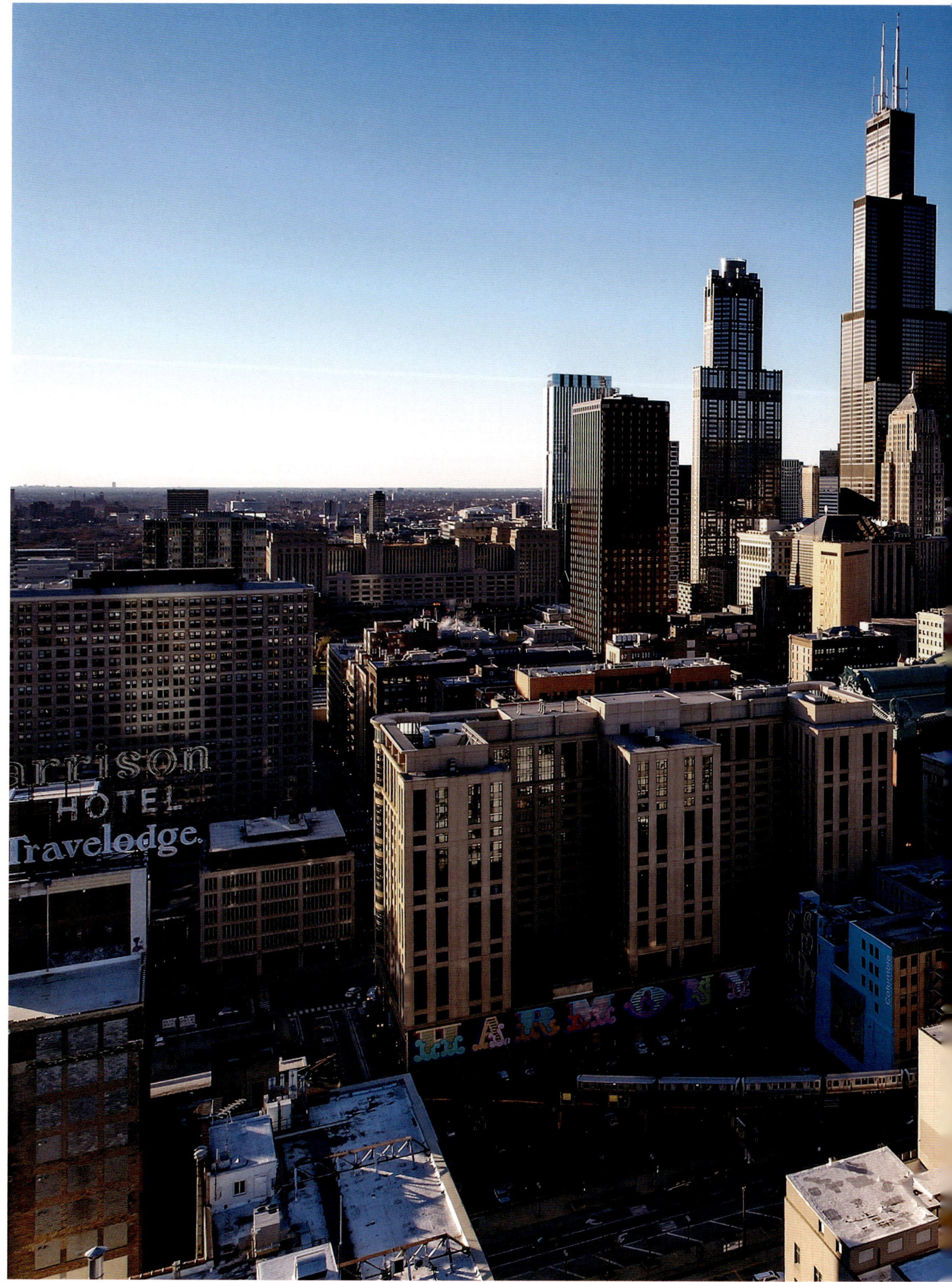

arrison
HOTEL
Travelodge.
HARMONY
Columbia

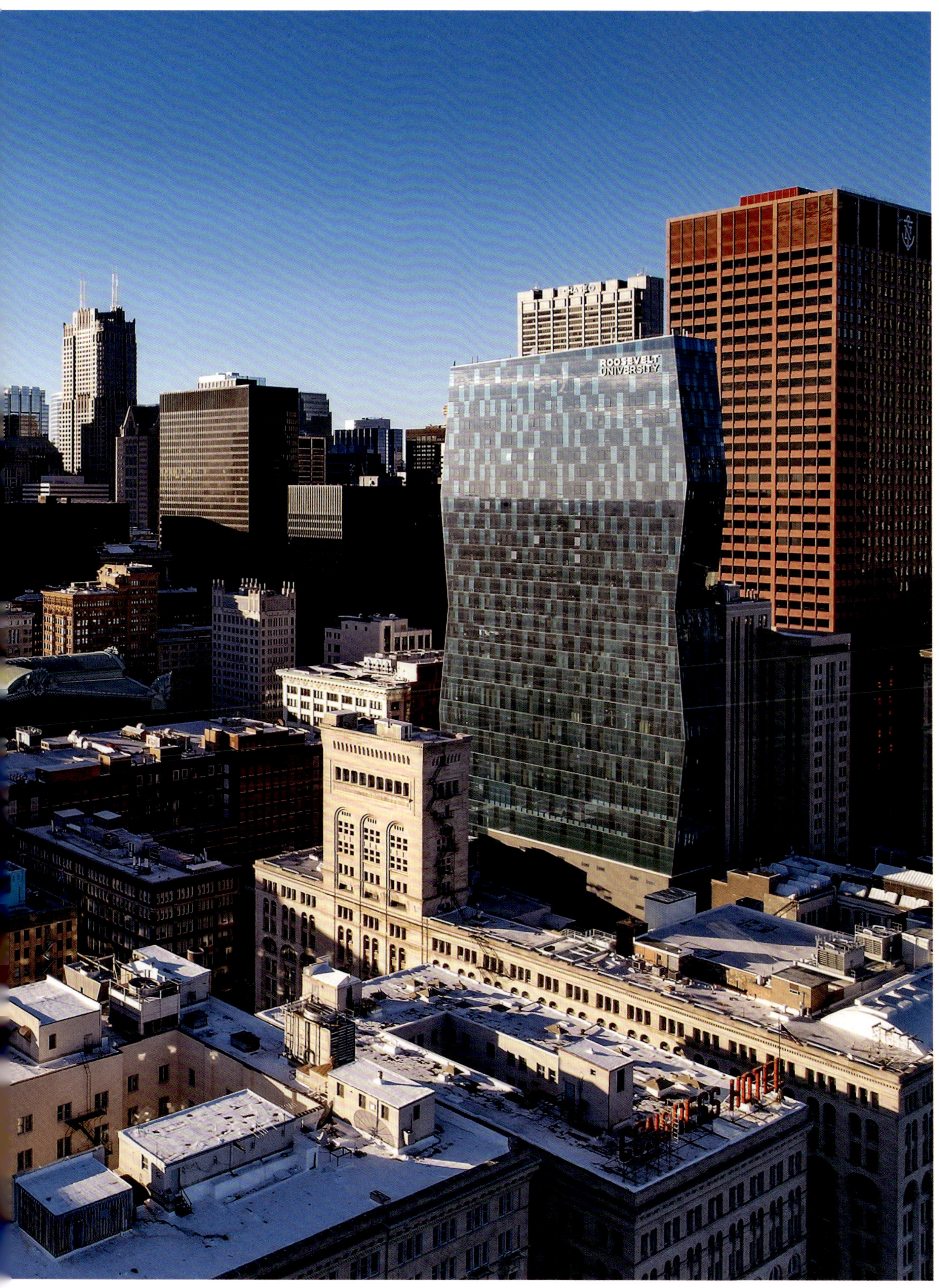

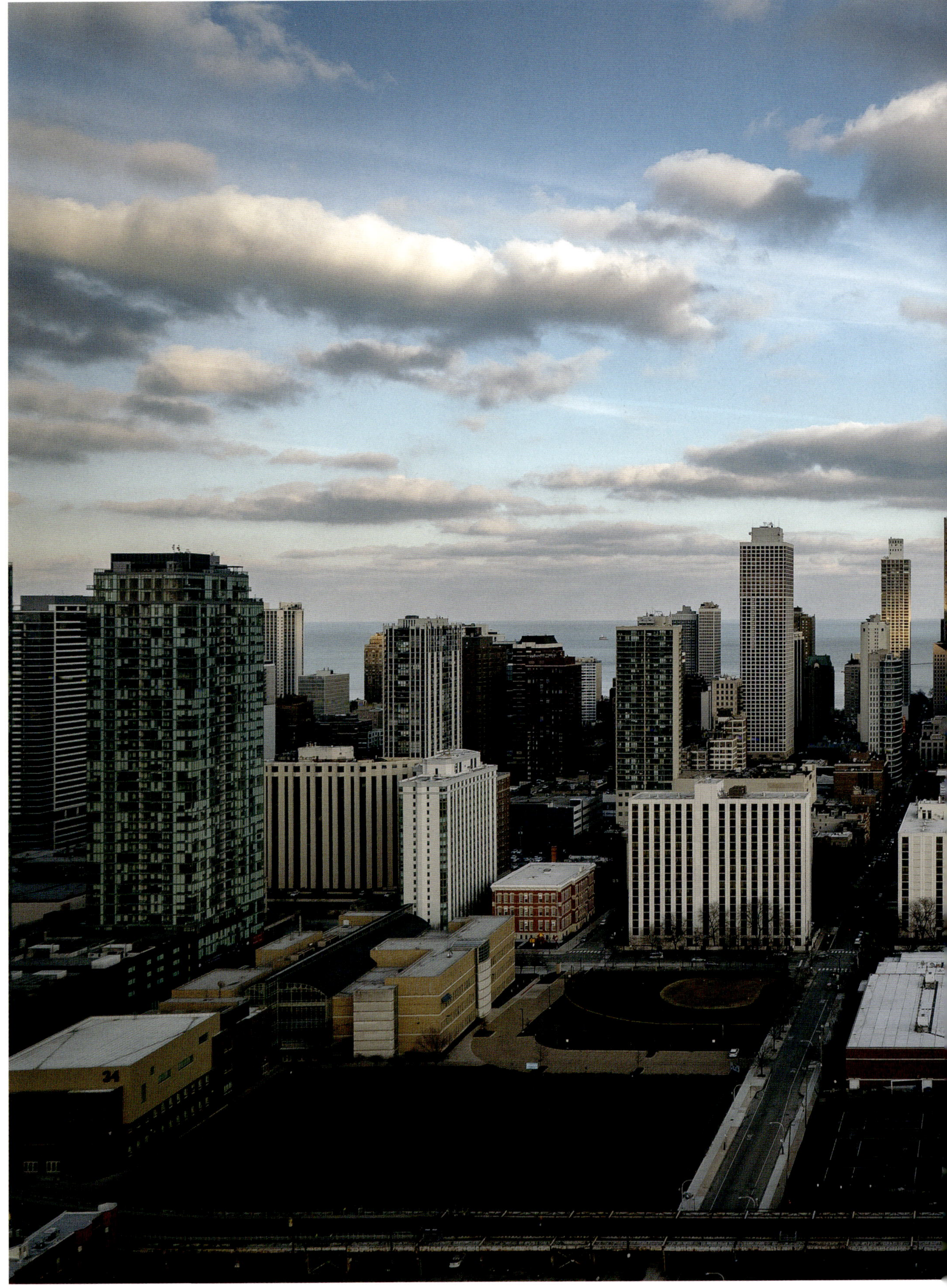

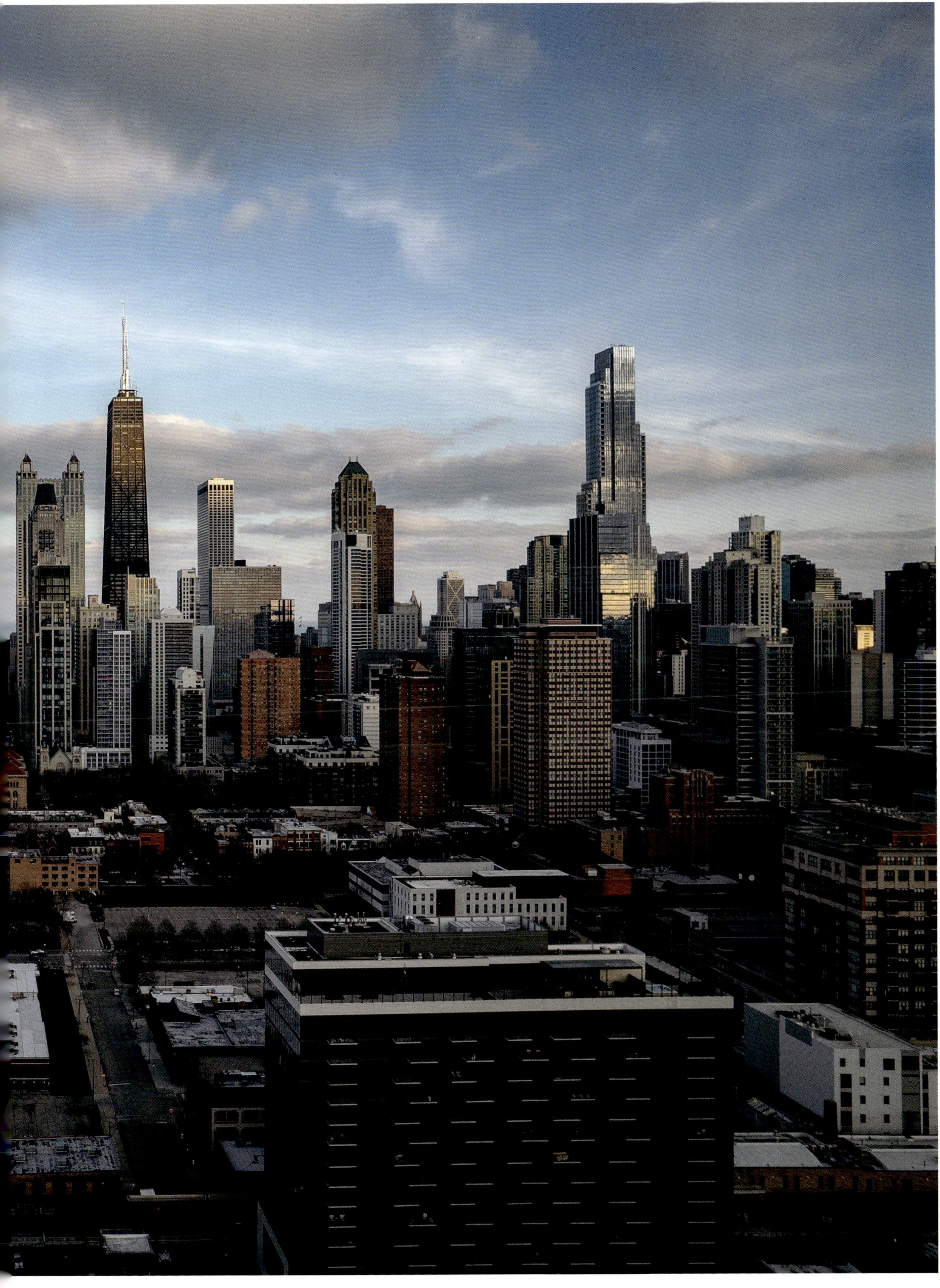

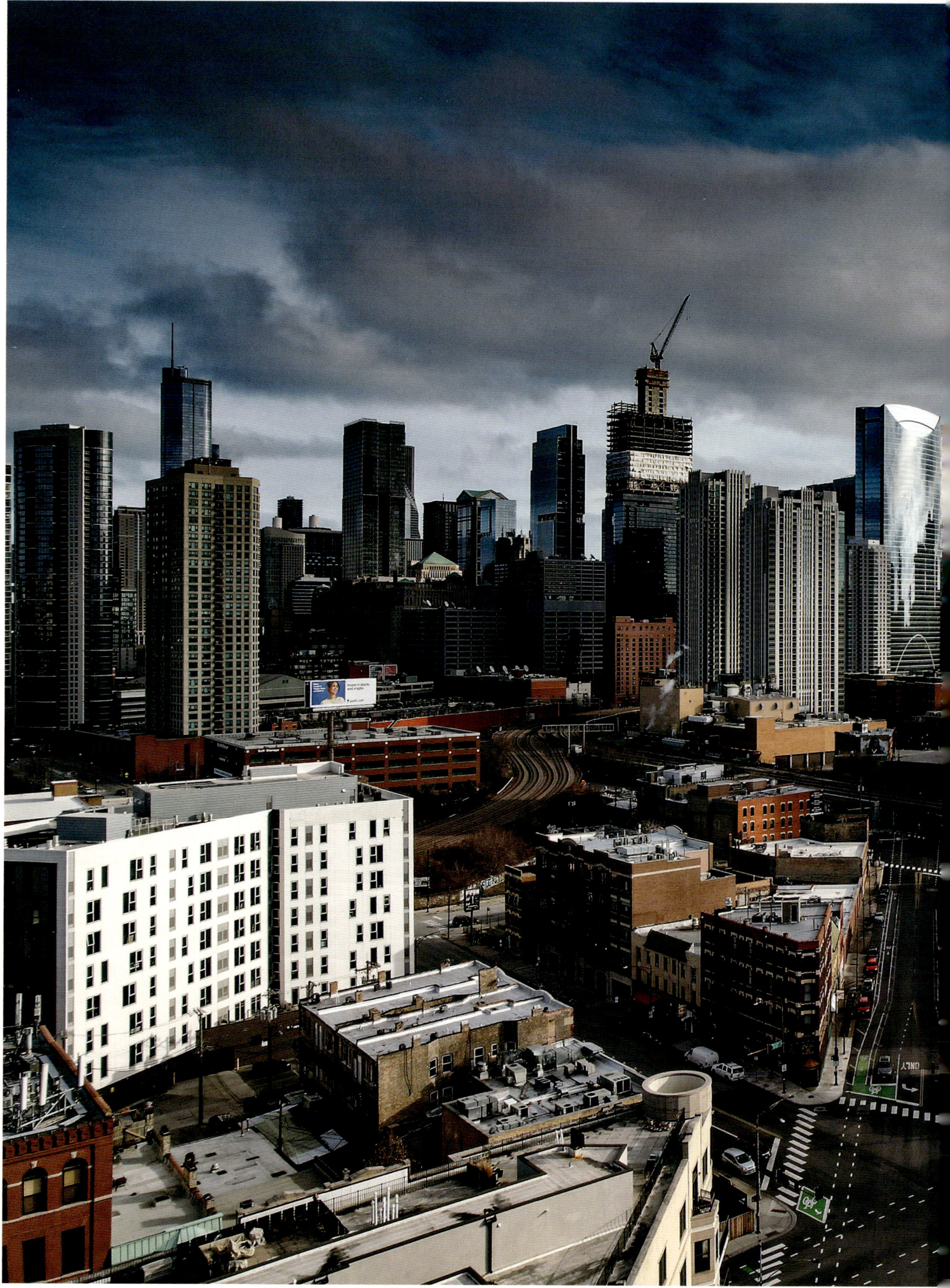

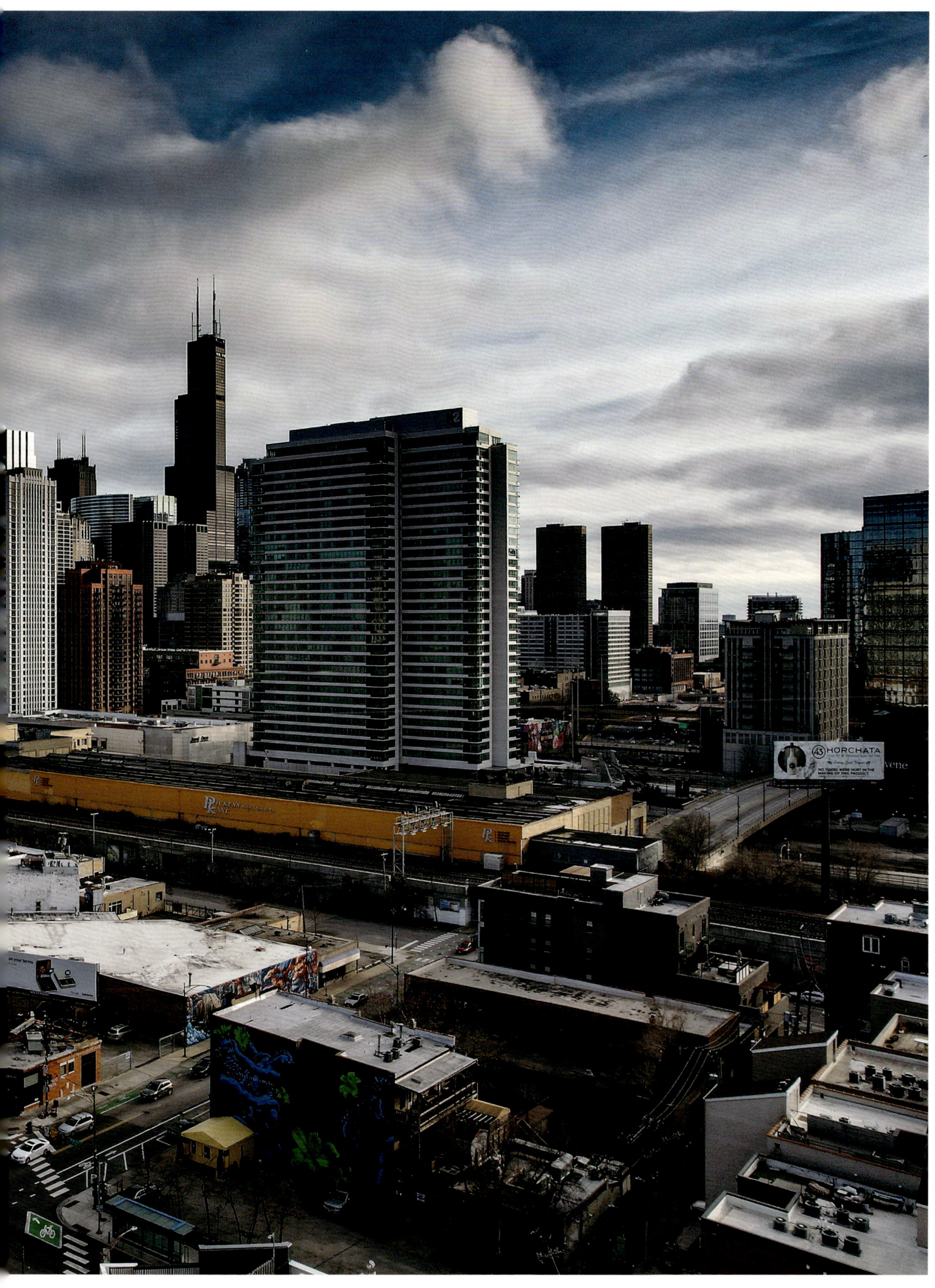

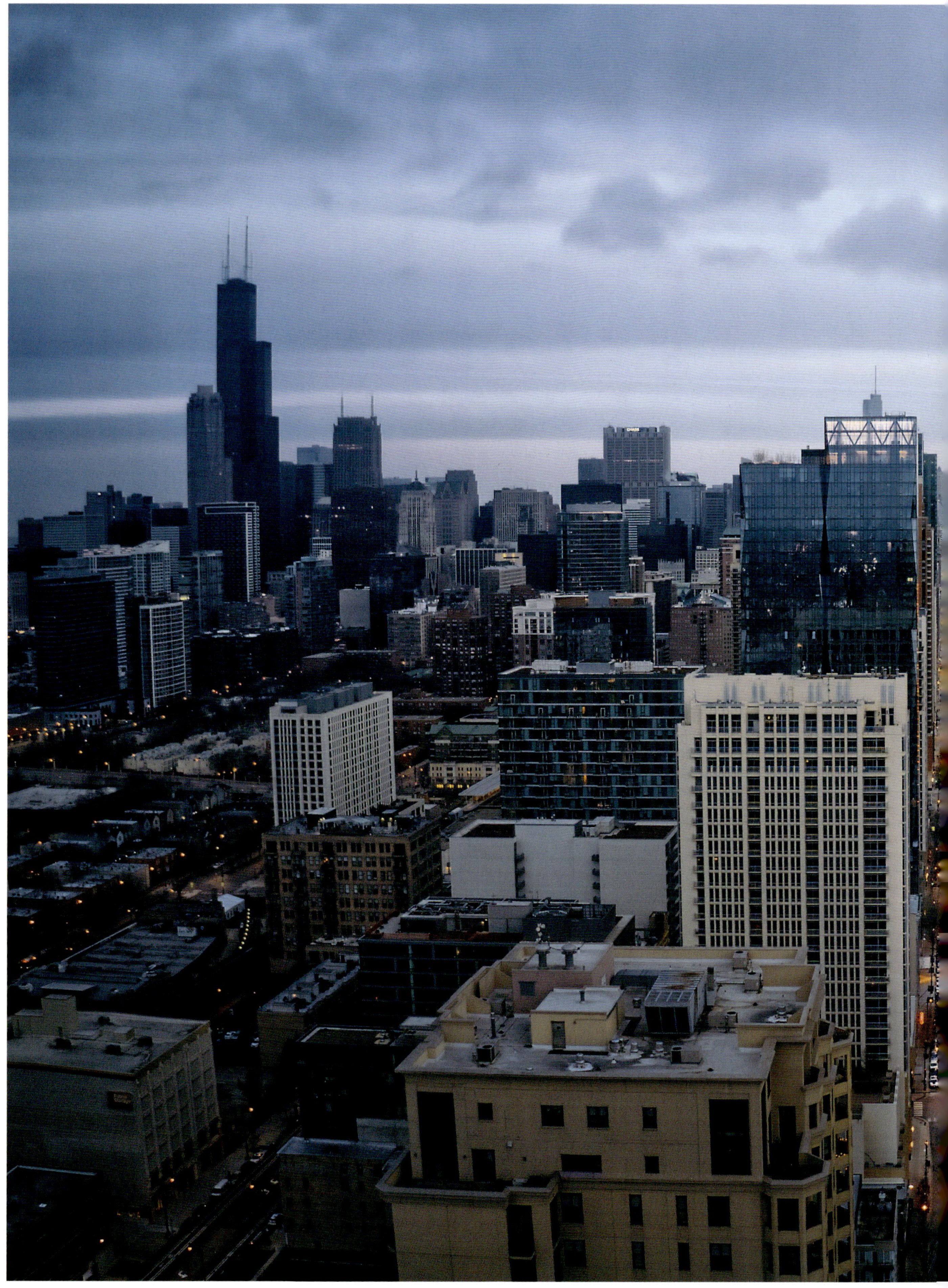

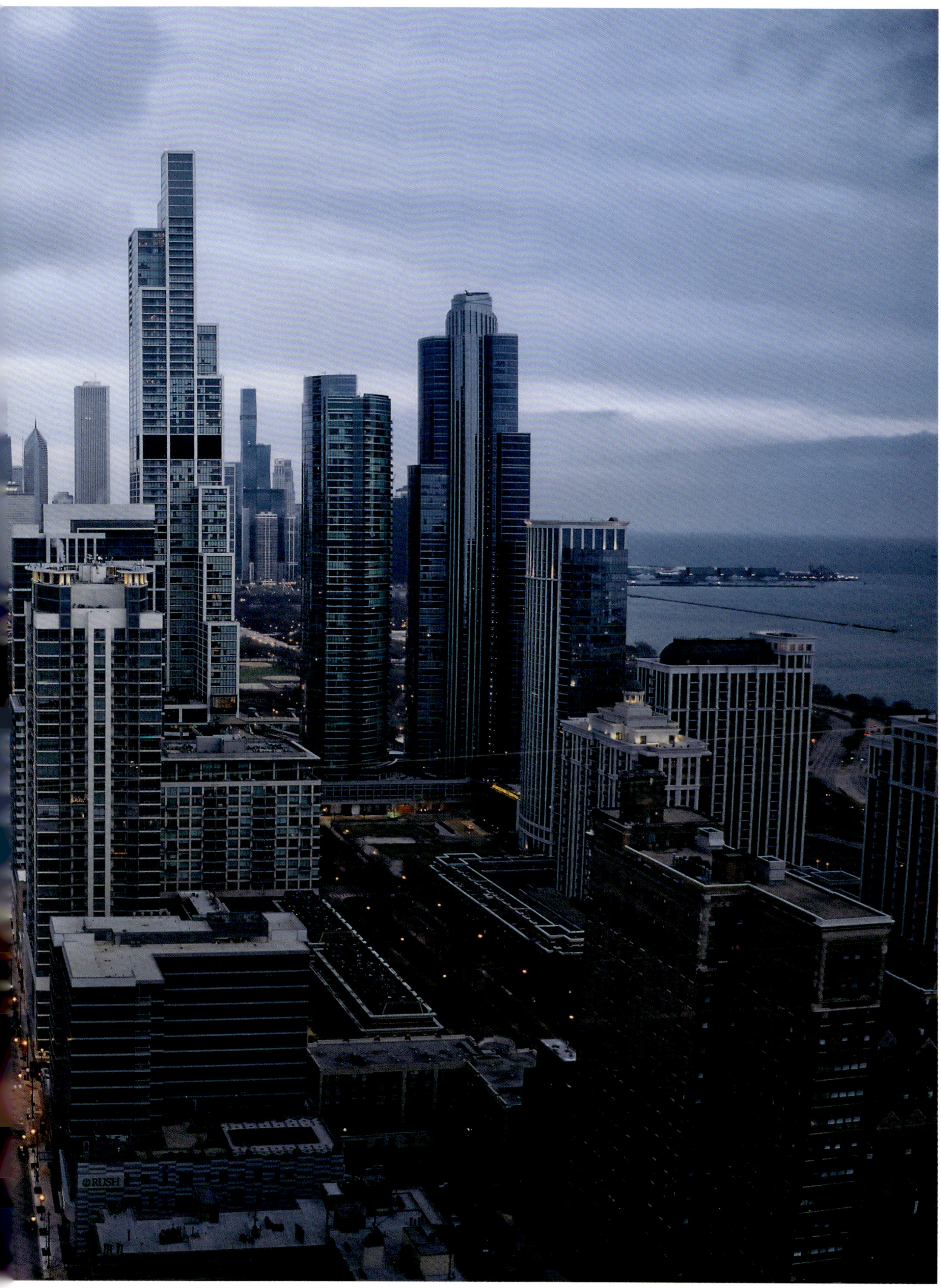

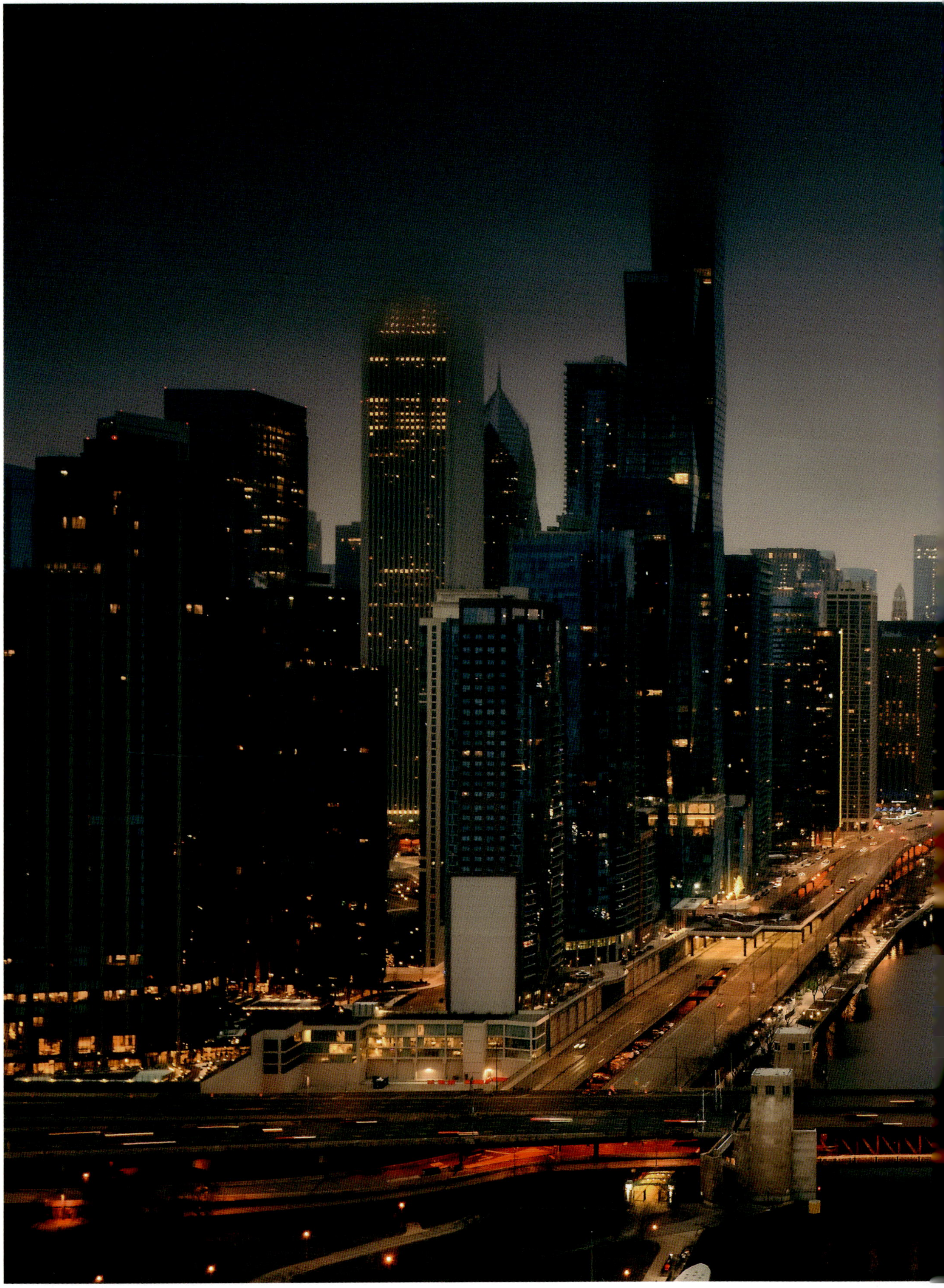

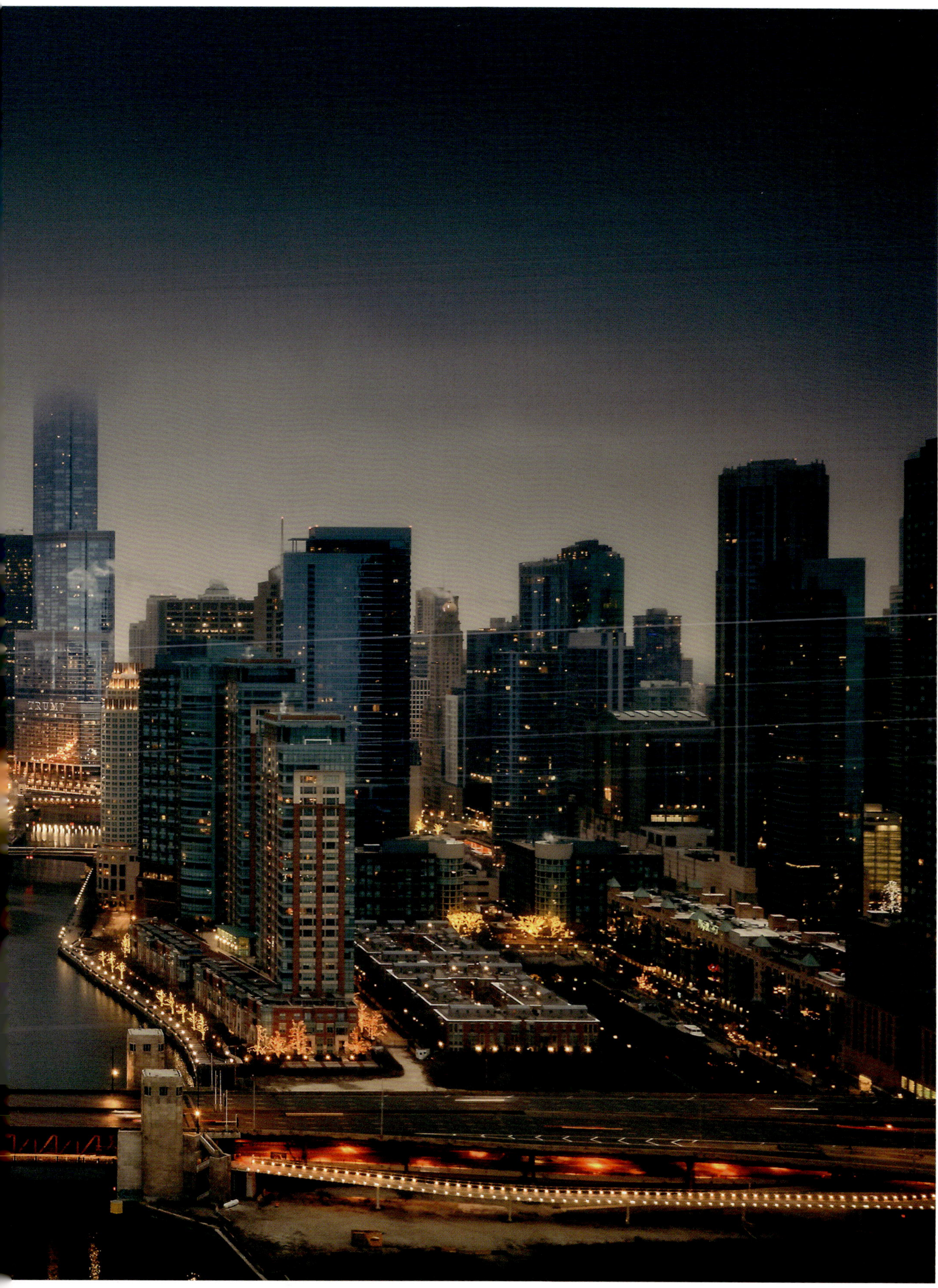

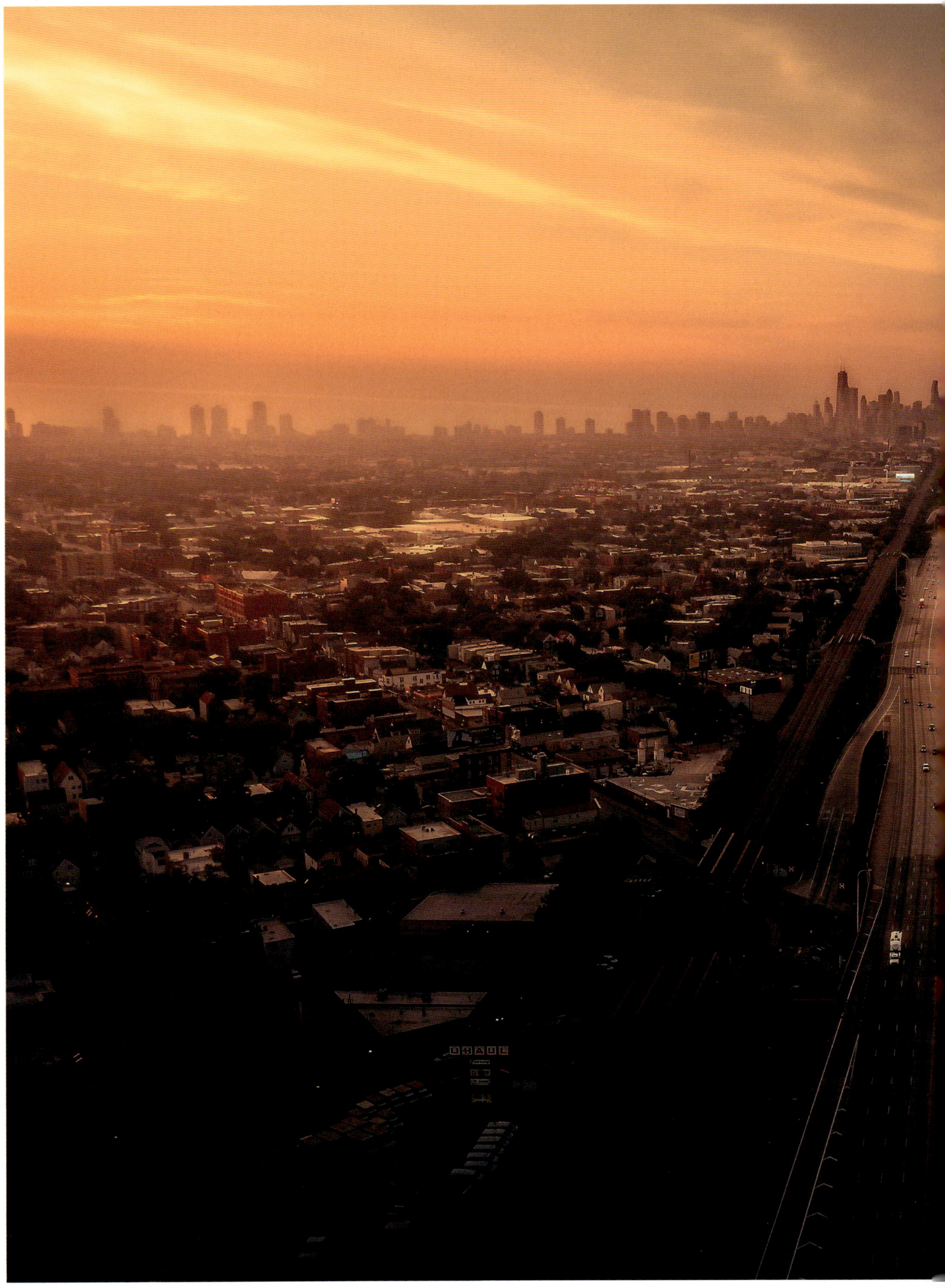

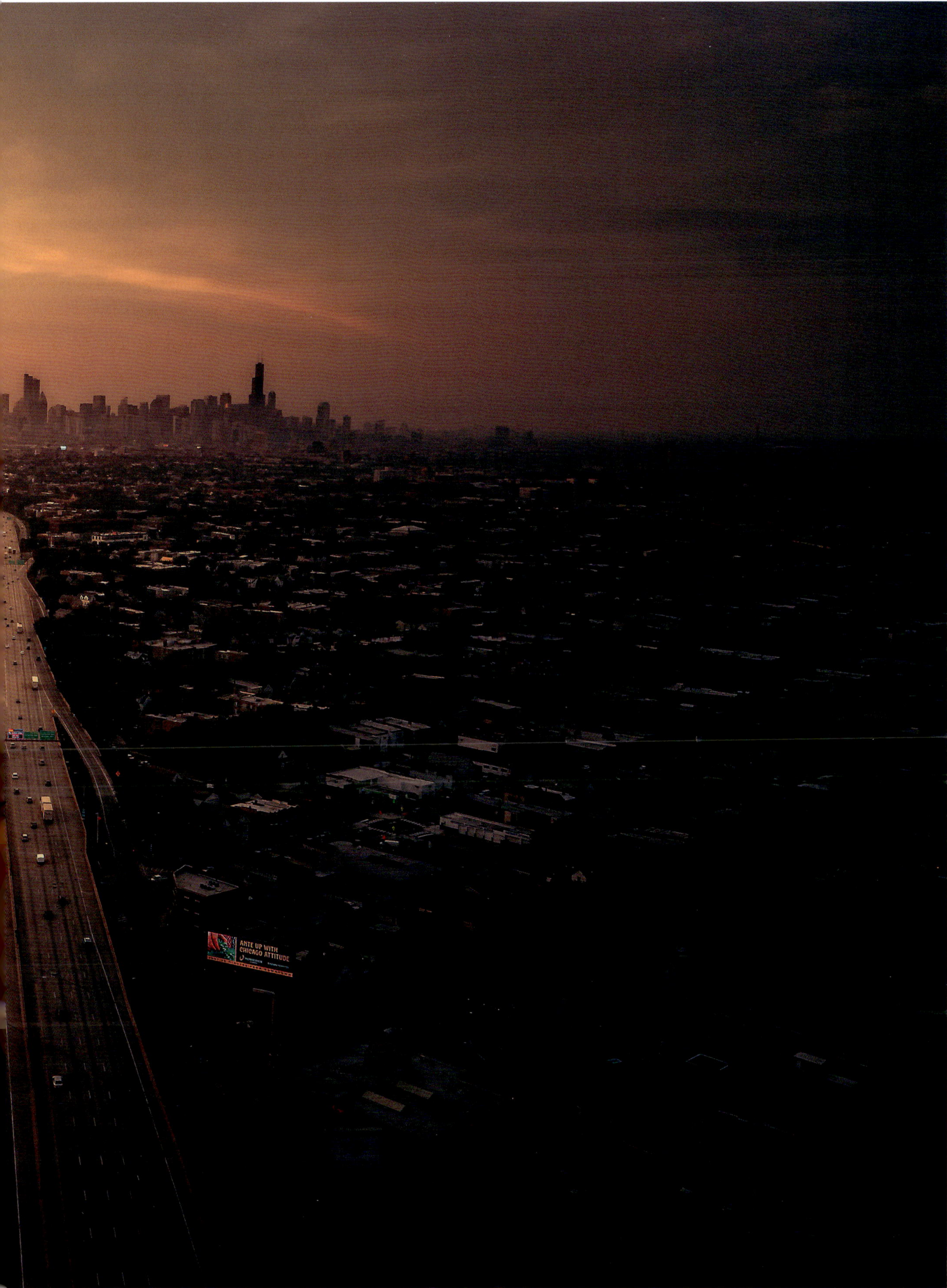
ANTE UP WITH
CHICAGO ATTITUDE

The Weather ★ Chicagoans are no strangers to the whims of Mother Nature, navigating a weather rollercoaster that includes bone-chilling winters, sweltering summers, and a sprinkle of unpredictable temperature twists throughout the year. In the Windy City, it's not unusual to spot locals in shorts on a balmy February day or shoveling snow amidst an unexpected April storm. These climatic extremes have not only shaped the city's resilient spirit but also forged a fascinating relationship between weather and architecture, defining Chicago's urban landscape in ways beyond imagination. ★ Architects have had to design buildings that can withstand the rigors of Chicago's climate, relying on robust materials, such as steel and concrete, to endure temperature fluctuations and weather-related stress. The result? Chicago's skyline wears its toughness proudly, with a distinctly "sturdy" aesthetic that mirrors the city's unyielding character. ★ Chicago's position on the shore of Lake Michigan makes it more prone to fog, particularly in the spring and fall when the lake is colder than the air. As fog weaves its magic, the city's skyline transforms, making the very tall buildings look as if they are disappearing into the sky. And if you happen to be above the fog and clouds, the buildings look as if they are appearing out of thin air. ★ This dynamic interplay between Chicago's weather and architectural prowess isn't just practical, it's downright picturesque. Imagine sleek, modern skyscrapers, their glass façades reflecting the pristine snow, or the play of sunlight on the Chicago River's surface. The city's palette evolves with the seasons, embracing vibrant hues that add an extra layer of uniqueness to its already iconic look.

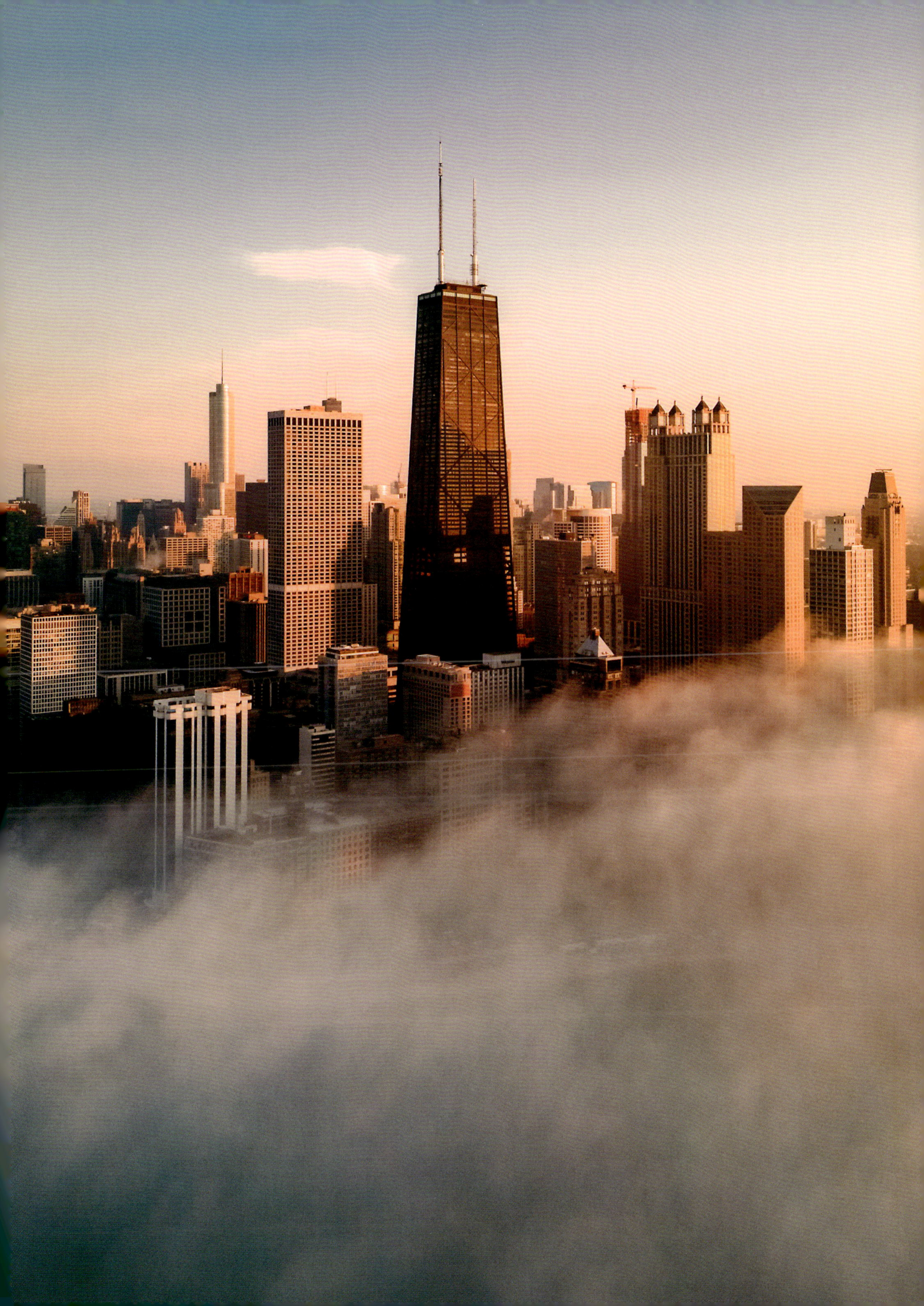

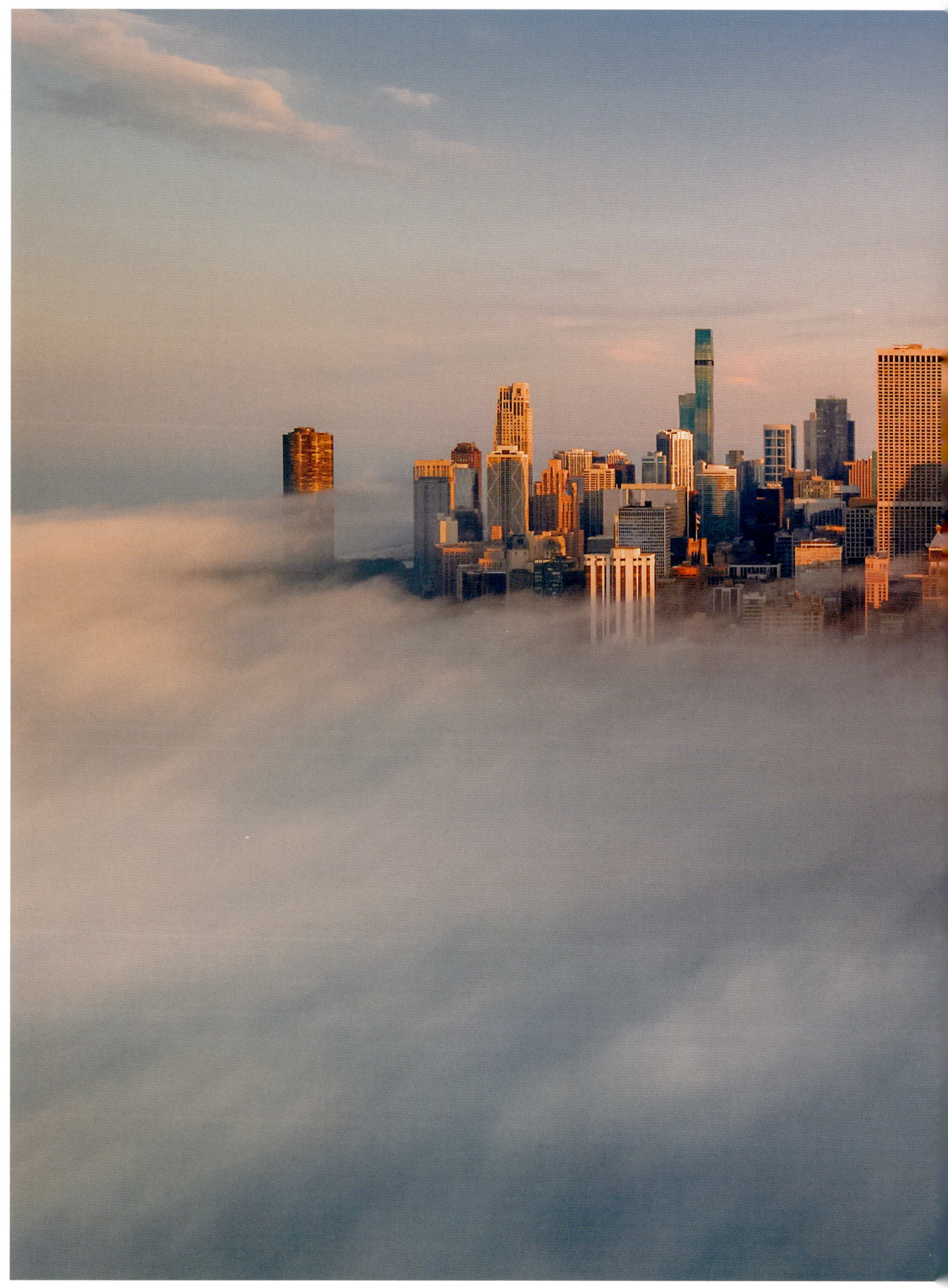

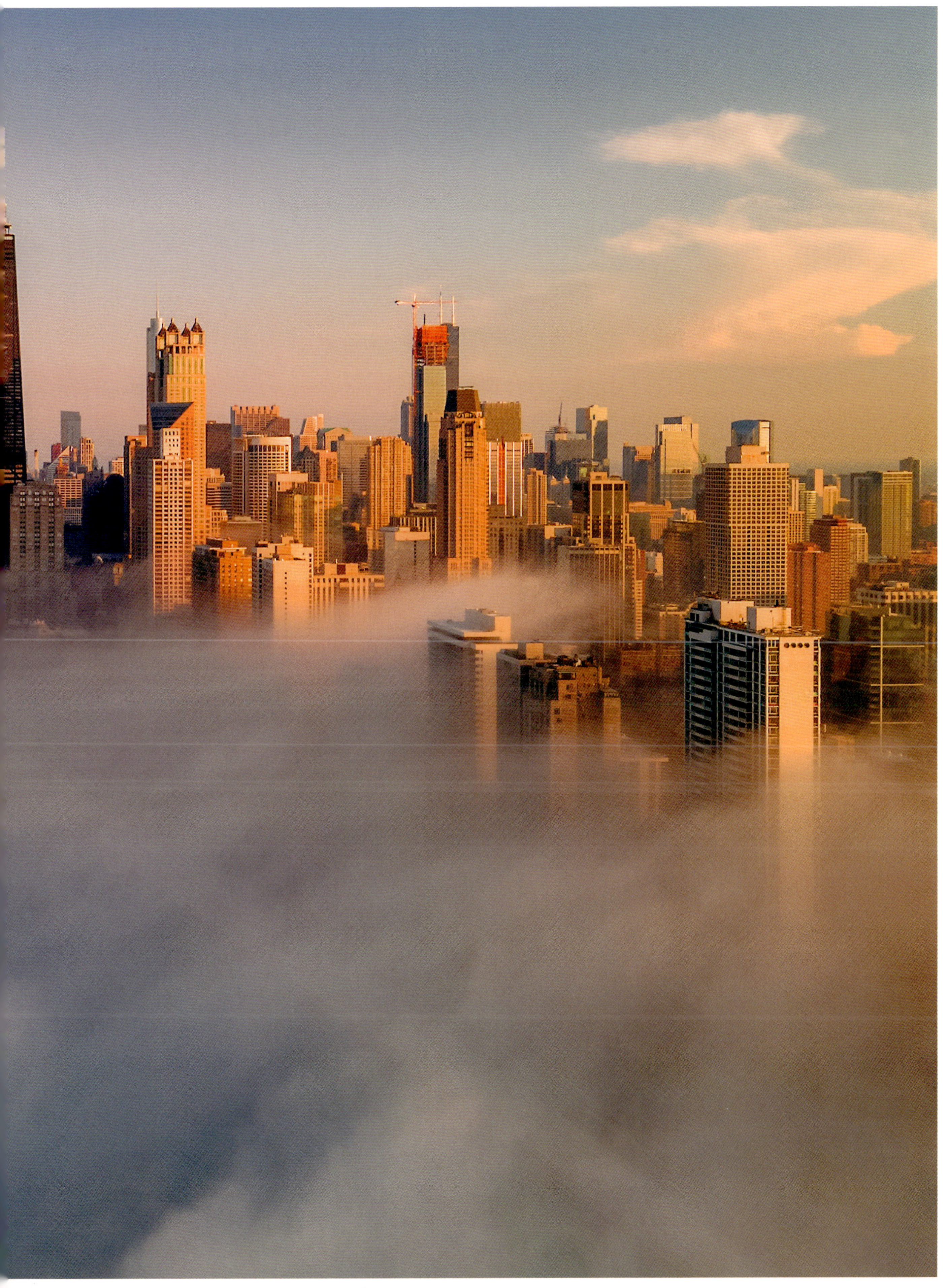

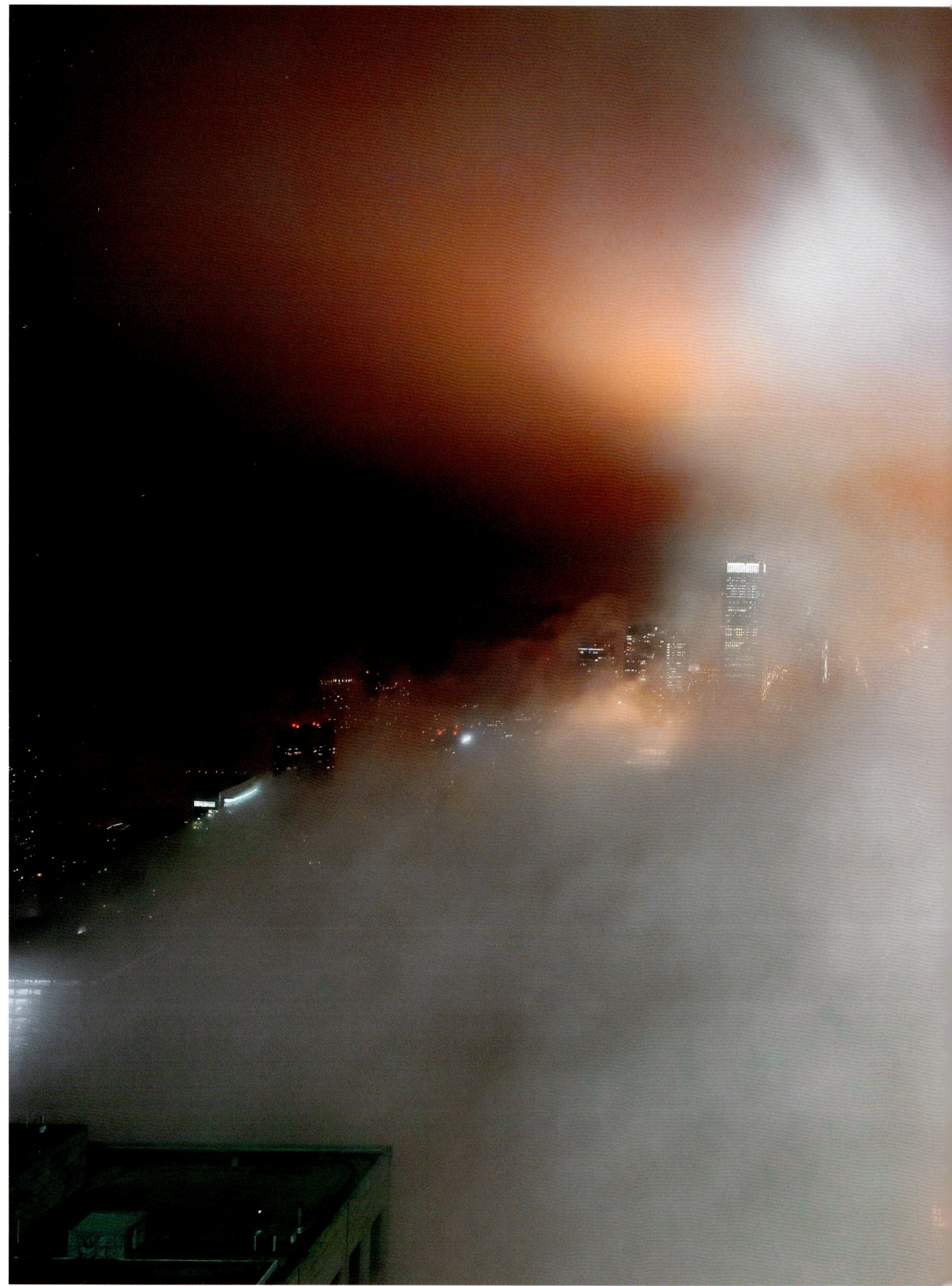

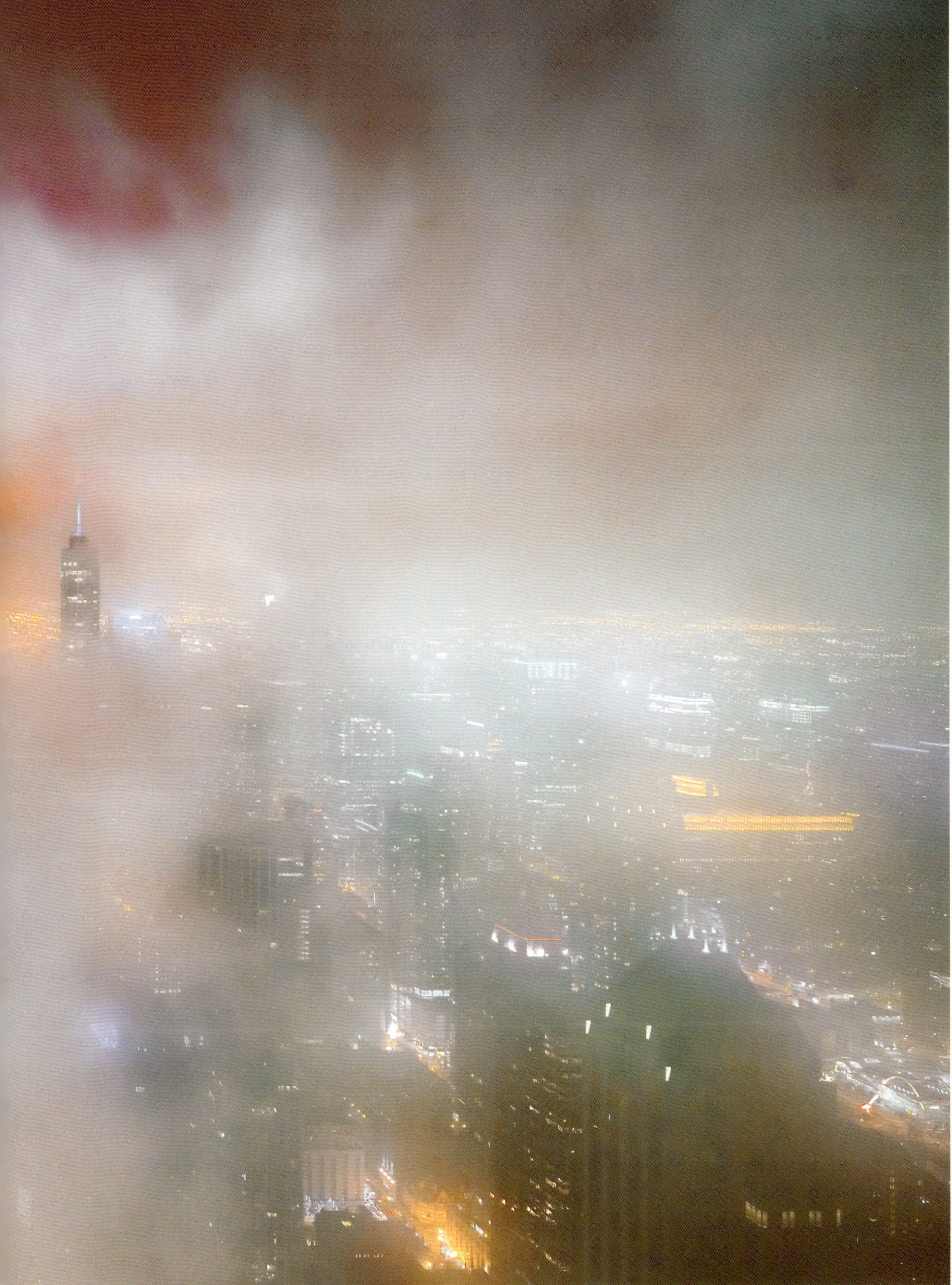

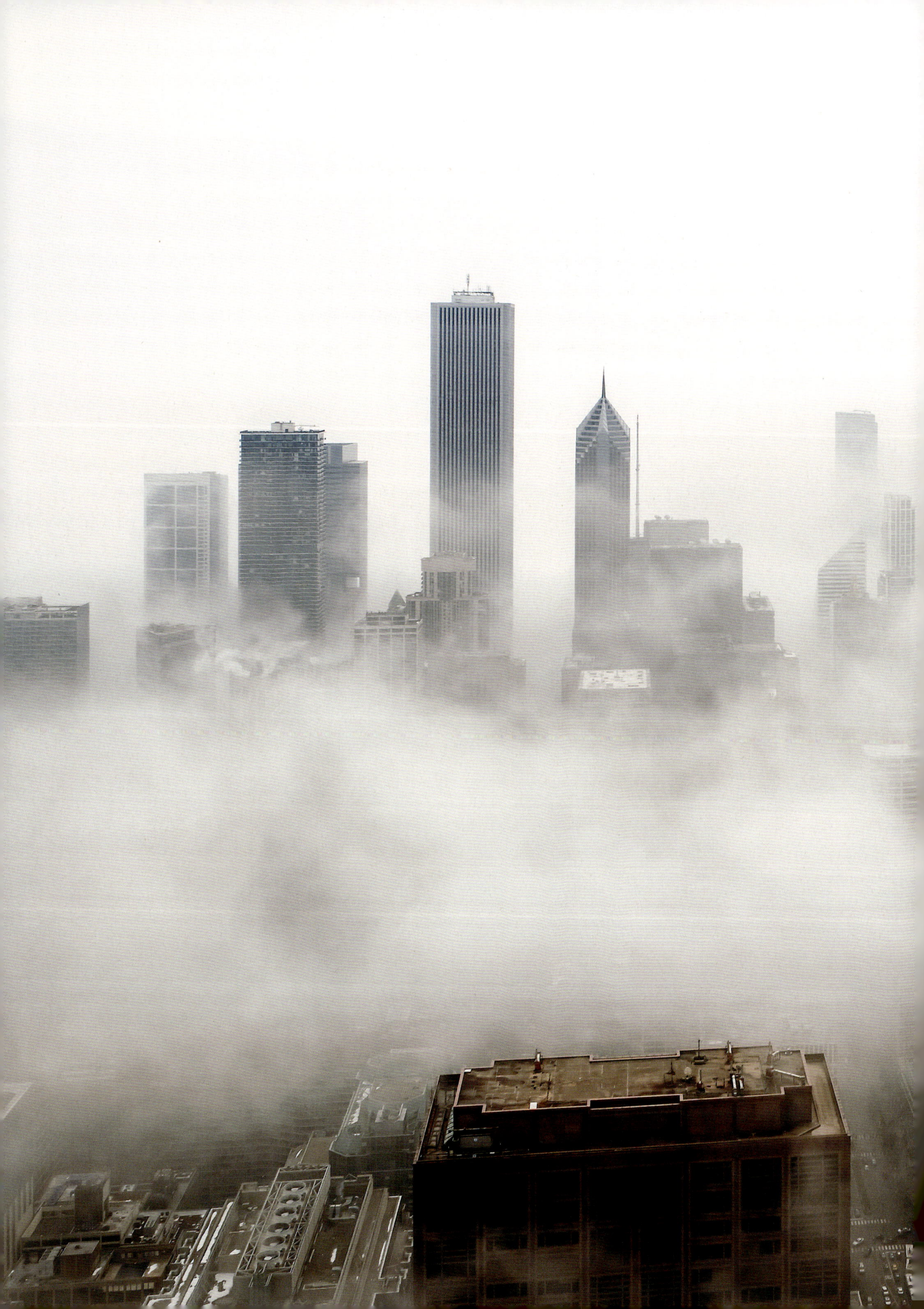

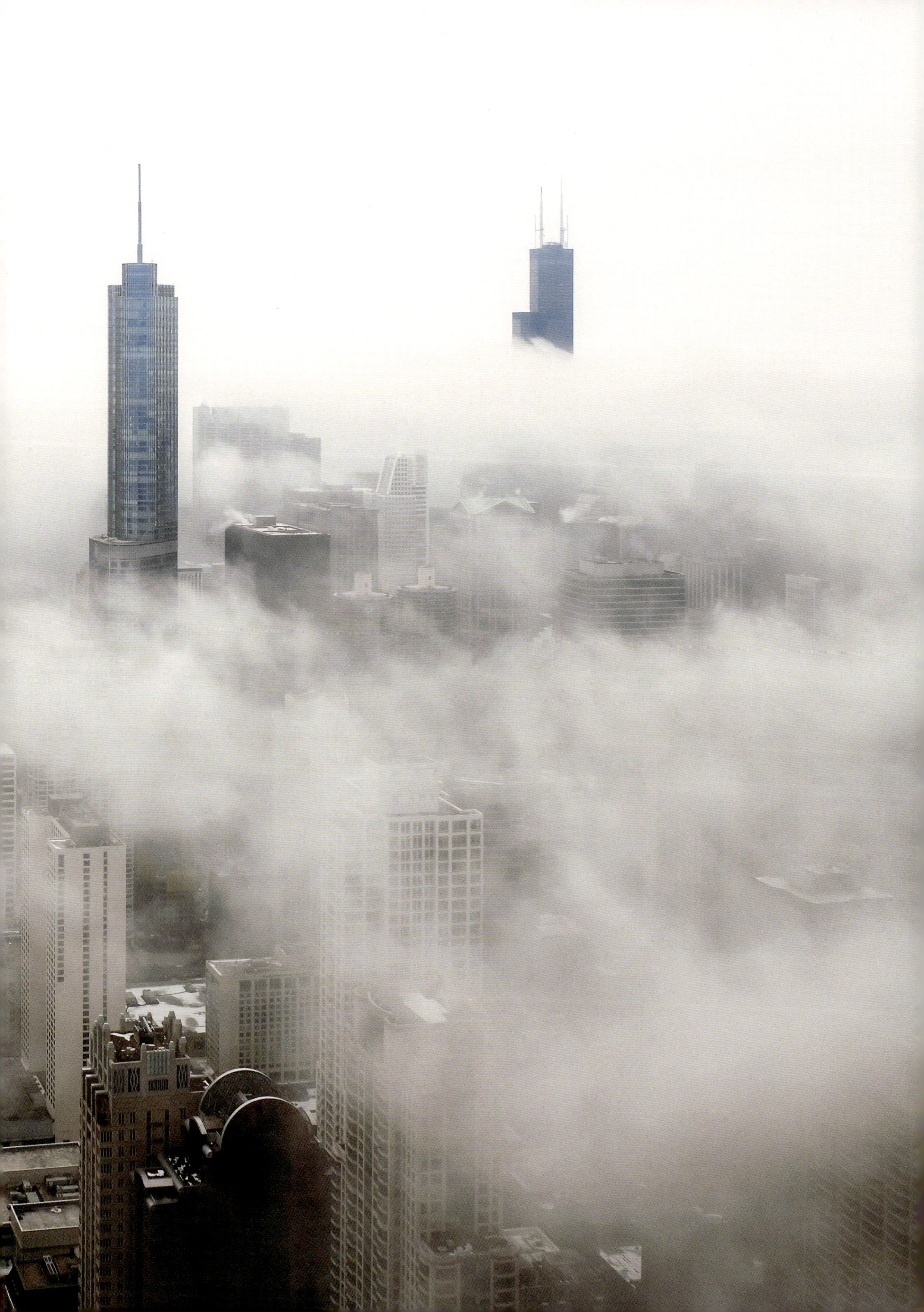

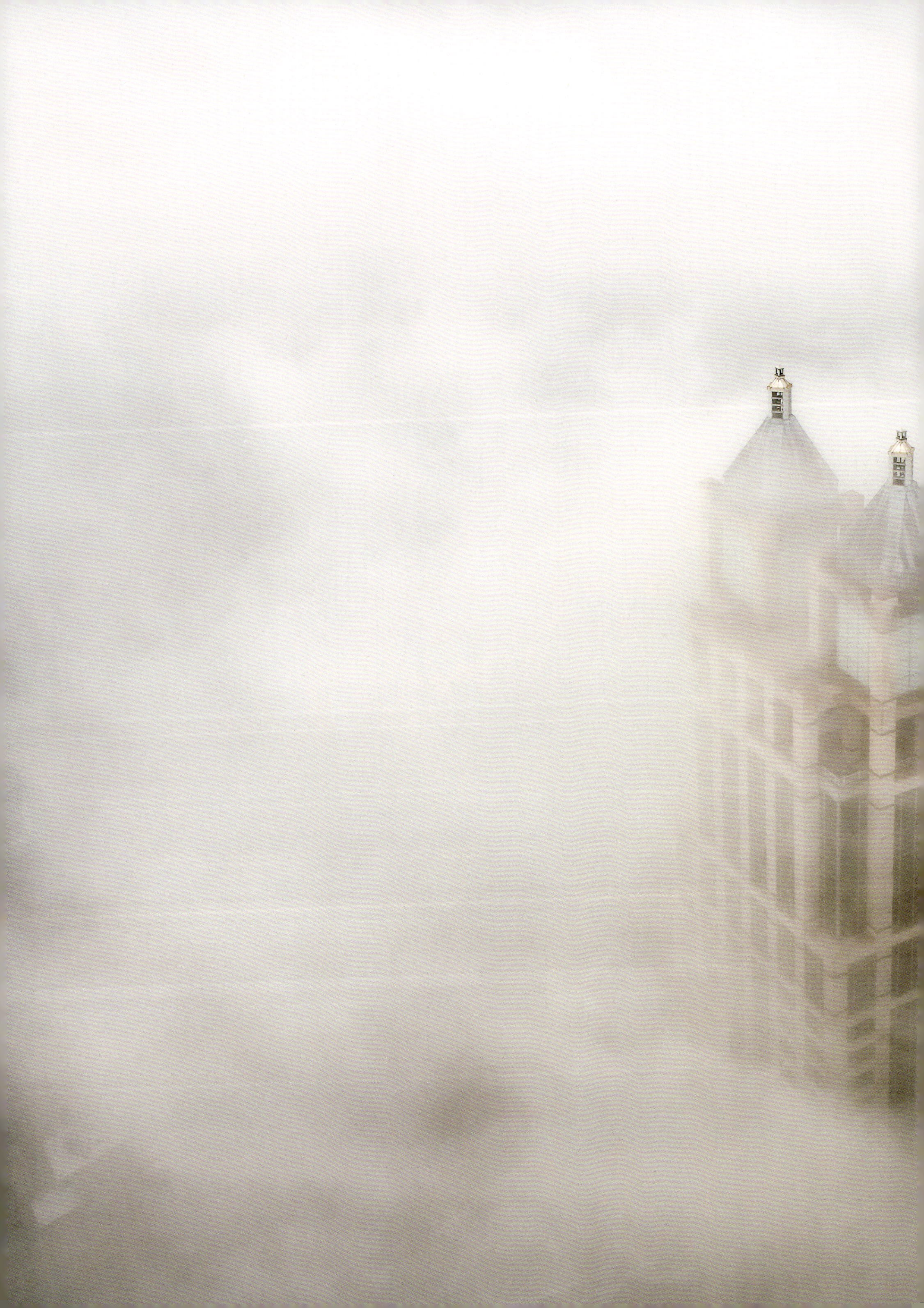

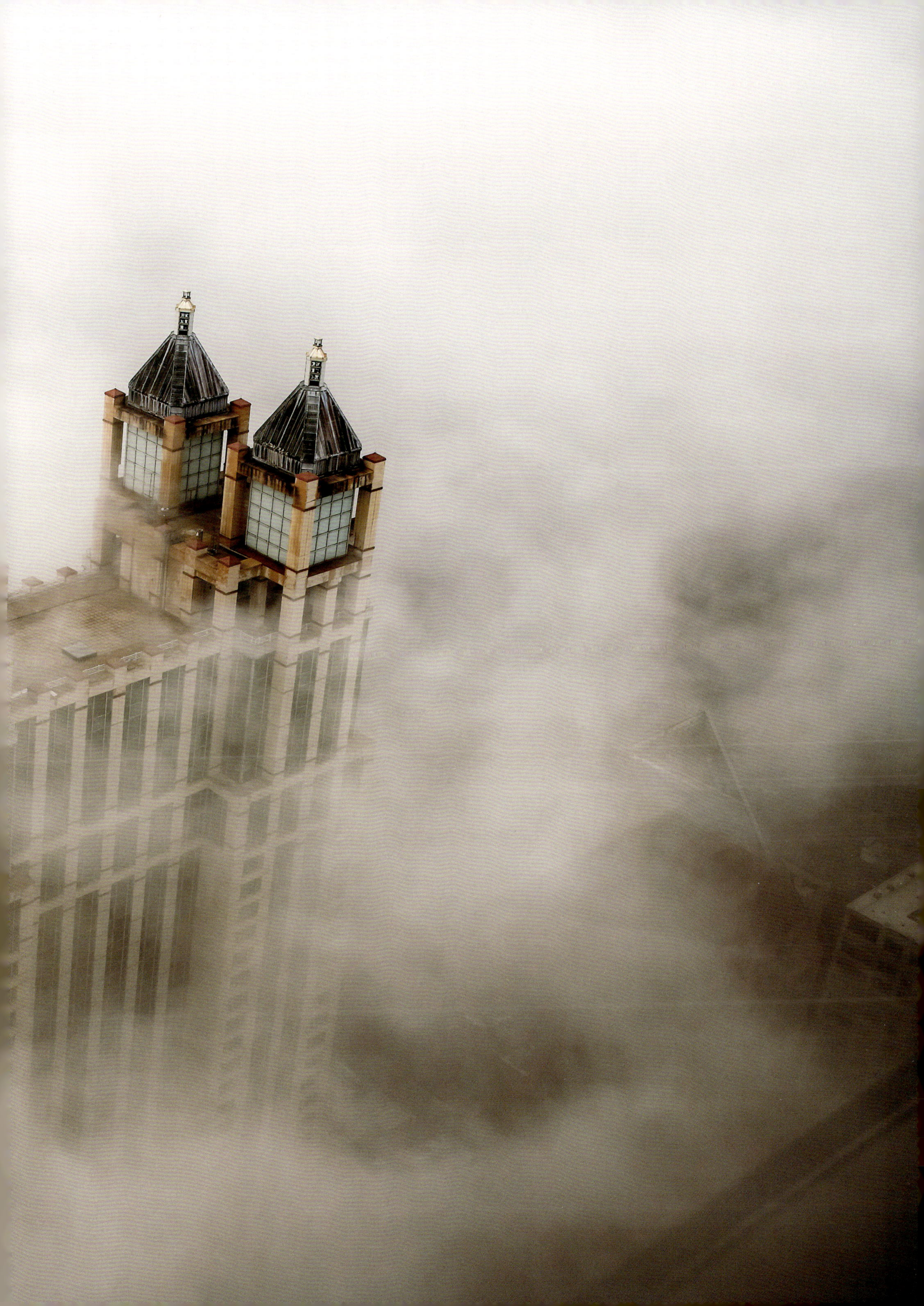

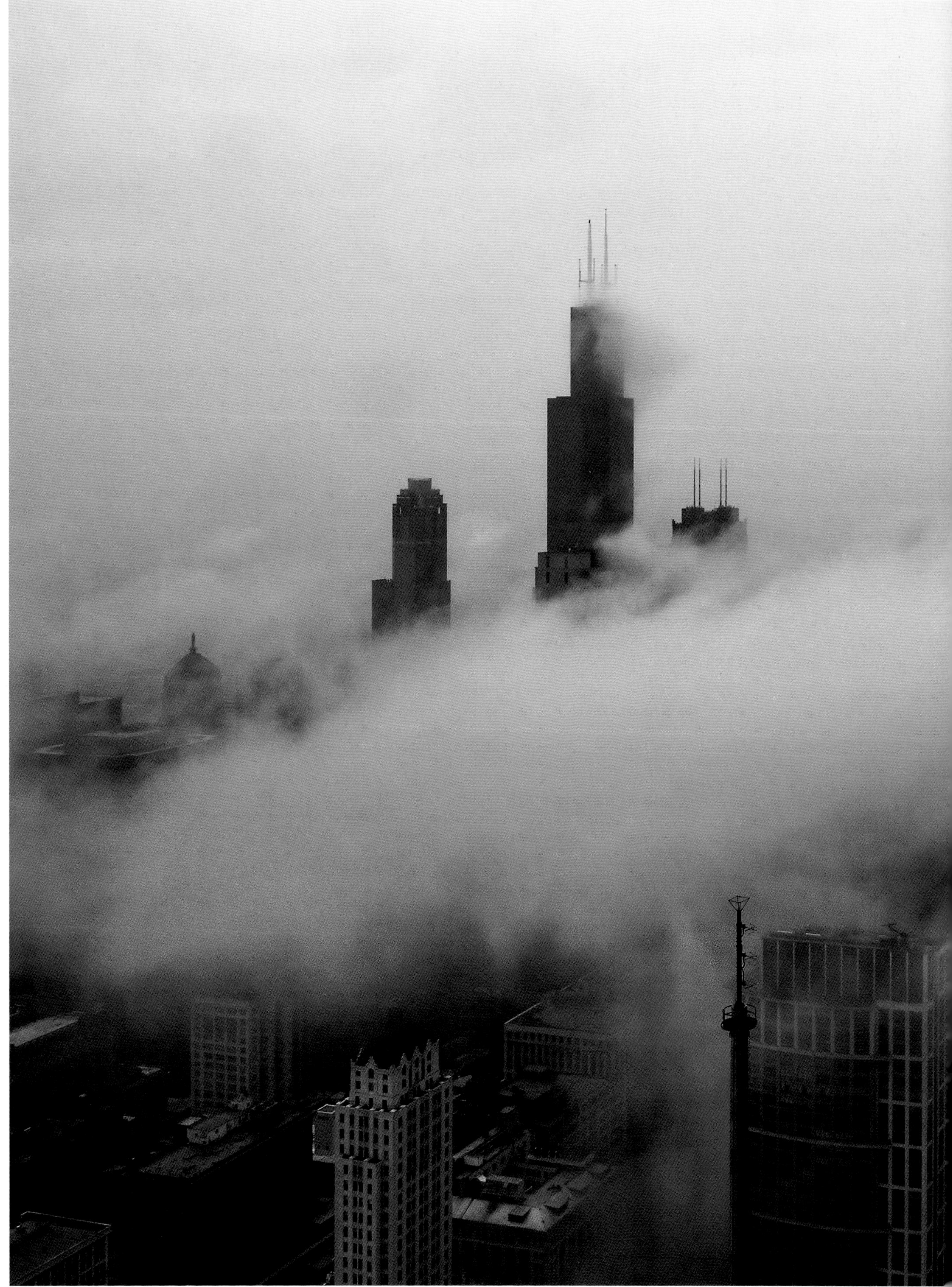

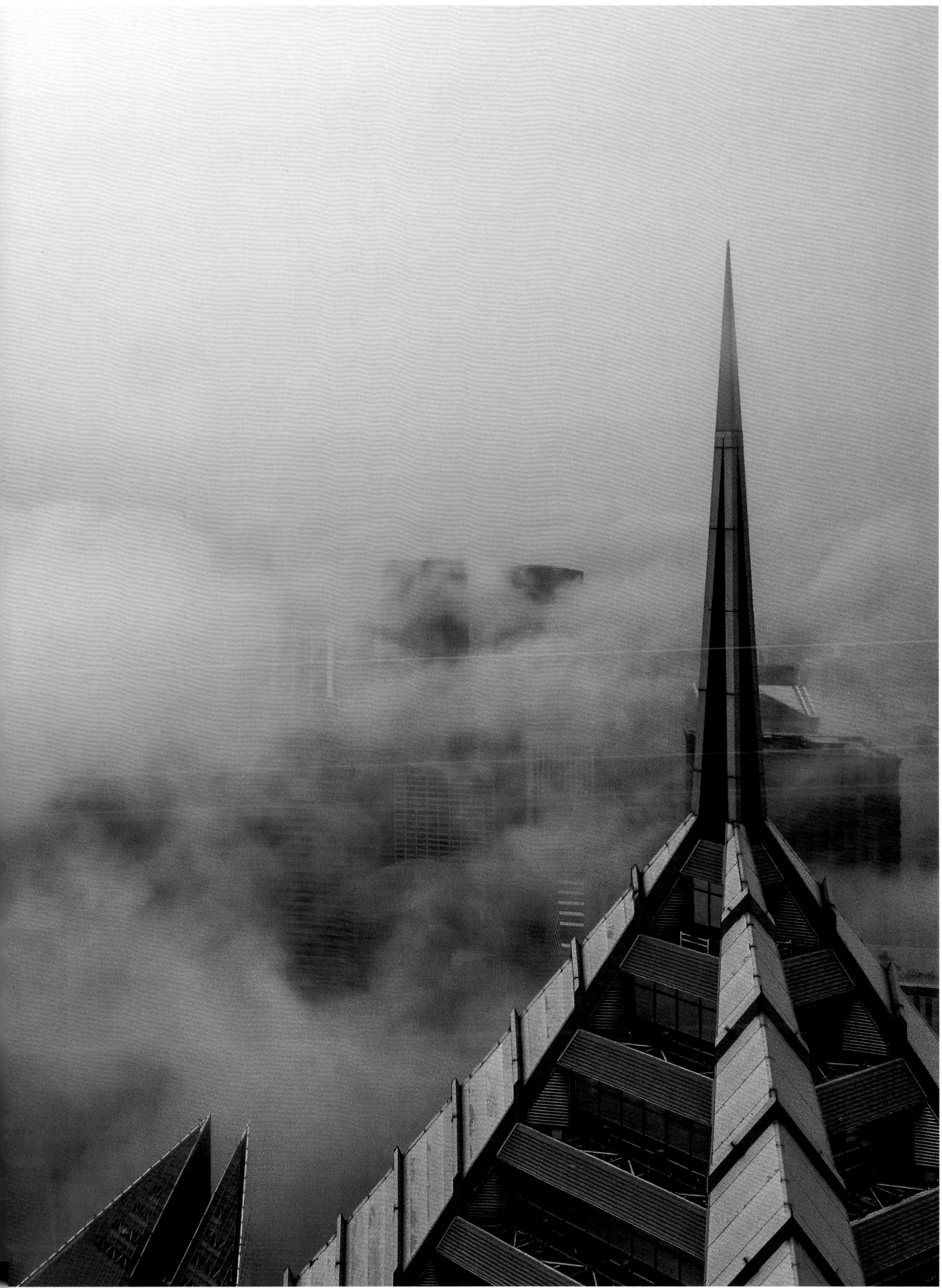

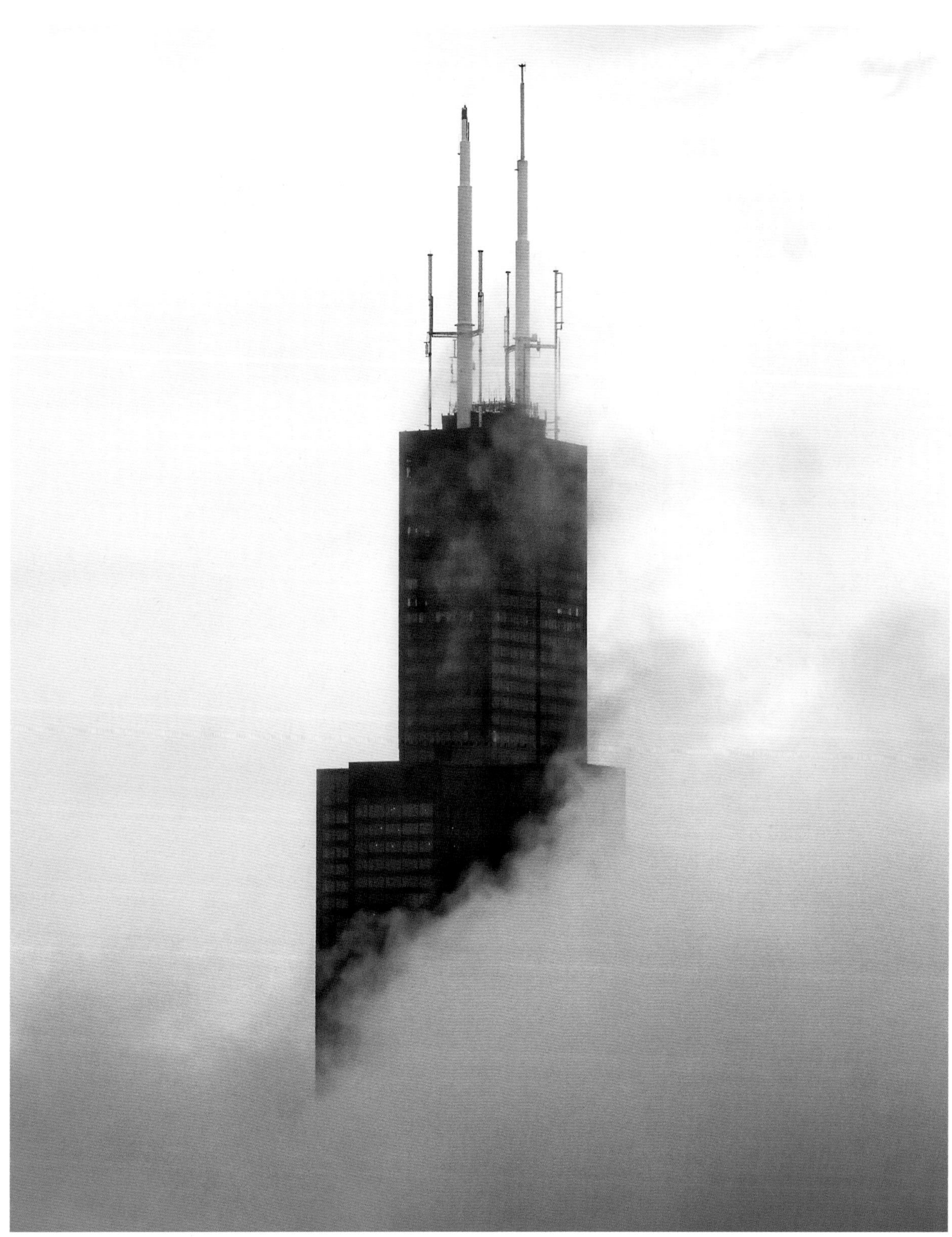

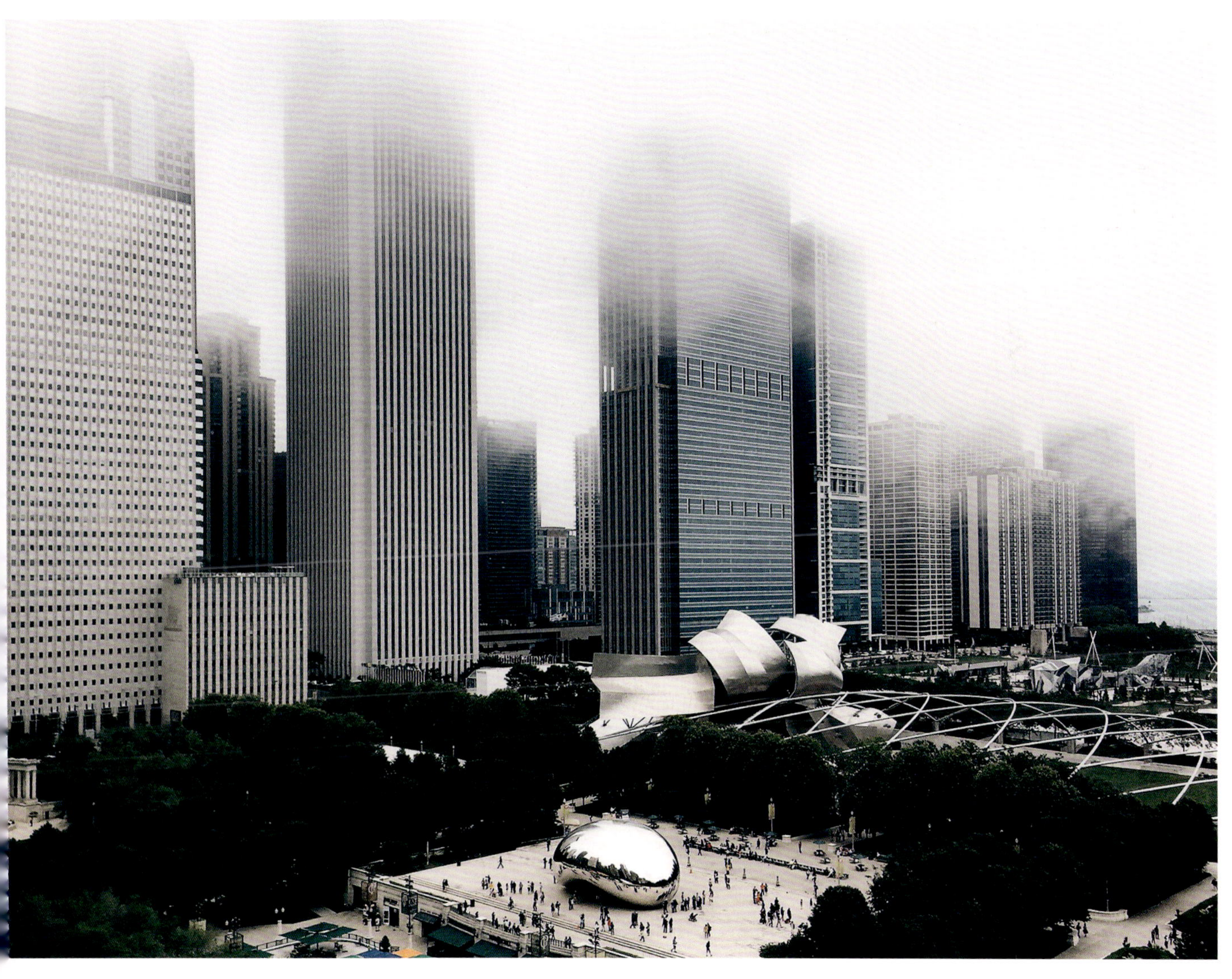

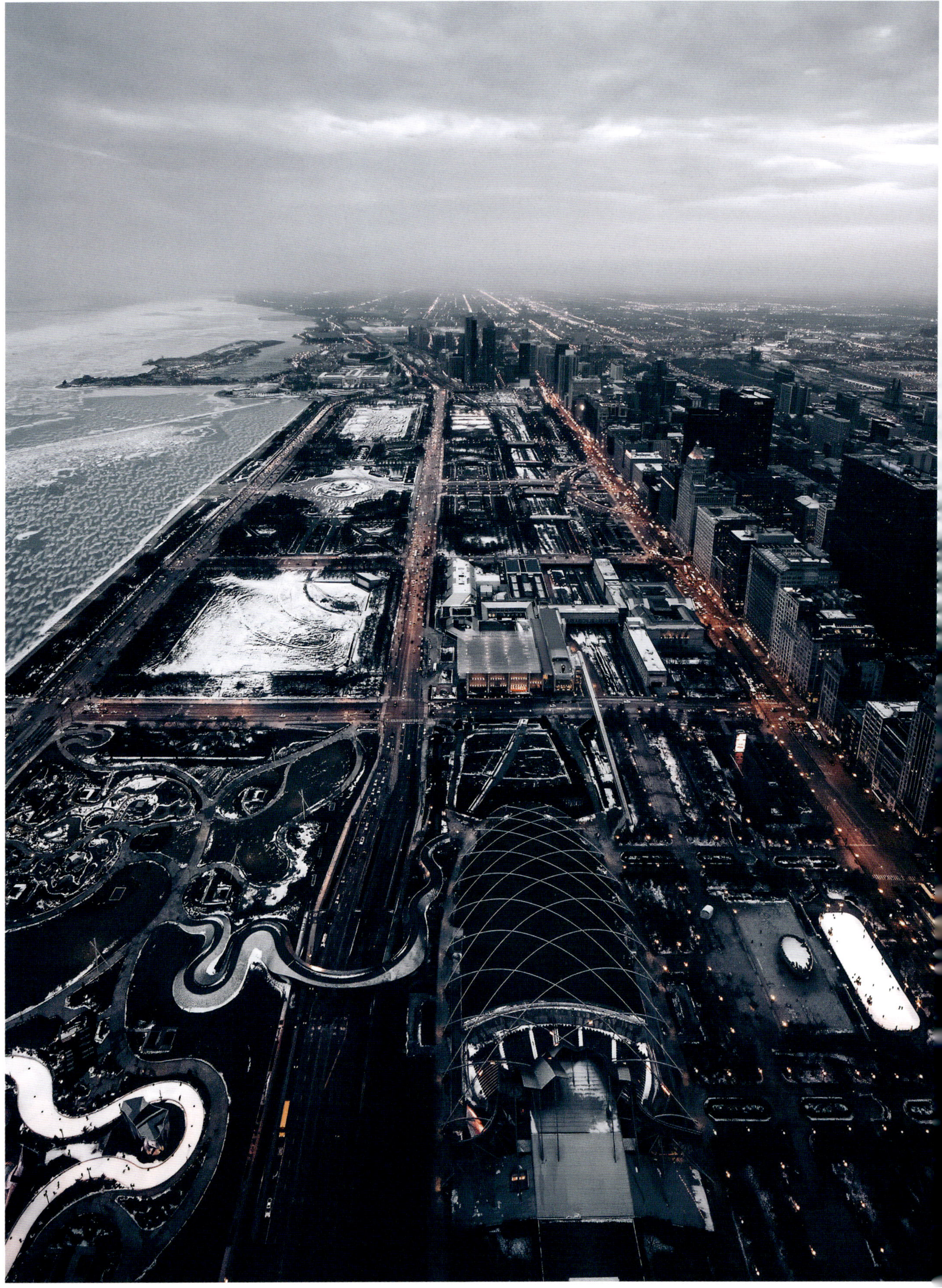

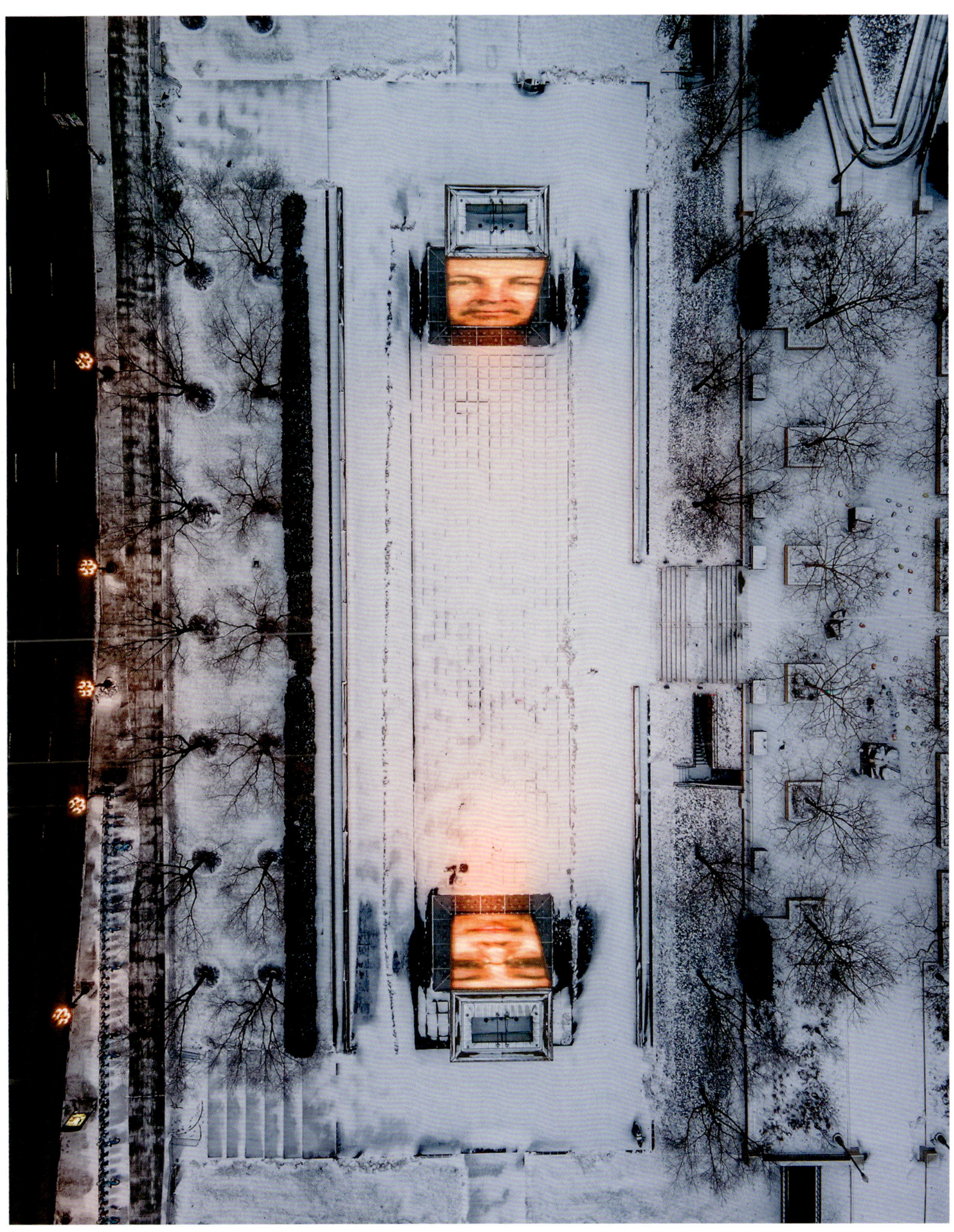

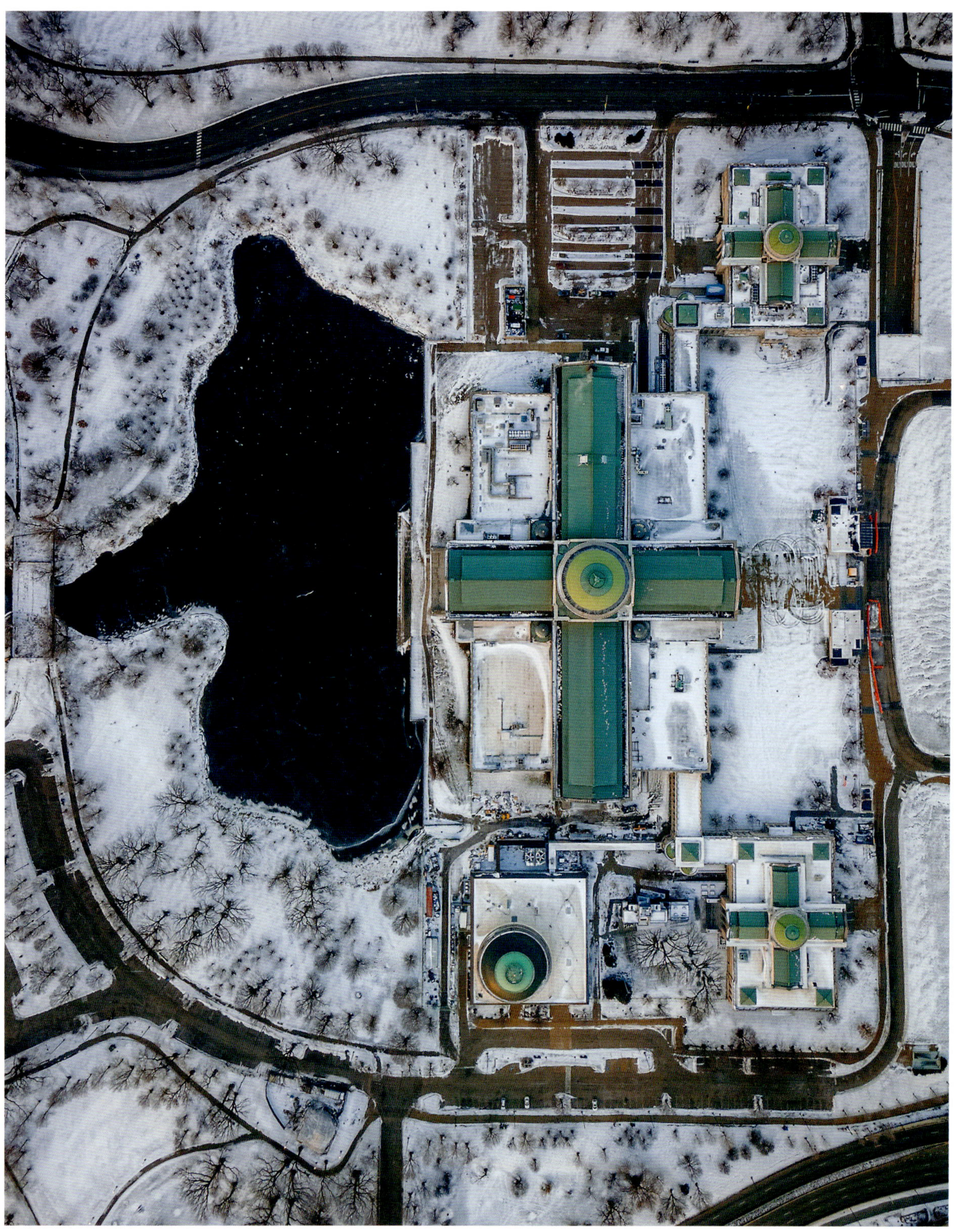

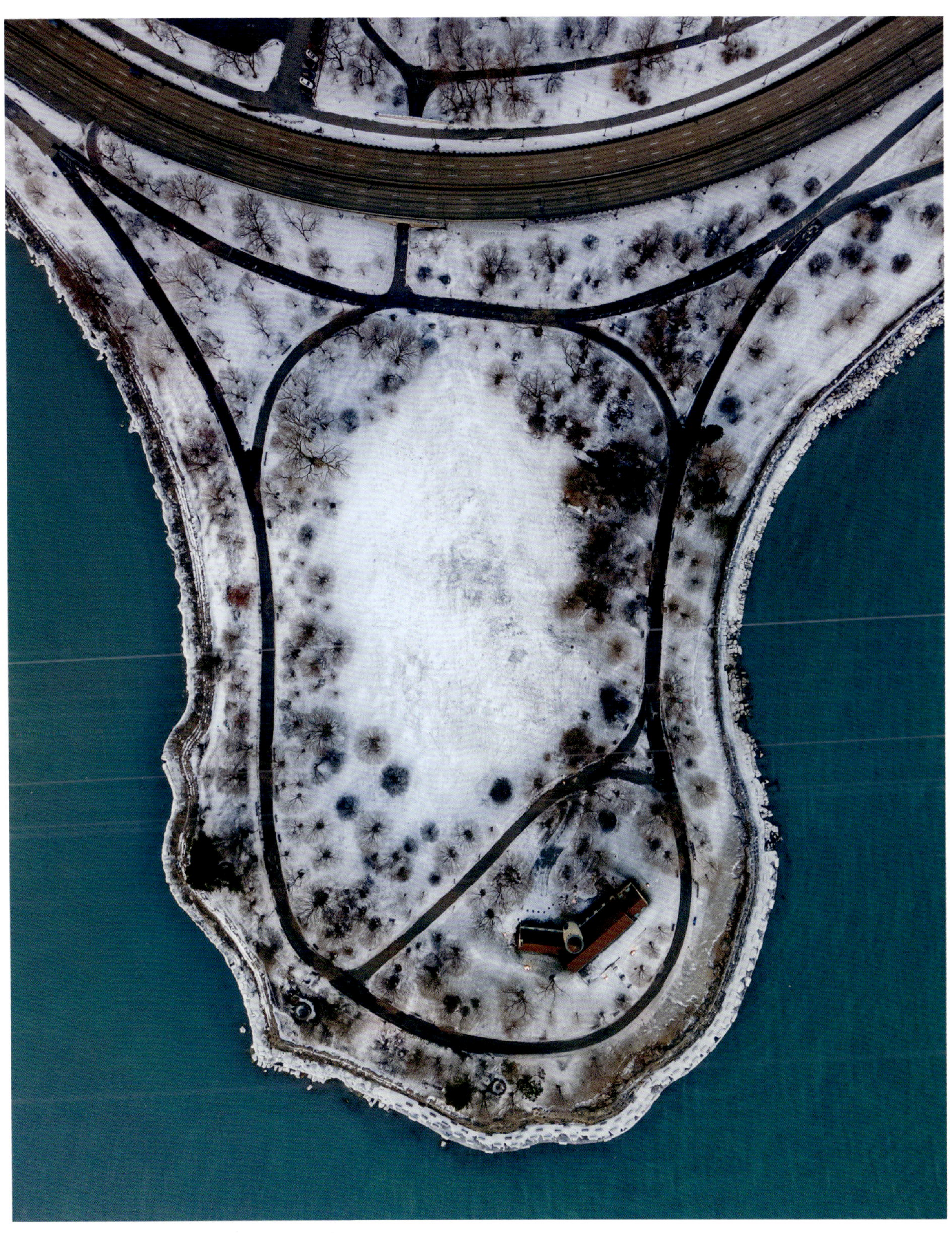

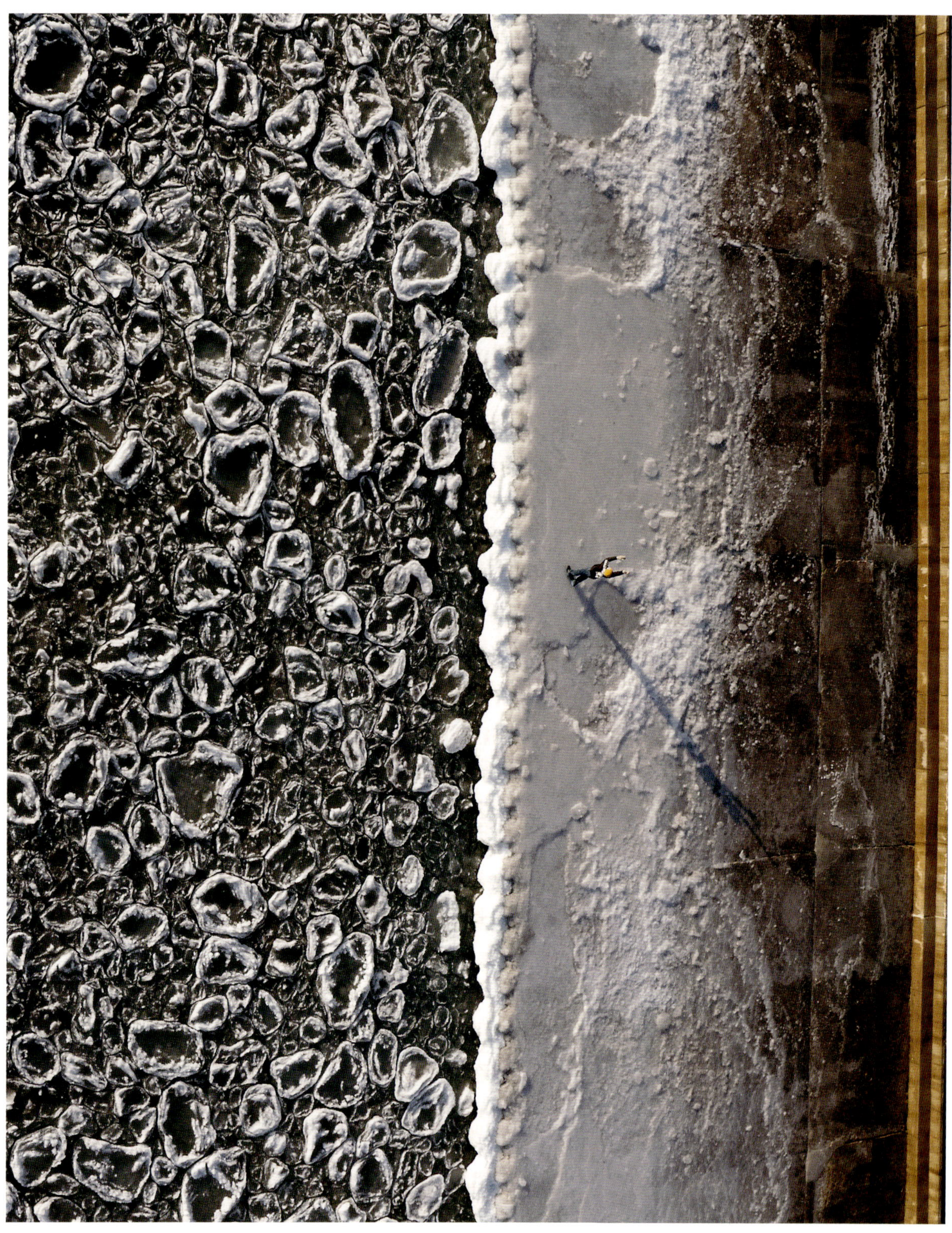

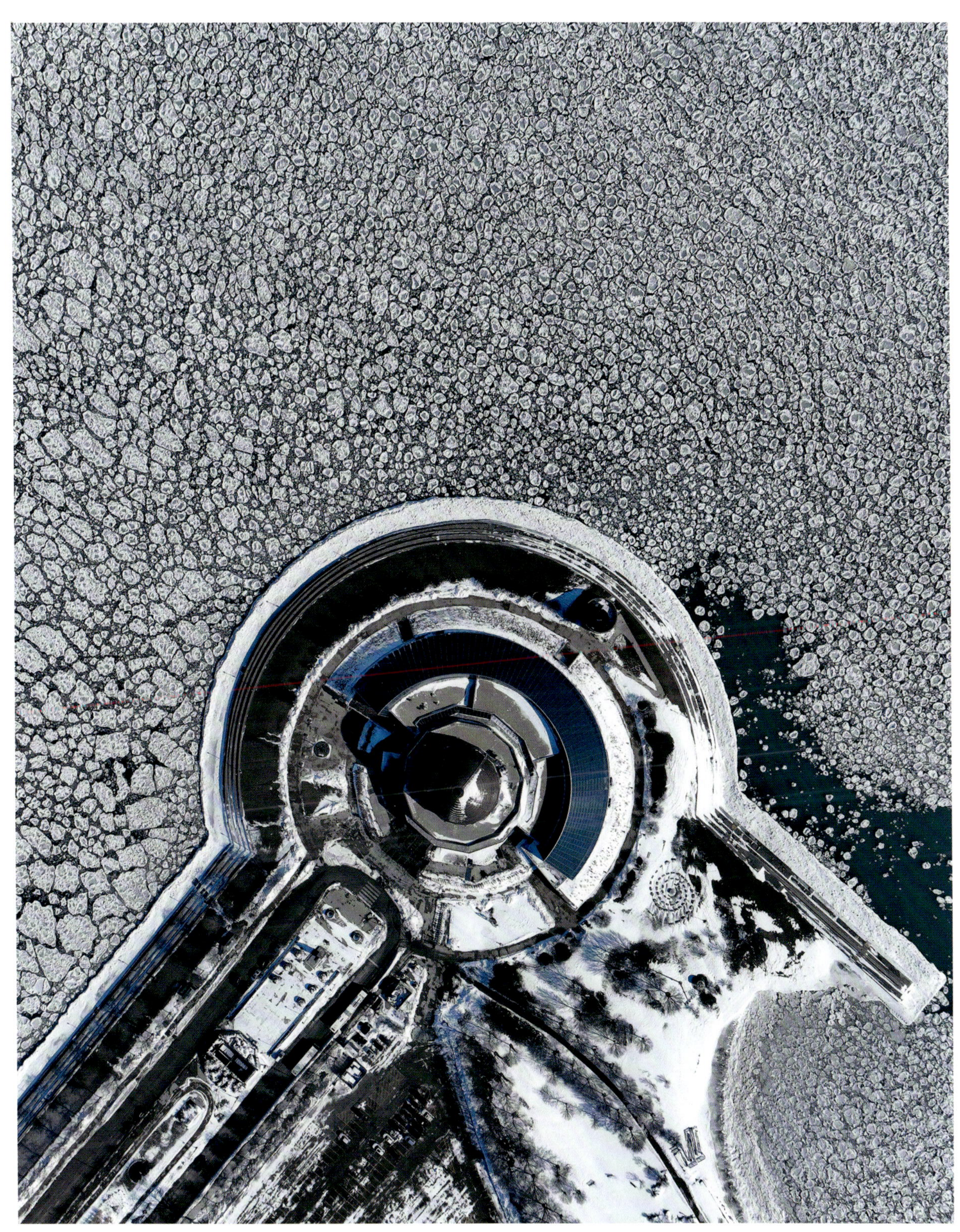

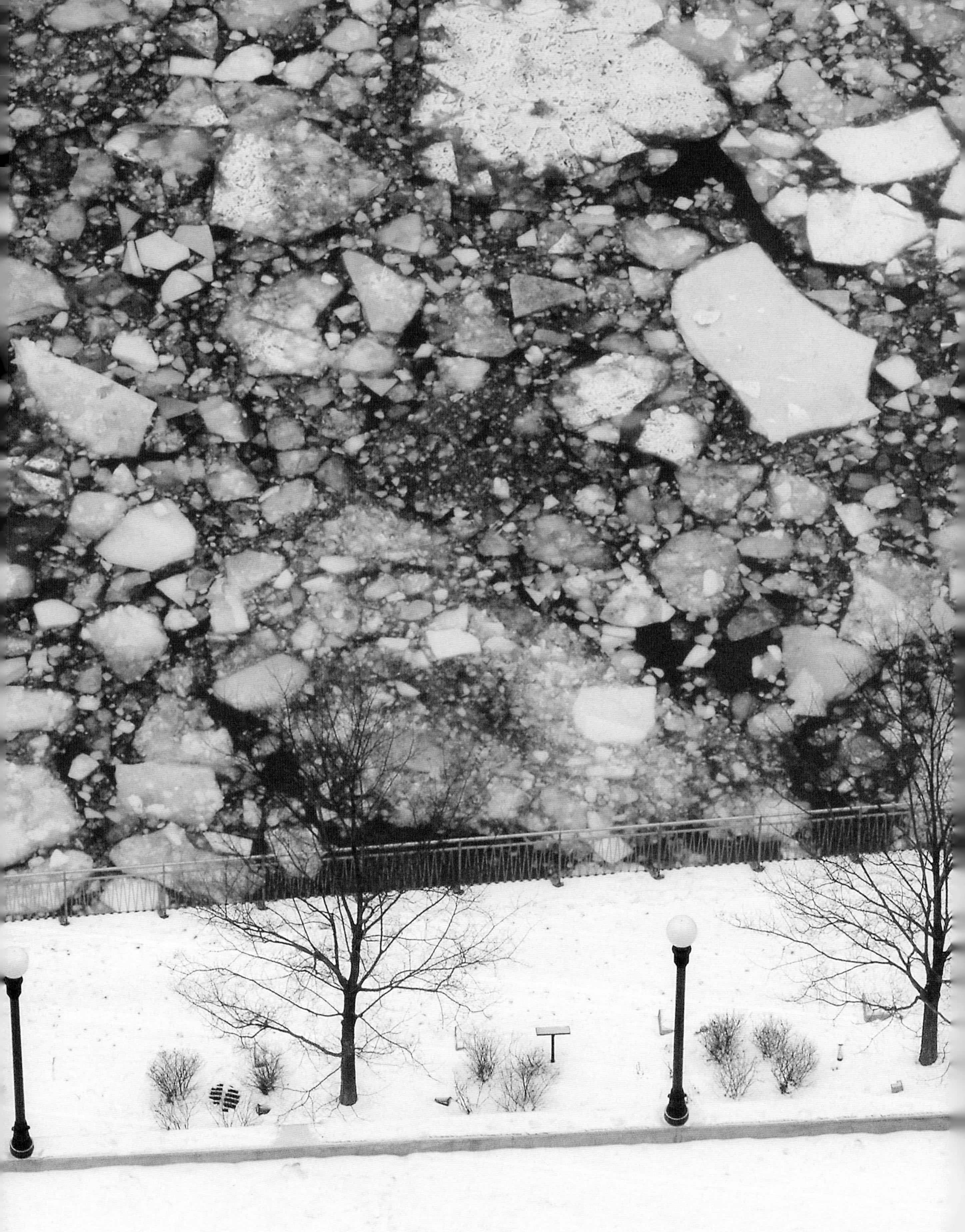

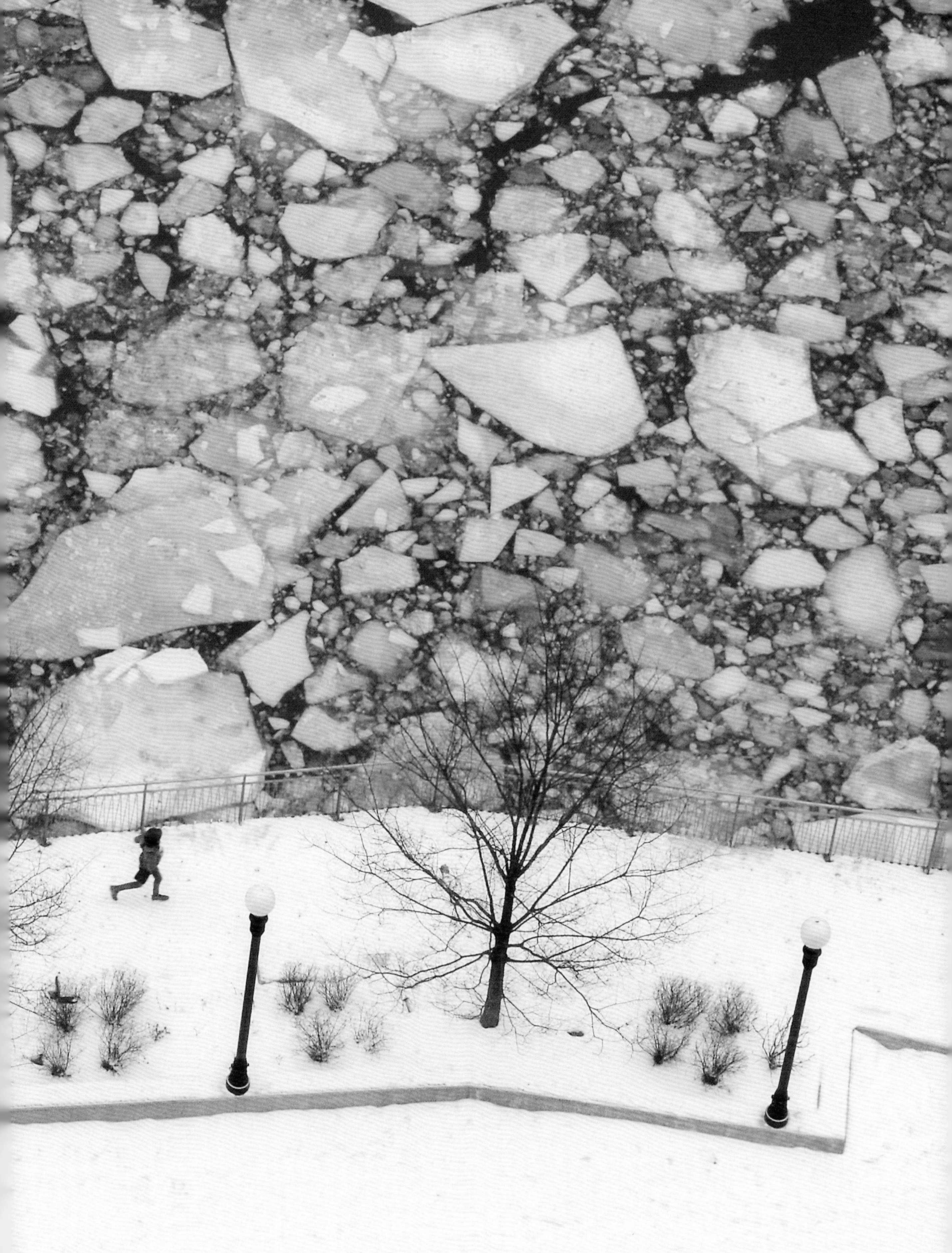

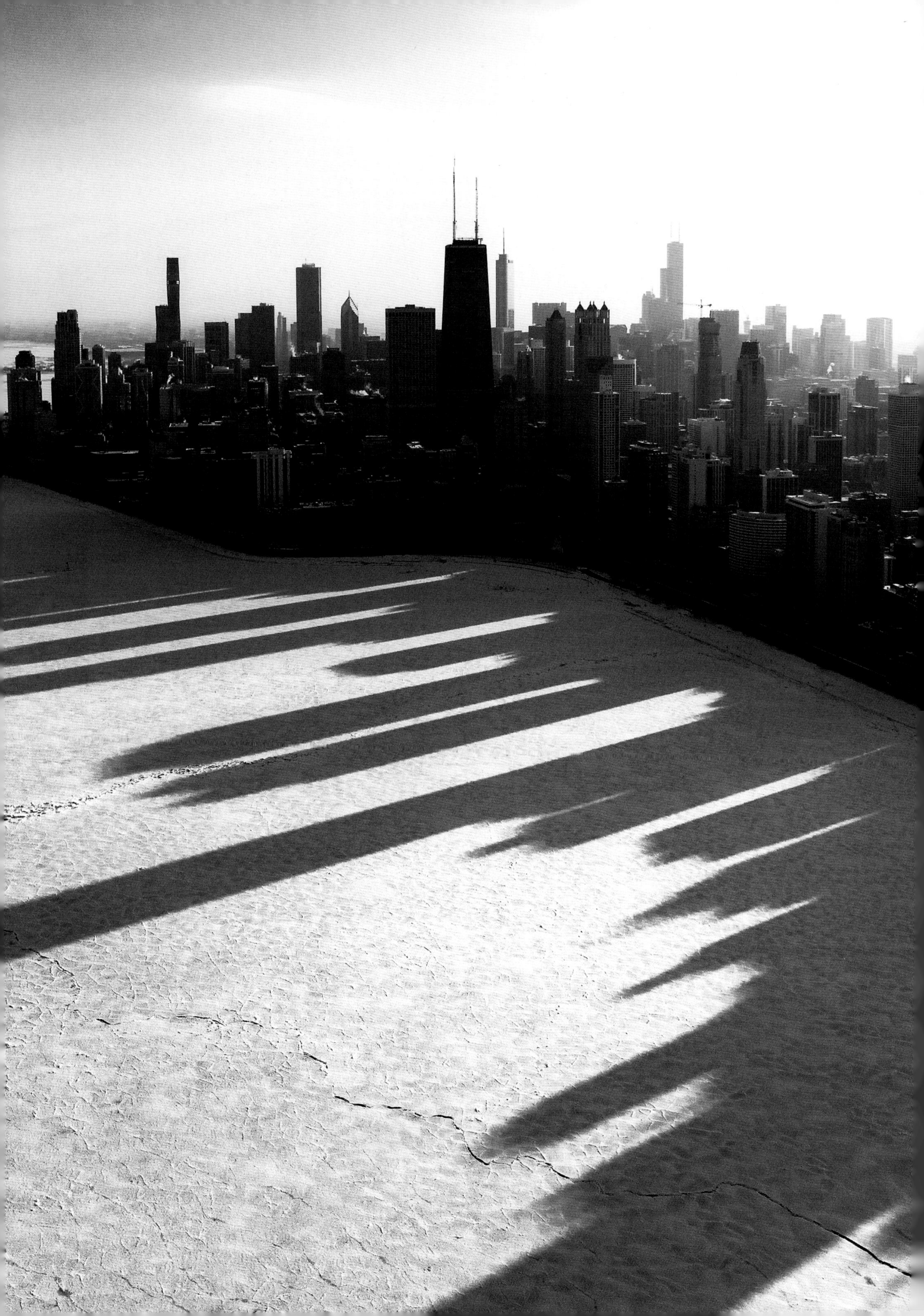

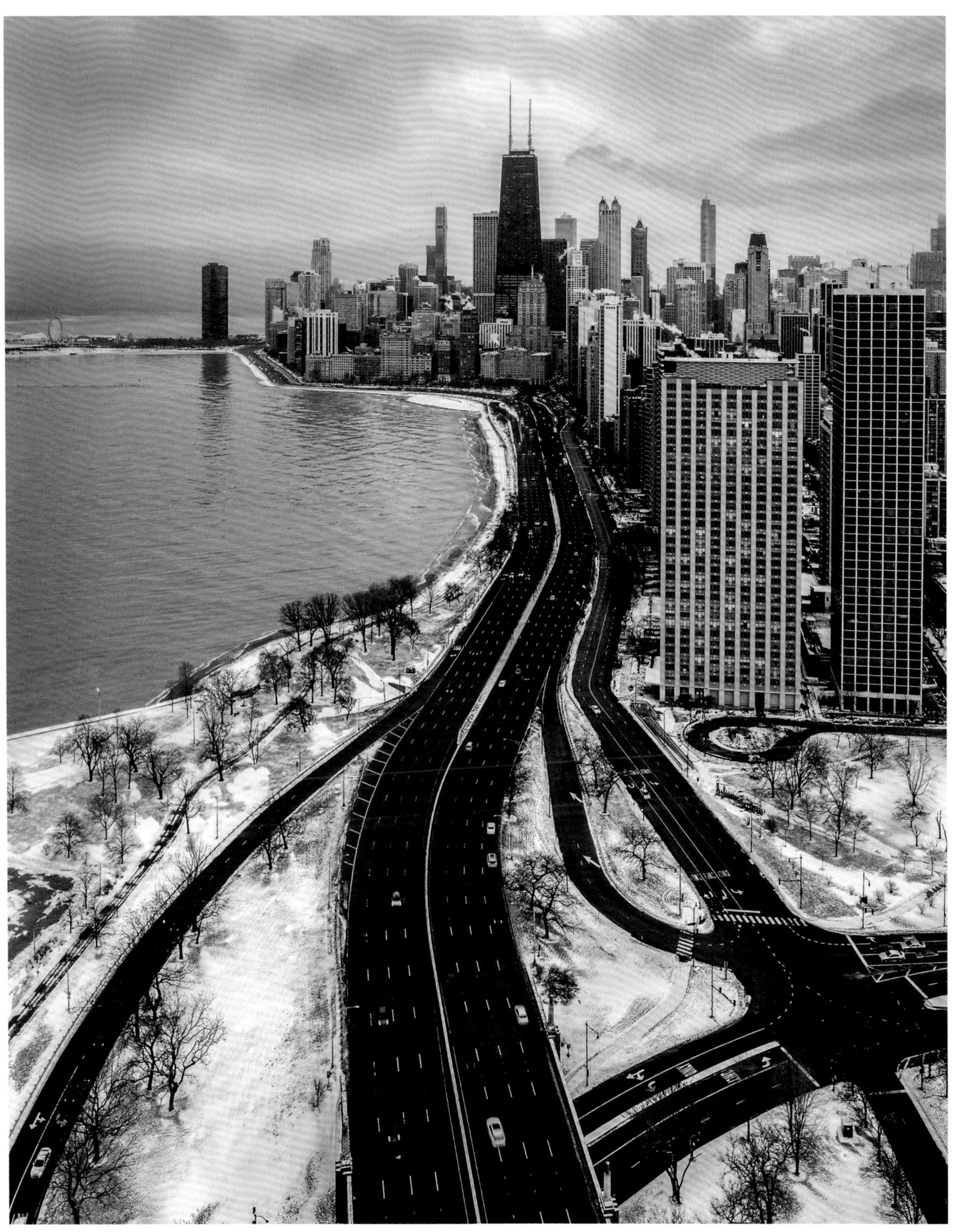

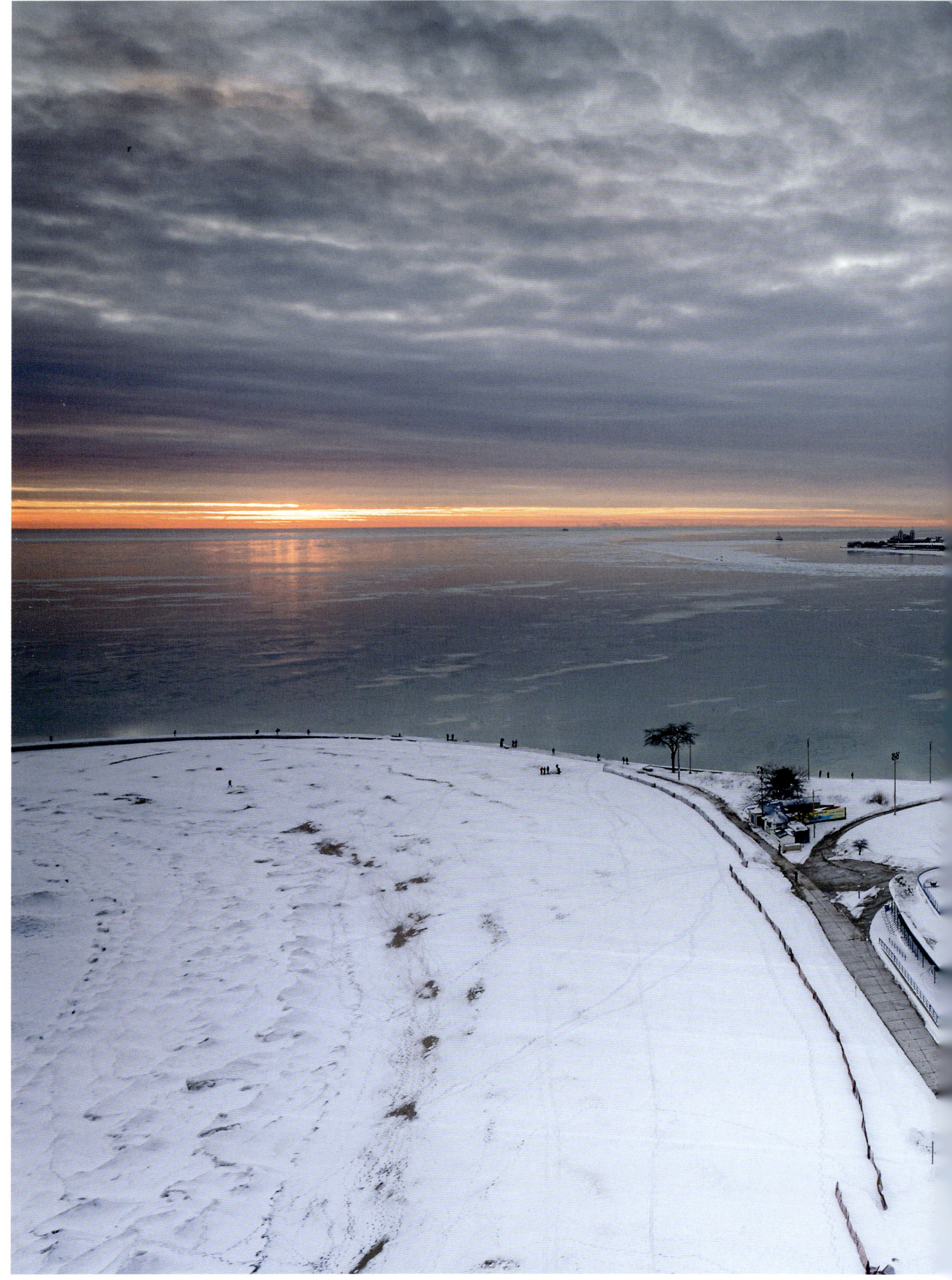

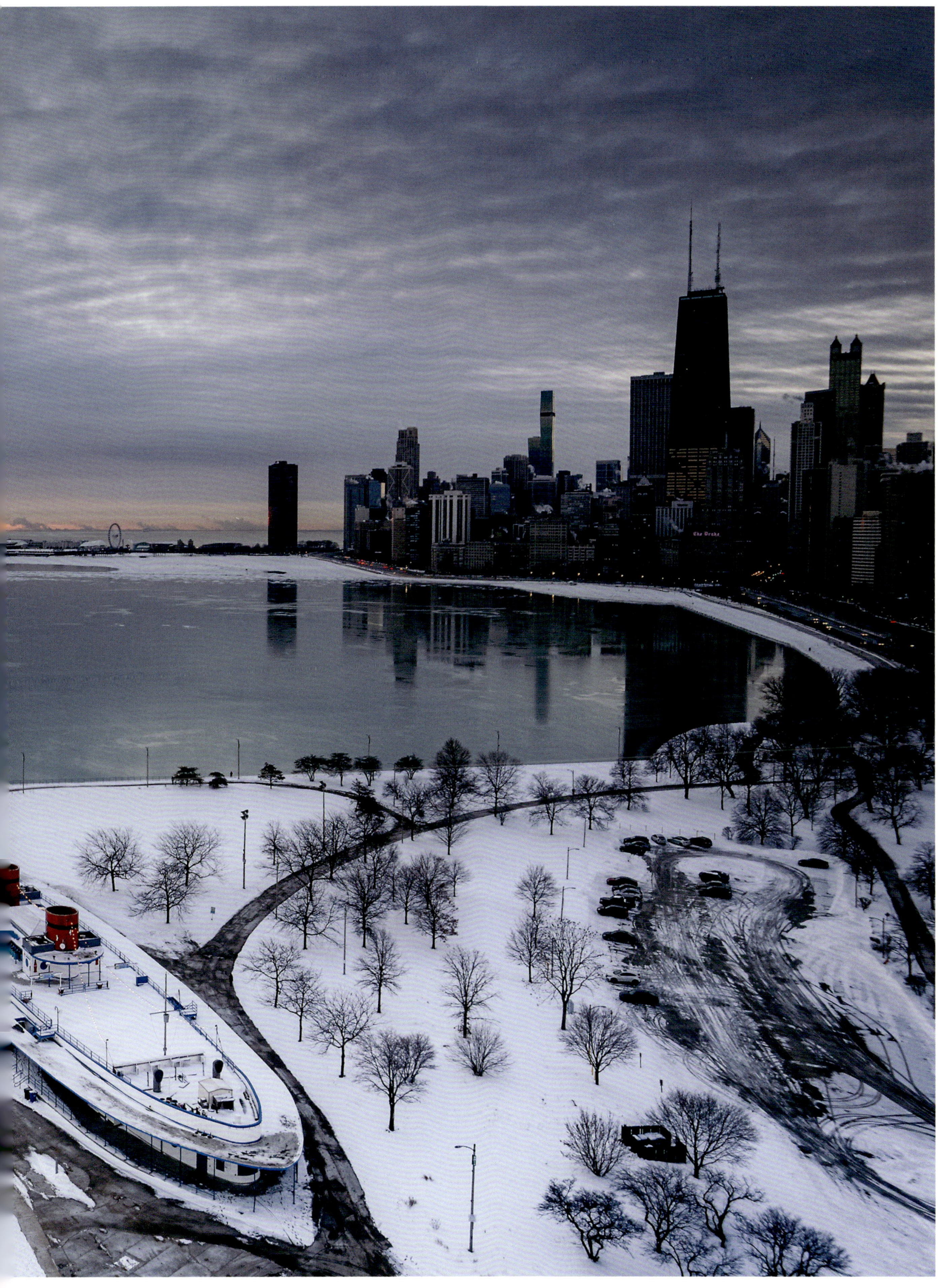

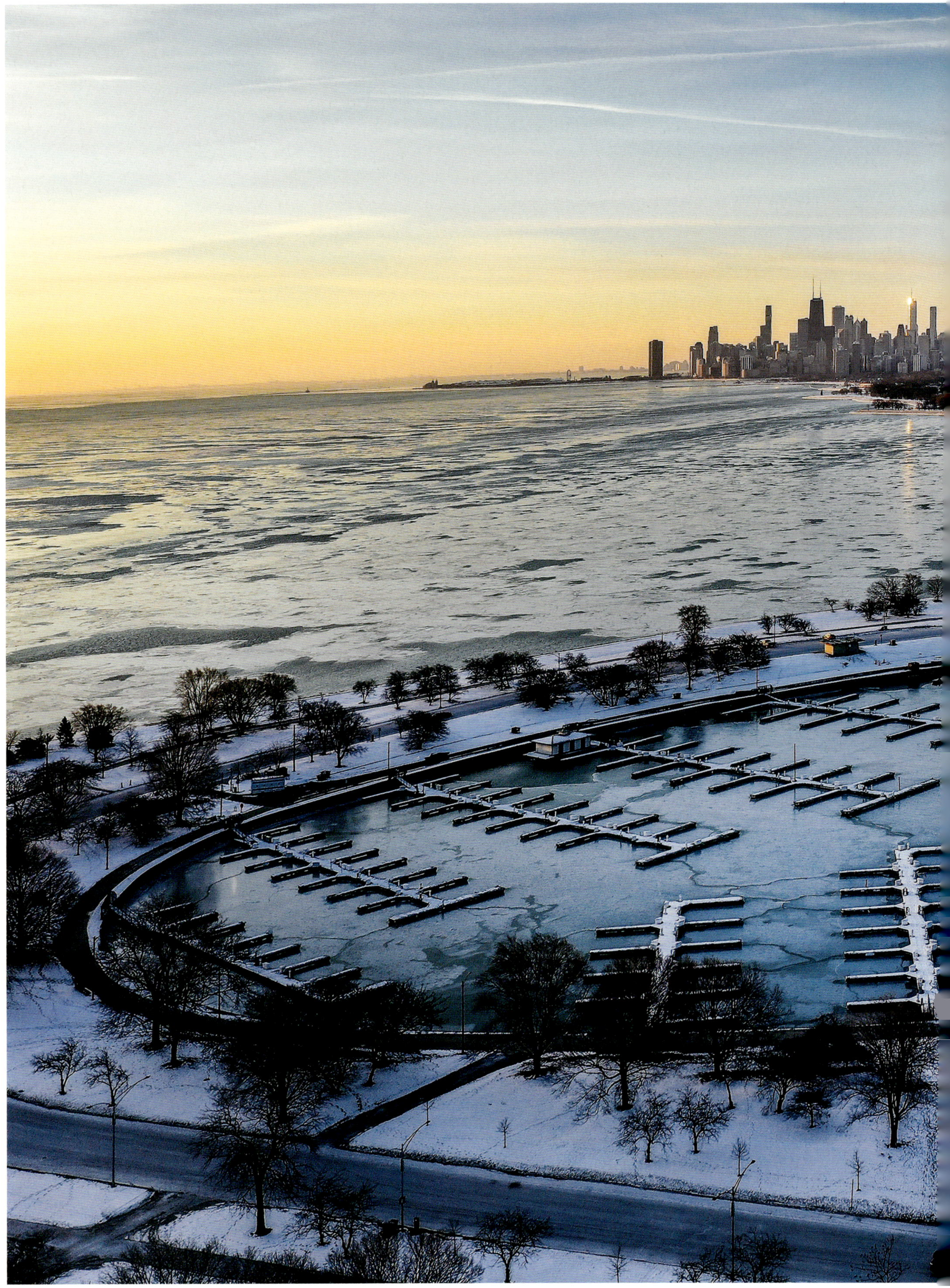

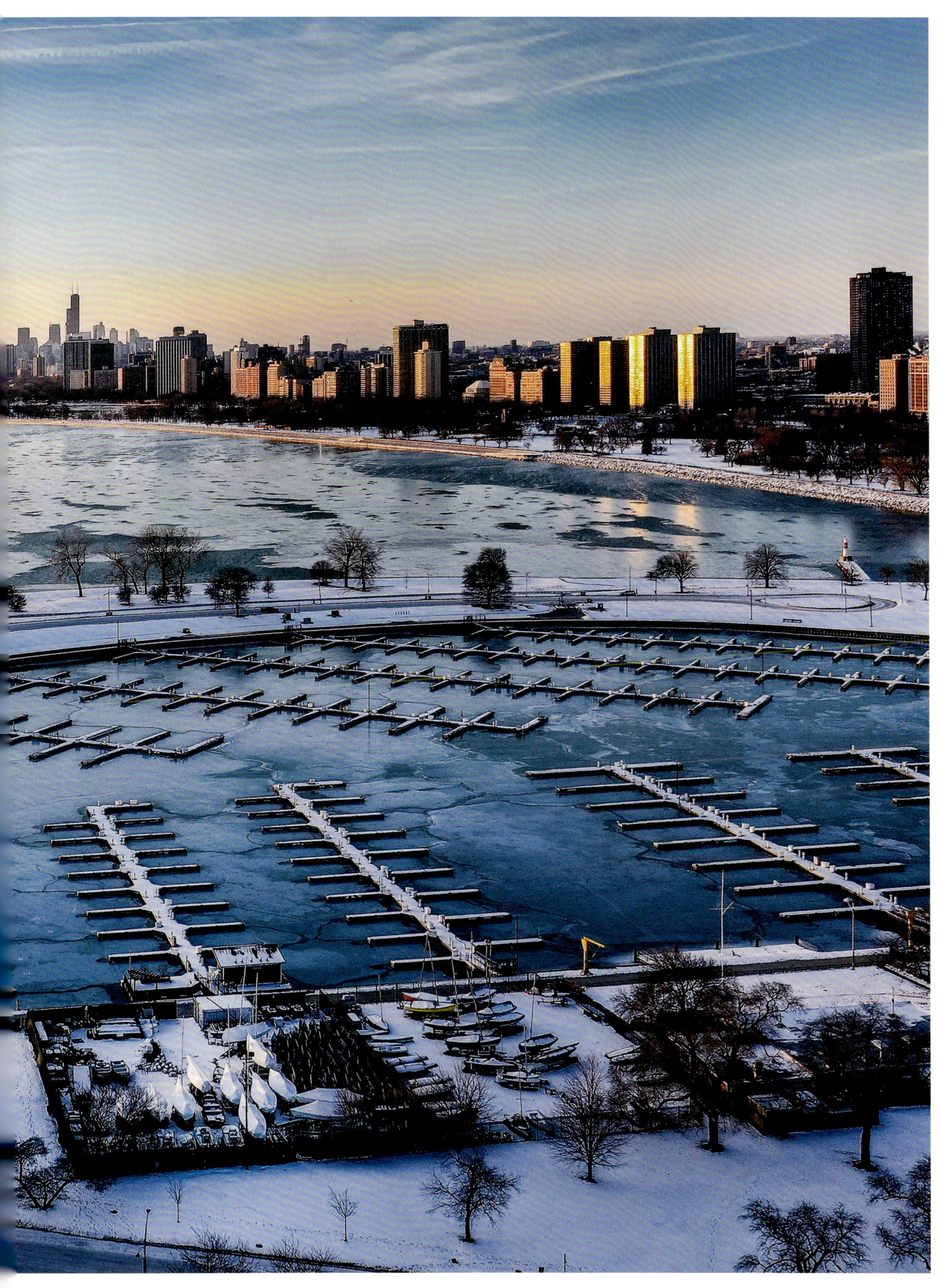

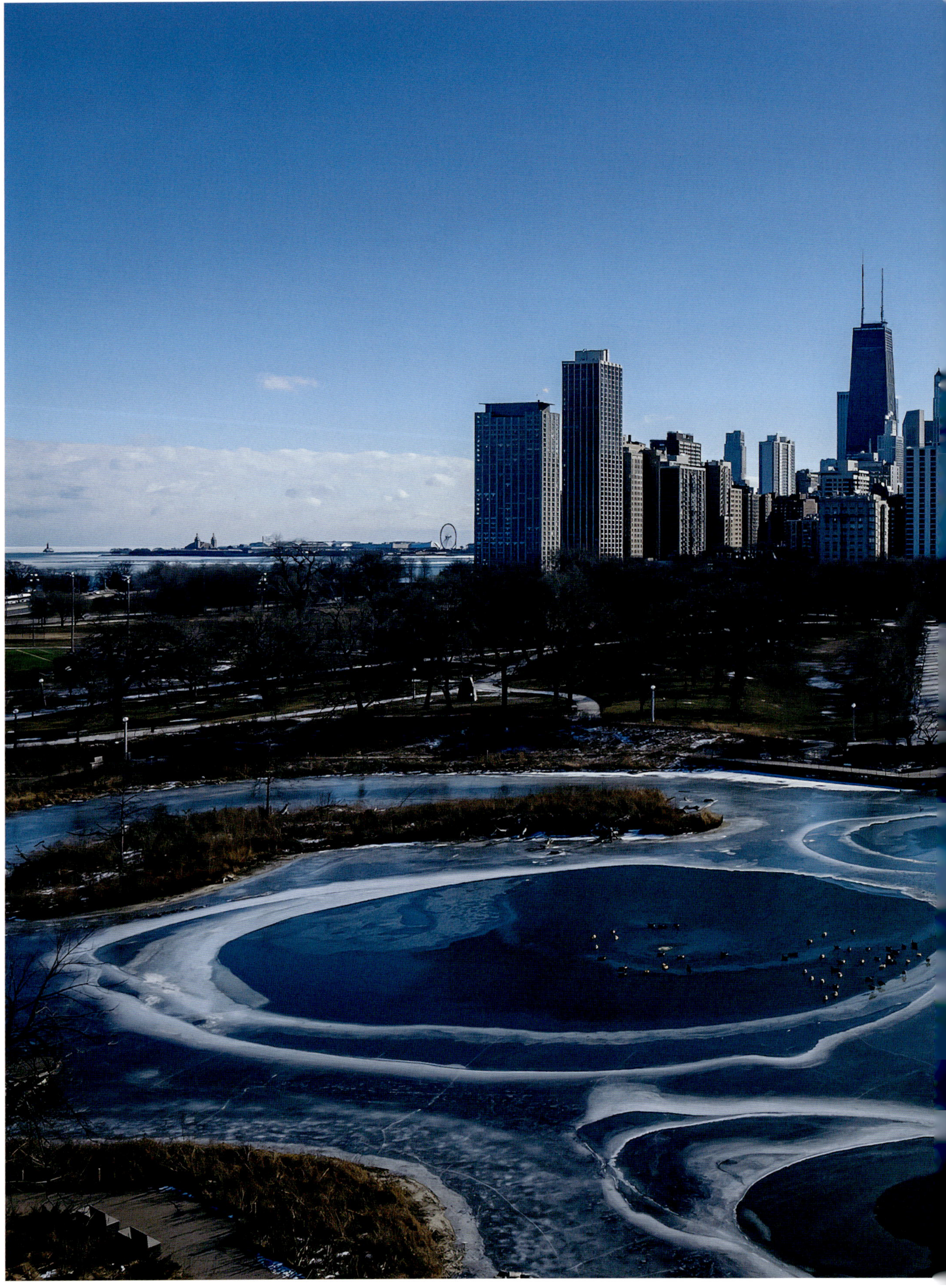

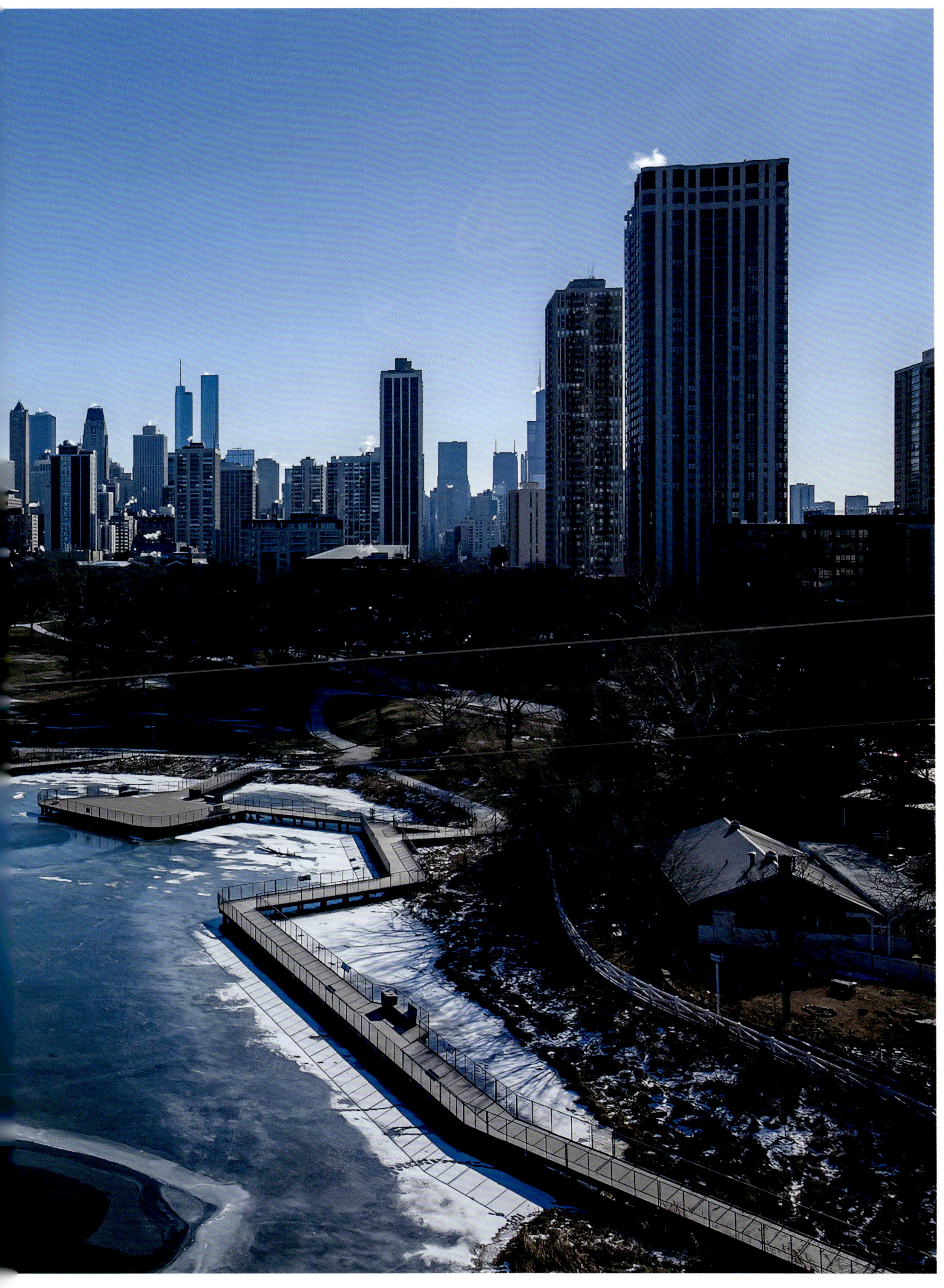

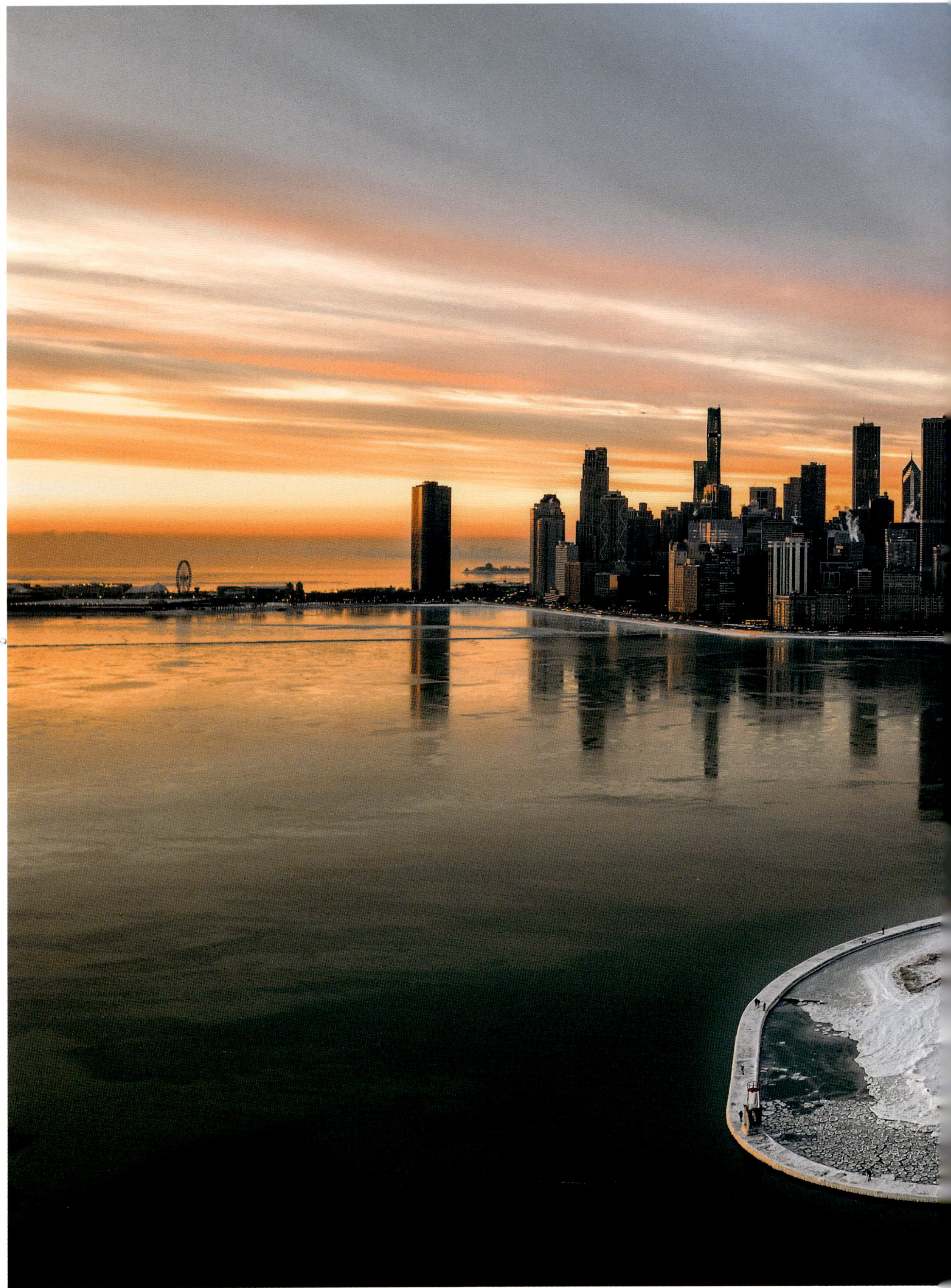

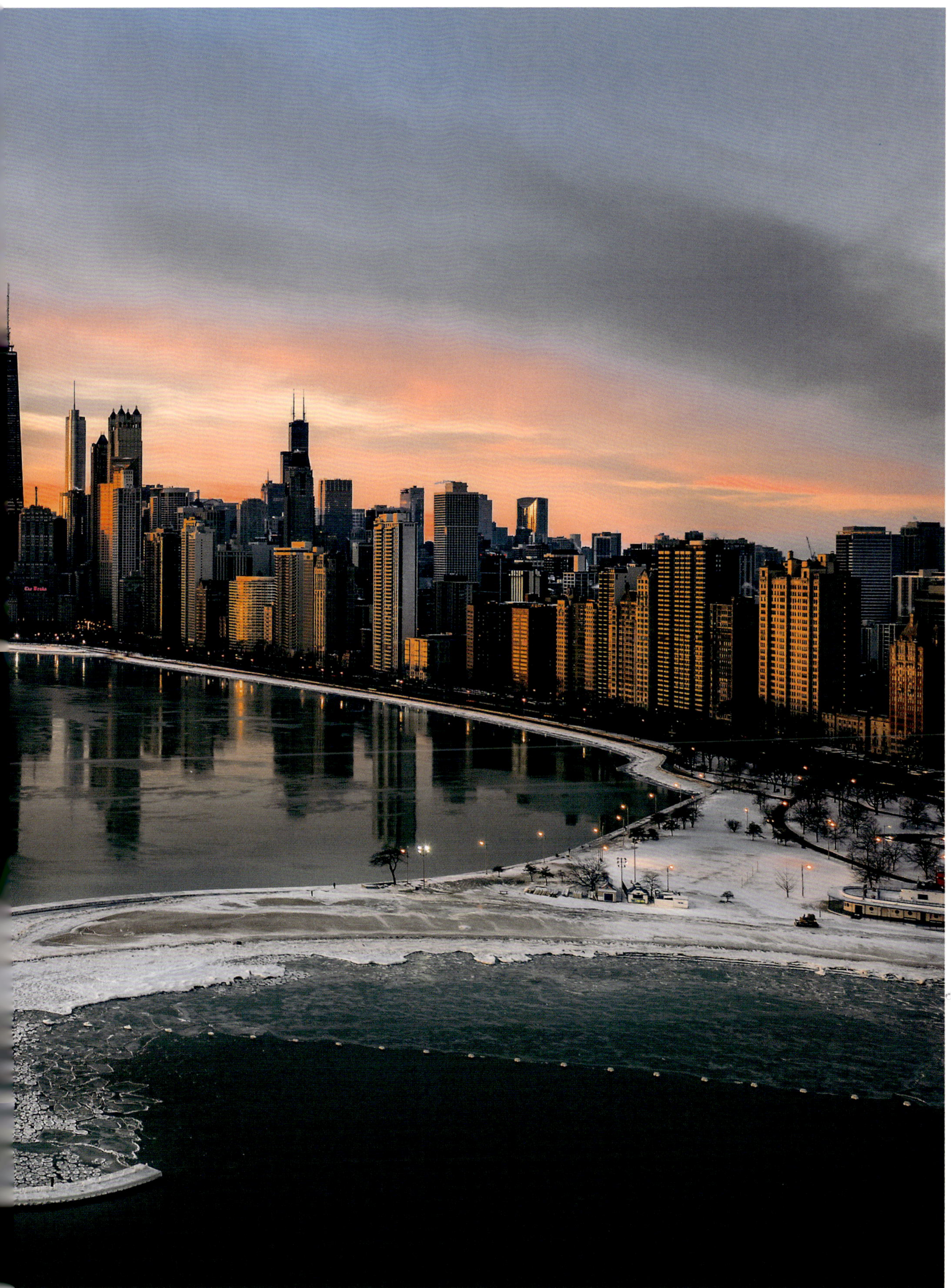

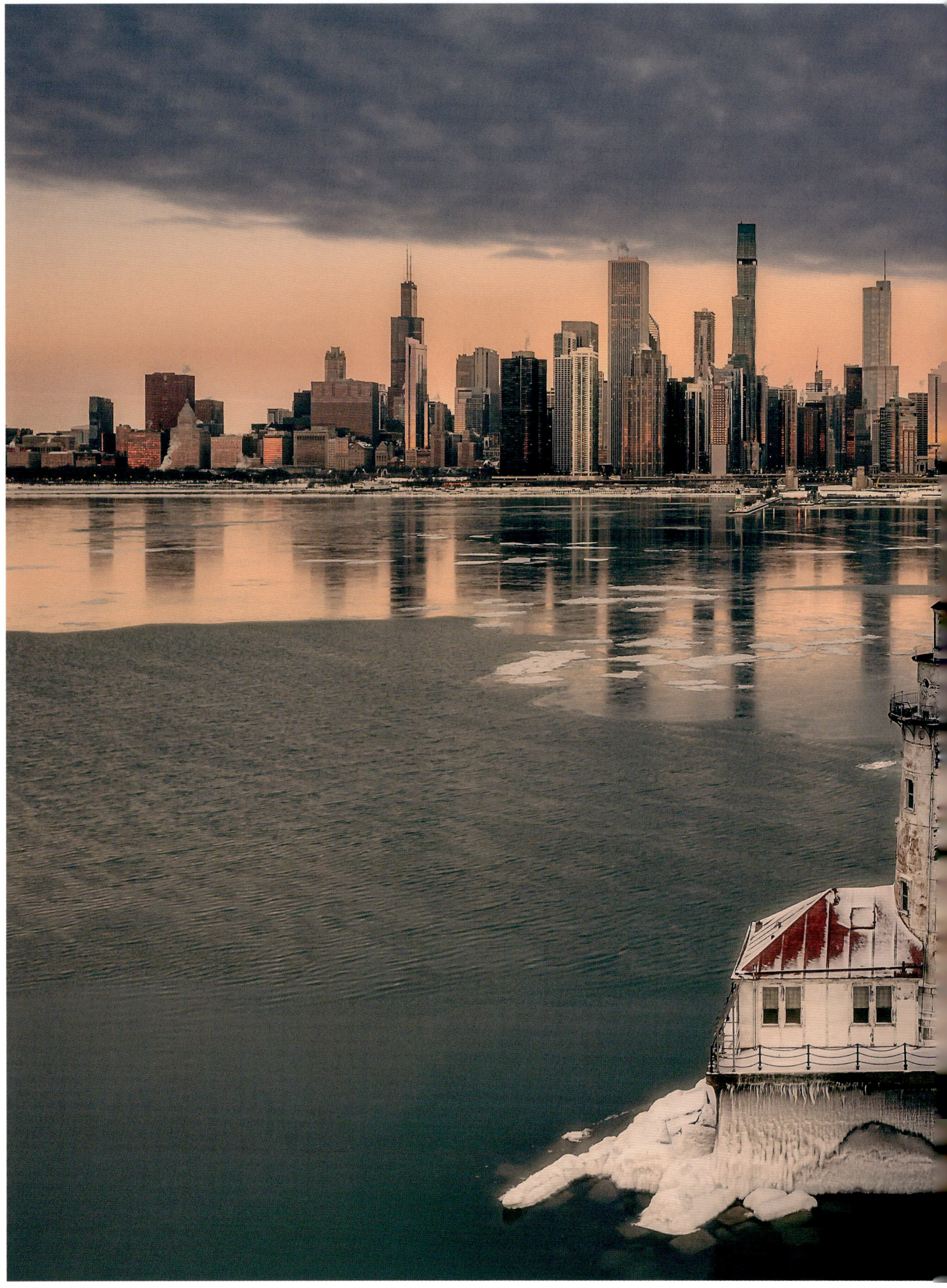

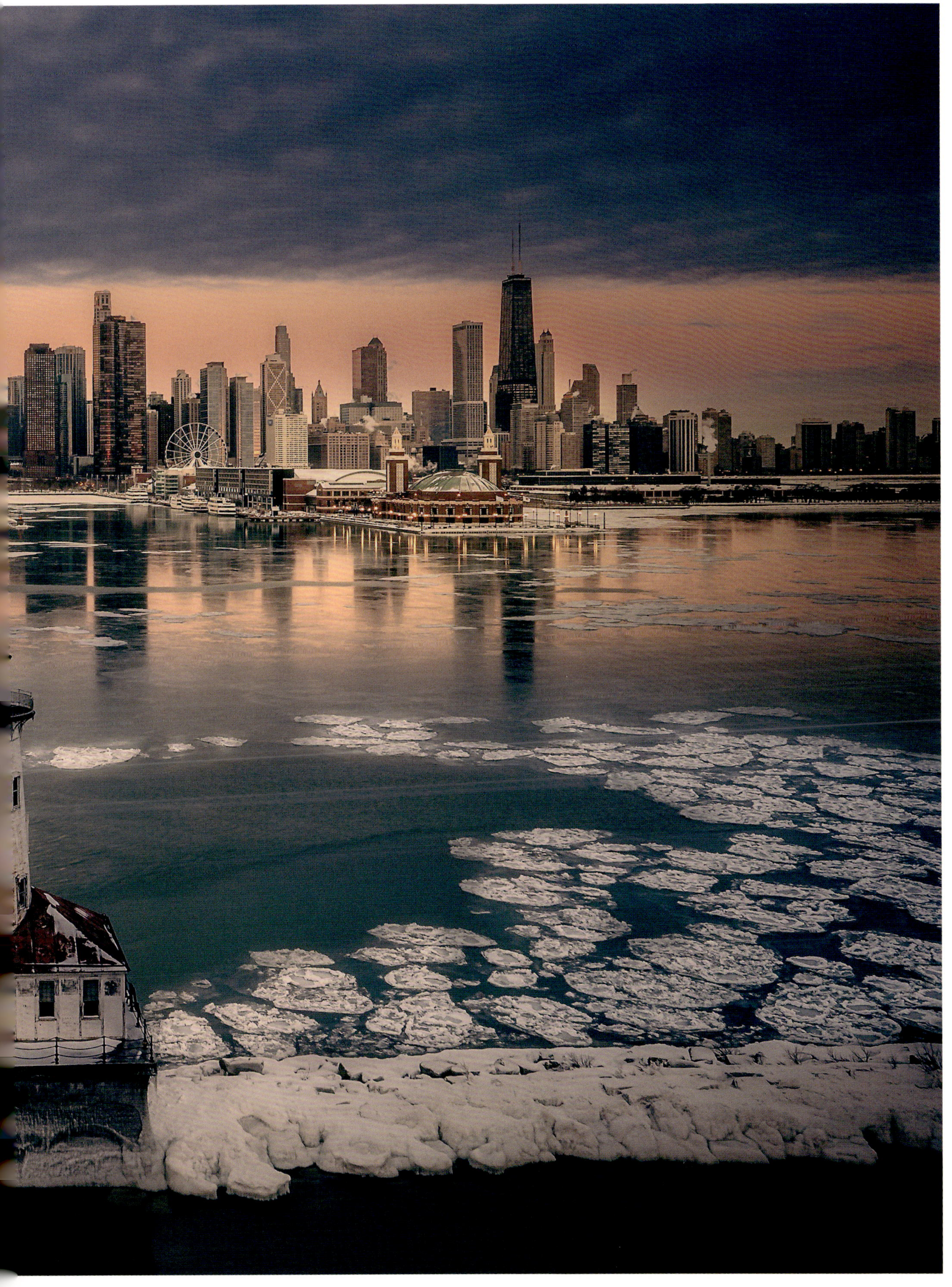

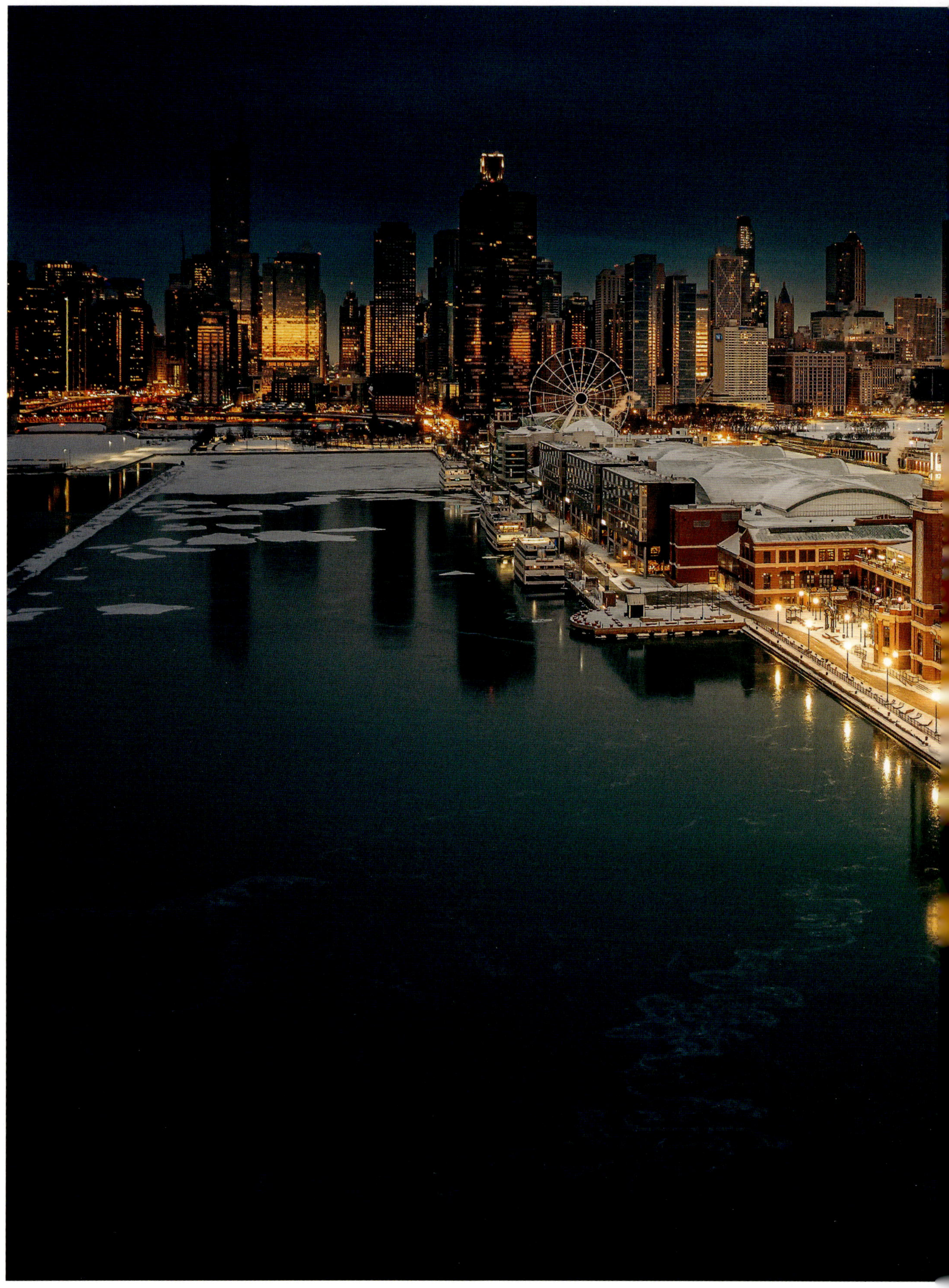

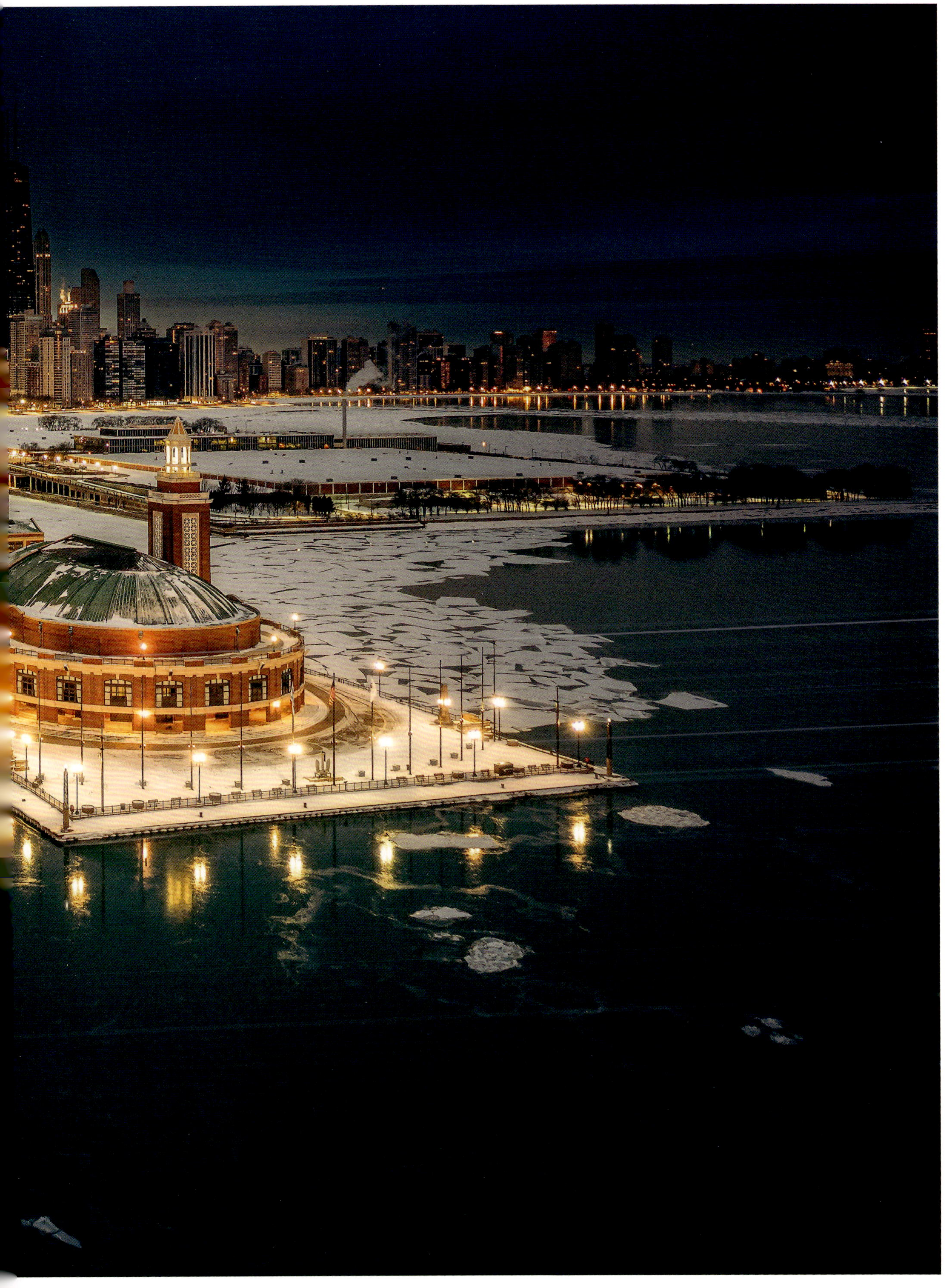

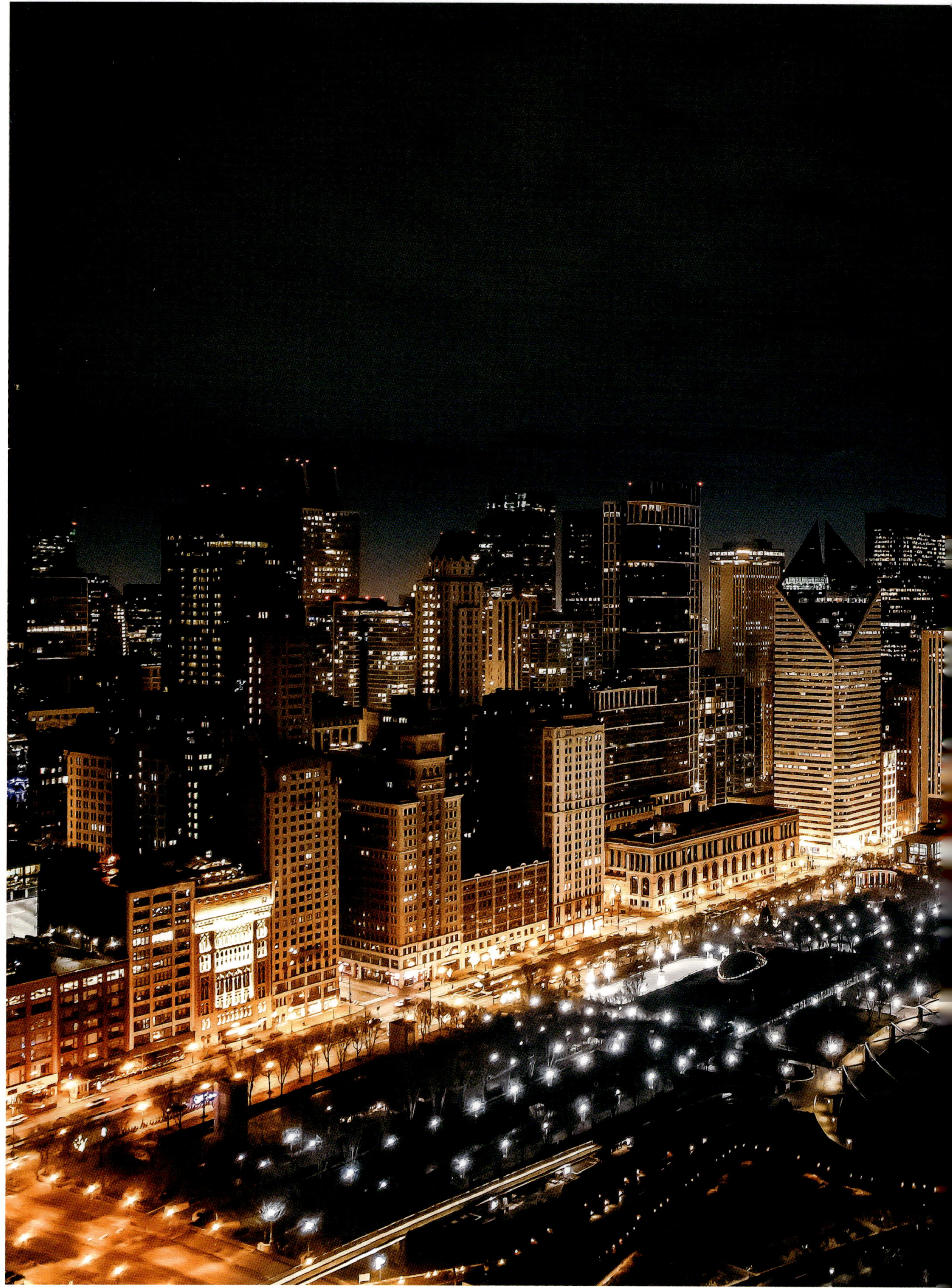

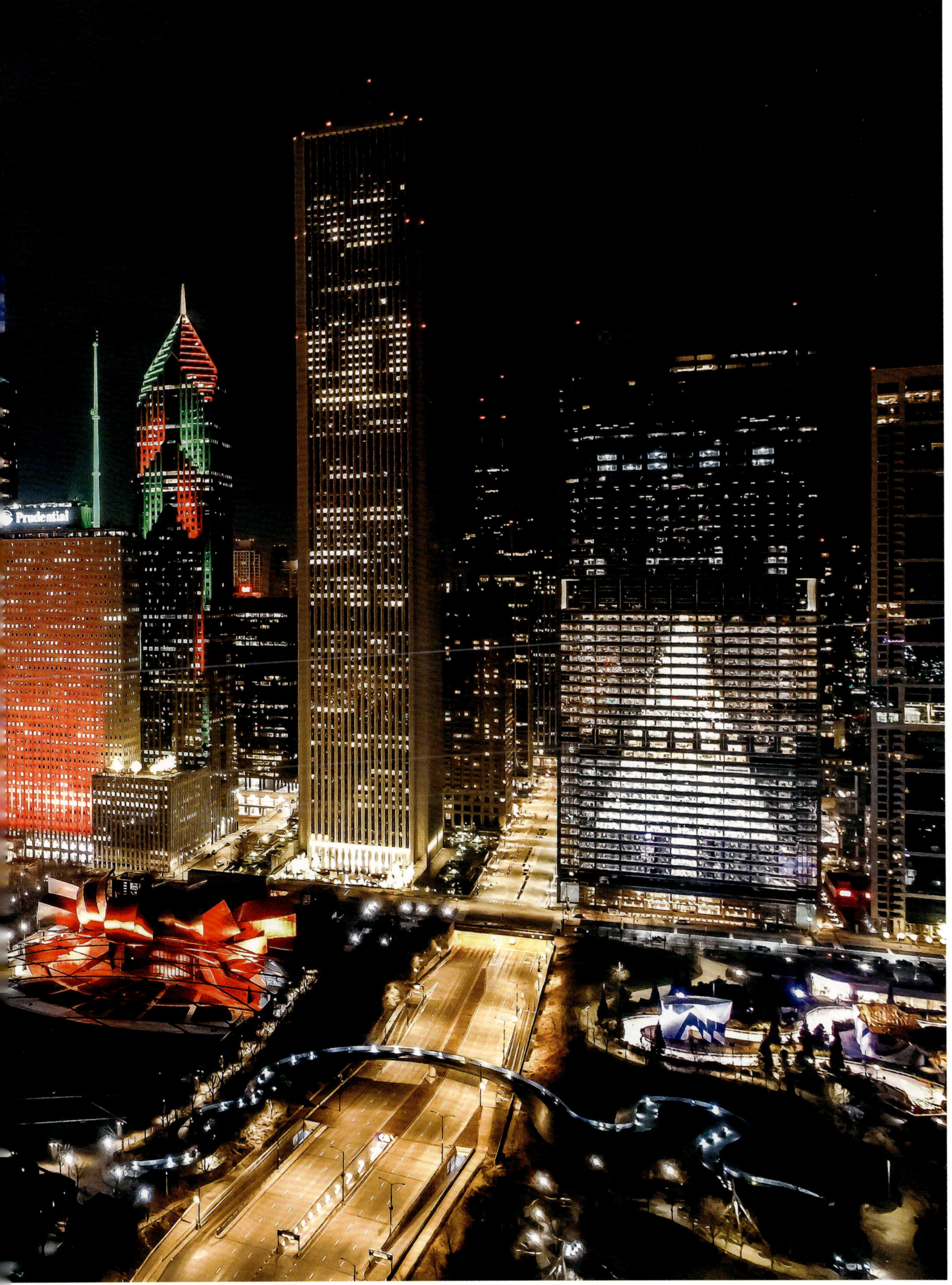

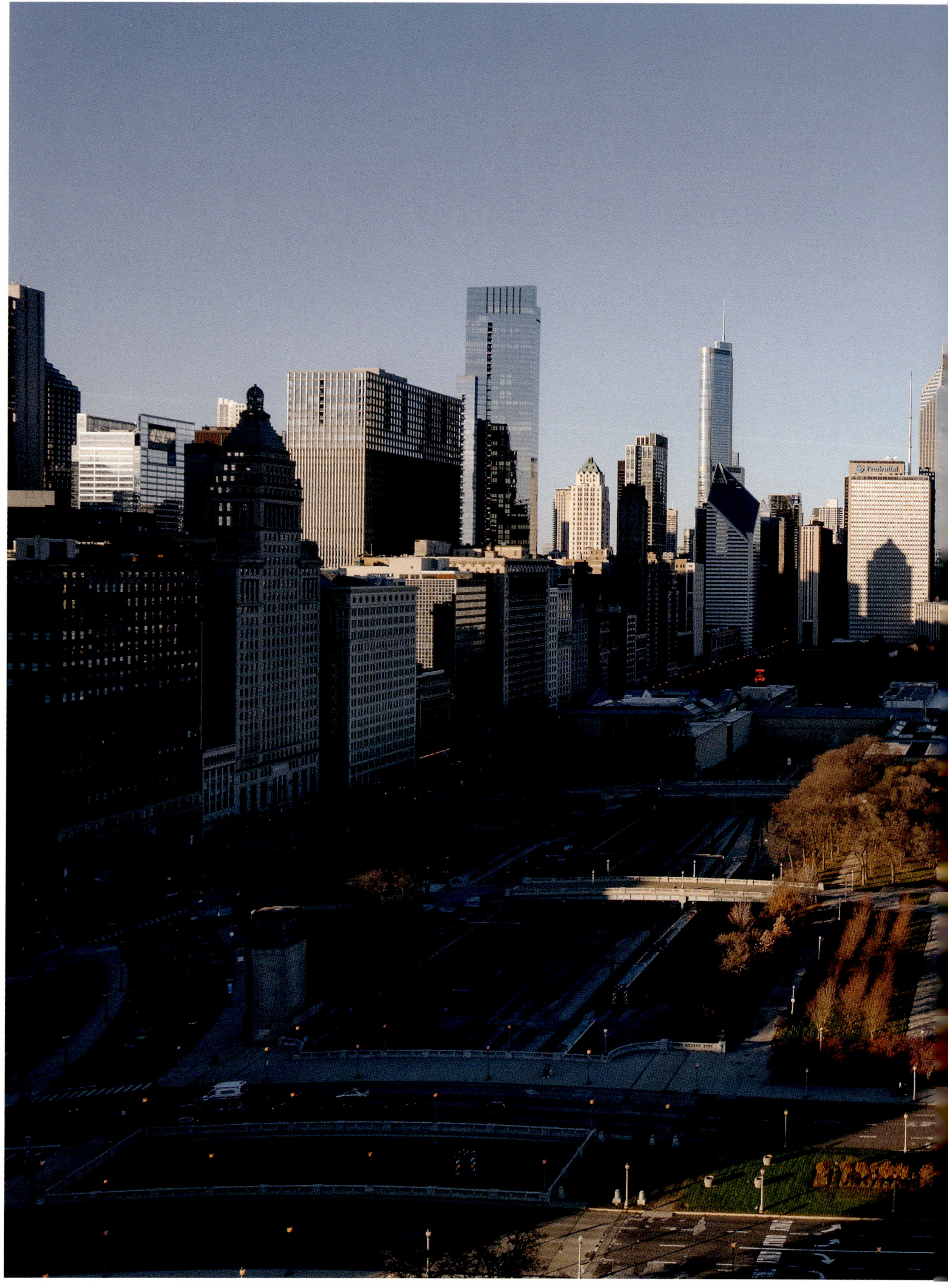

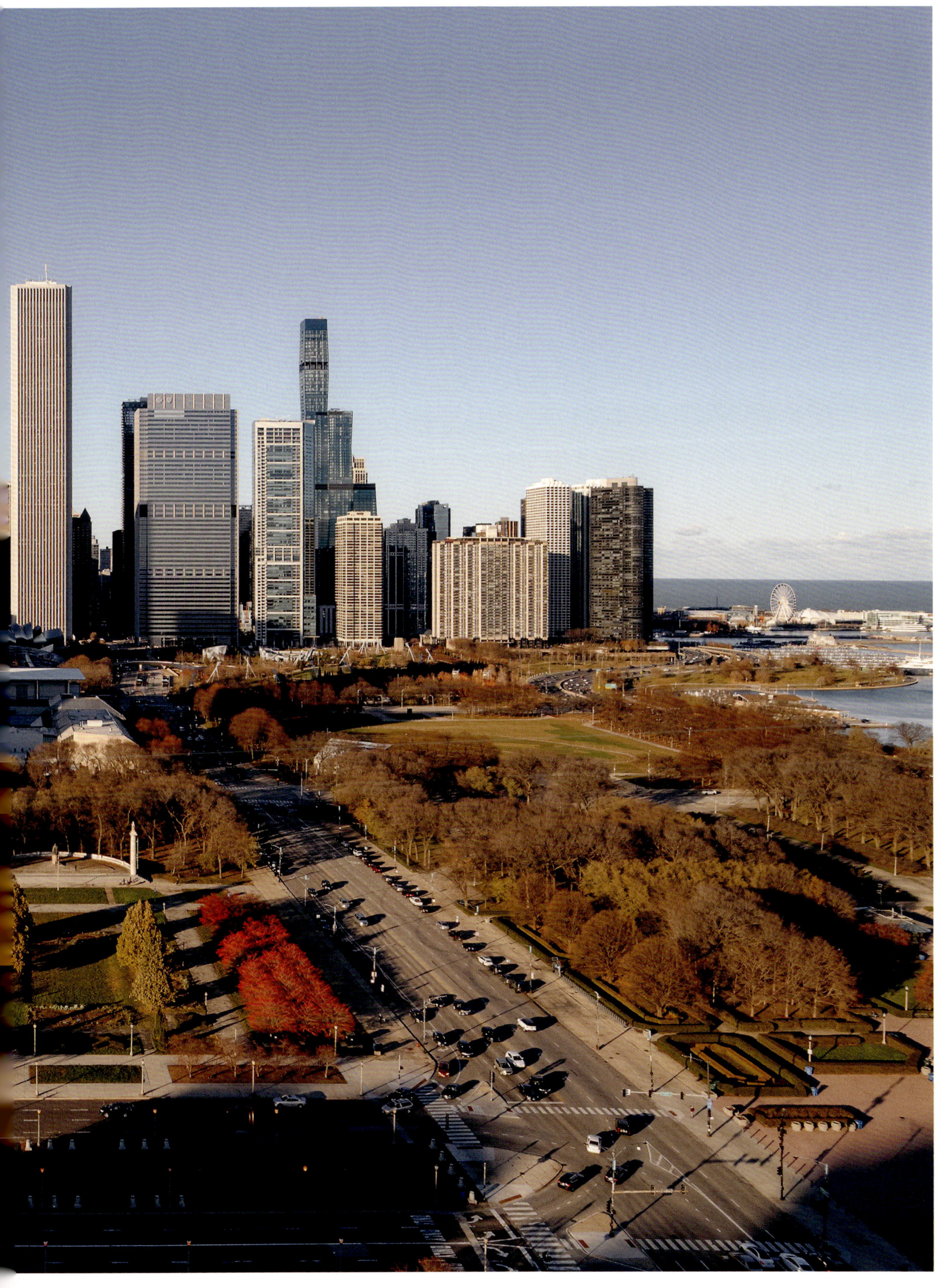

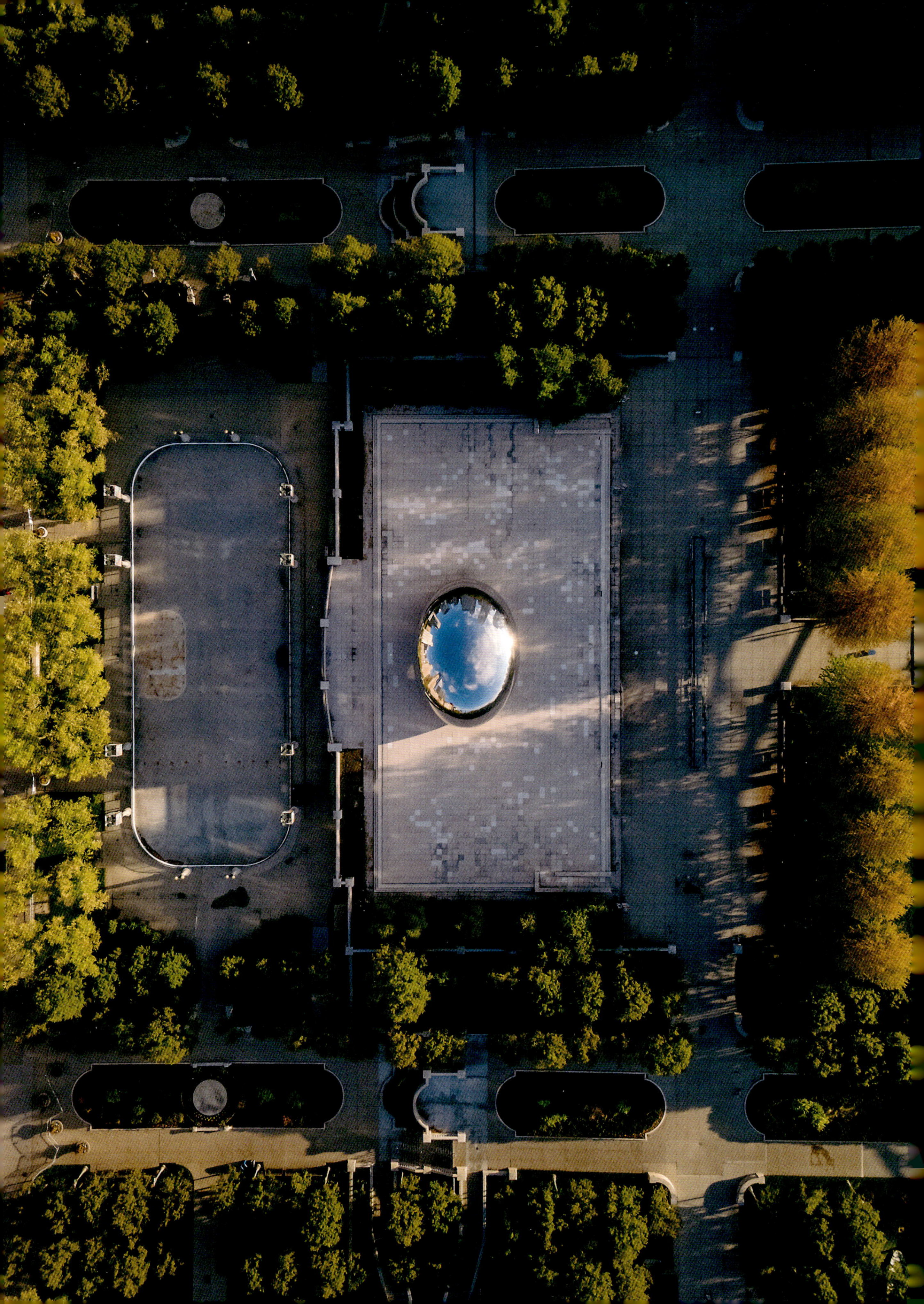

Life in Chicago ✳ Celebrated for its kaleidoscope of lively public spaces, Chicago is one of those cities where people love to come together outside. From iconic spaces to lesser-known hidden gems tucked away in neighborhoods, public parks shine. ✳ In the heart of the city lies Millennium Park, home to green space, public art and programming. Its Cloud Gate sculpture, affectionately dubbed "The Bean," has become a shimmering symbol of Chicago since its unveiling in 2004. Crafted by British artist Anish Kapoor, this stainless steel masterpiece reflects the city's skyline and visitors. The park also boasts Jay Pritzker Pavilion, a stunning outdoor amphitheater designed by the legendary Frank Gehry. Hosting everything from live concerts to film screenings, it's a testament to Chicago's commitment to blending art seamlessly into urban life. ✳ From the majestic Buckingham Fountain to the Museum Campus — home to the Shedd Aquarium, the Field Museum, and the Adler Planetarium — Grant Park is steeped in history. Once the site of the 1893 World's Columbian Exposition, it now plays host to the world-renowned Lollapalooza music festival and other major outdoor events. ✳ Stretching over 1200 acres along Lake Michigan's shore, Lincoln Park is a green oasis on the city's north side. Featuring walking and biking trails, sports fields, and playgrounds, Lincoln Park is also home to Lincoln Park Zoo and the Peggy Notebaert Nature Museum. ✳ The lakefront paths and free beaches provide an escape from the hustle and bustle of city life. Whether running or cycling along the shore, catching a beach volleyball game, or taking in breathtaking views of the iconic skyline and the lights of Navy Pier, the lakefront offers the perfect way to unwind and savor the beauty of Chicago's waterfront. ✳ Whether in the shadow of towering skyscrapers or amidst the greenery of a park, Chicago's vibrant commitment to making every space an opportunity for shared experiences is clear. Welcome to a city where the outdoors isn't just a backdrop, it's the main event.

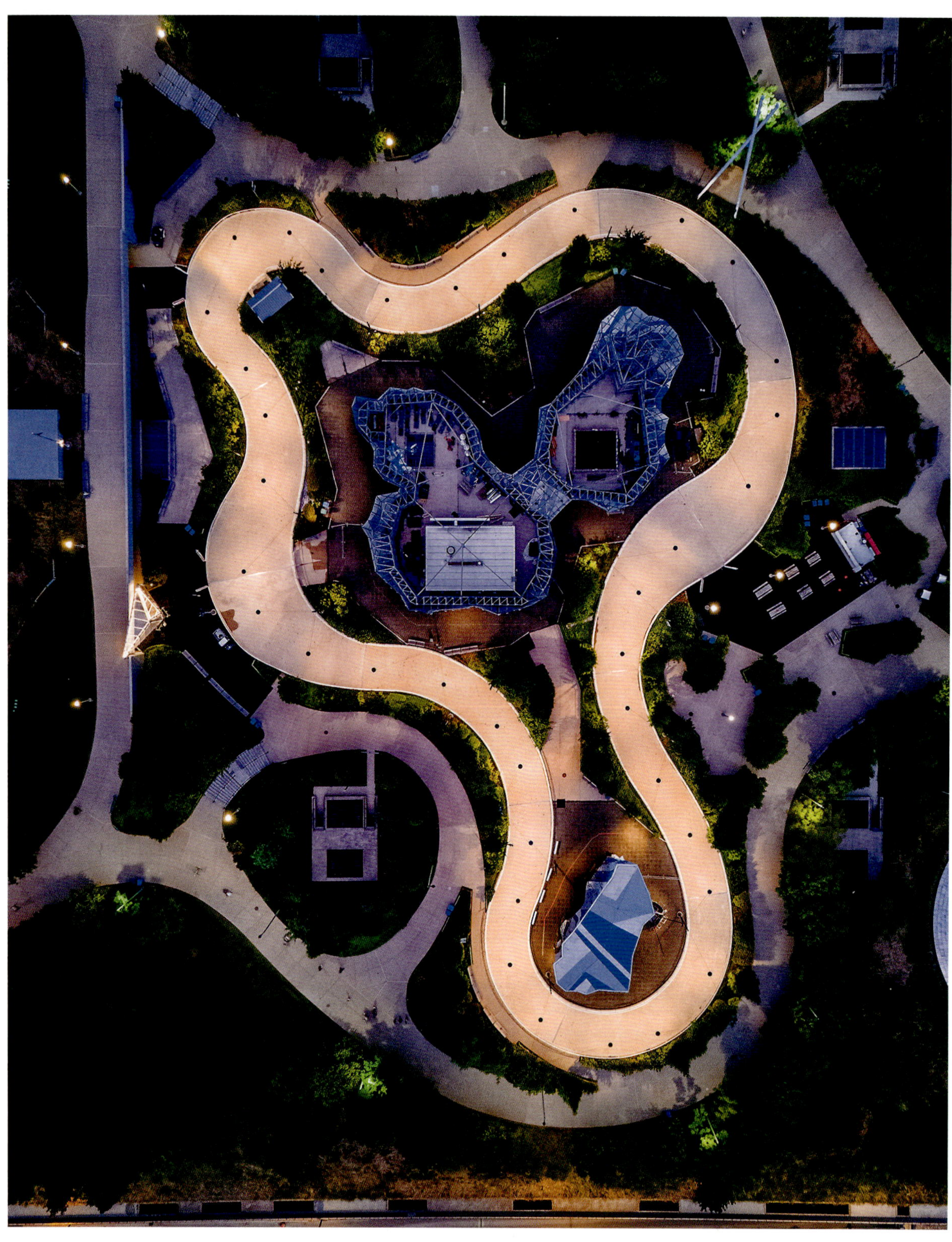

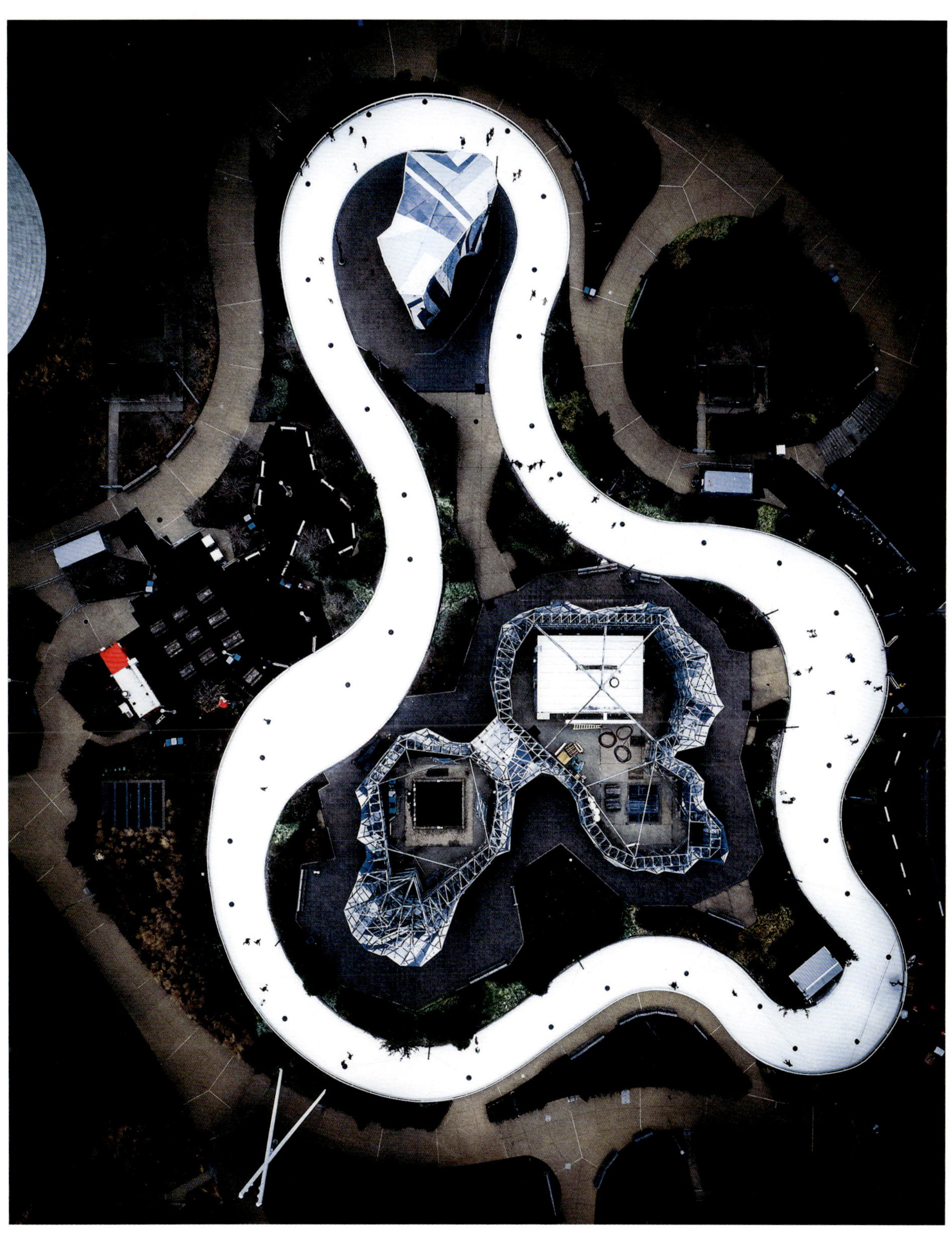

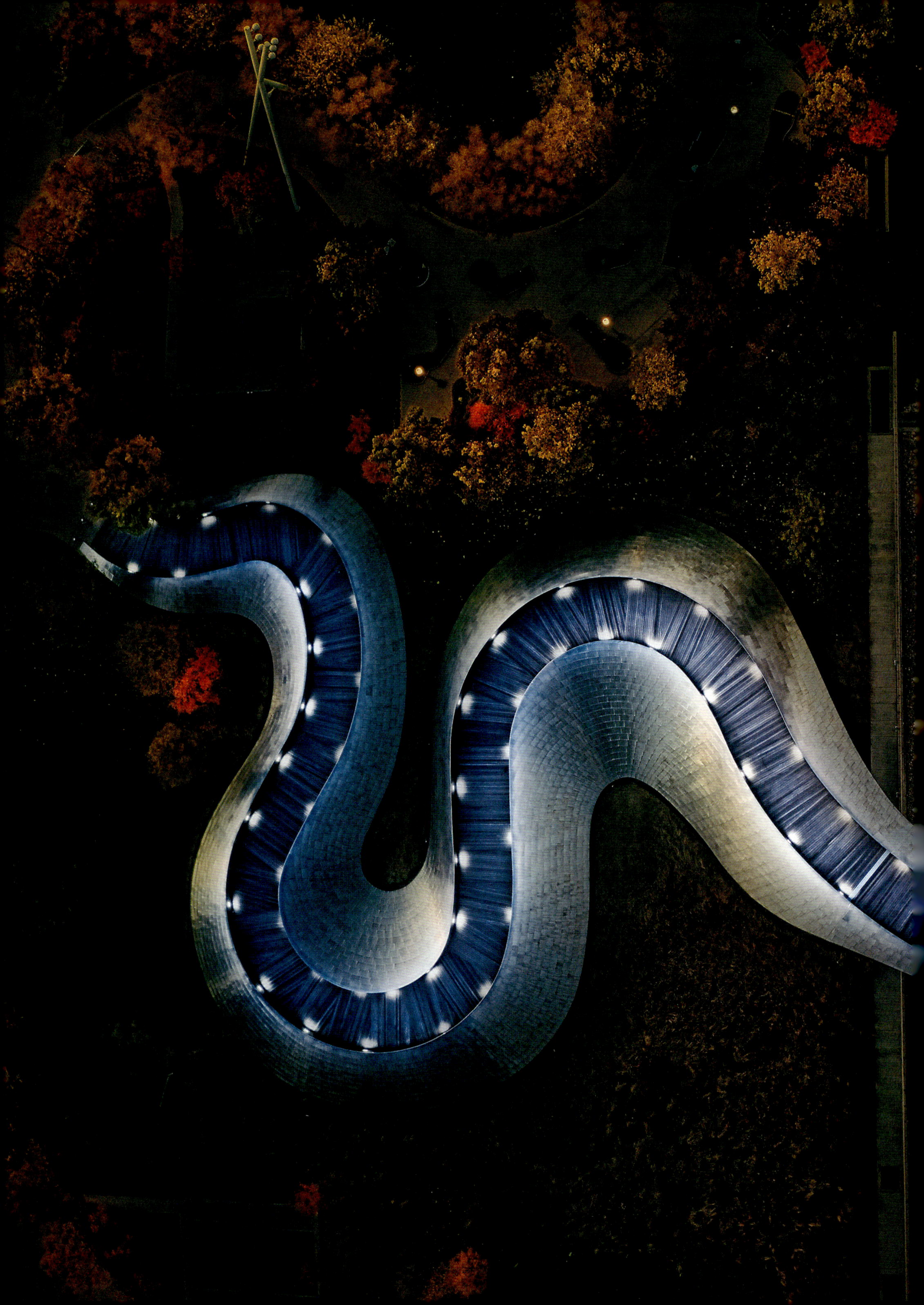

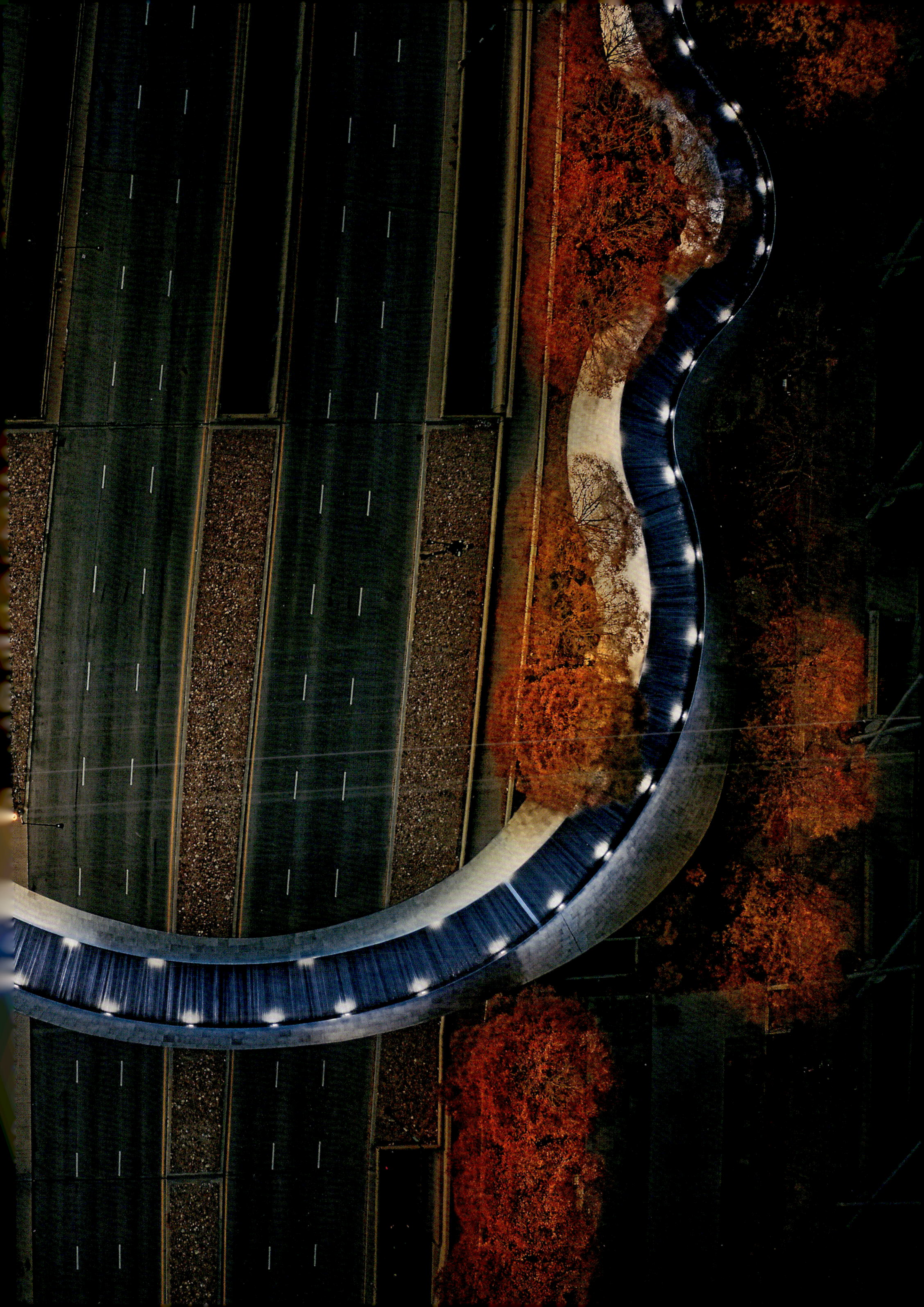

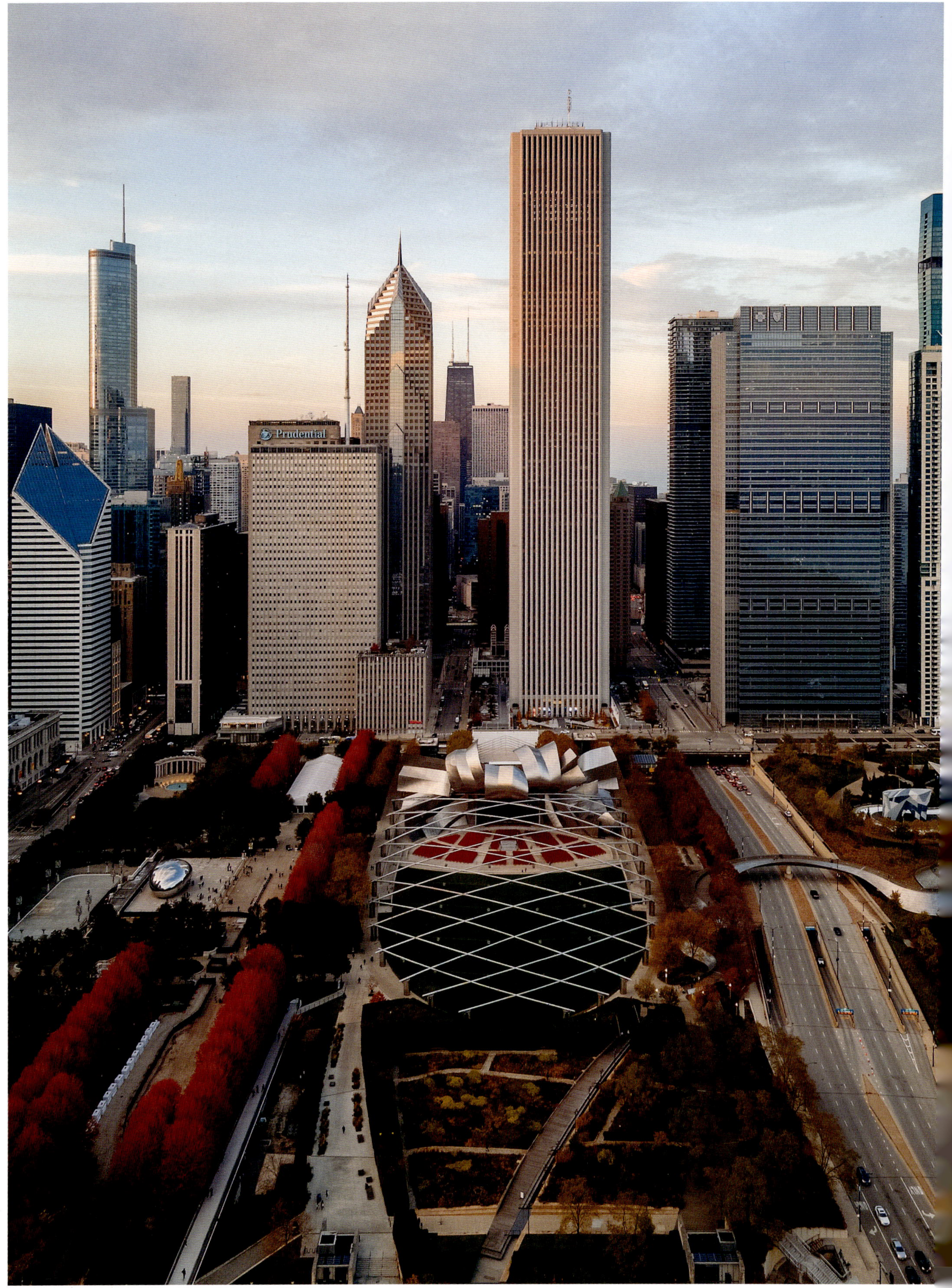

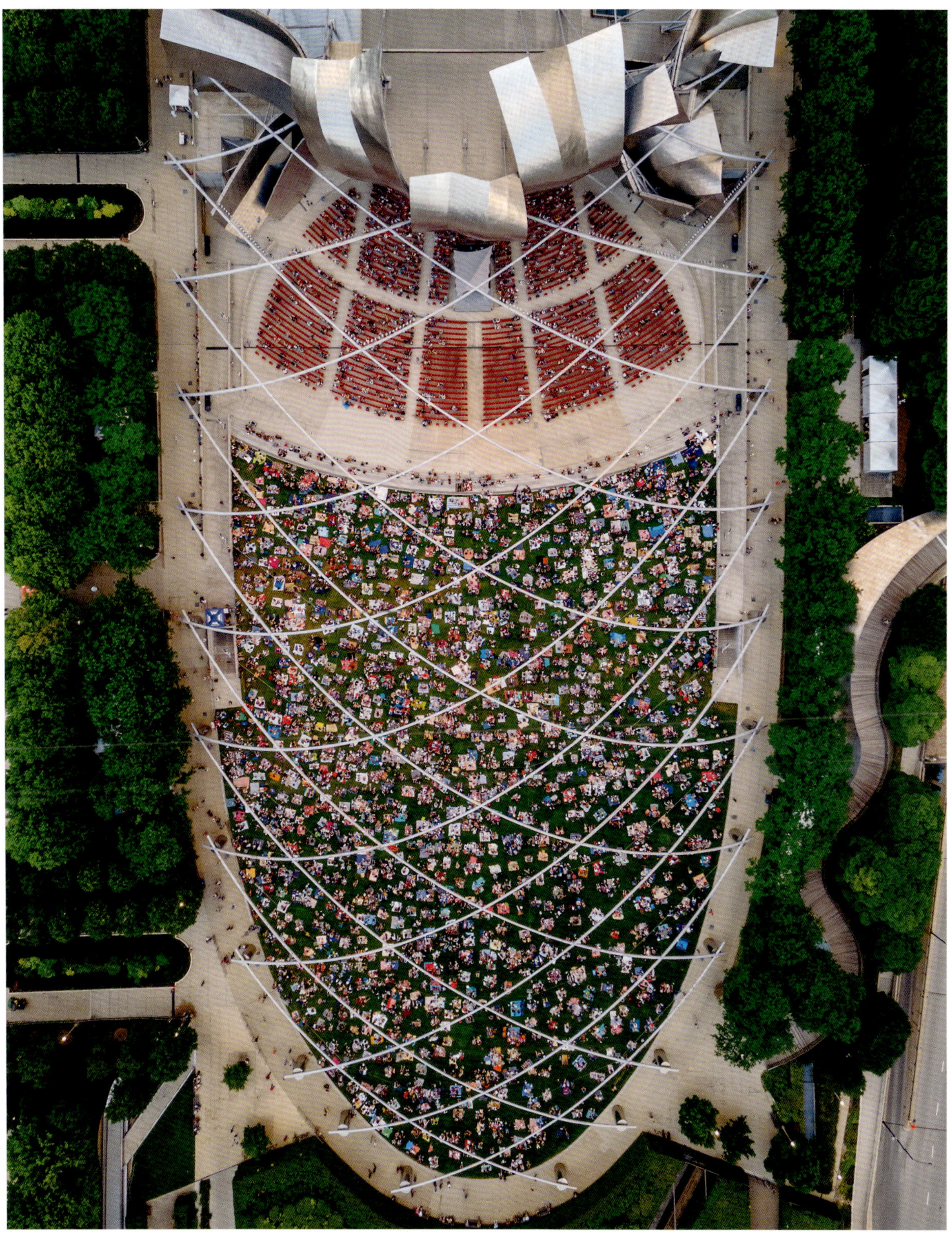

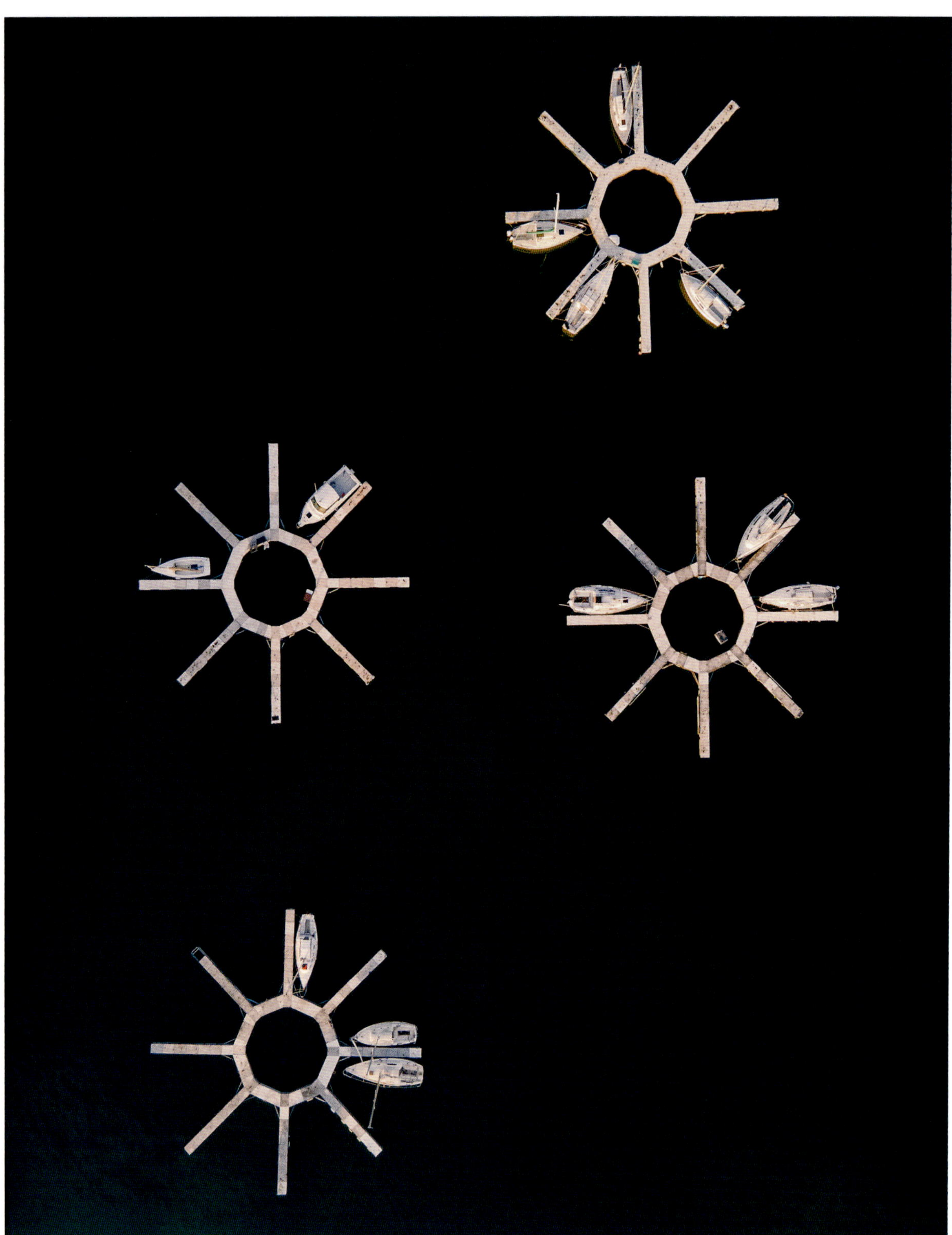

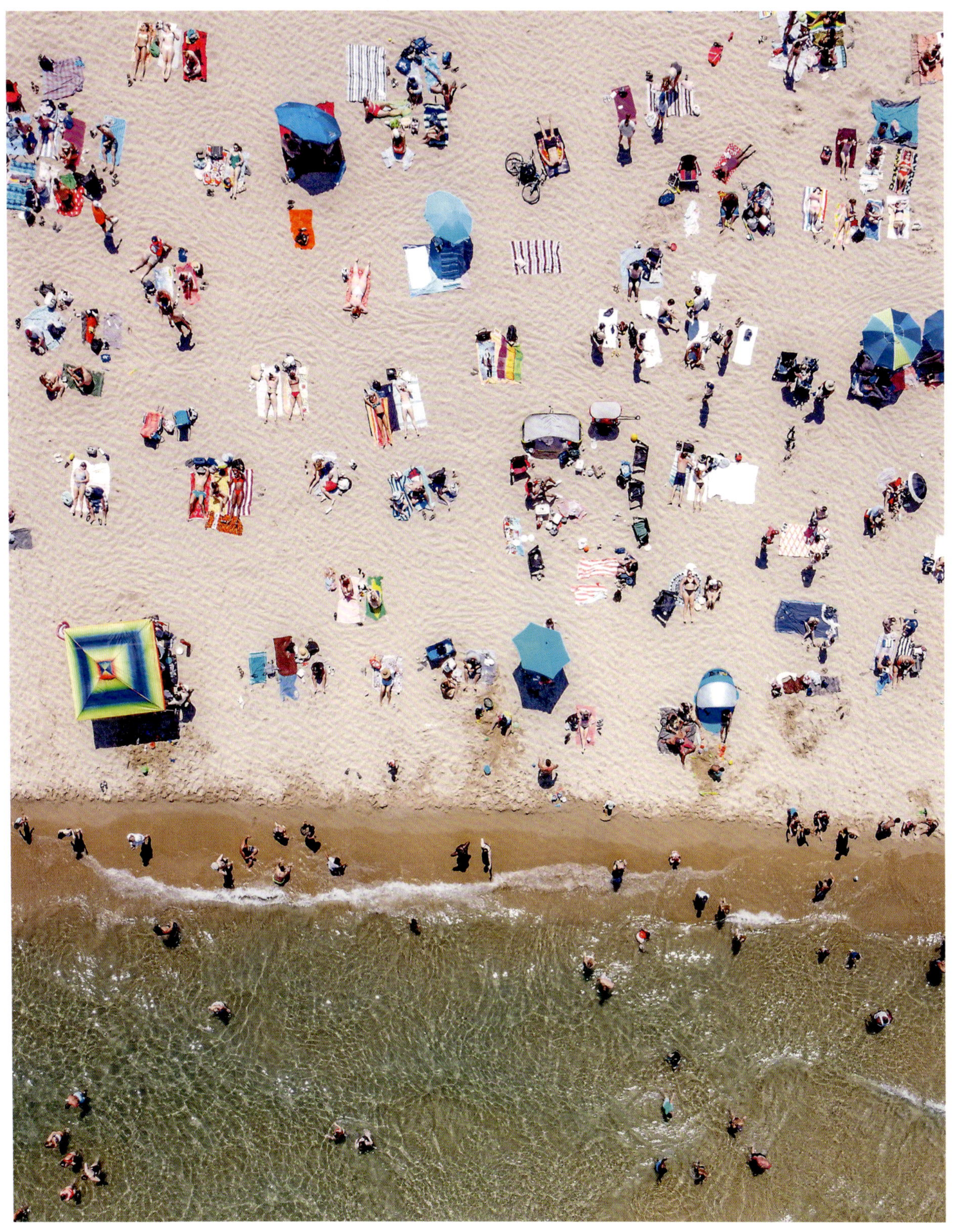

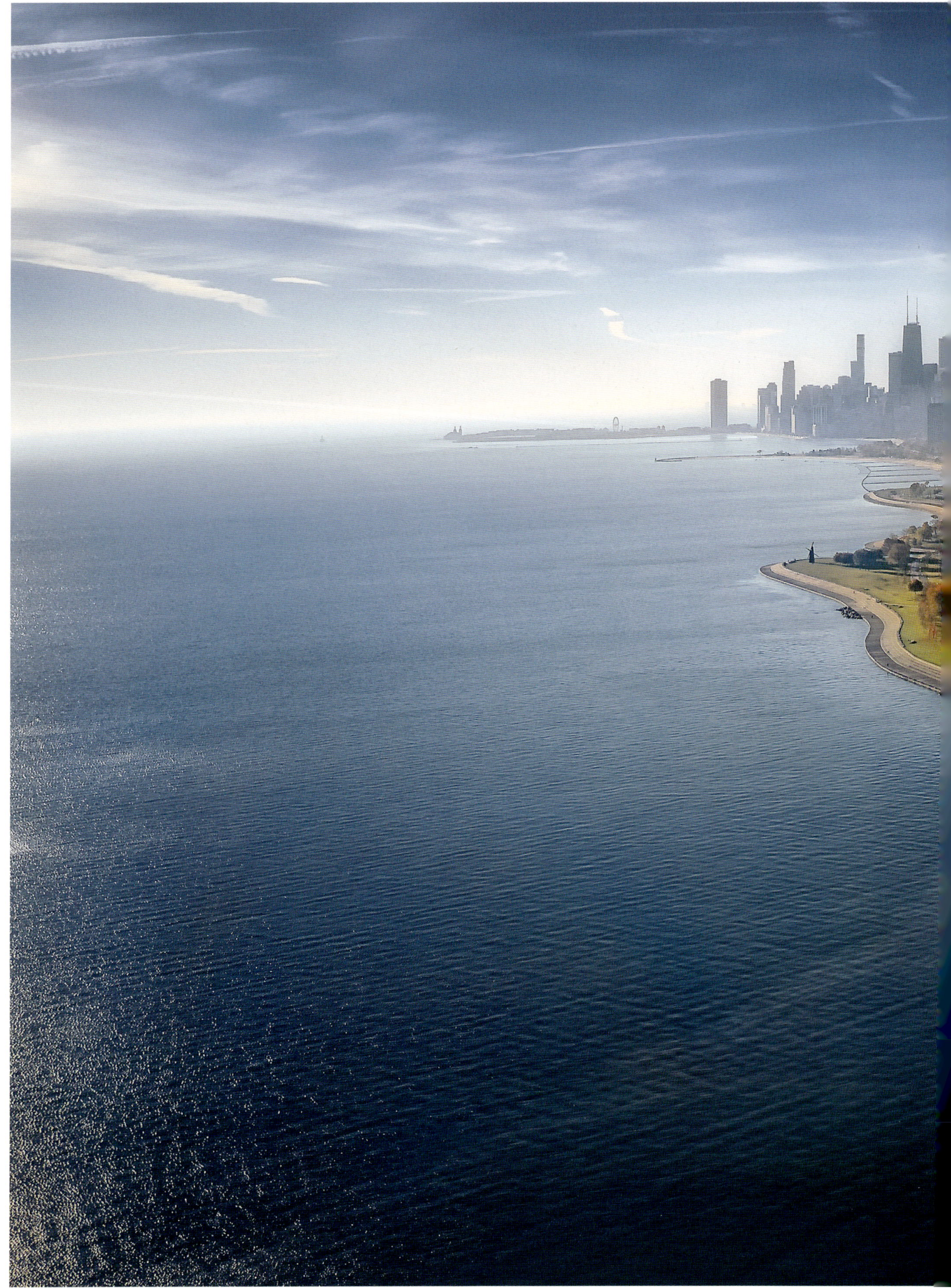

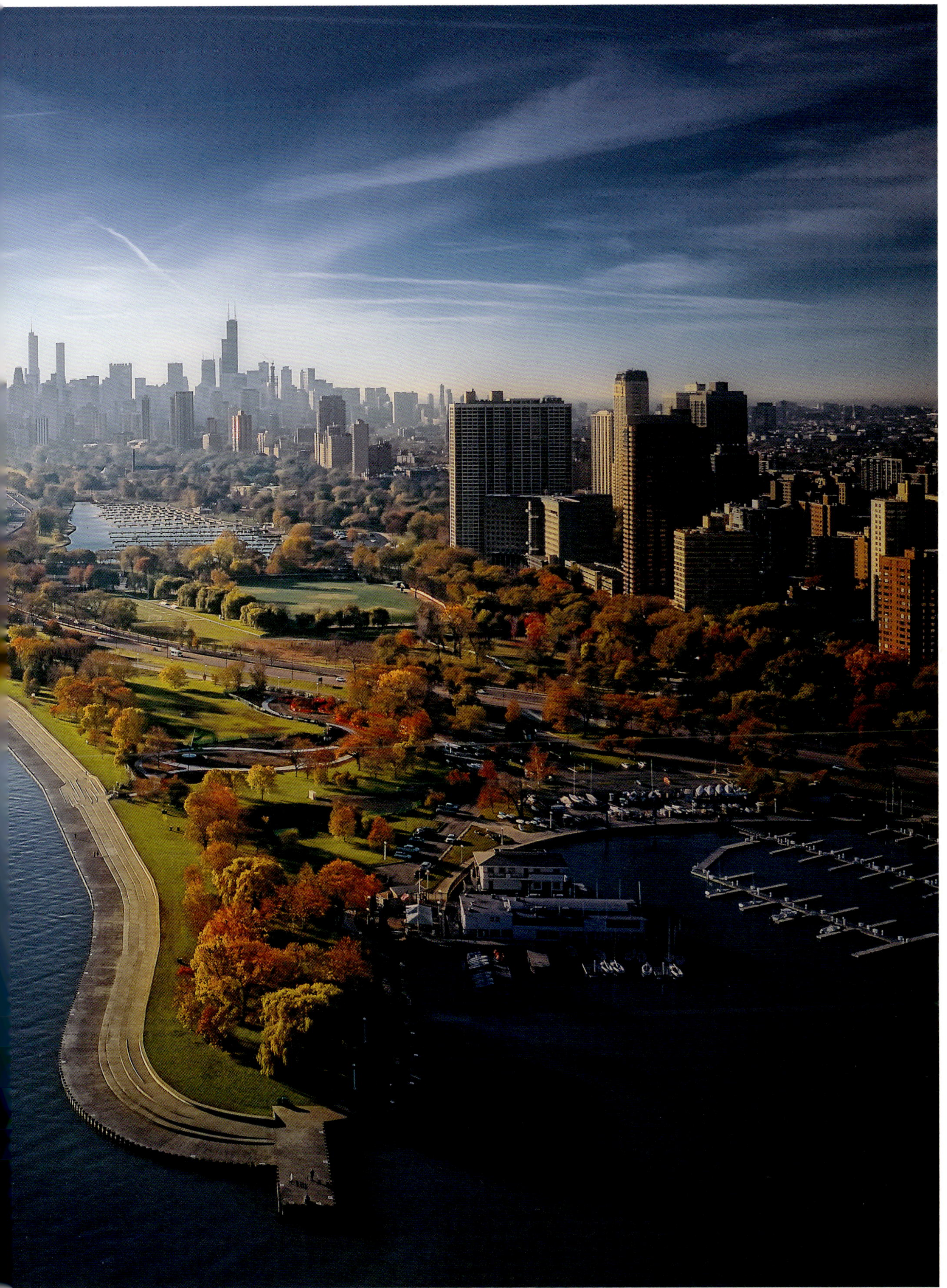

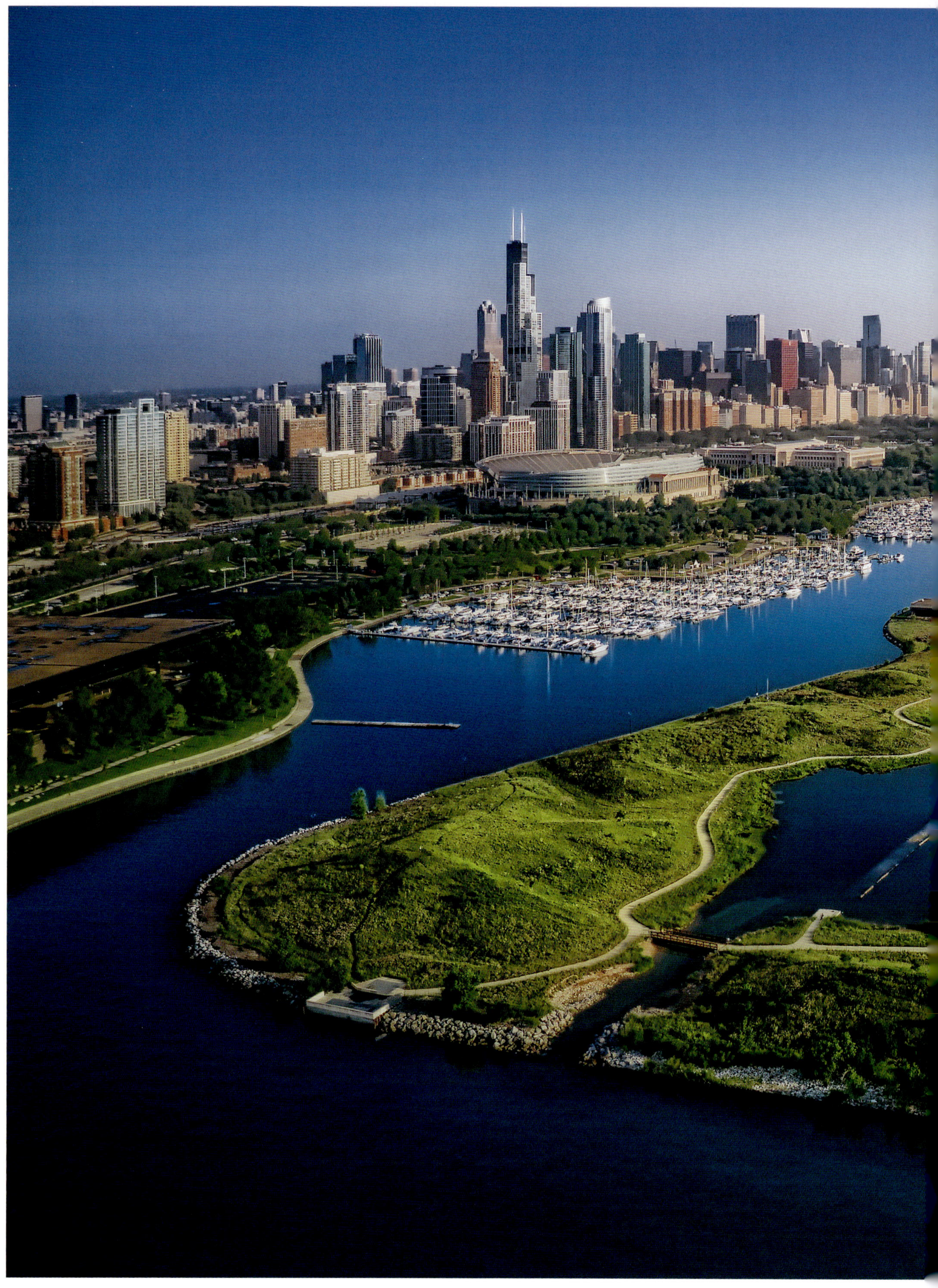

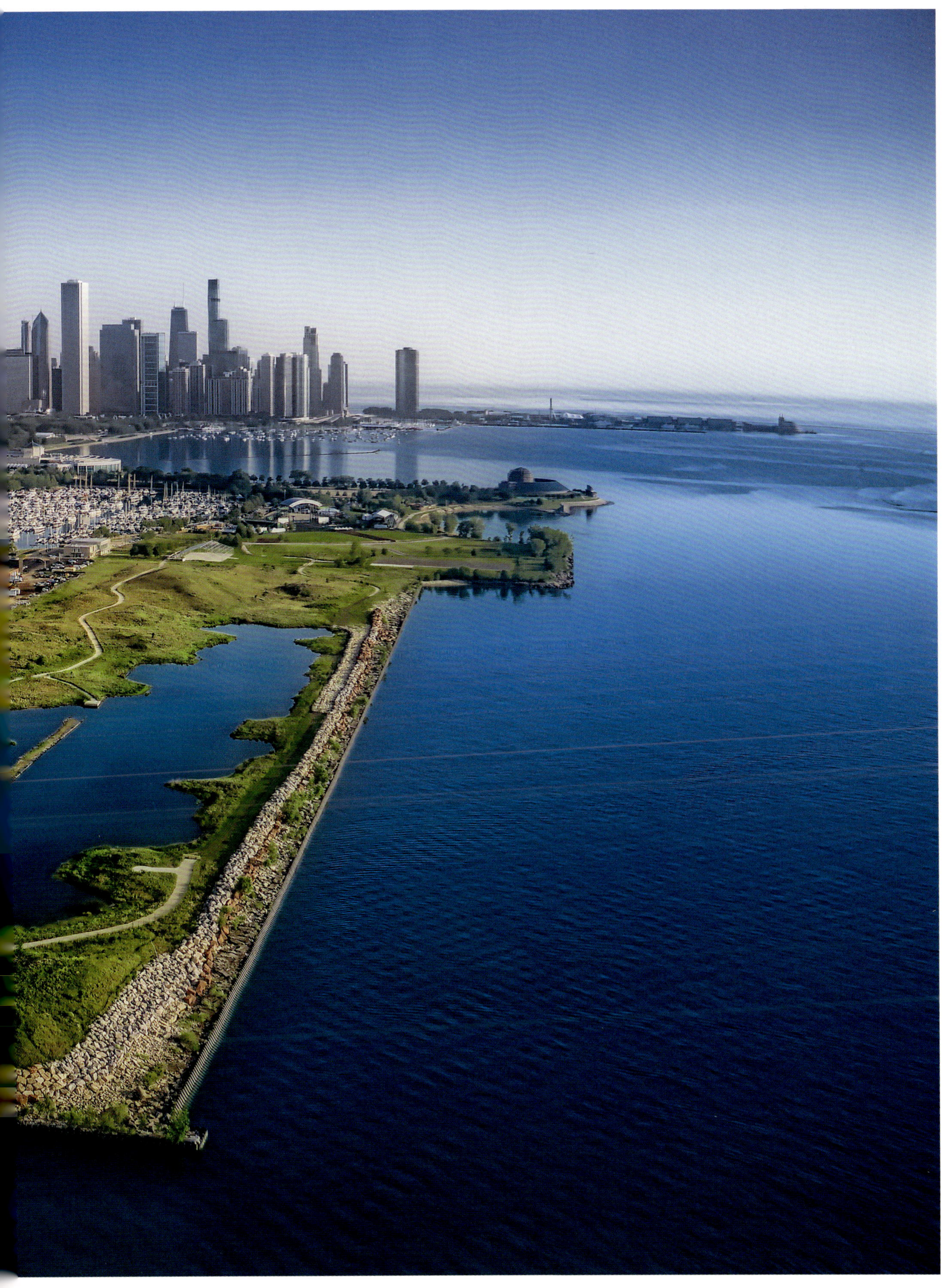

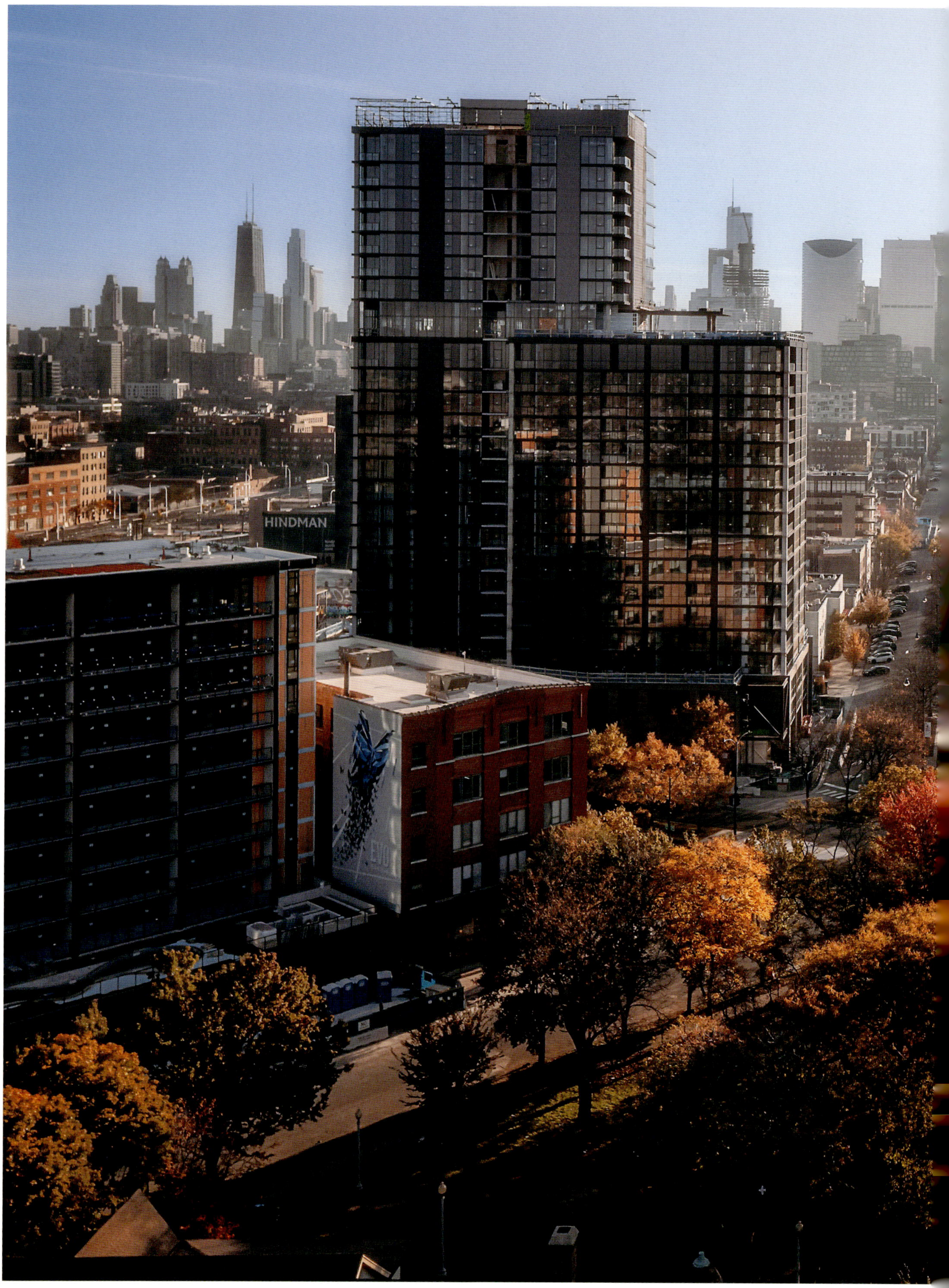
HINDMAN

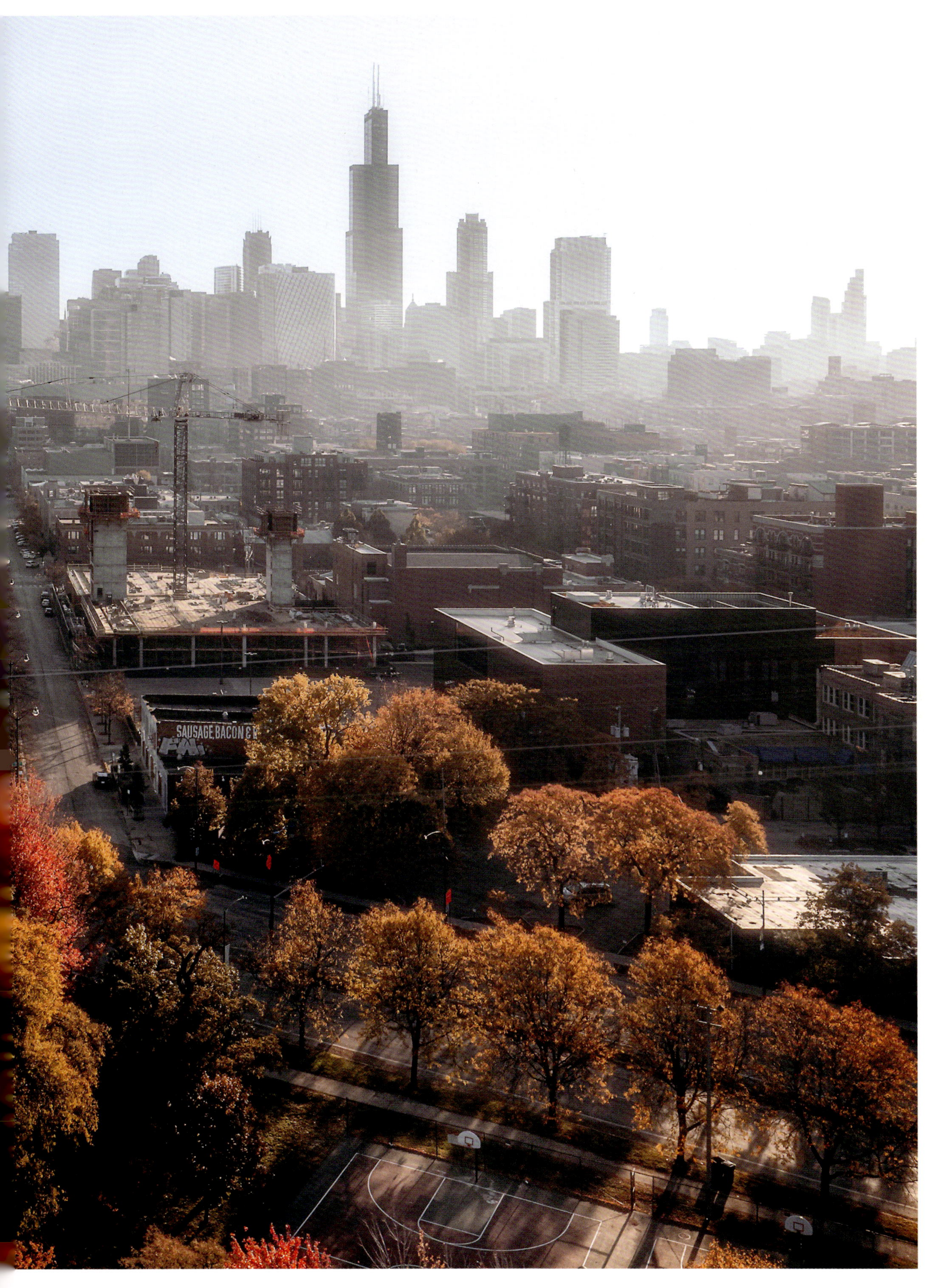

SAUSAGE, BACON &

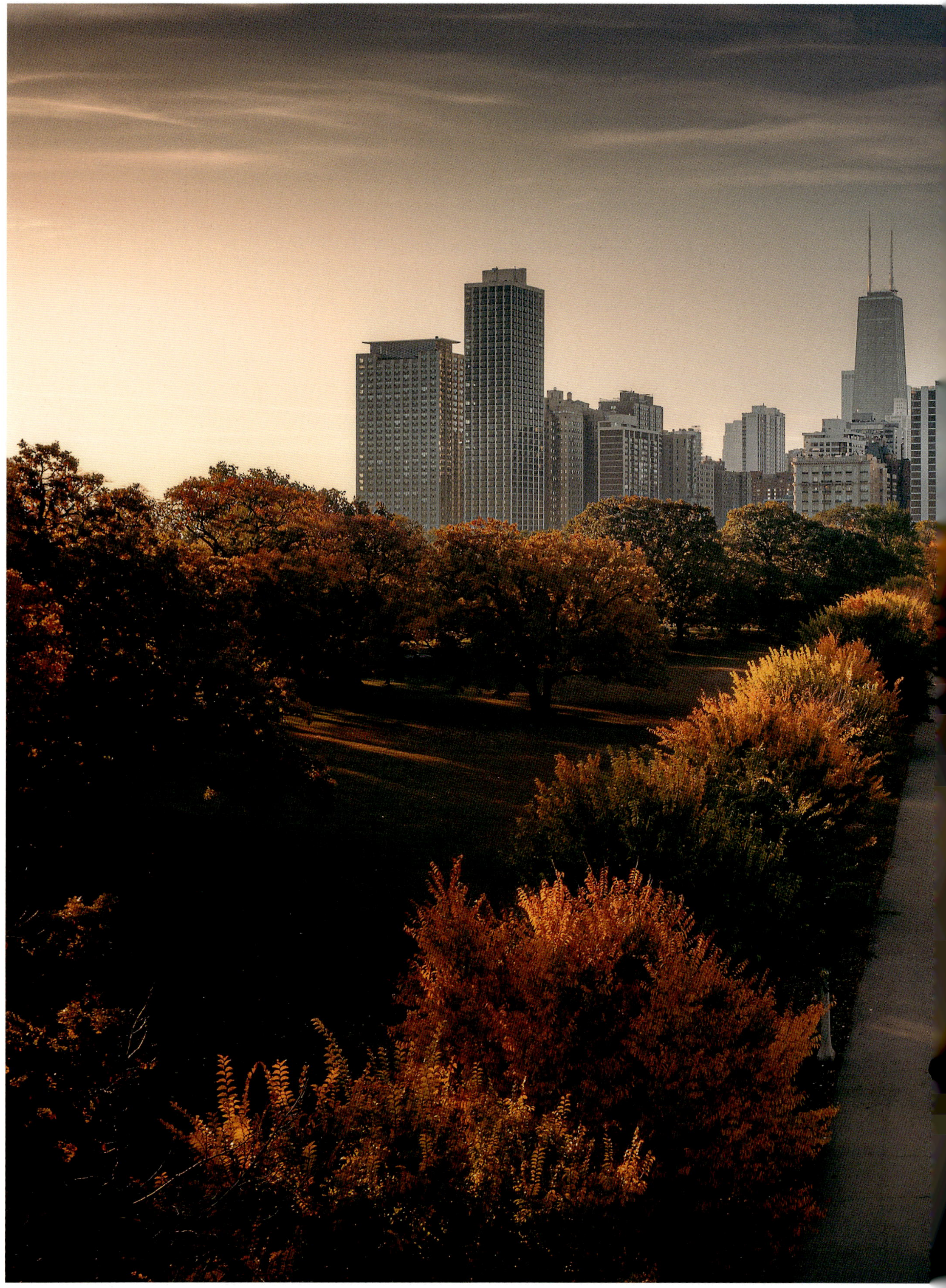

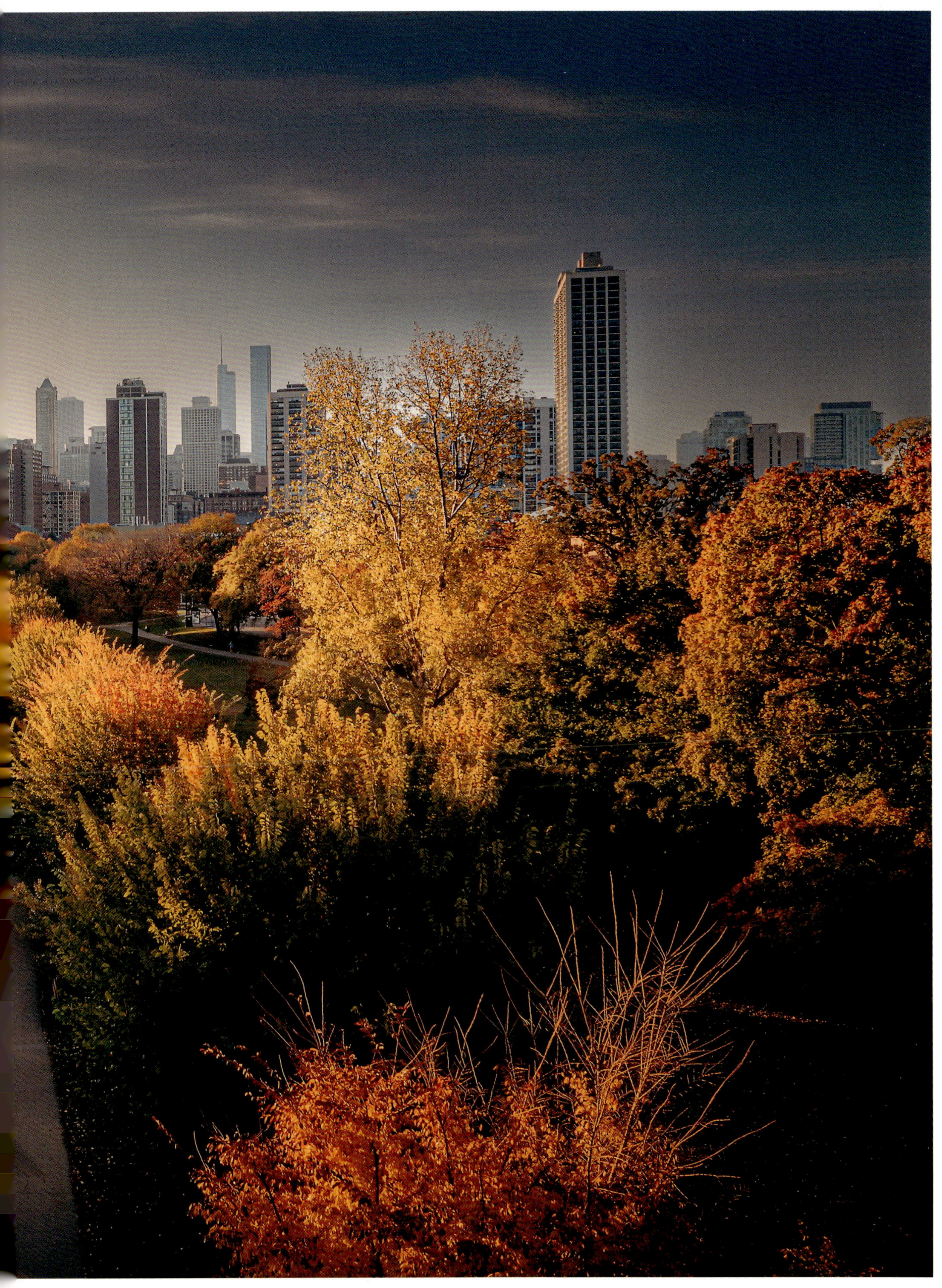

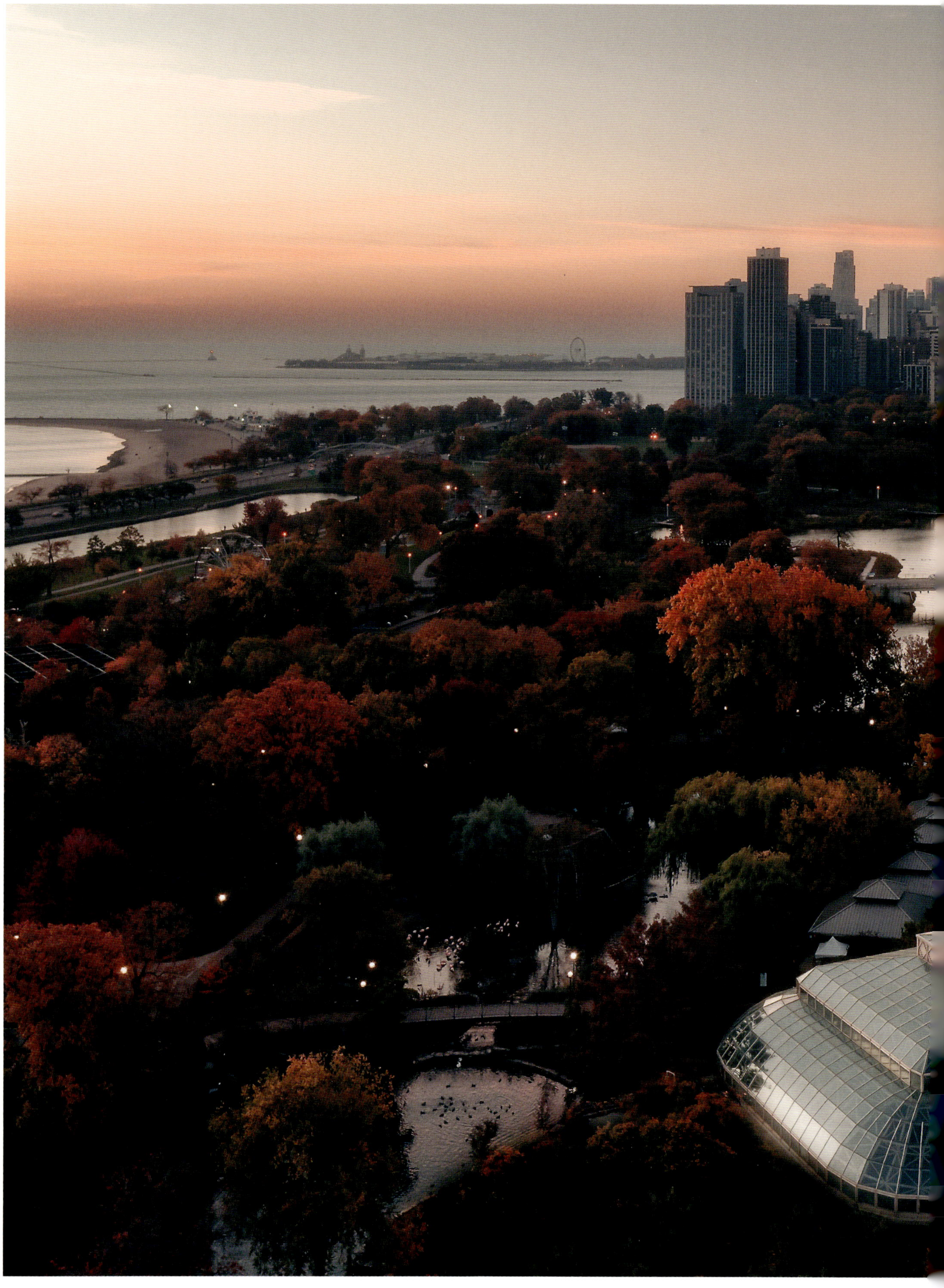

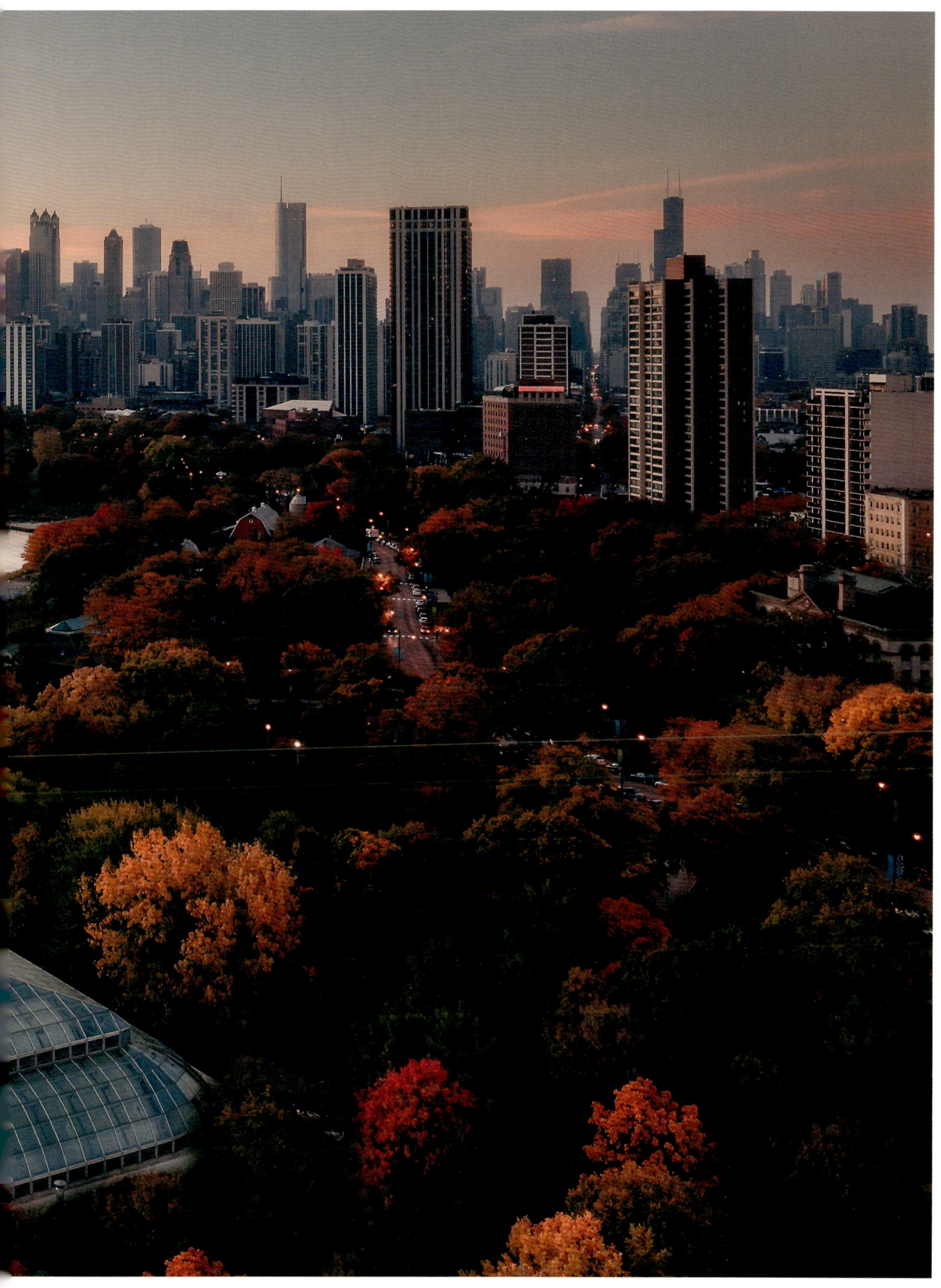

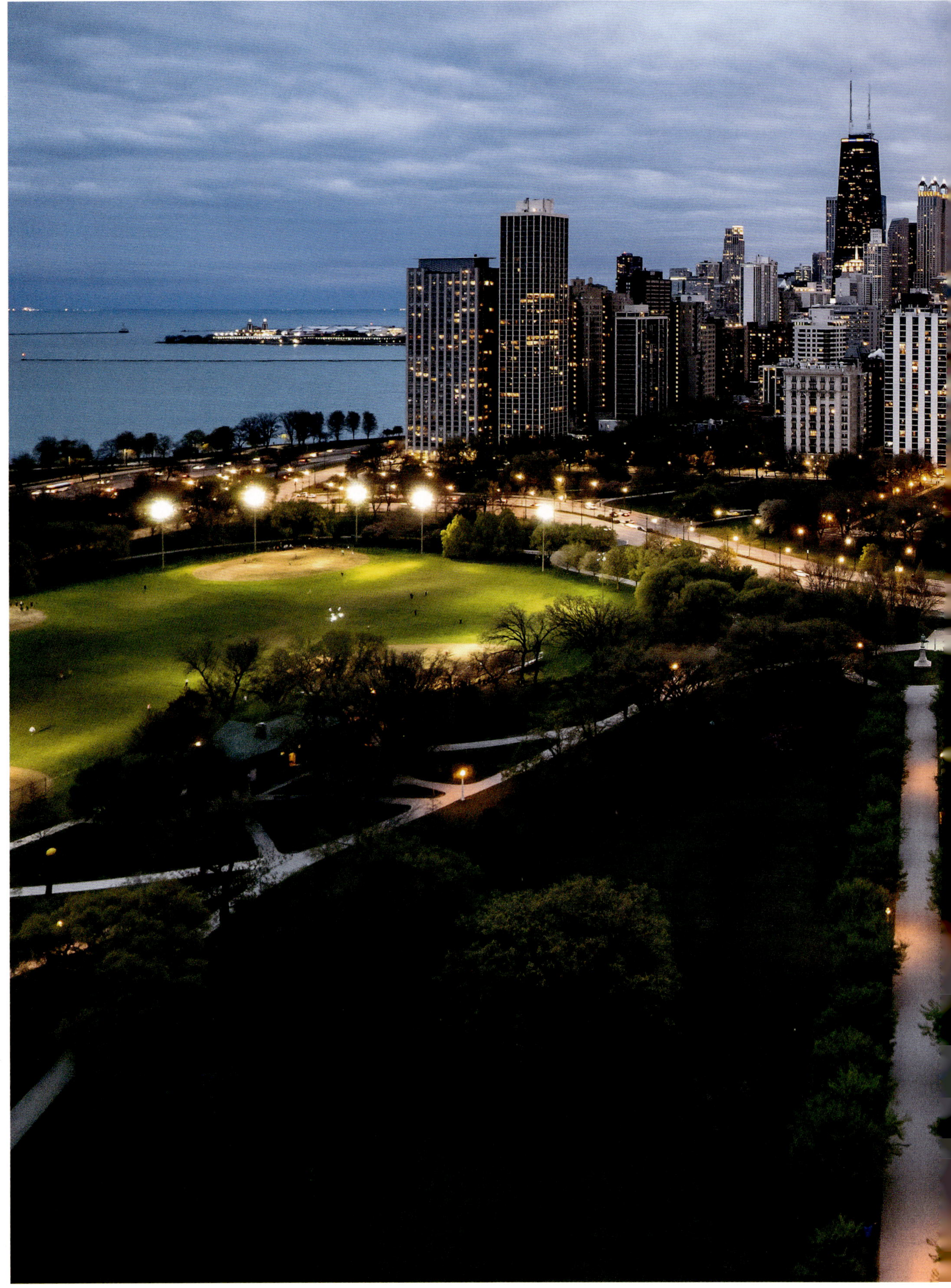

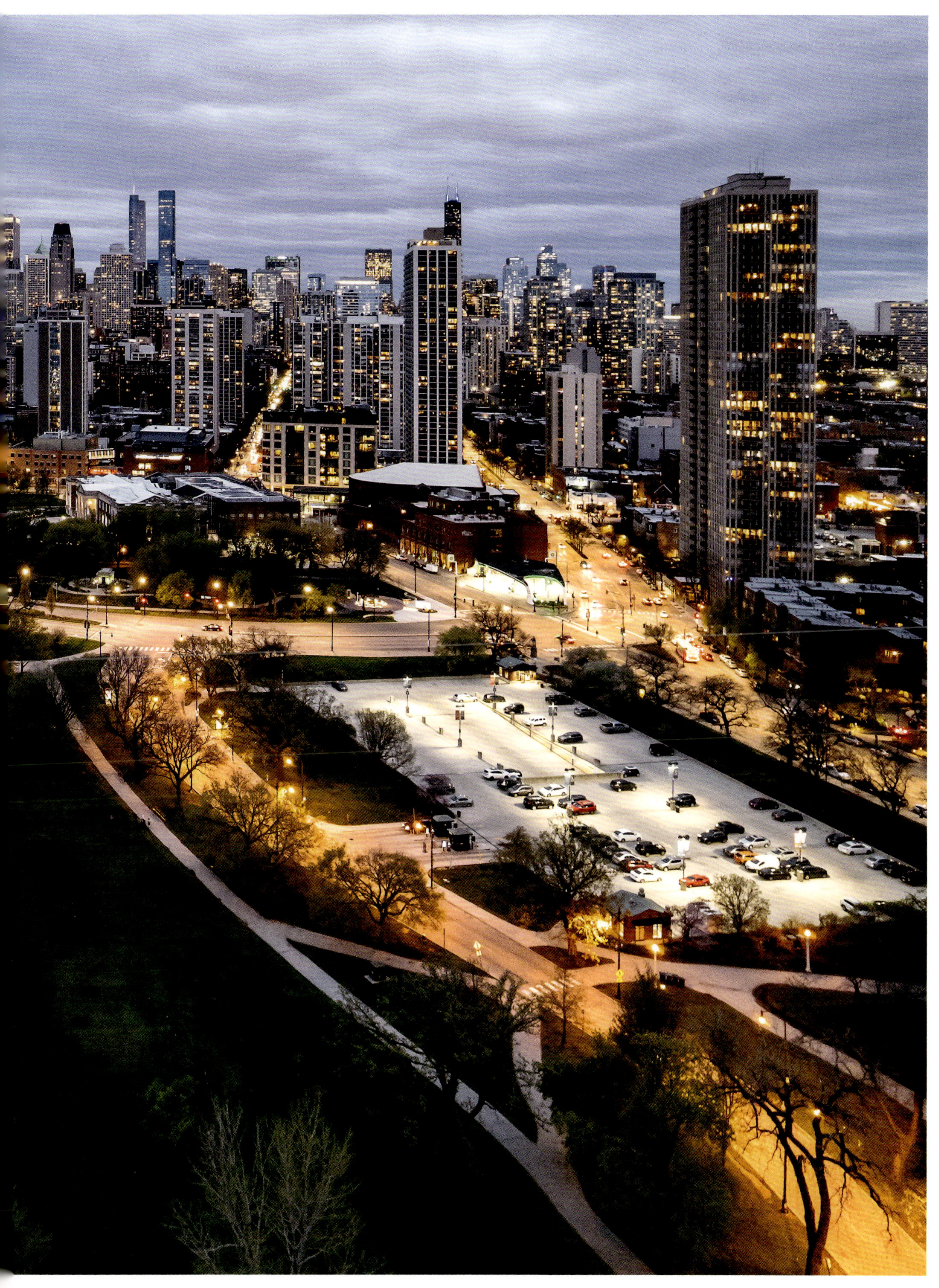

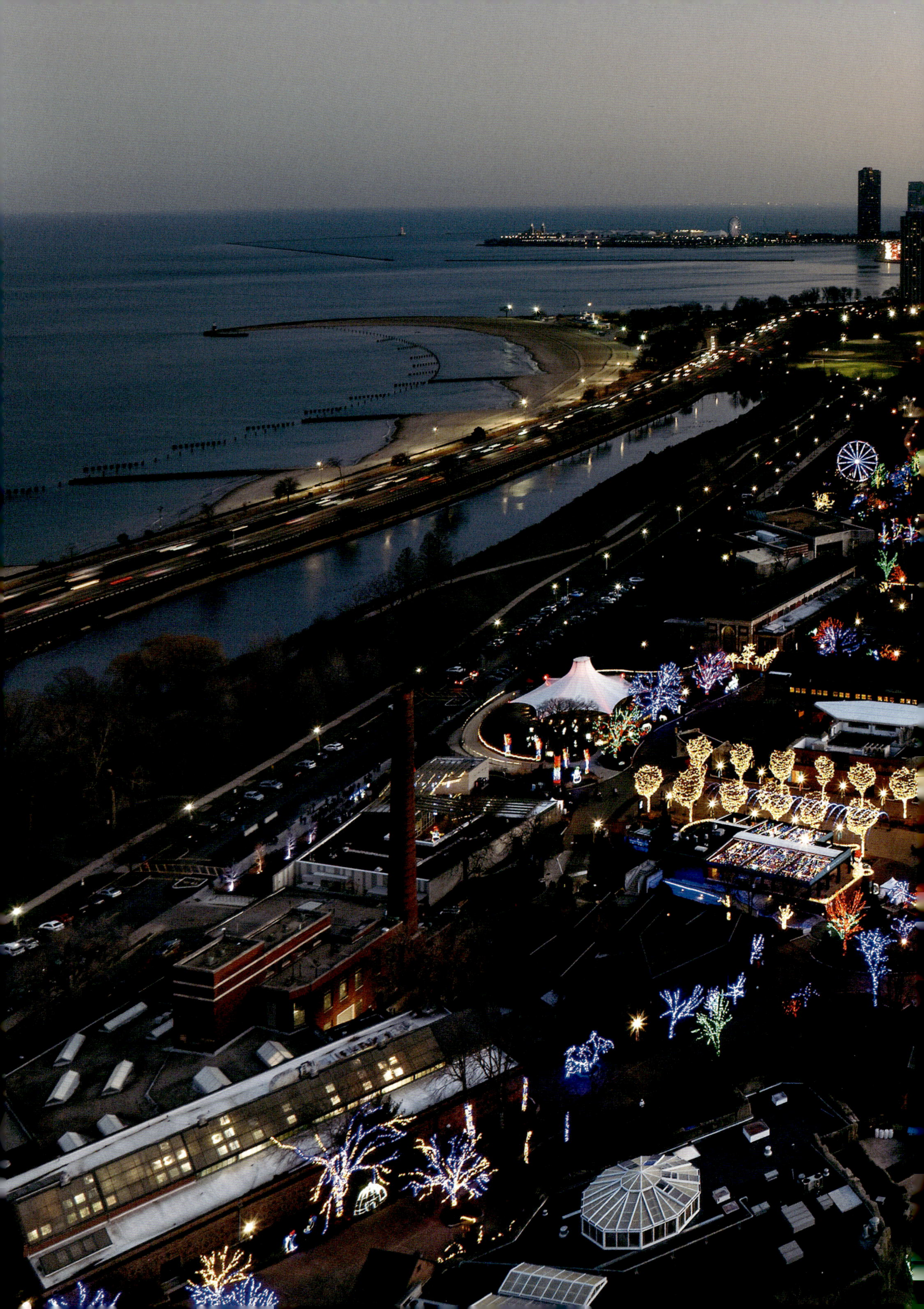

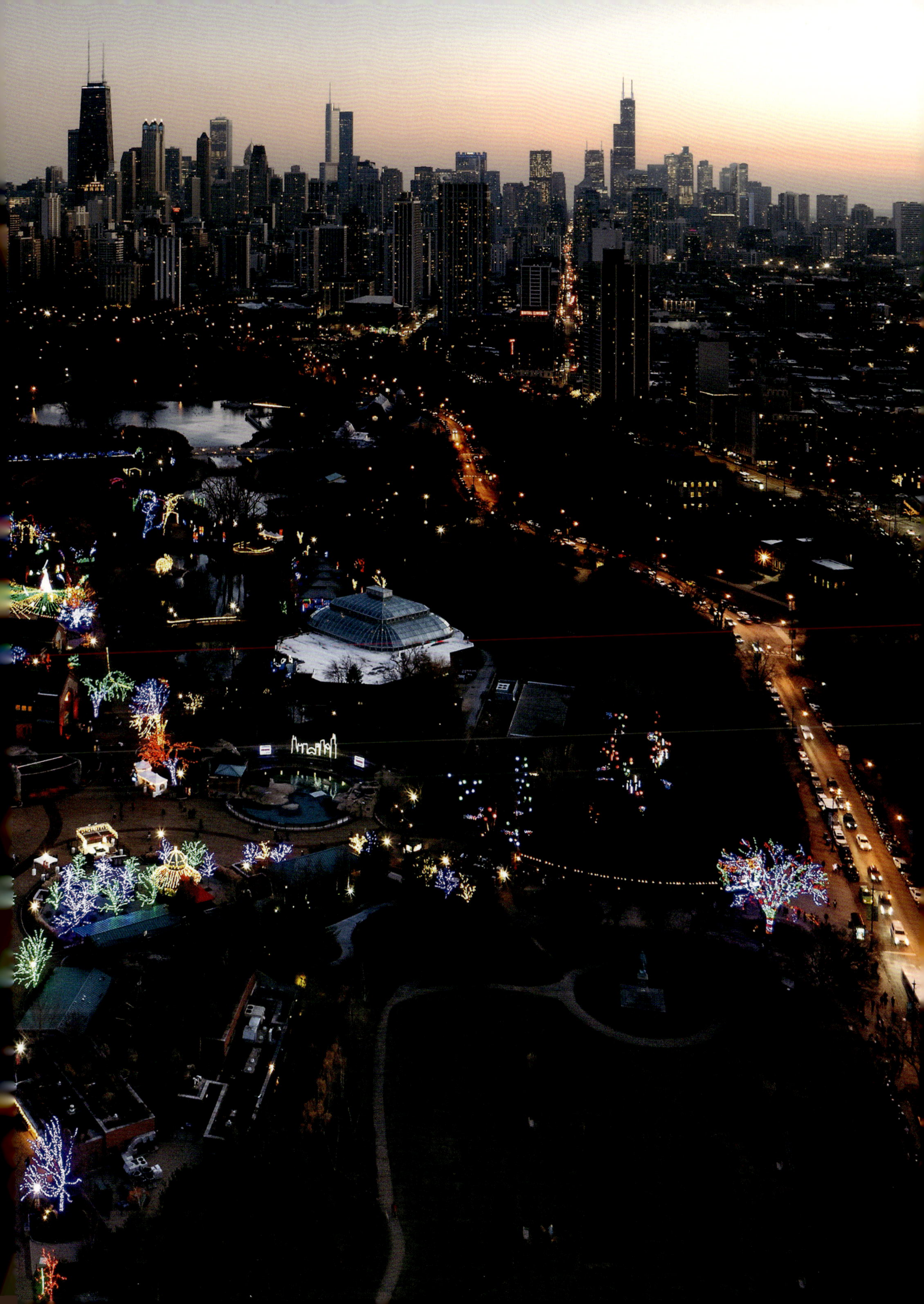

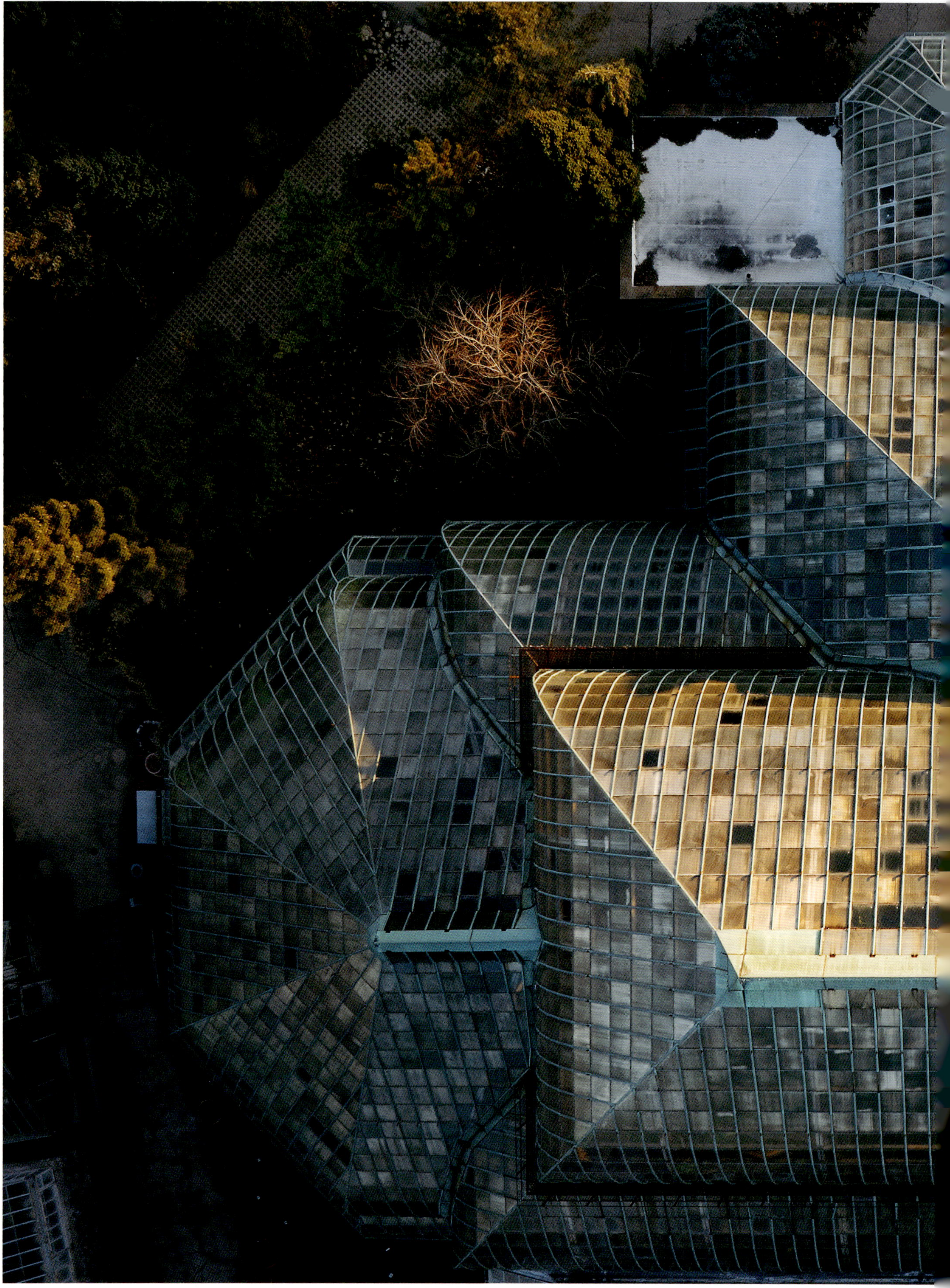

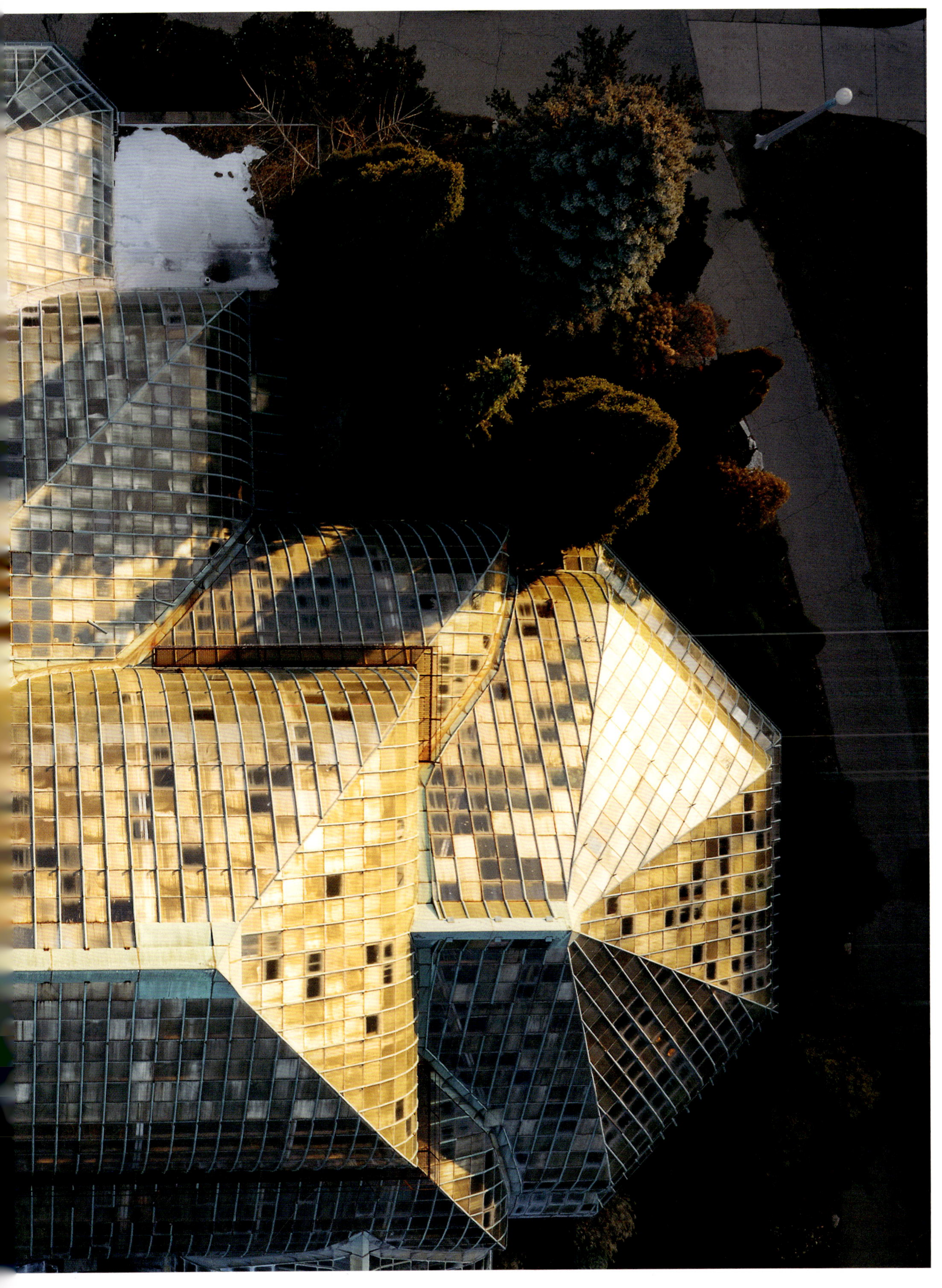

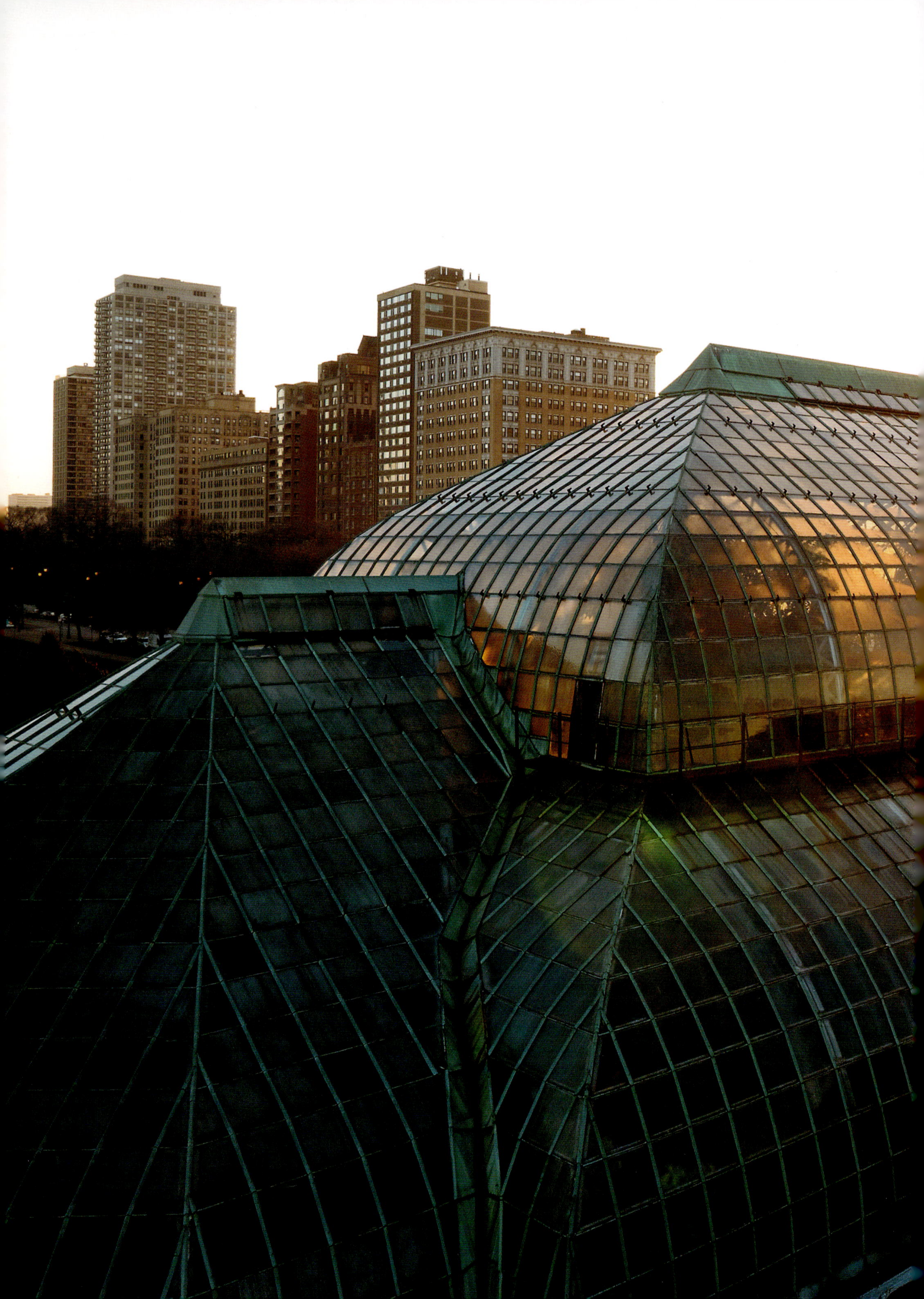

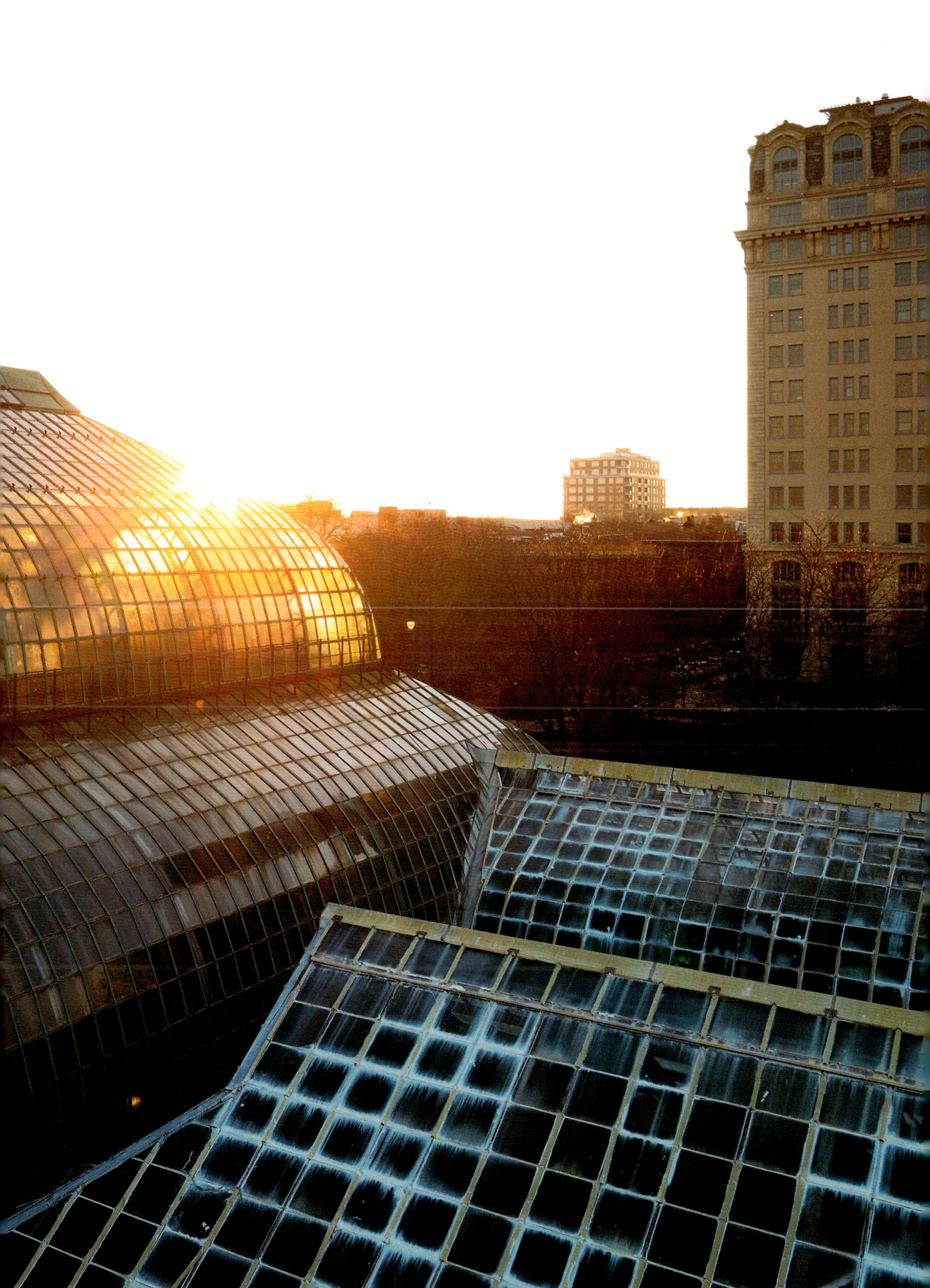

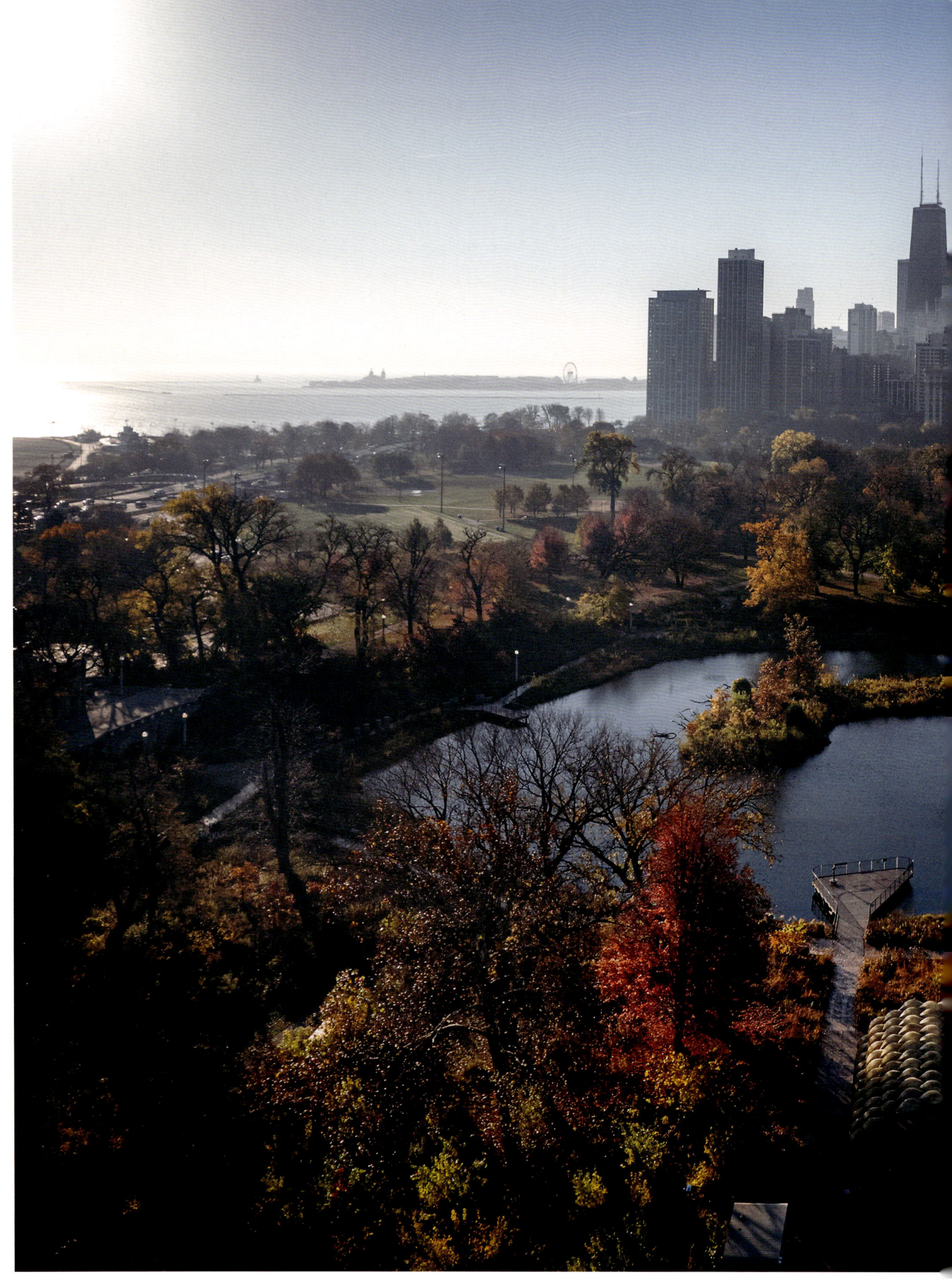

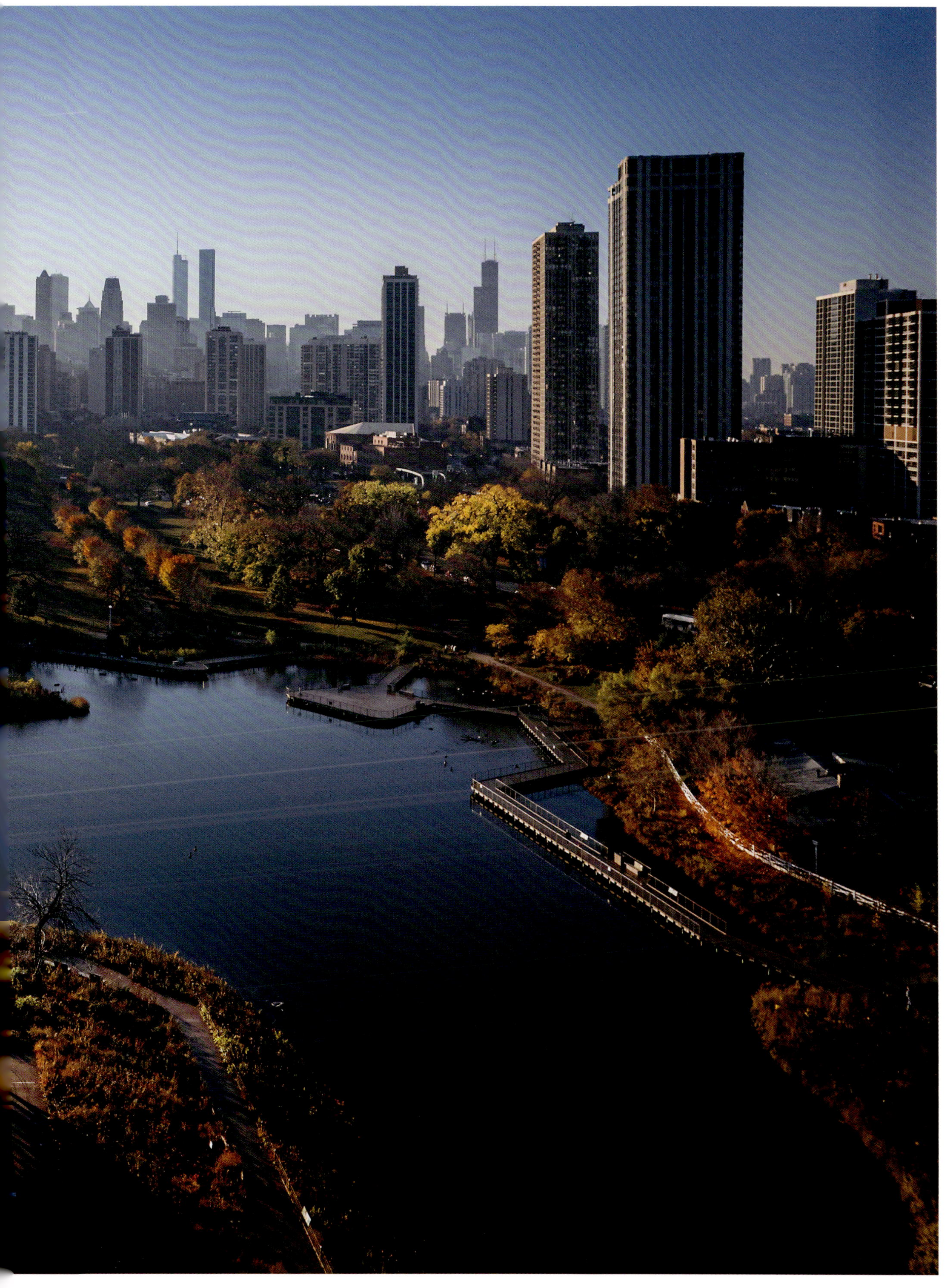

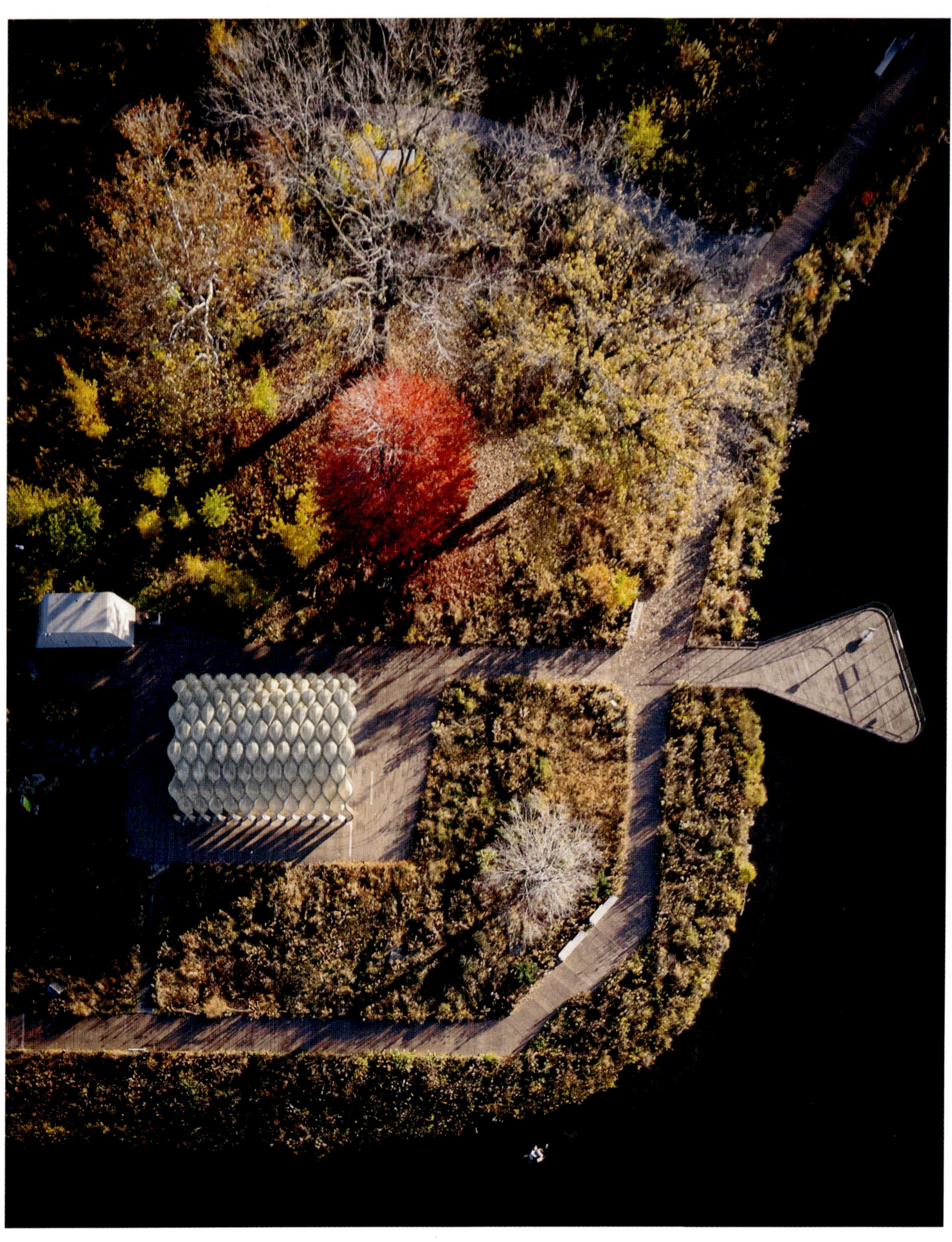

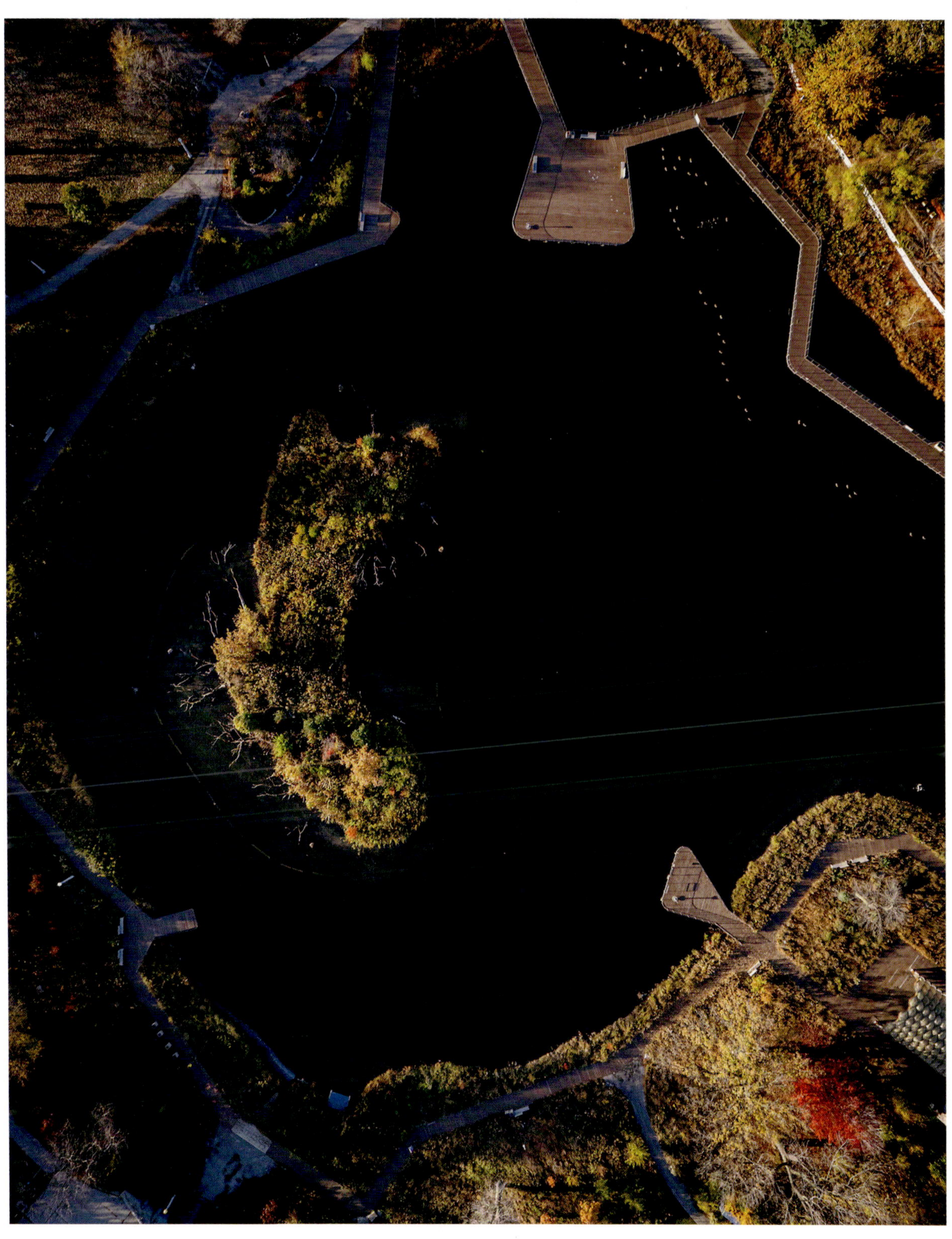

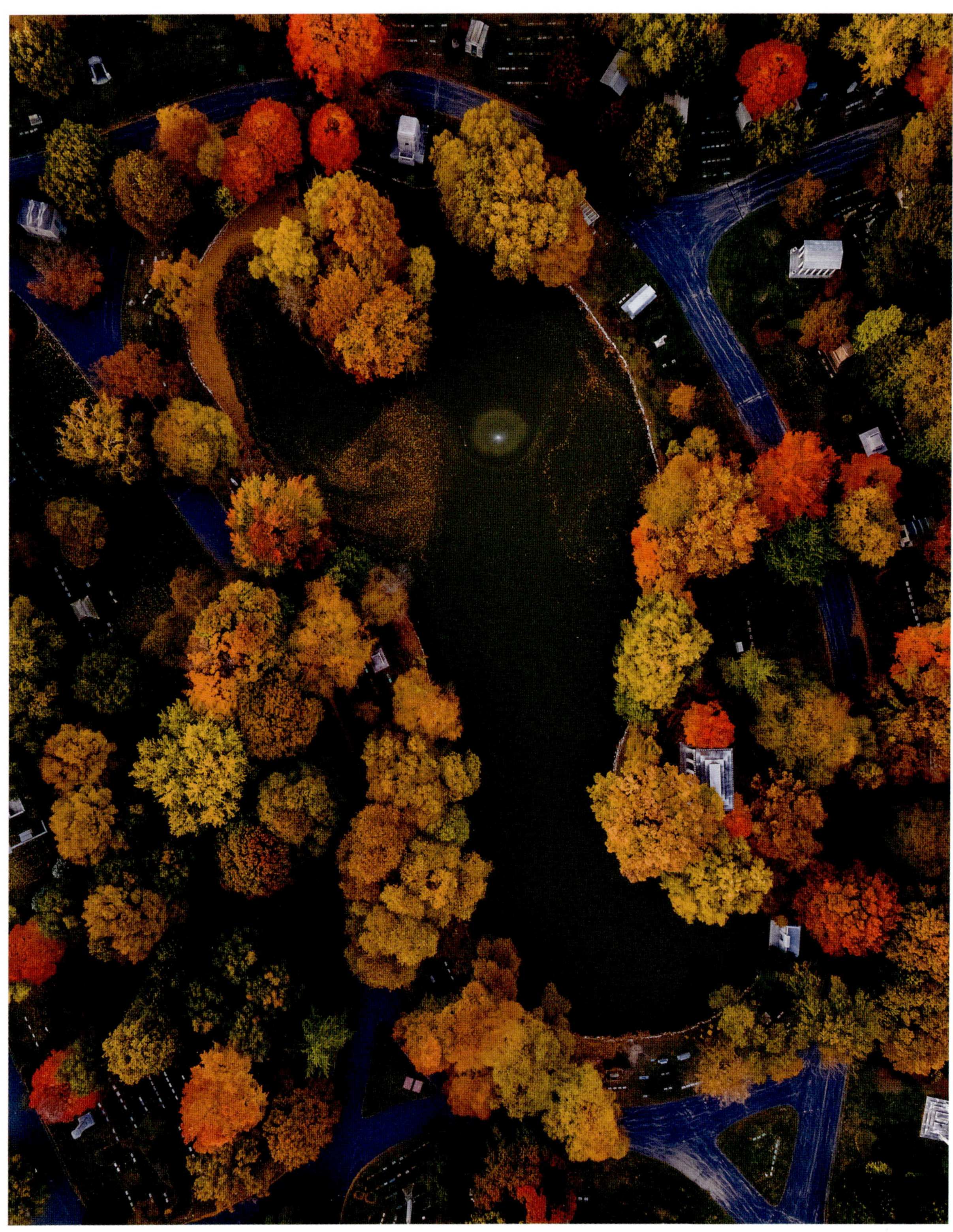

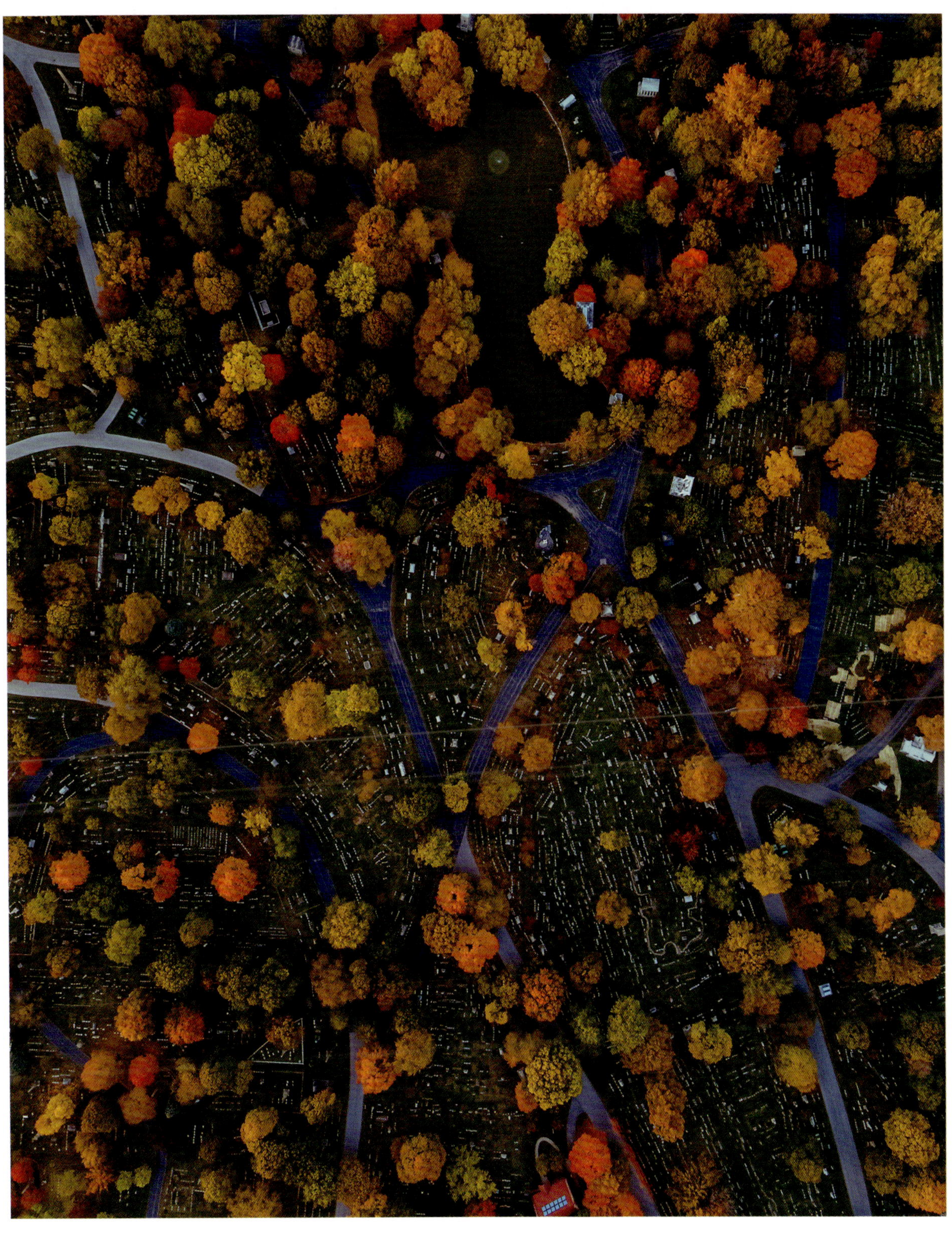

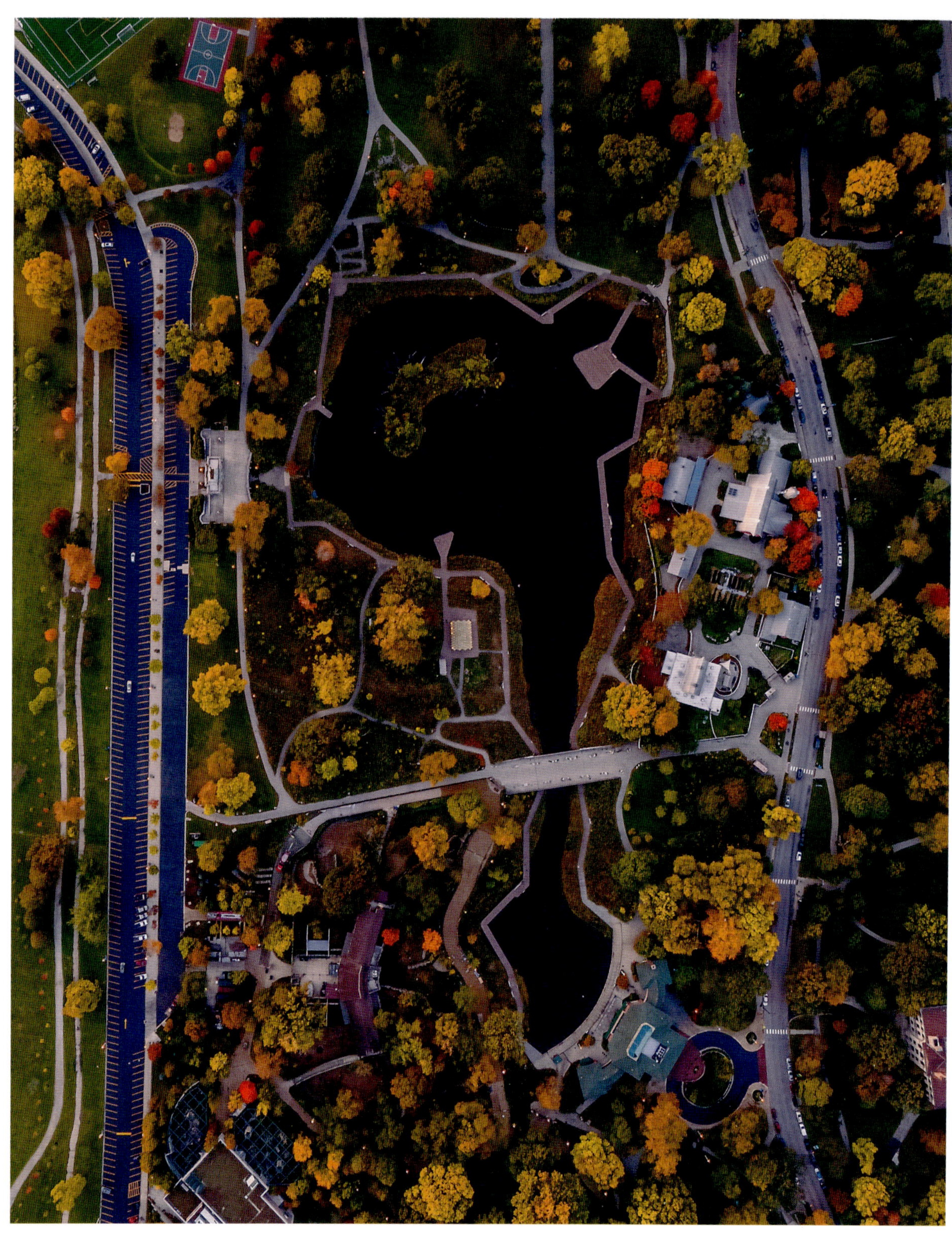

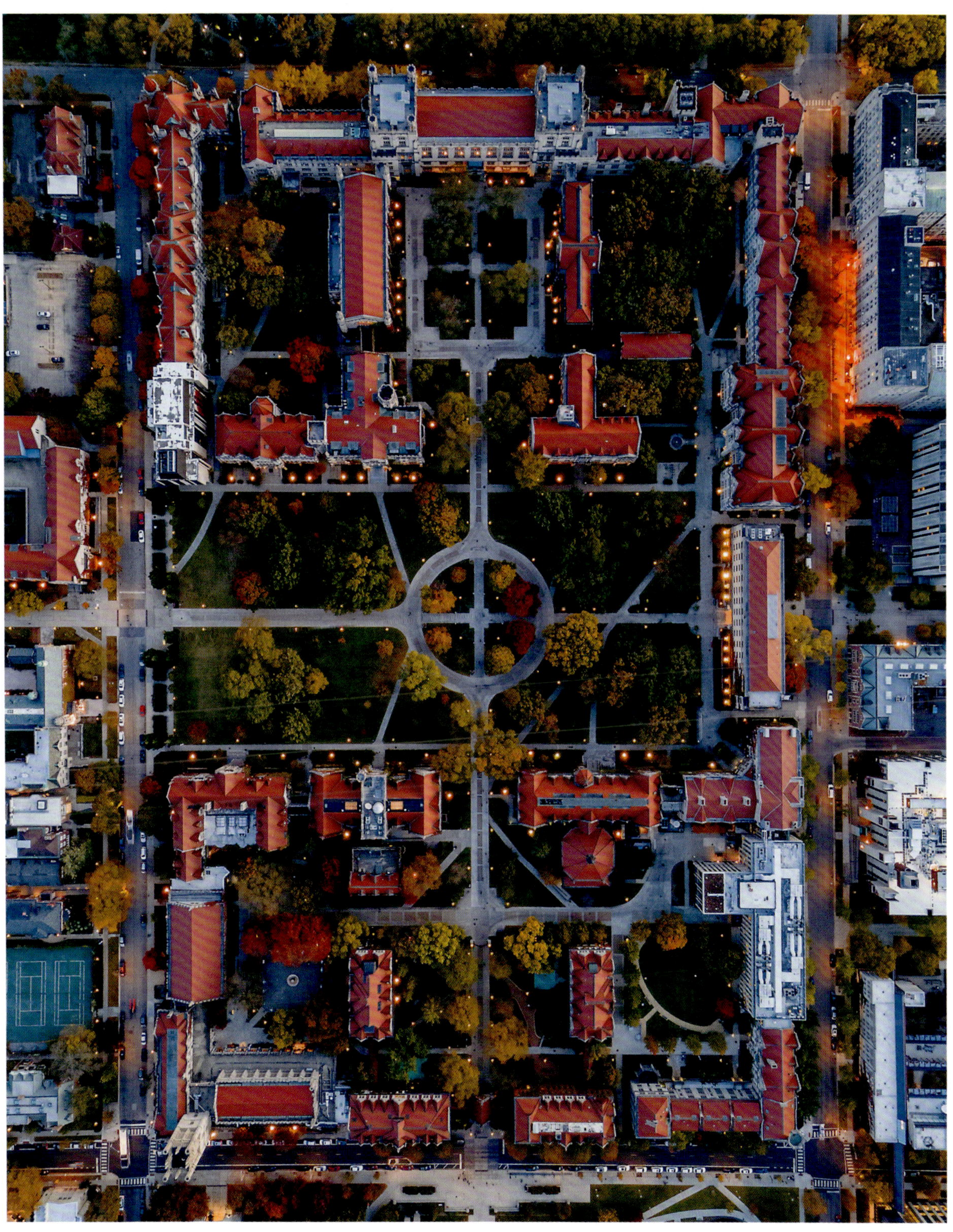

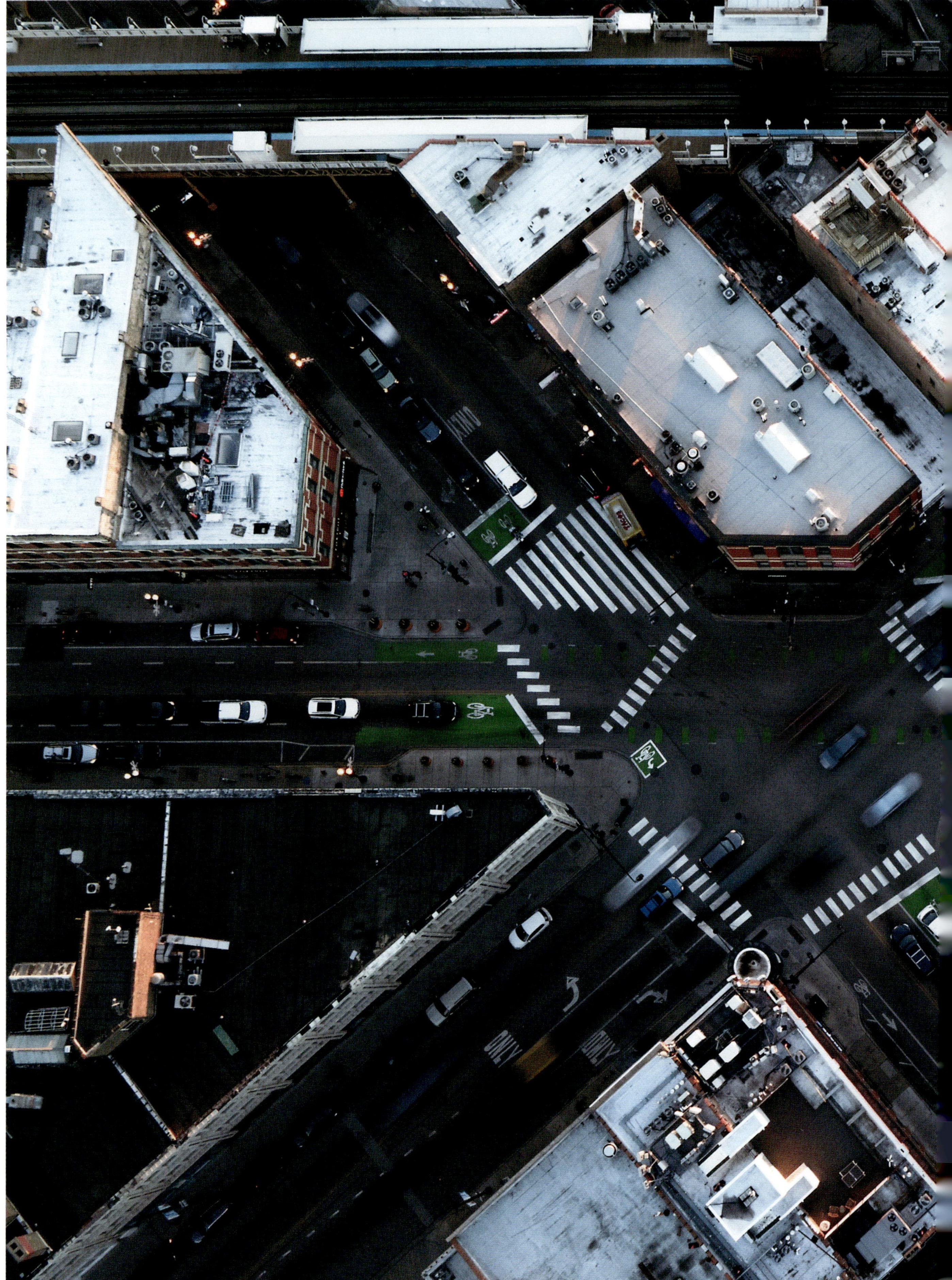

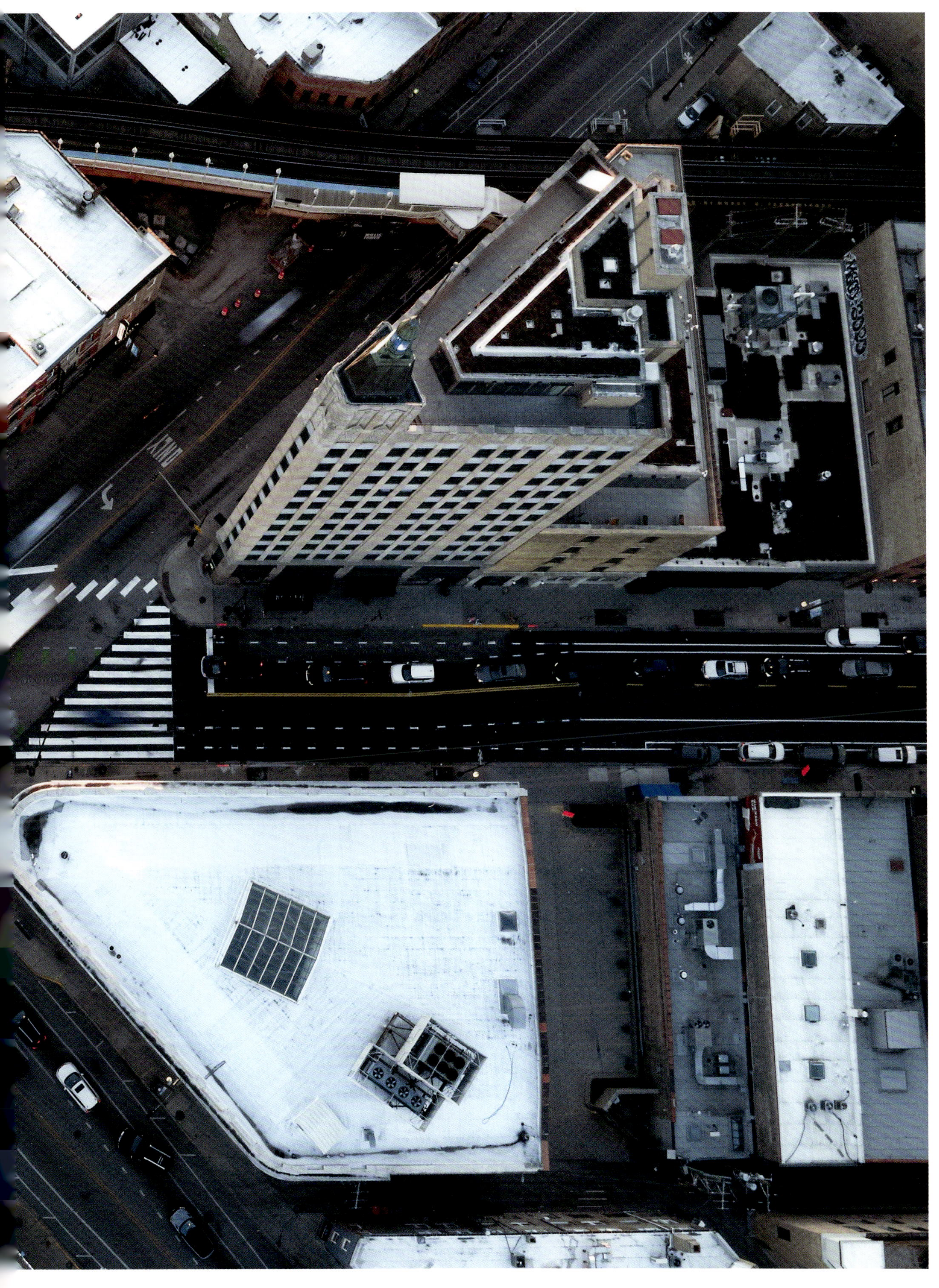

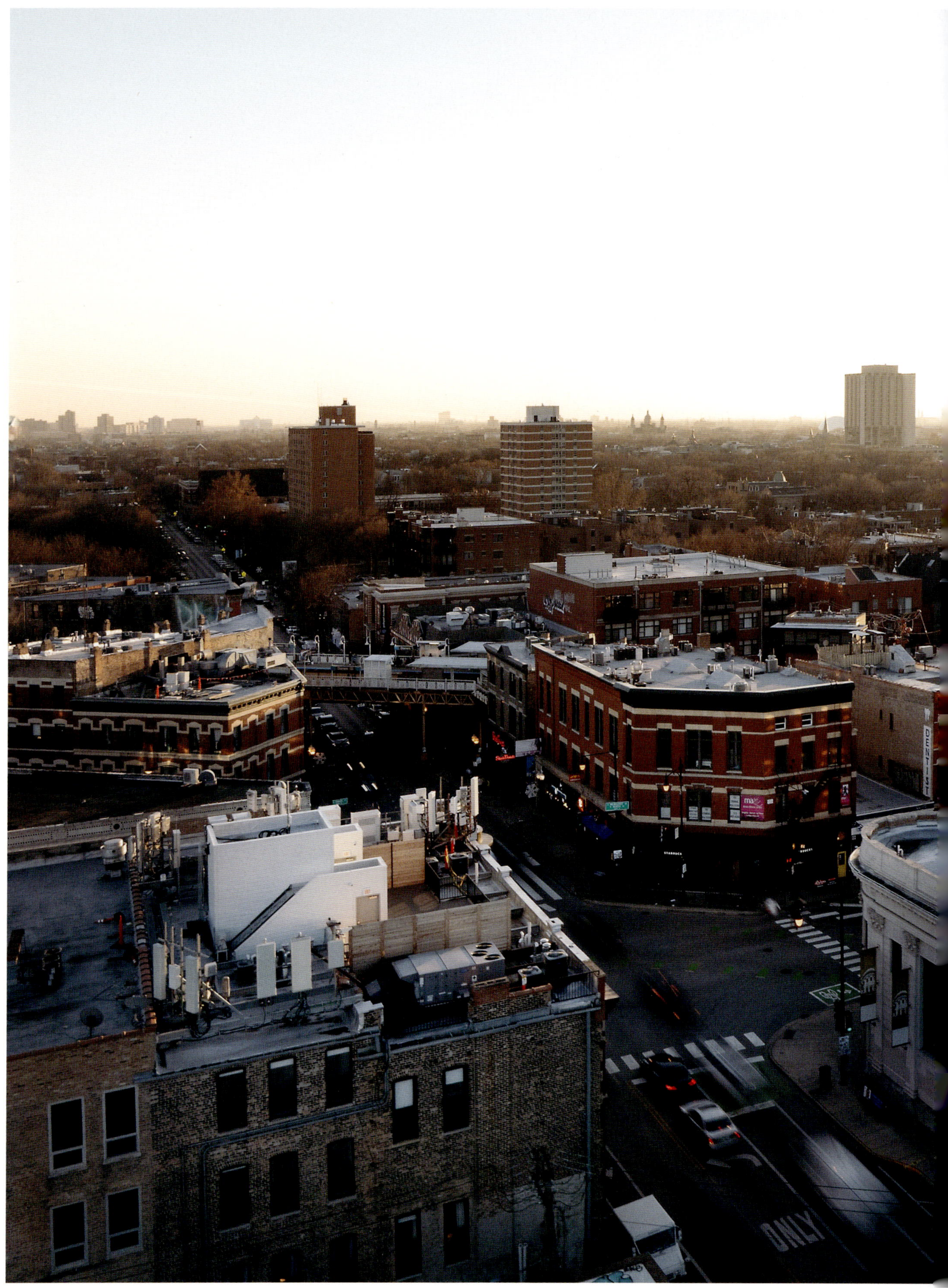

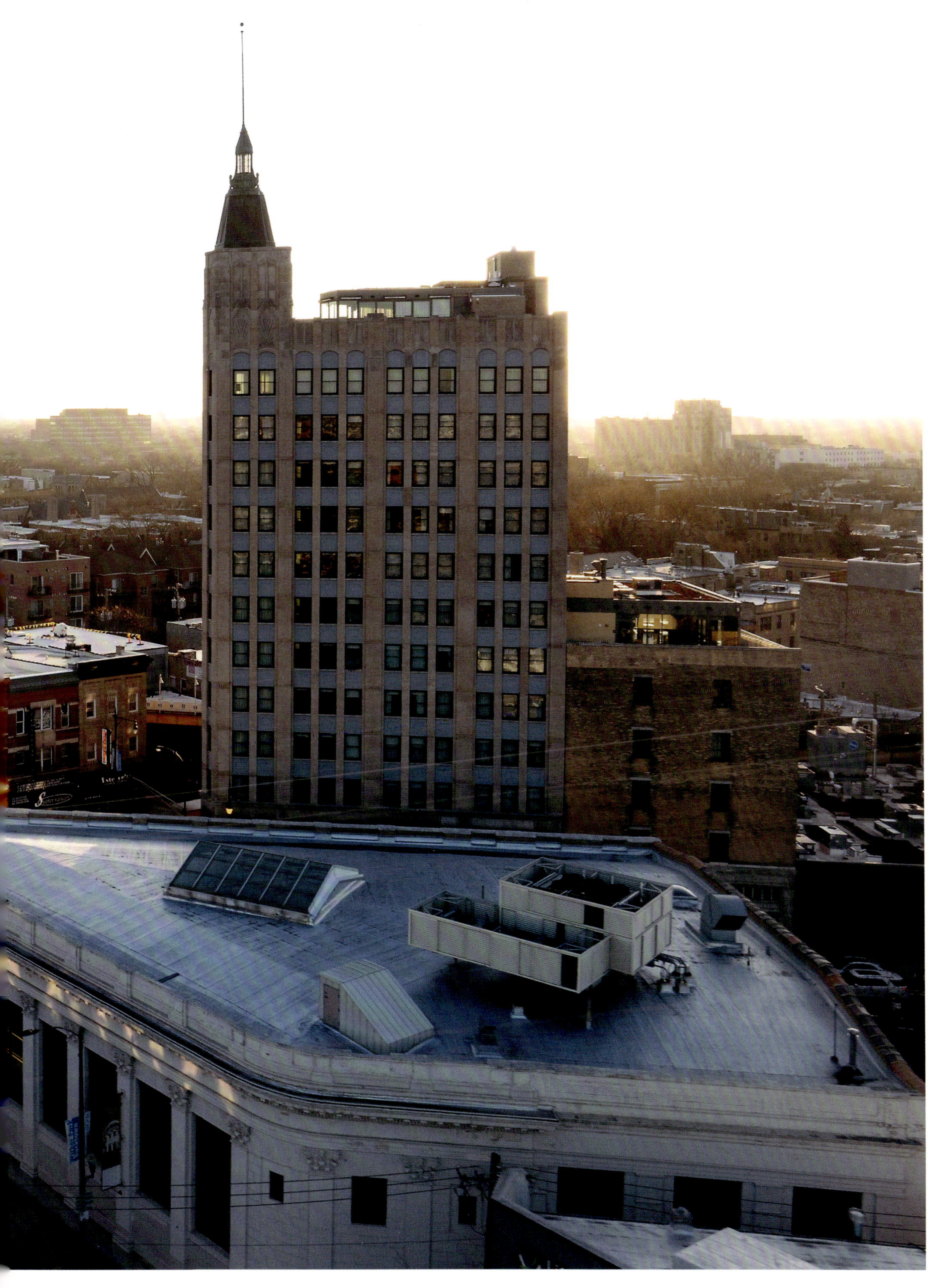

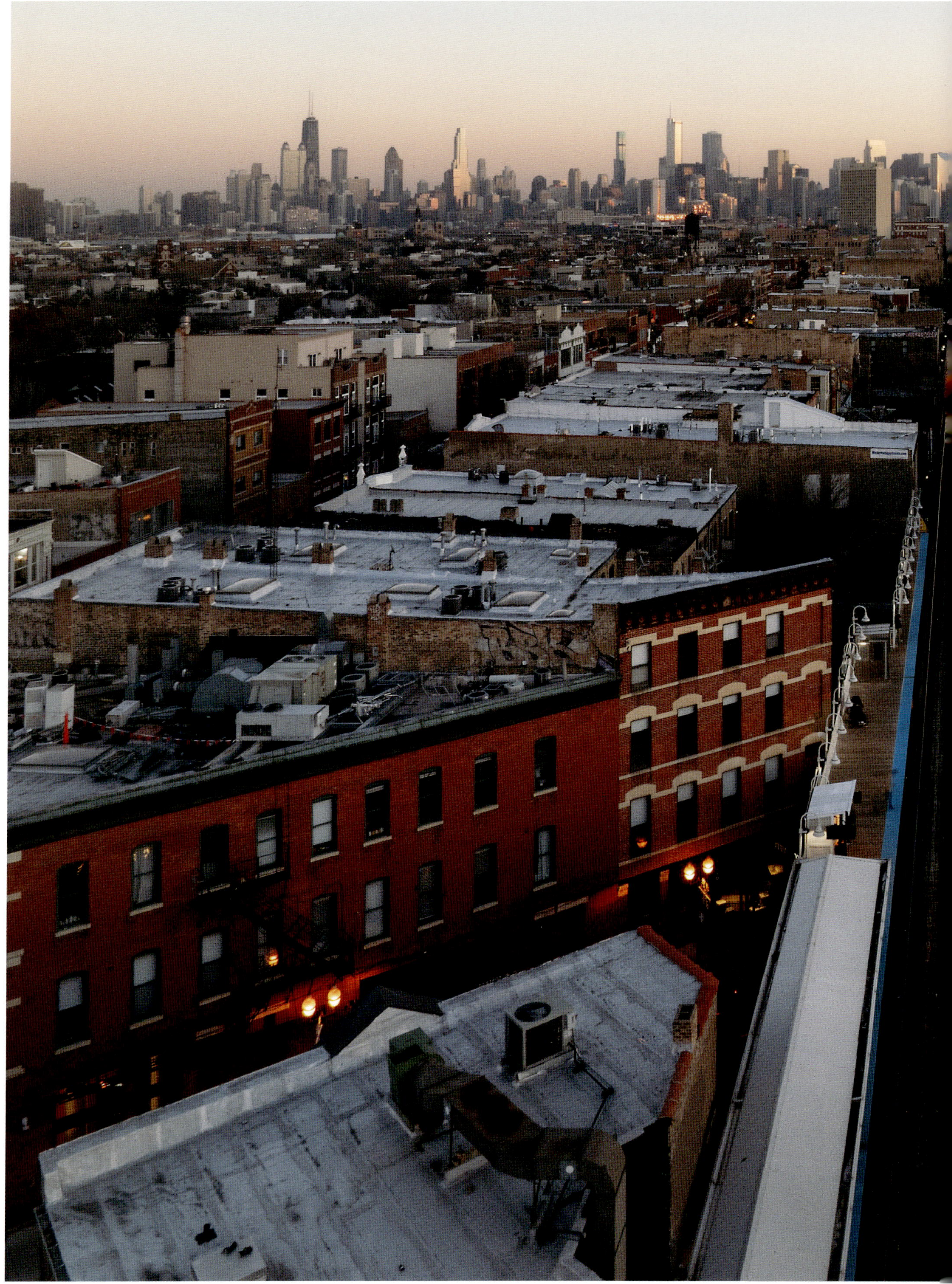

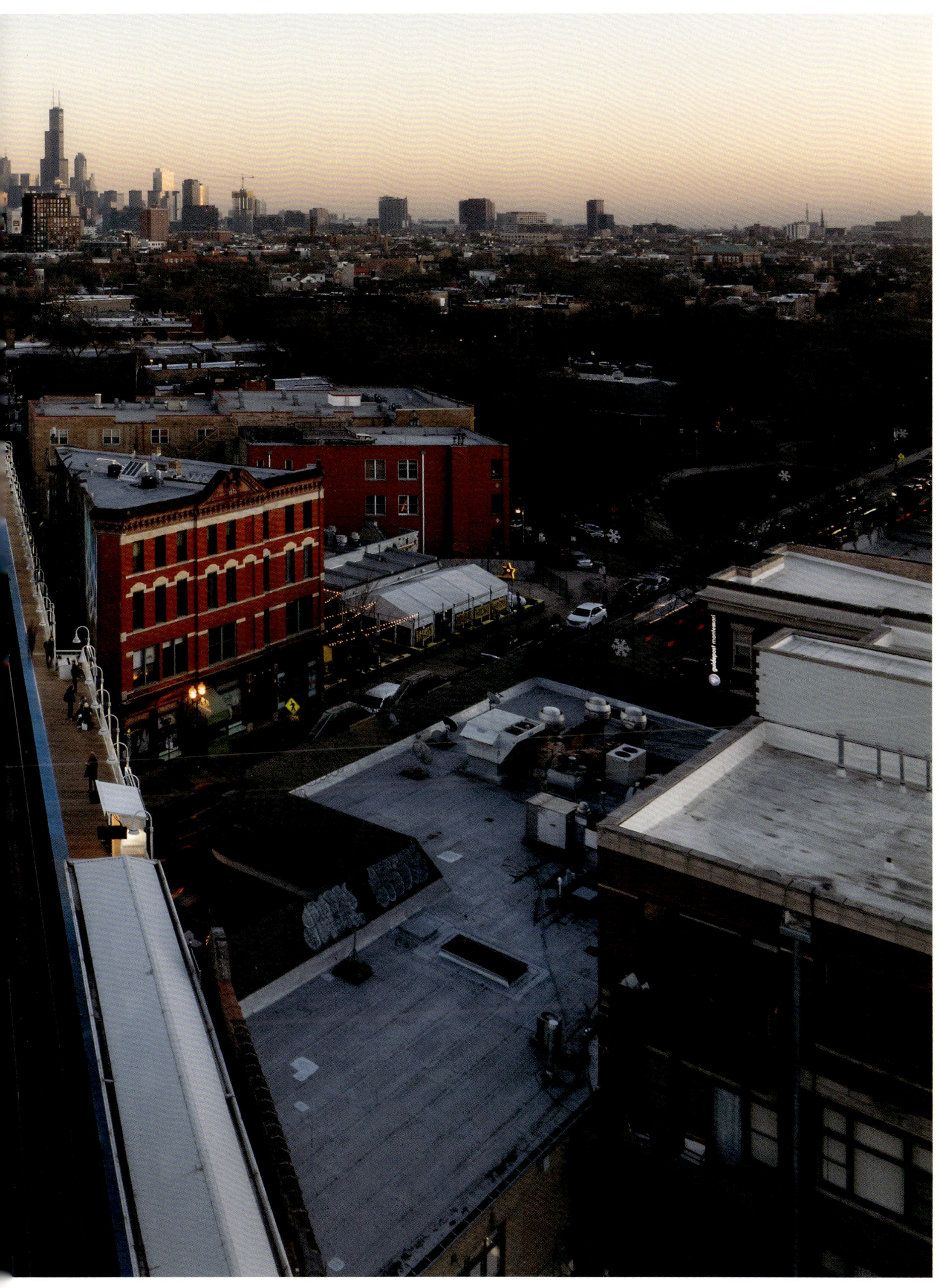

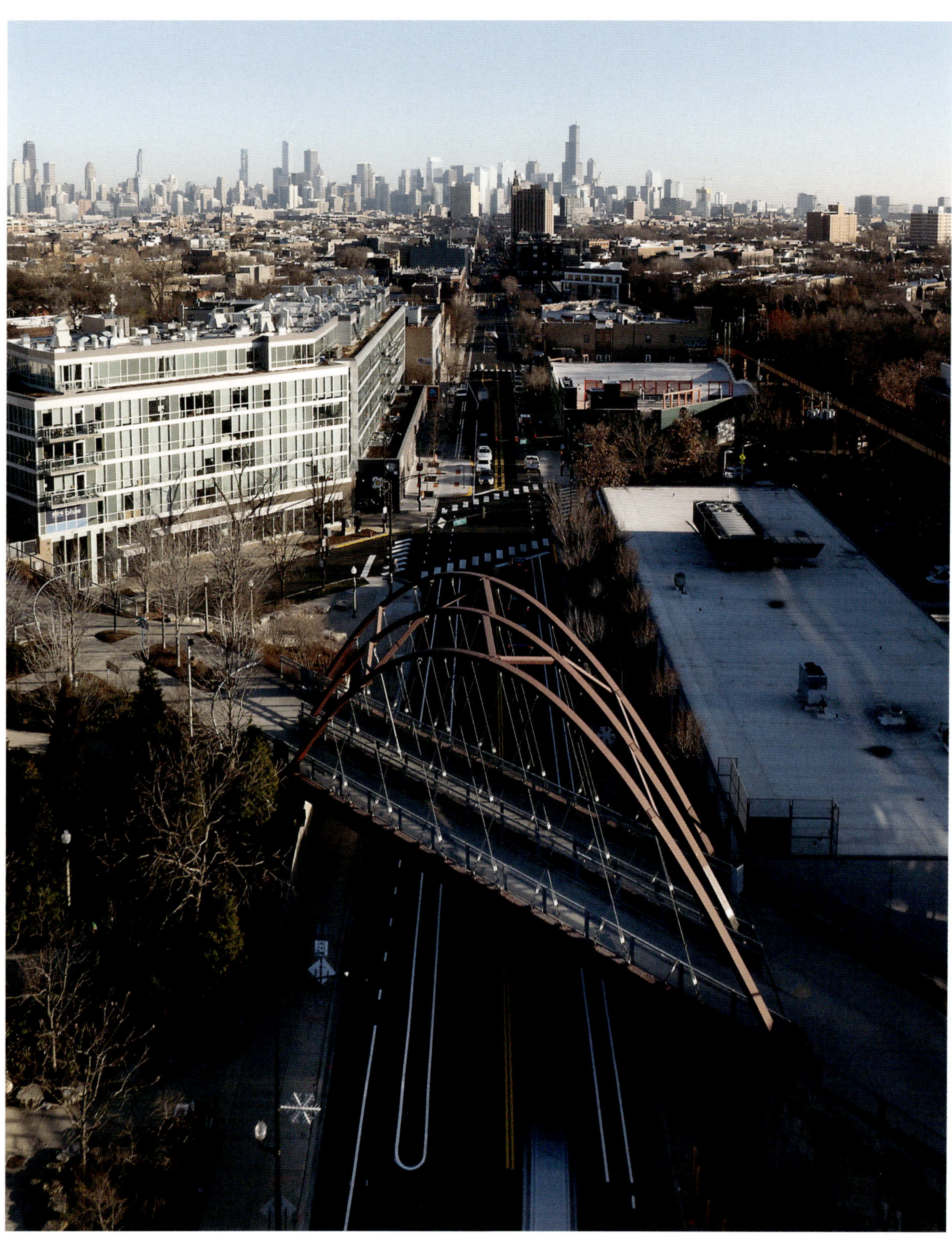

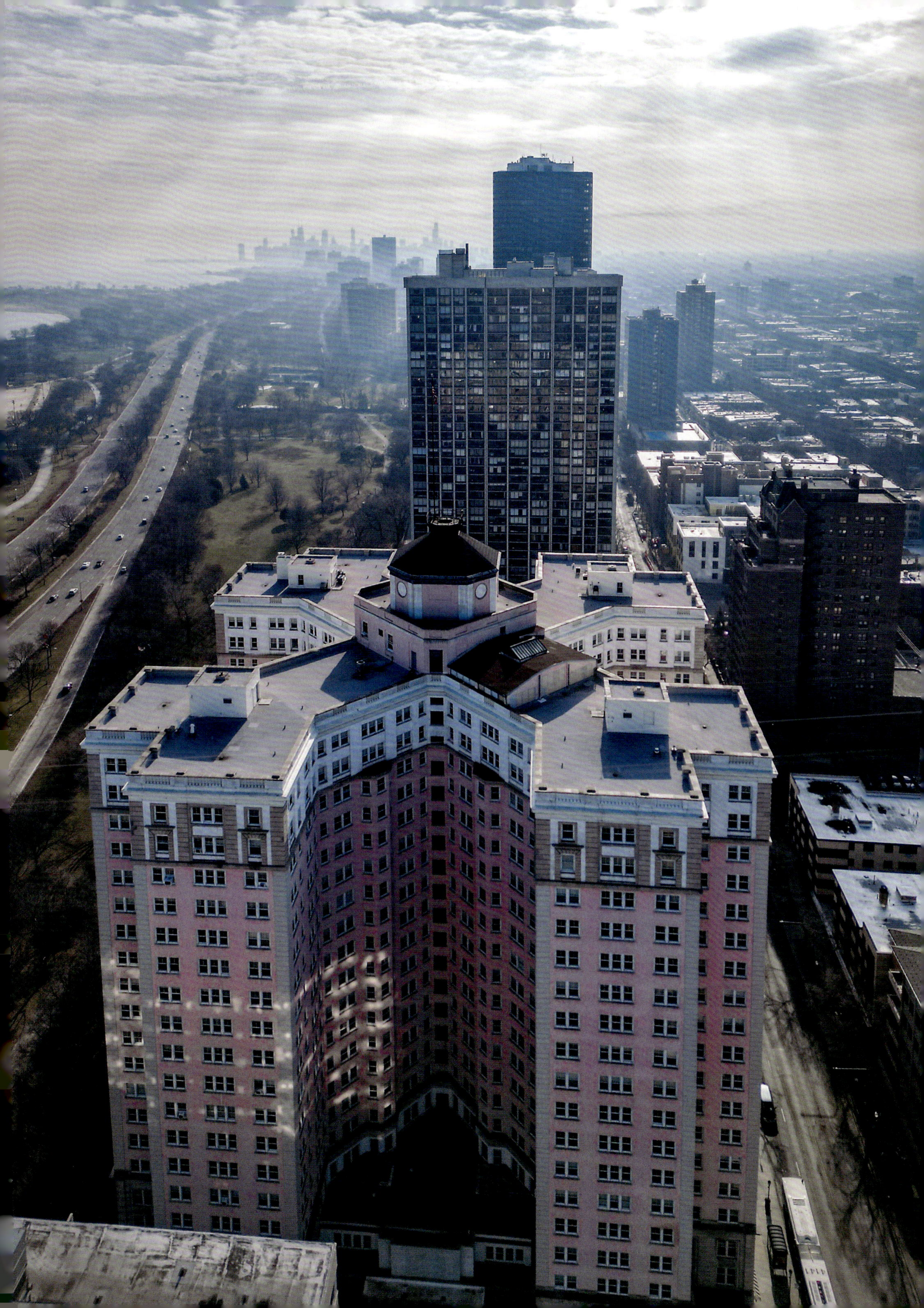

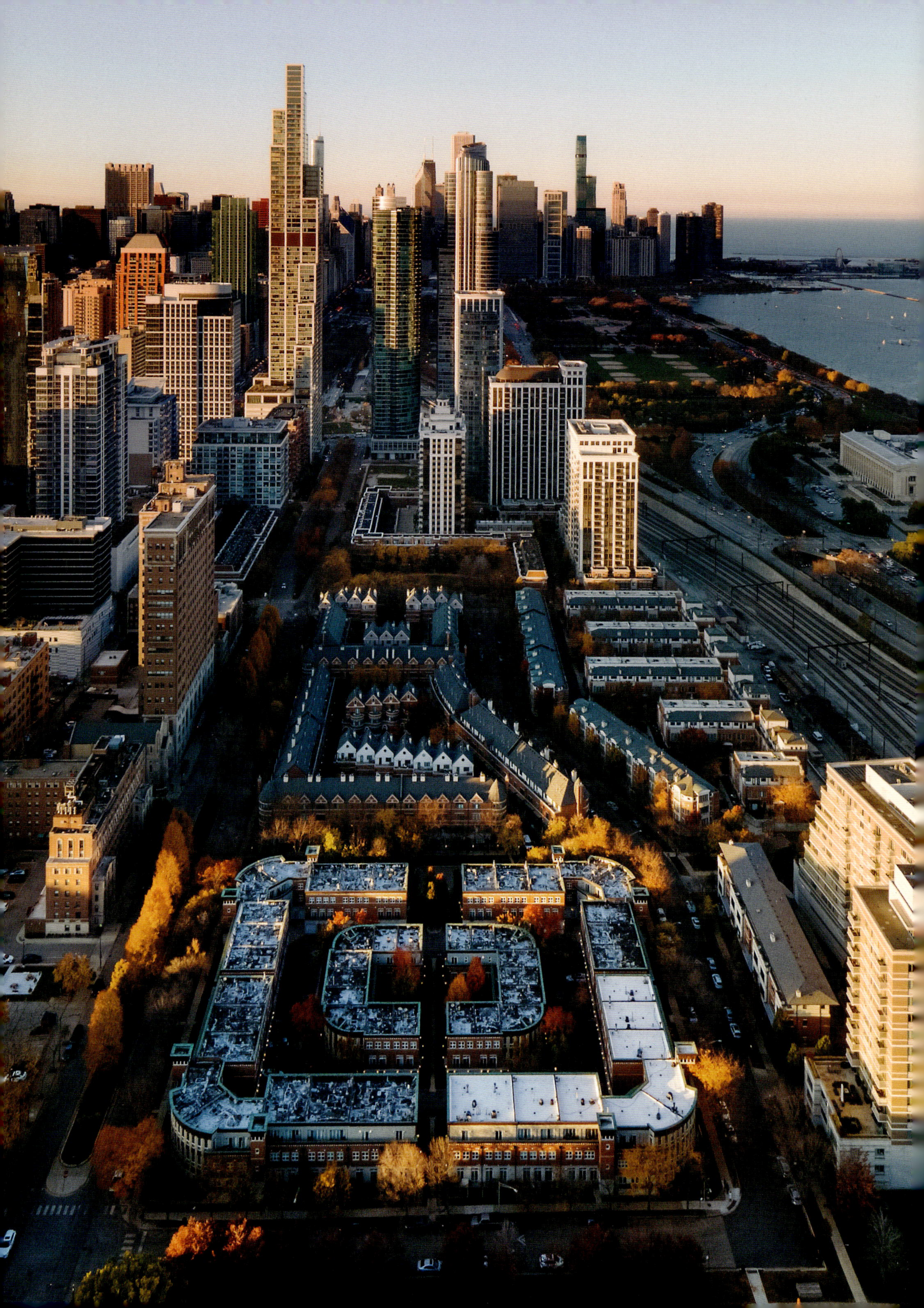

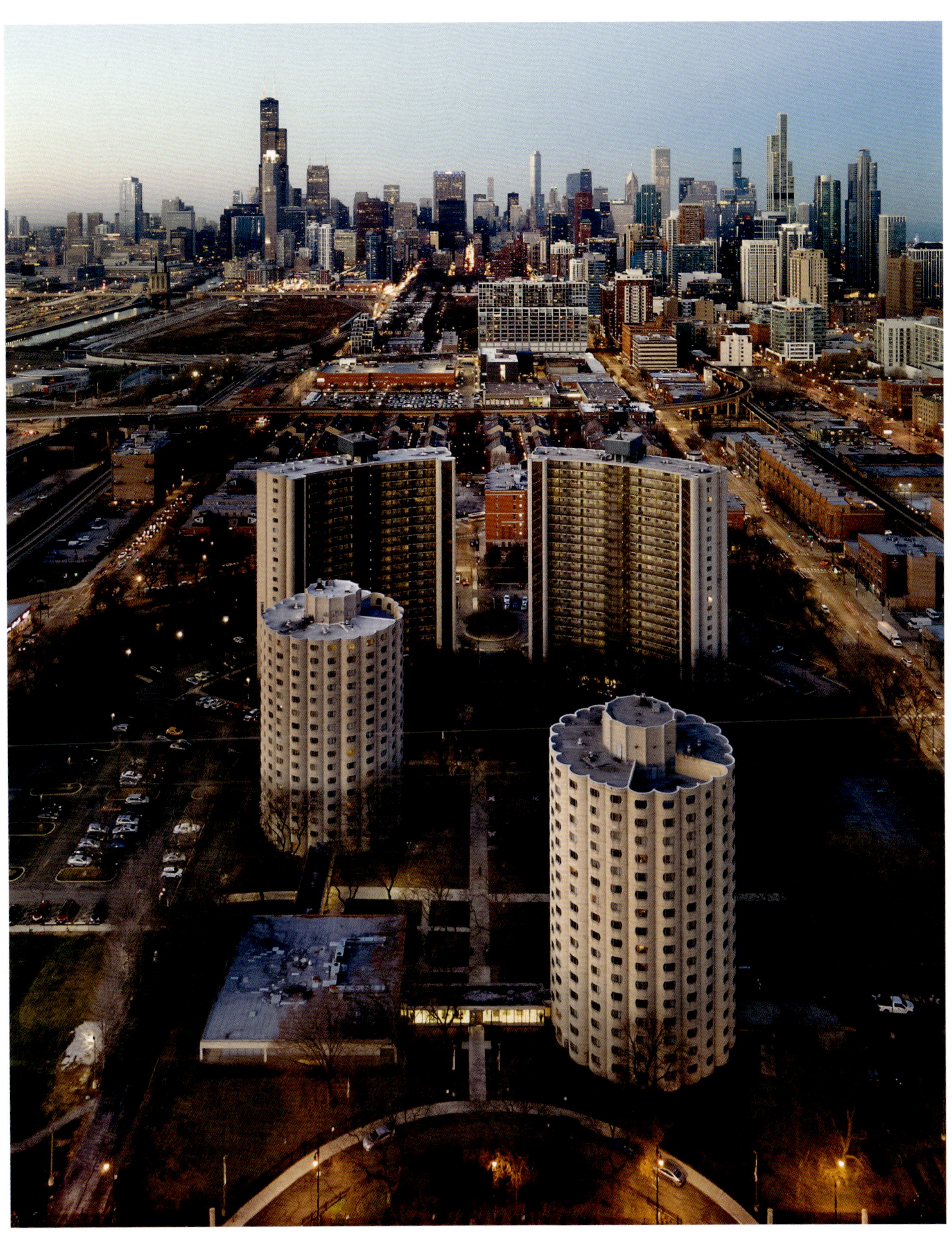

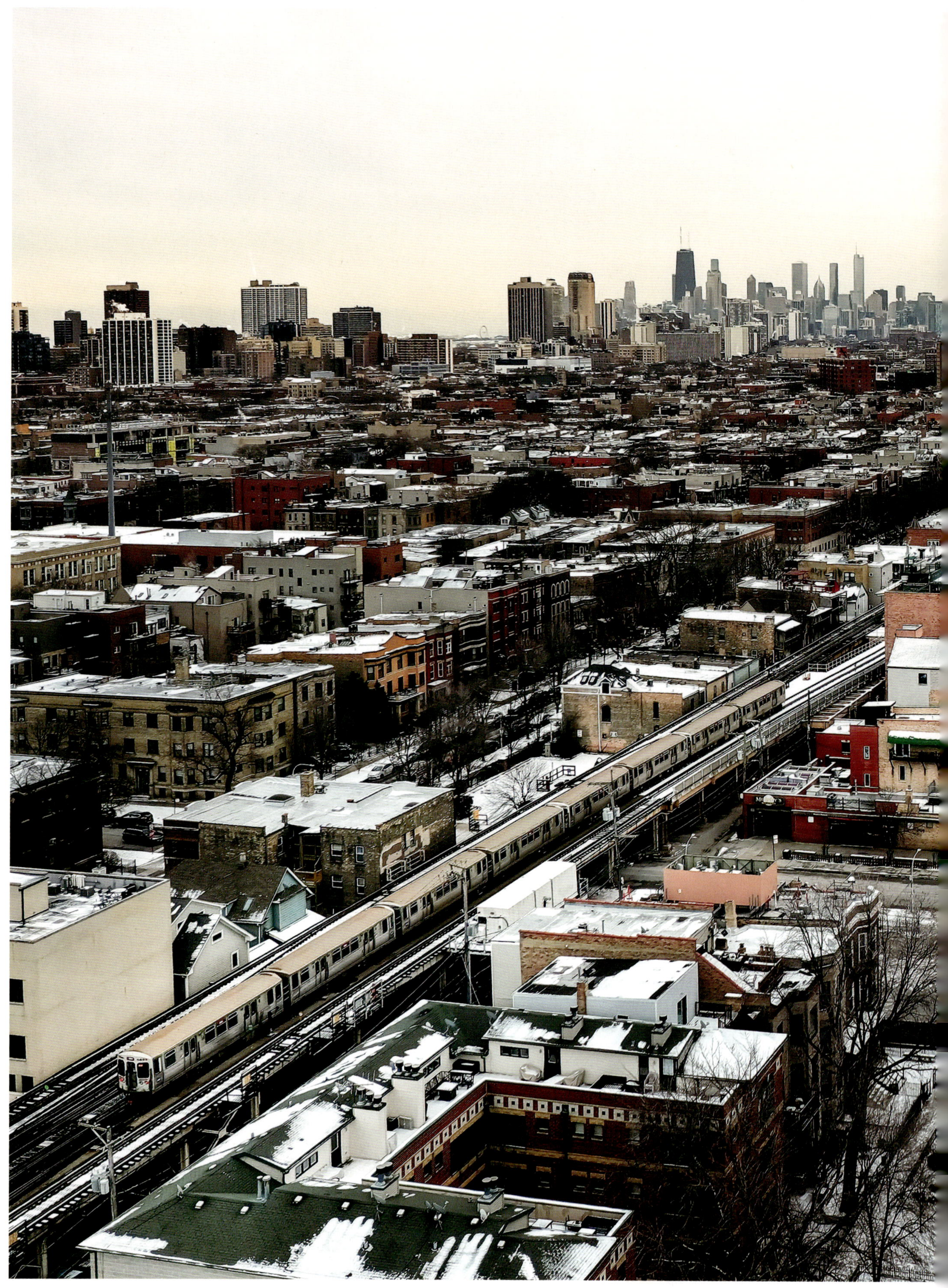

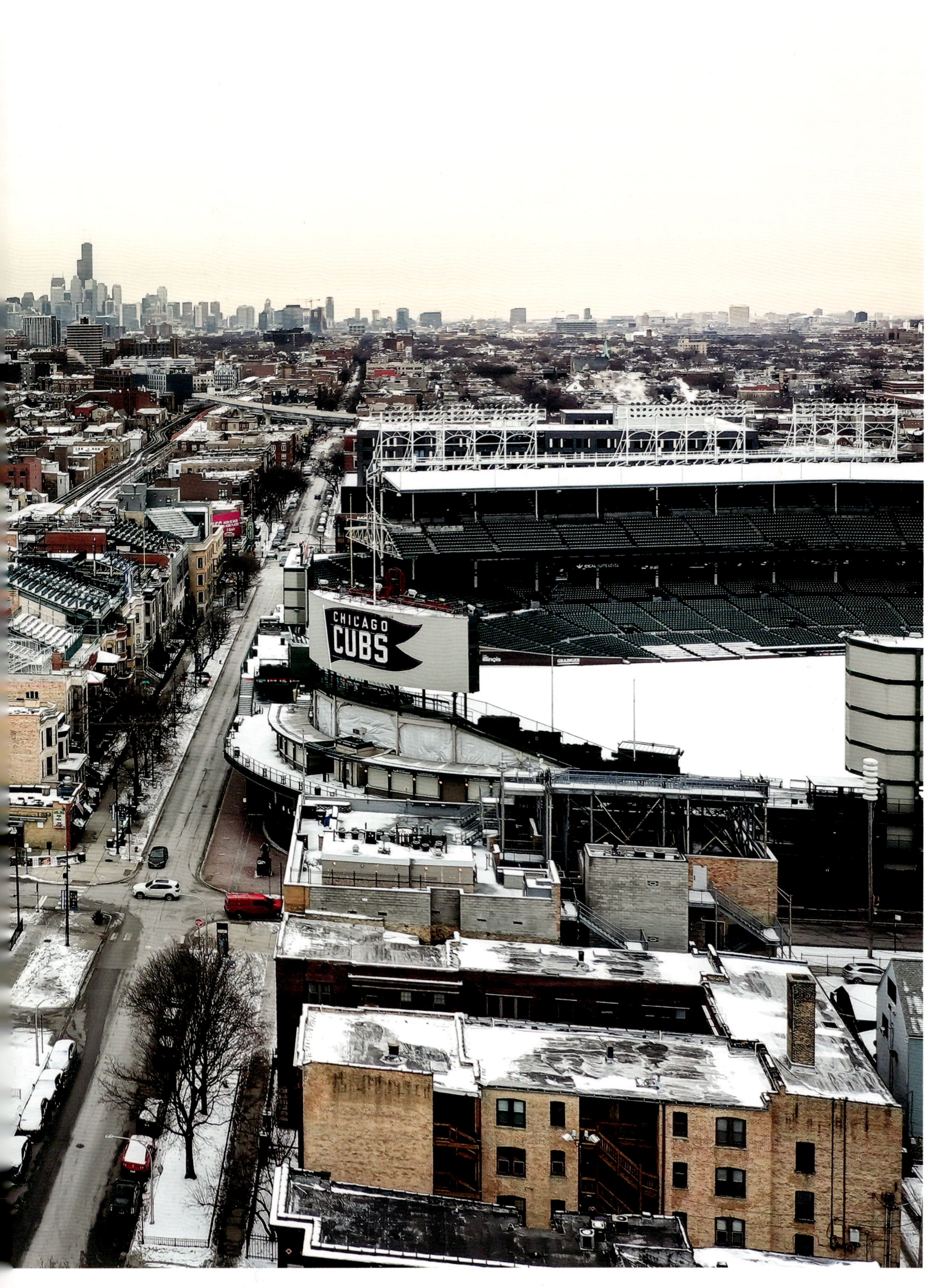

CHICAGO
CUBS

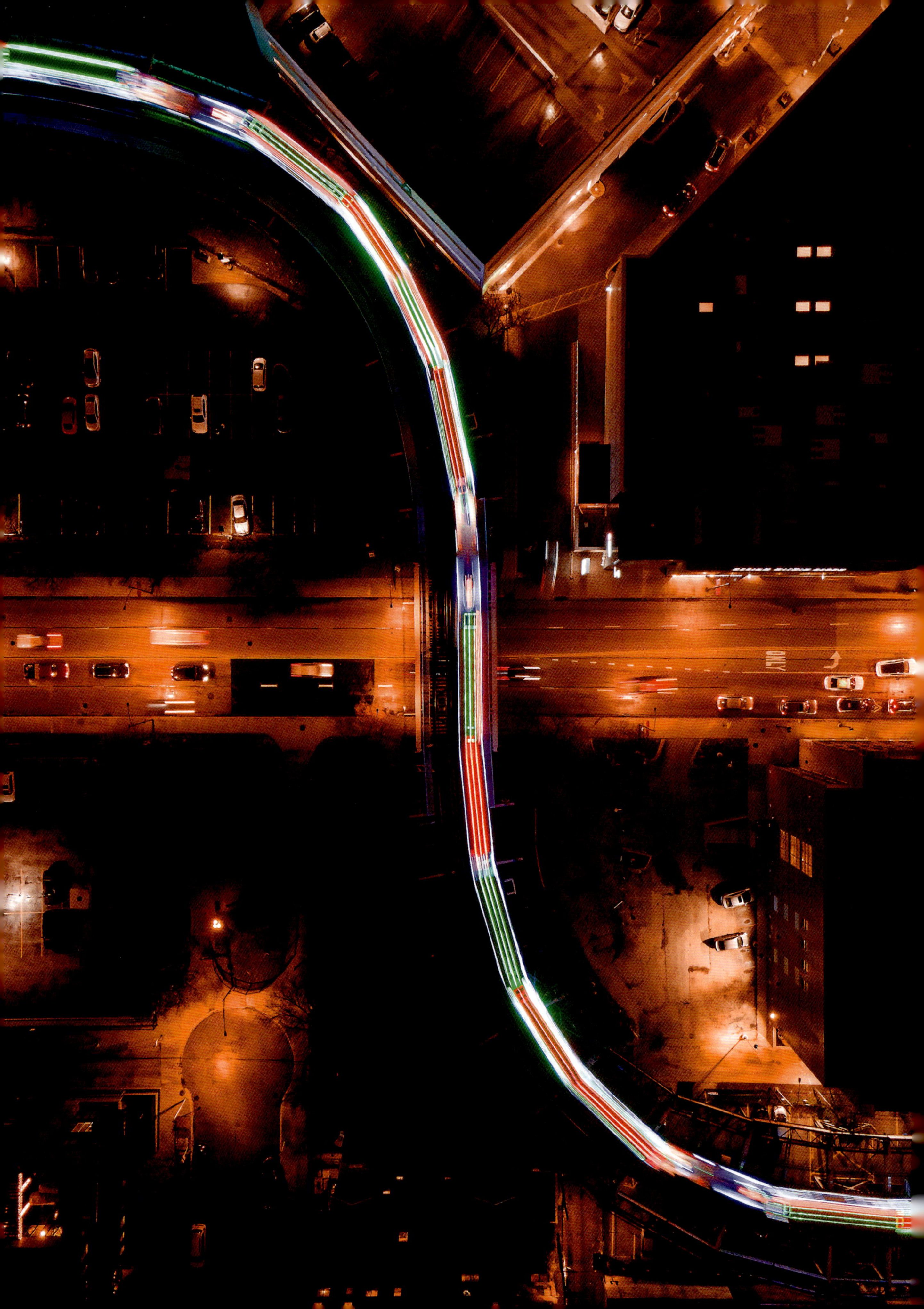

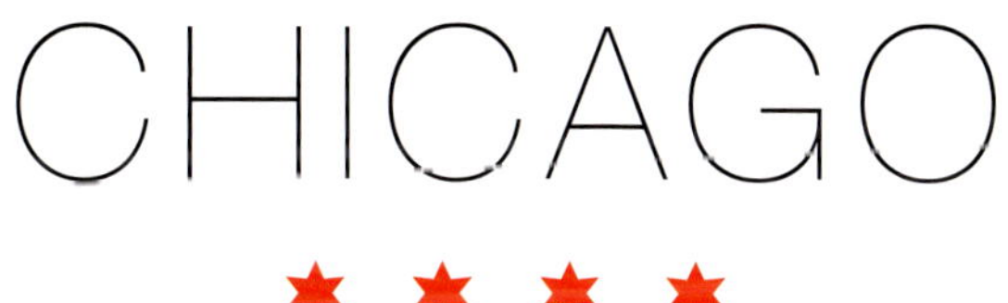

ABOVE & ACROSS
CHICAGO

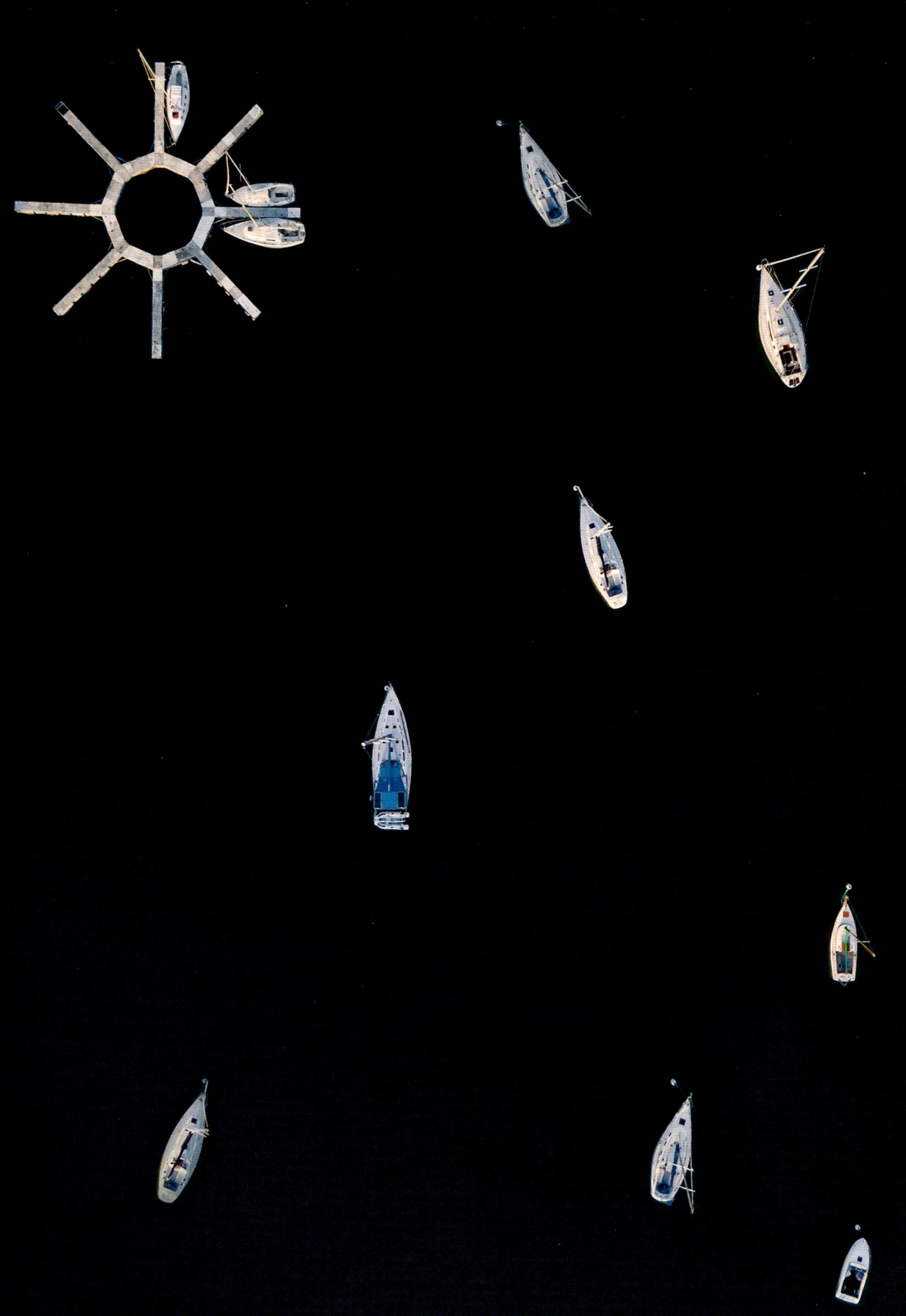

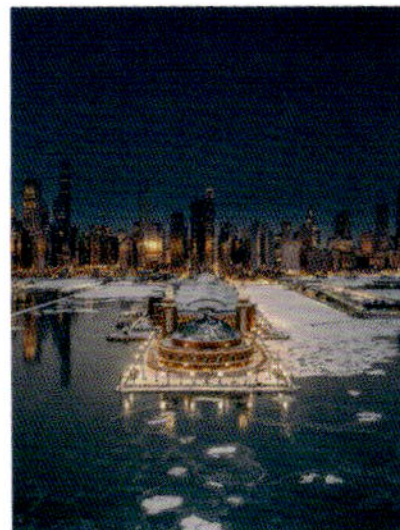

Front Cover Adam Pearson
View of Navy Pier

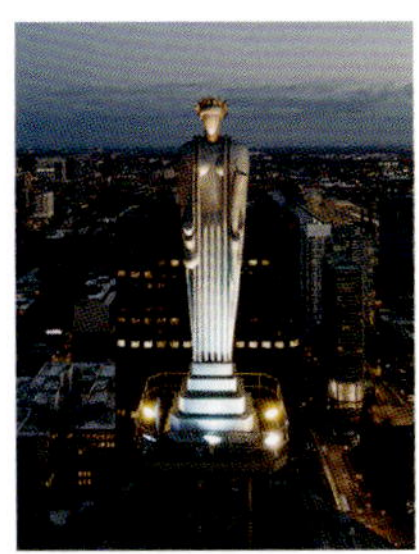

2 Daniel Moreno
View of the Chicago Board of
Trade Building

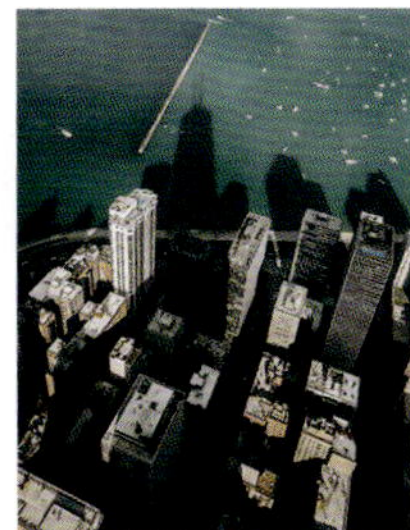

4 Sonja Weiss
Above Streeterville

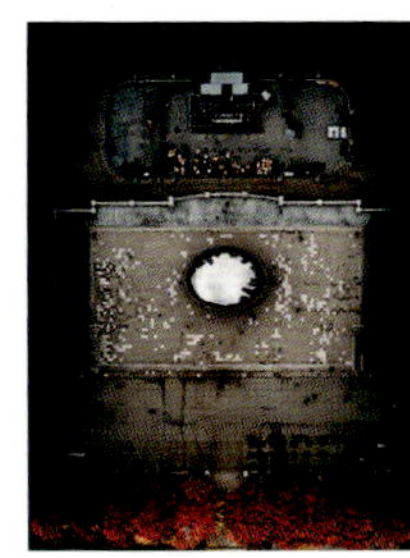

6 Dominika Brzykcy
Above Cloud Gate

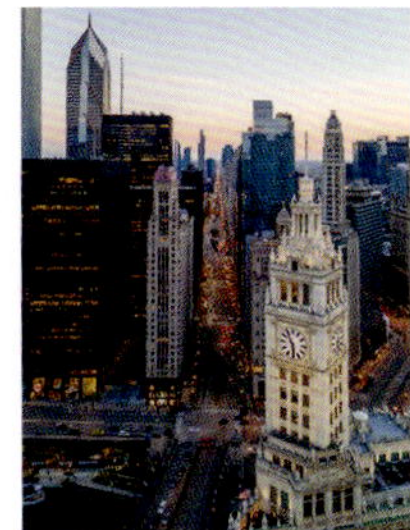

9 Daniel Moreno
View of the Wrigley Building
and Michigan Avenue

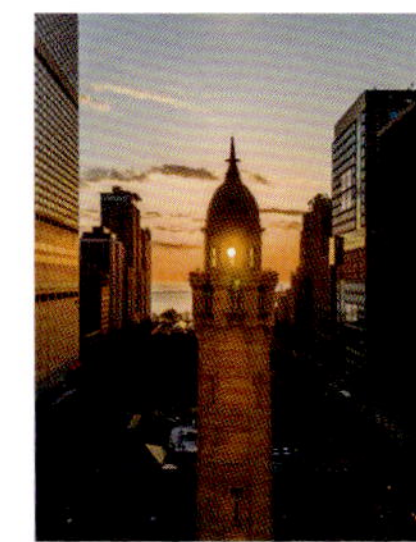

11 Daniel Moreno
View of the Chicago
Water Tower

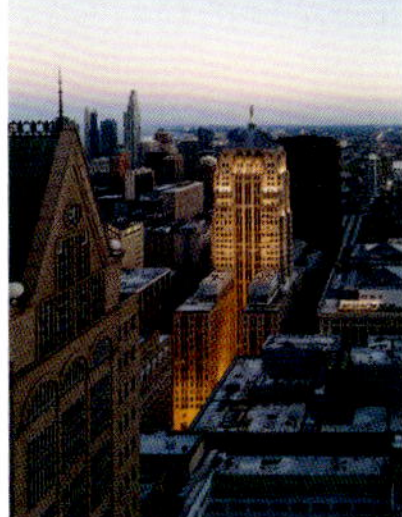

12 Daniel Moreno
View of the Loop

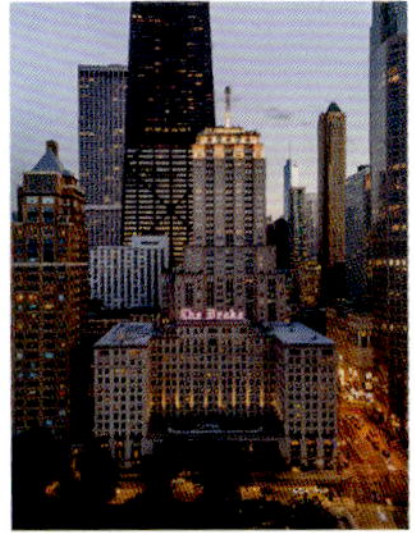

13 Daniel Moreno
View of The Drake

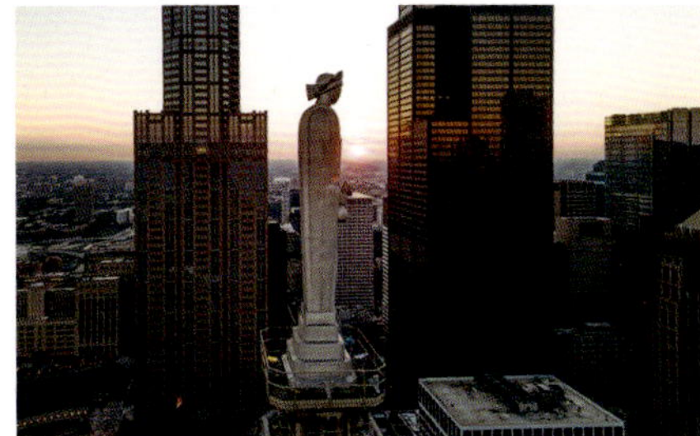

14-15 Daniel Moreno
View of Willis Tower and the Loop

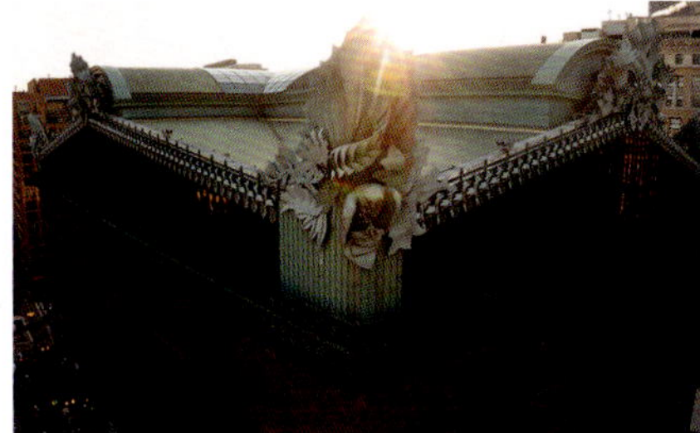

16-17 Terry Maday
View of the Harold Washington Library Center

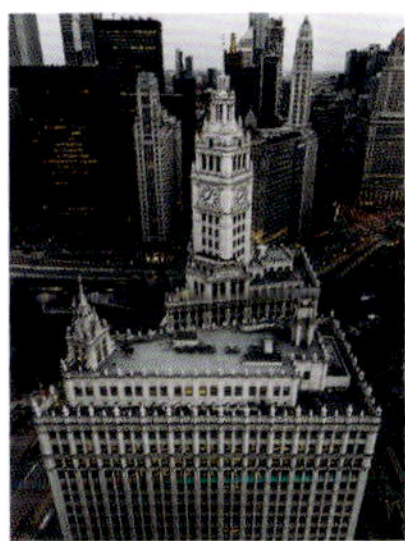

18 Max Leitner
View of the Wrigley Building

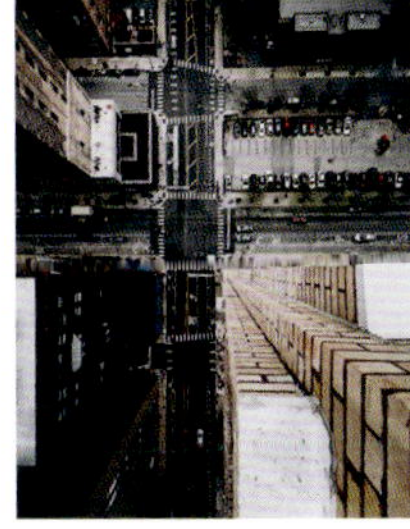

19 Max Leitner
Above West Harrison Street

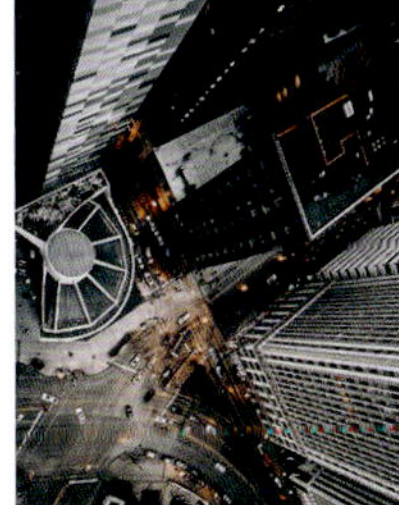

20 Alex Sheyn
Above East Wacker Drive

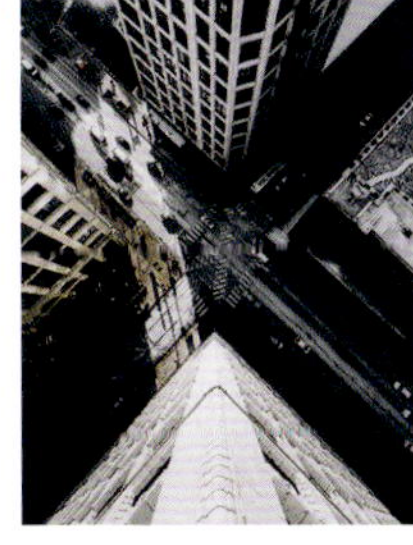

21 Max Leitner
Above West Jackson Boulevard
and South State Street

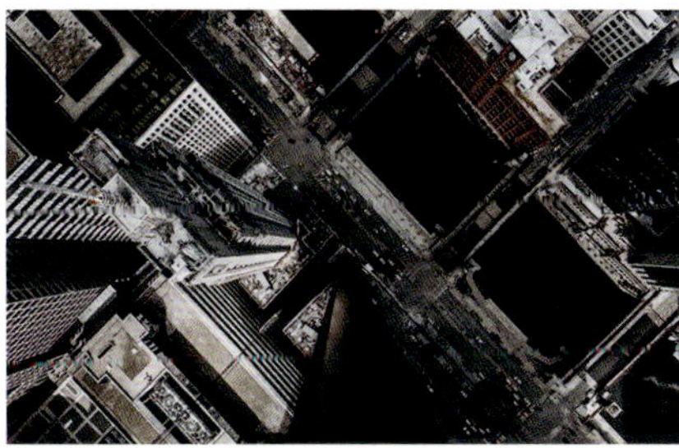

22-23 Max Leitner
Above the Chicago River and West Wacker Drive

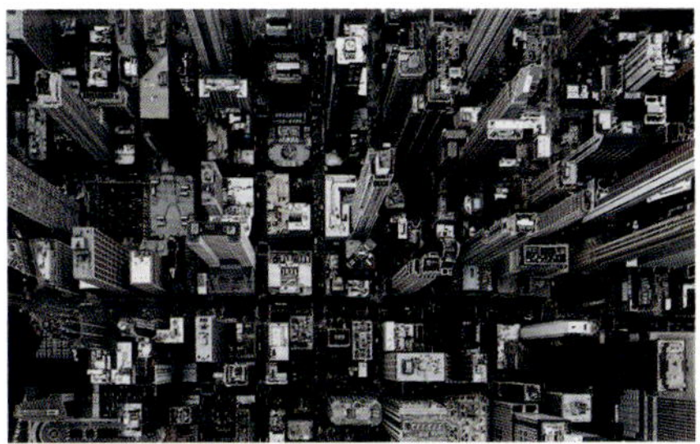

24-25 Max Leitner
Above Michigan Avenue

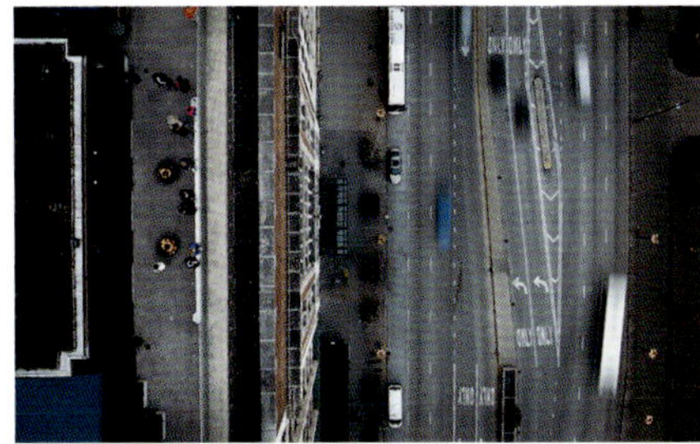

26-27 Terry Maday
Above Michigan Avenue

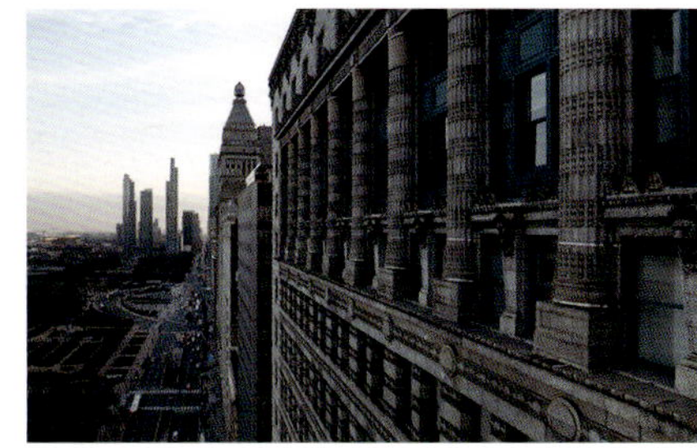

28-29 Terry Maday
View of the Peoples Gas Building

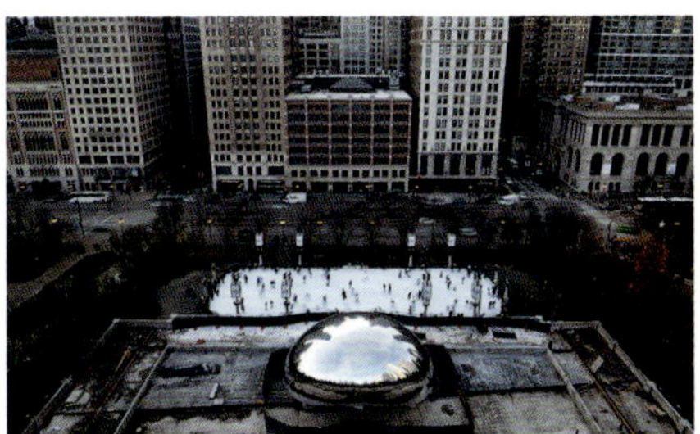

30-31 Terry Maday
View of Cloud Gate and the McCormick Tribune Plaza

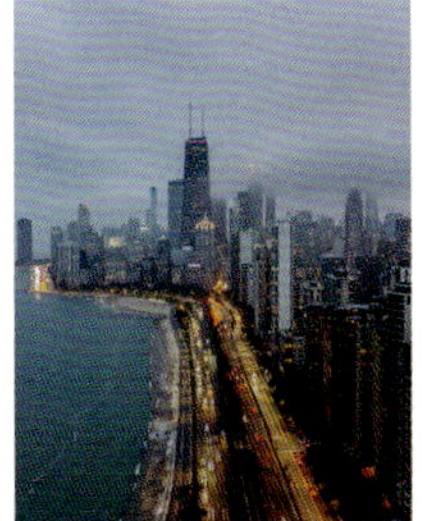

33 Daniel Schindler
View of North DuSable Lake
Shore Drive

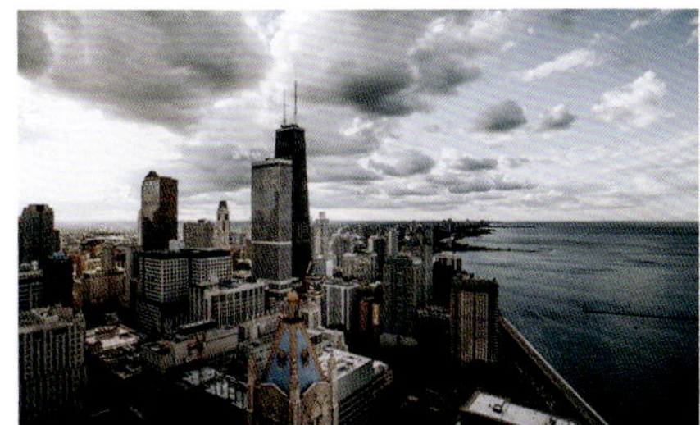

34-35 Alberto Santiago
View of Streeterville

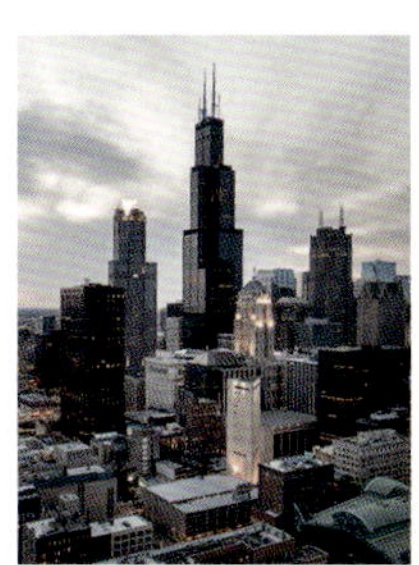

36 Jason Lumsden
View of Willis Tower and
downtown Chicago

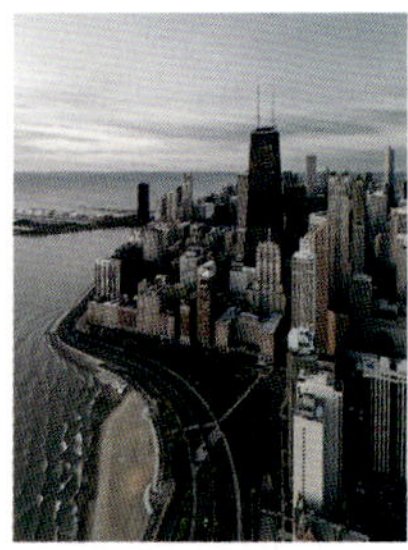

37 Jason Lumsden
View of Streeterville and North DuSable Lake Shore Drive

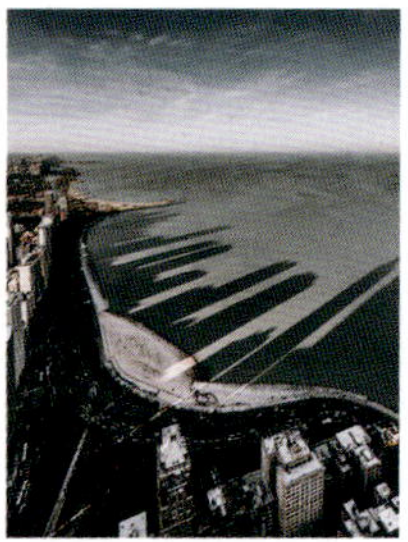

38 Nick Crawford
Above Oak Street Beach and Lake Michigan

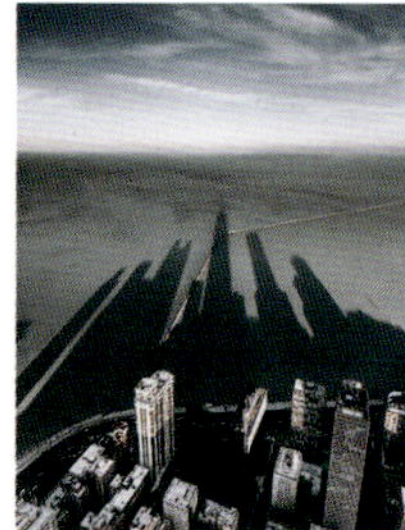

39 Nick Crawford
Above Streeterville and Lake Michigan

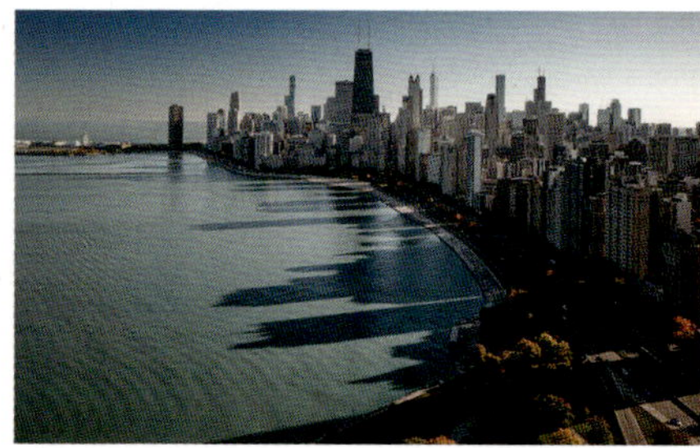

40-41 Adam Pearson
View of Lake Michigan and the Chicago skyline

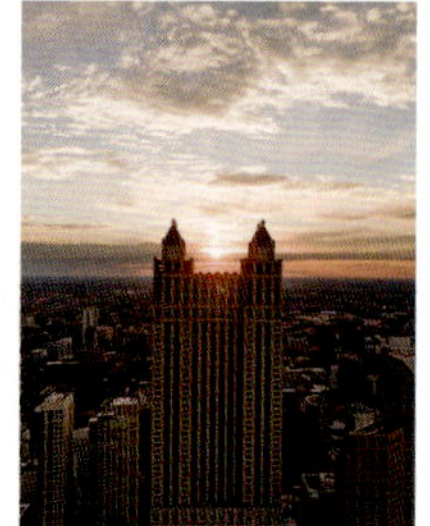

42 Daniel Moreno
View of 900 North Michigan

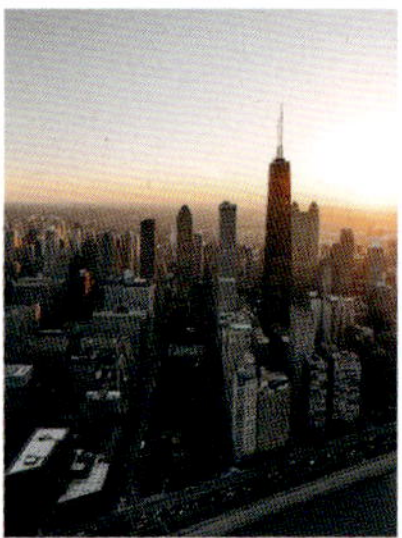

43 Sonja Weiss
View of Streeterville and the Museum of Contemporary Art Chicago

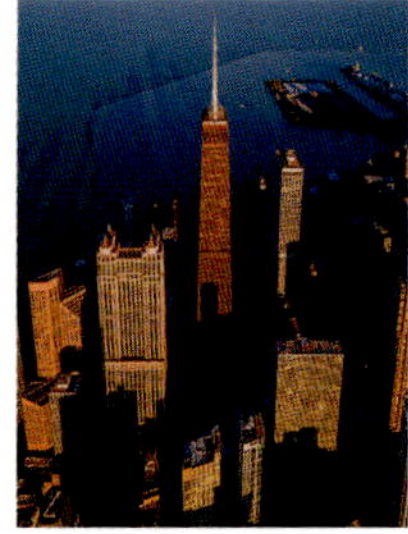

44 Daniel Moreno
View of 875 North Michigan and Streeterville

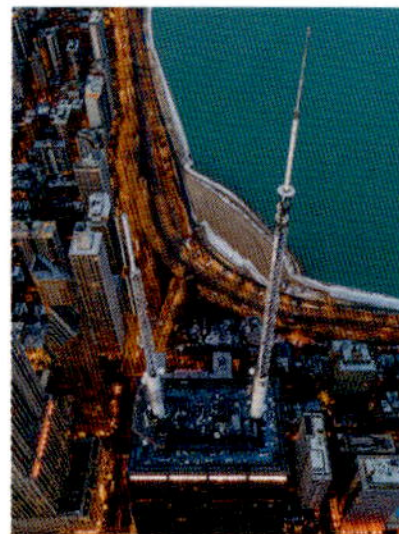

45 Daniel Moreno
Above 875 North Michigan and Oak Street Beach

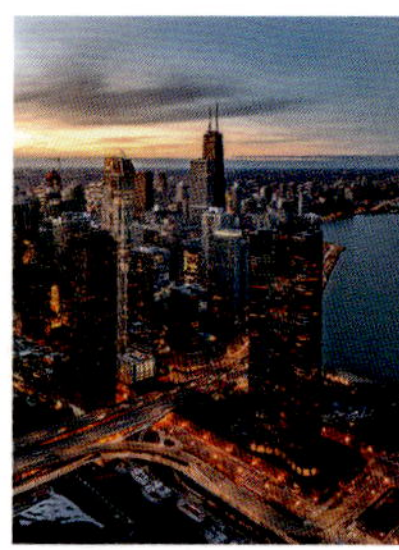

46 Jason Lumsden
View of Streeterville

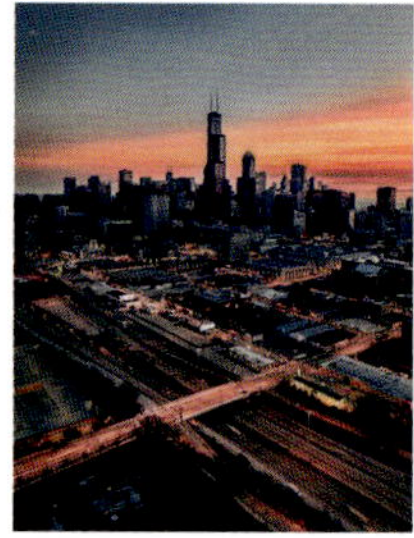

47 Jason Lumsden
View of I-90 and downtown Chicago

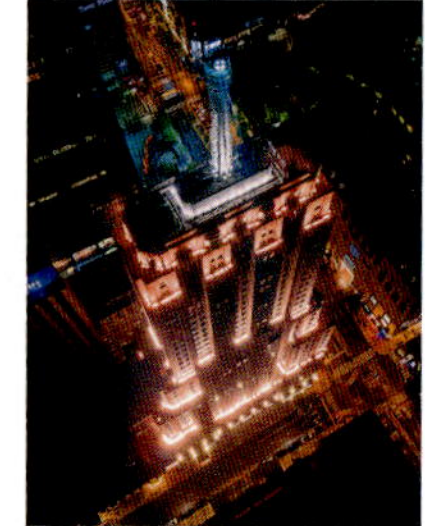

48 Daniel Moreno
Above the Palmolive Building

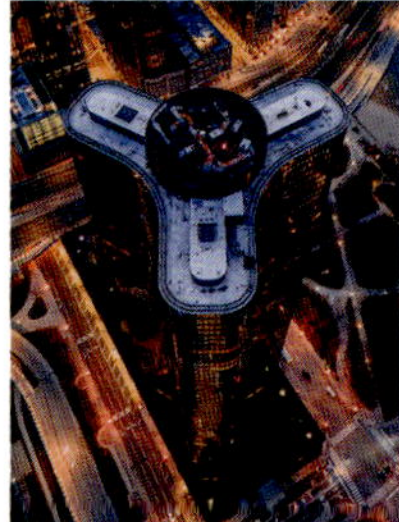

49 Daniel Moreno
Above Lake Point Tower

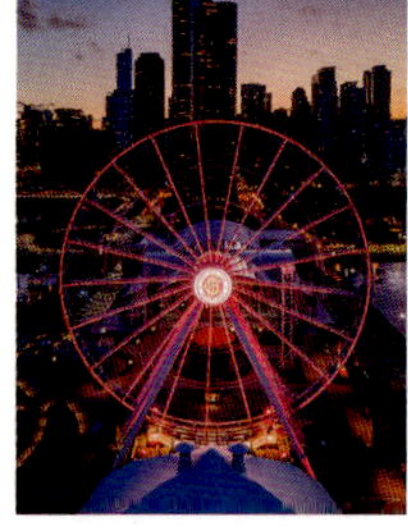

50 Daniel Moreno
View of Centennial Wheel, Navy Pier

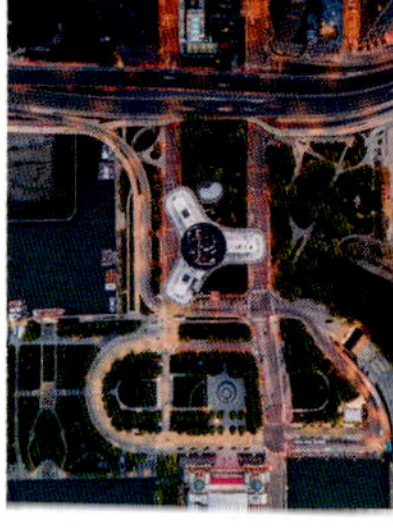

51 Daniel Moreno
Above Lake Point Tower

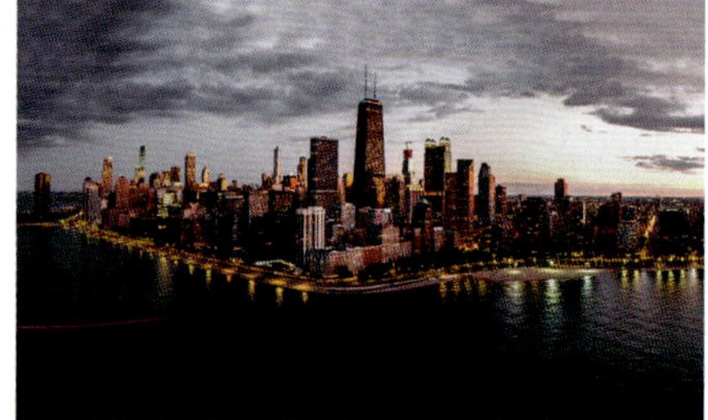

52-53 Daniel Schindler
View of the Chicago skyline

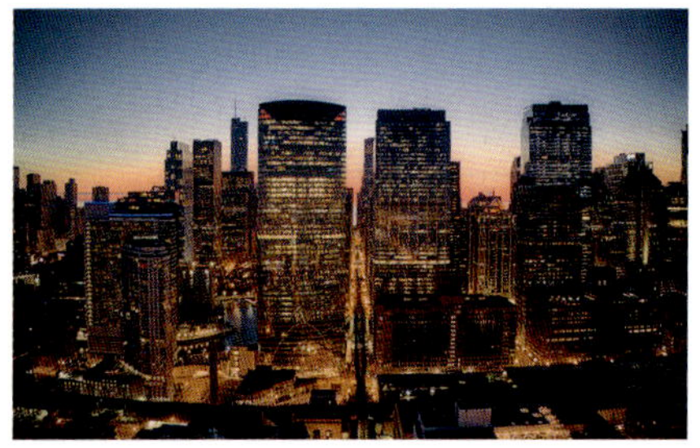

54-55 Adam Pearson
View of West Lake Street and downtown Chicago

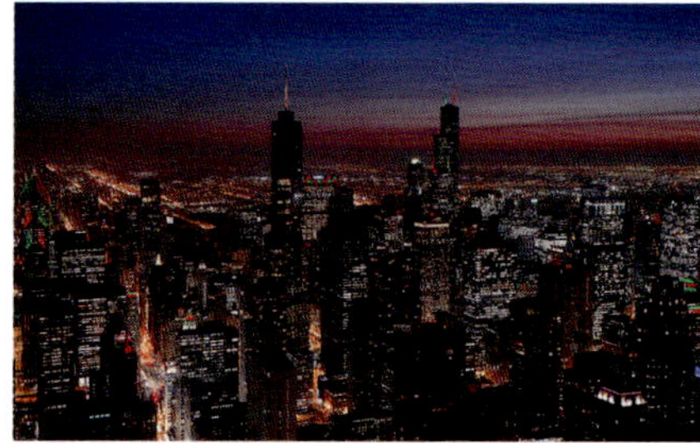

56-57 David Sowa
View of downtown Chicago

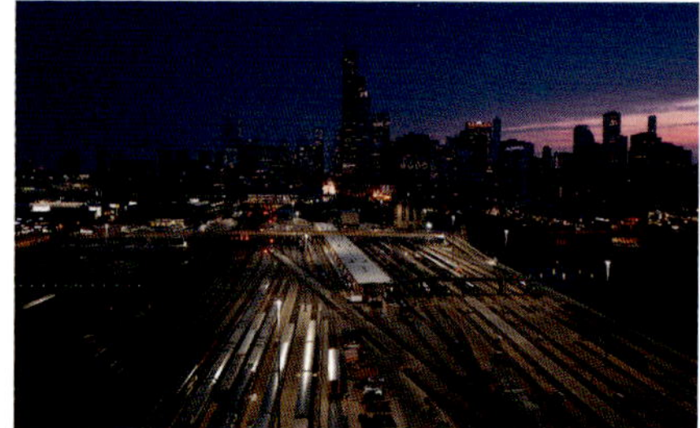

58-59 Adam Pearson
View of the Amtrak Chicago Car Yard

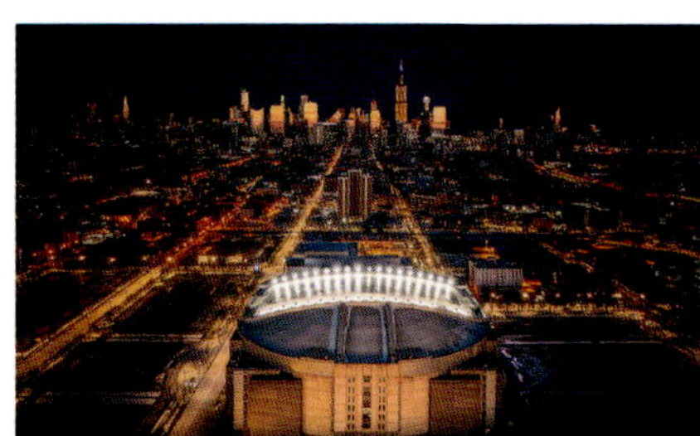

60-61 Adam Pearson
View of the United Center

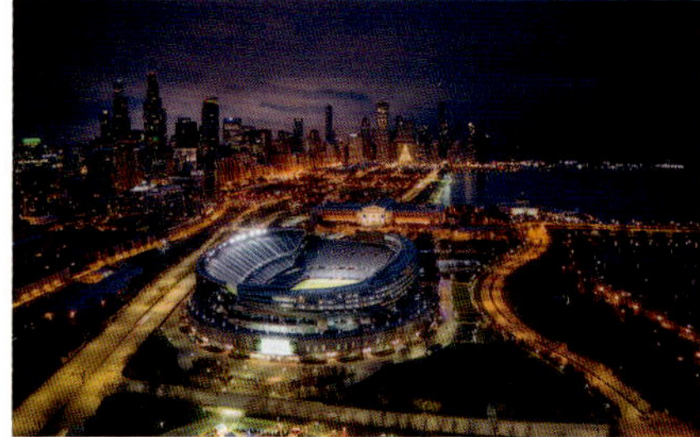

62-63 Adam Pearson
View of Soldier Field

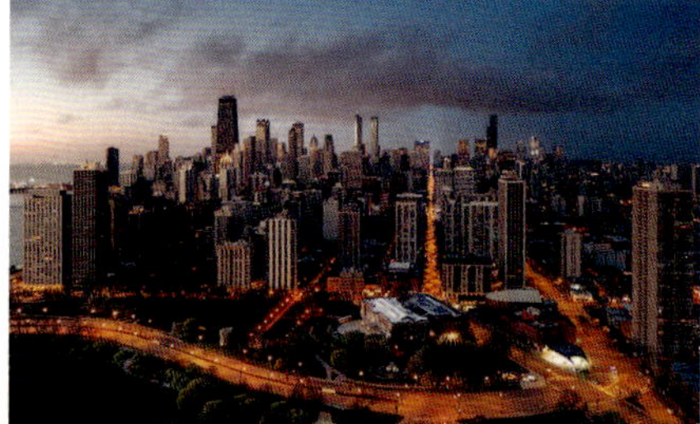

64-65 Adam Pearson
View of the Chicago History Museum and Gold Coast

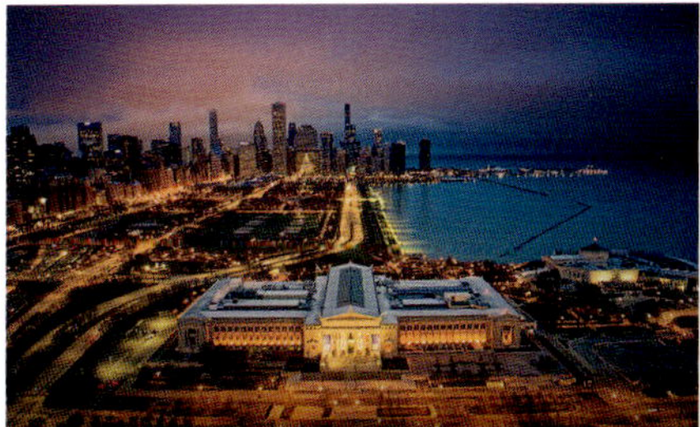

66-67 Adam Pearson
View of the Field Museum

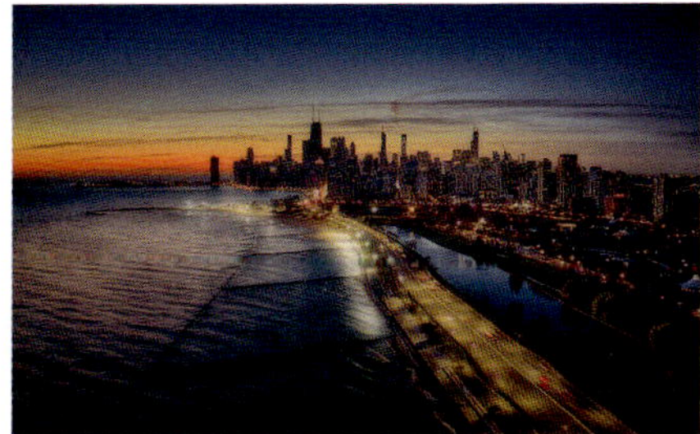

68-69 Adam Pearson
View of Lincoln Park Zoo and the Chicago skyline

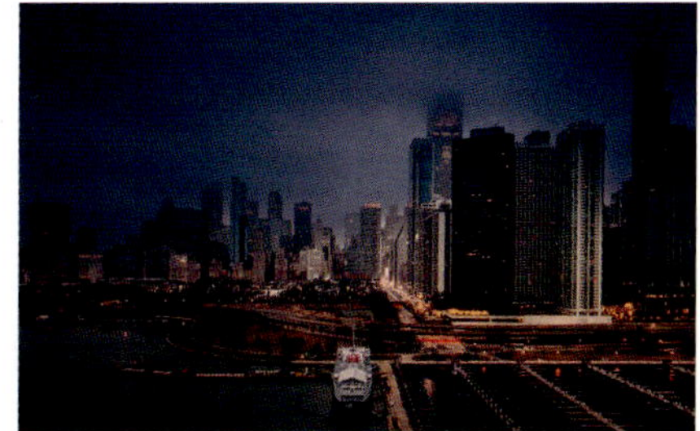

70-71 Adam Pearson
View of DuSable Harbor and East Randolph Street

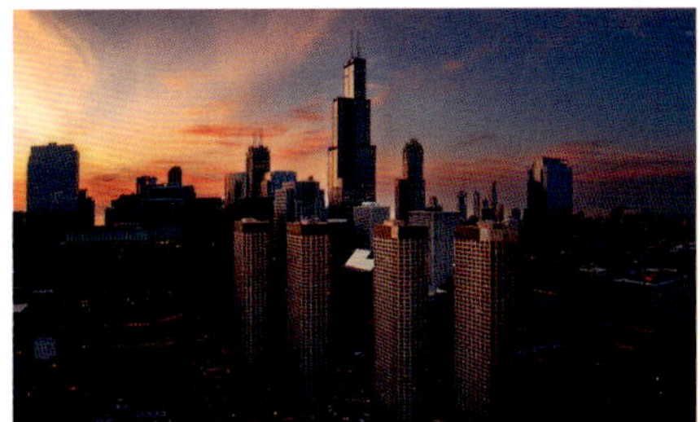

72-73 Adam Pearson
View of the Presidential Towers

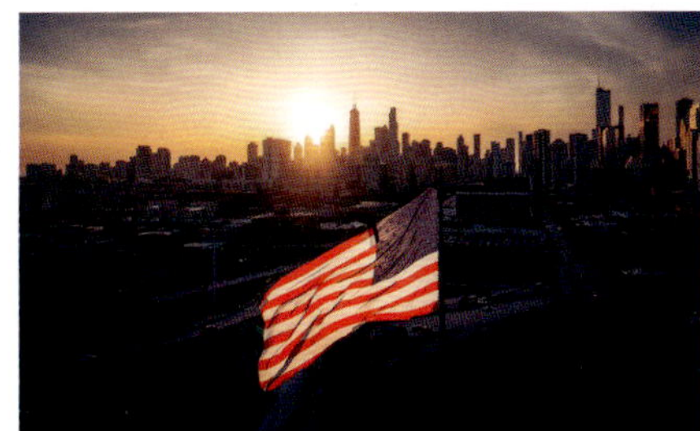

74-75 Adam Pearson
View of the Chicago skyline

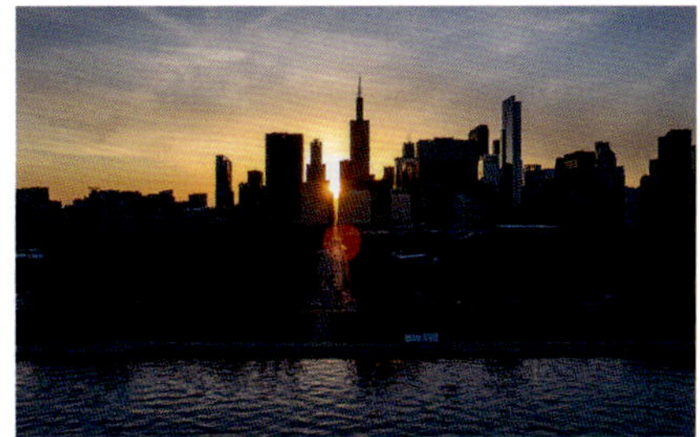

76-77 Dominika Brzykcy
View of East Jackson Boulevard

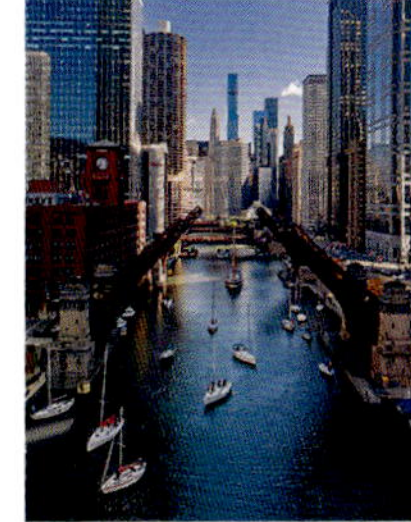

79 Daniel Moreno
View of the Chicago River and
North LaSalle Drive Bridge

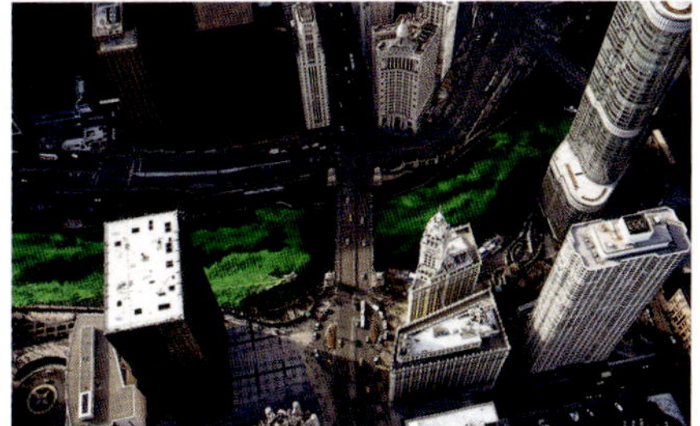

80-81 David Sowa
Above the Chicago River and DuSable Bridge

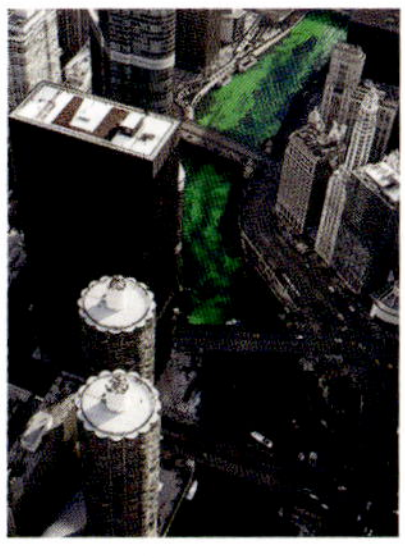

82 David Sowa
Above the Chicago River

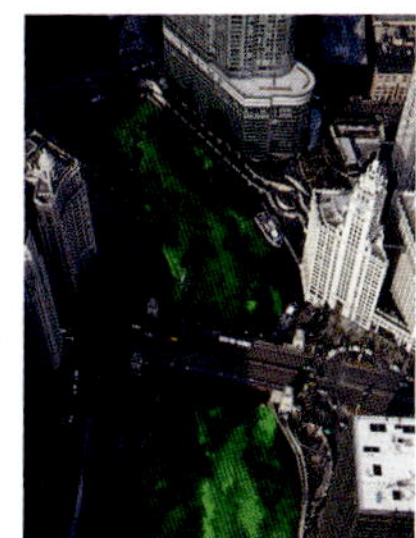

83 David Sowa
Above the Chicago River and
DuSable Bridge

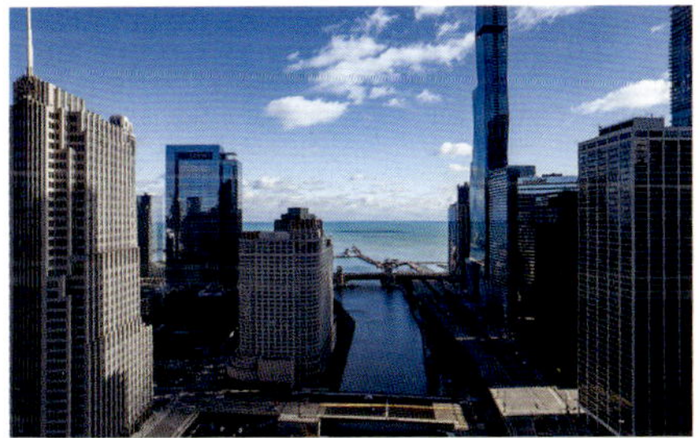

84-85 Dominika Brzykcy
View of the Chicago River and Lake Michigan

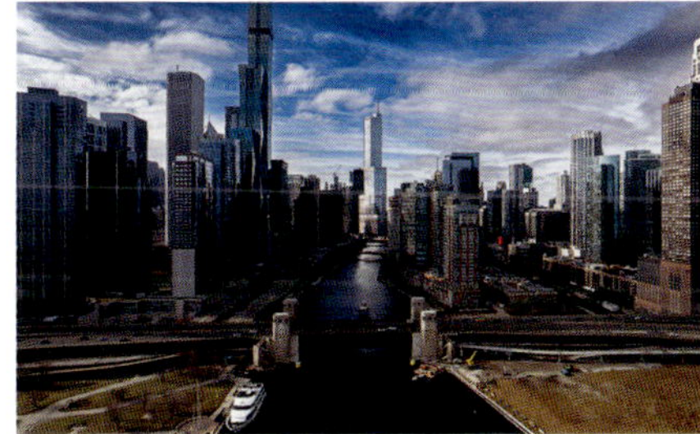

86-87 Dominika Brzykcy
View of the Chicago River and North DuSable Lake Shore Drive

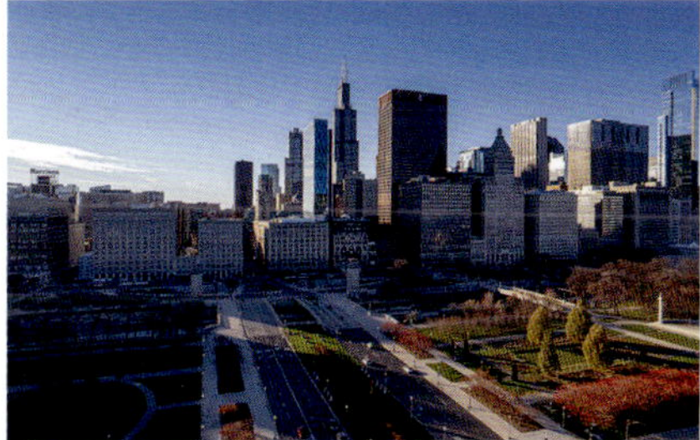

88-89 Dominika Brzykcy
View of East Ida B. Wells Drive and Michigan Avenue

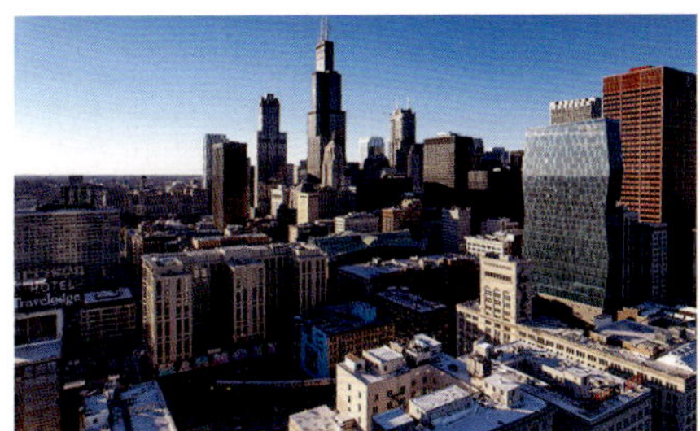

90-91 Dominika Brzykcy
View of the Loop

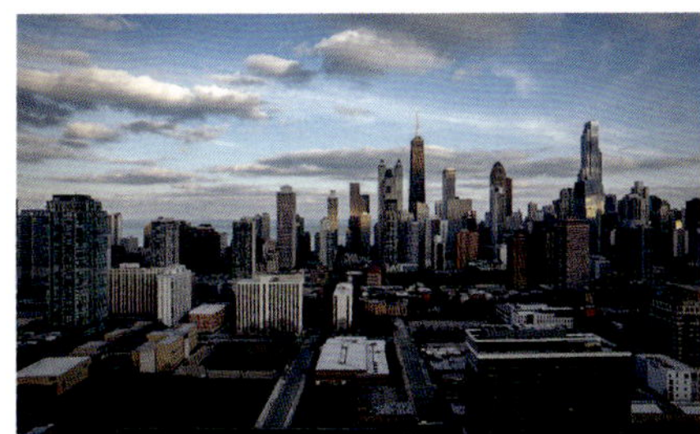

92-93 Dominika Brzykcy
View of West Oak Street and the Chicago skyline

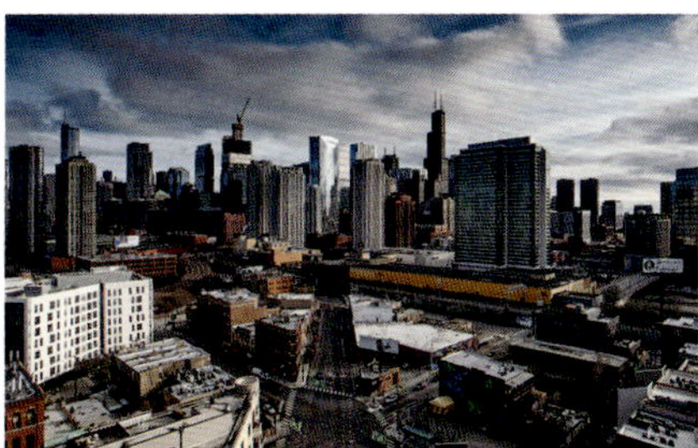

94-95 Dominika Brzykcy
View of North Halsted Street

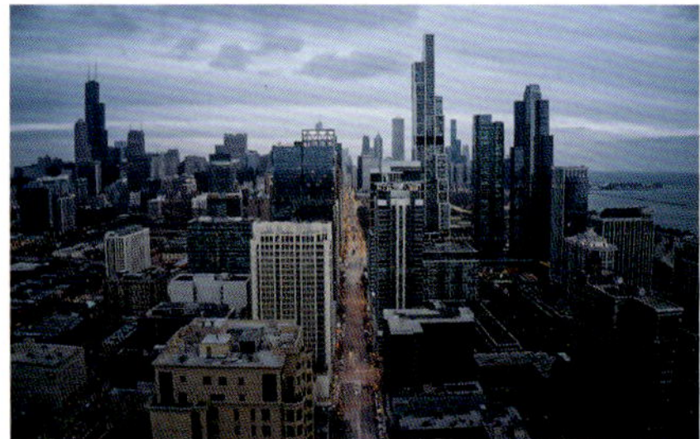

96-97 Adam Pearson
View of South Michigan Avenue

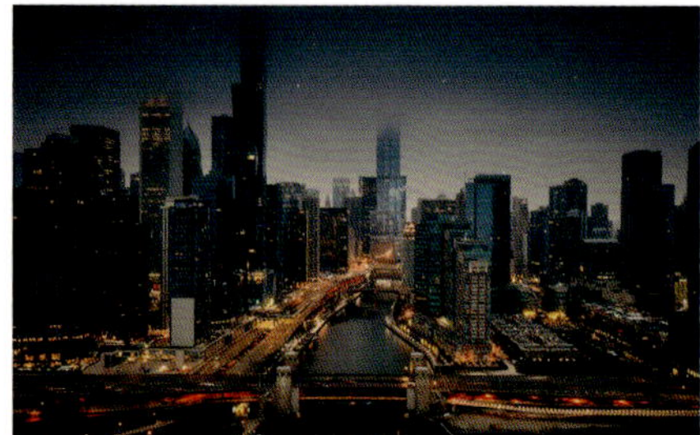

98-99 Adam Pearson
View of the Chicago River and North DuSable Lake Shore Drive

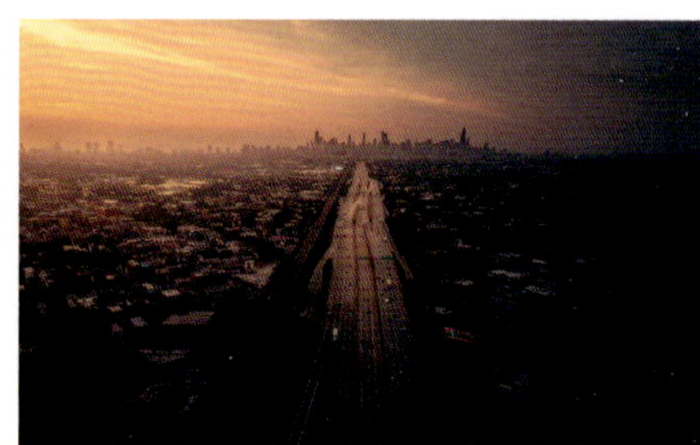

100-101 Adam Pearson
View of the Chicago skyline

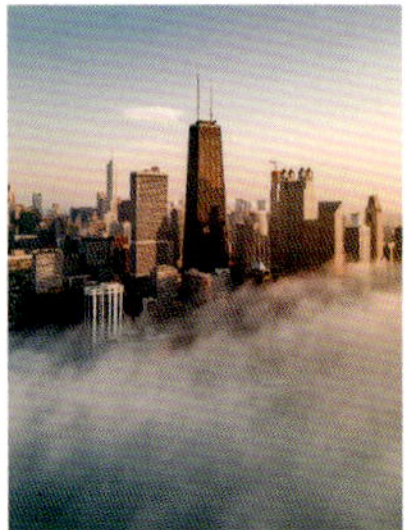

103 Daniel Moreno
View of 875 North Michigan
and Streeterville

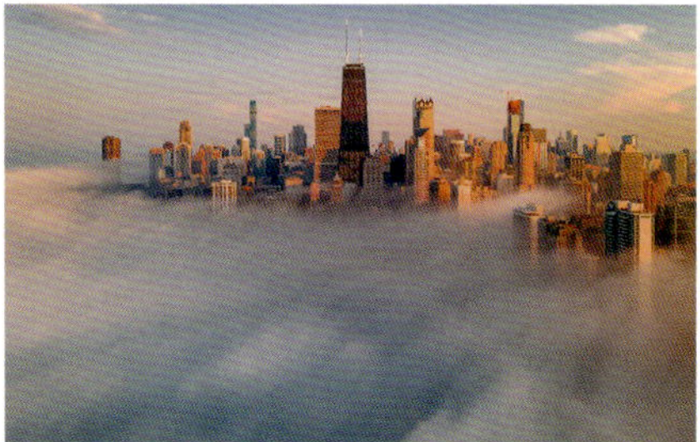

104-105 Daniel Moreno
View of the Chicago skyline

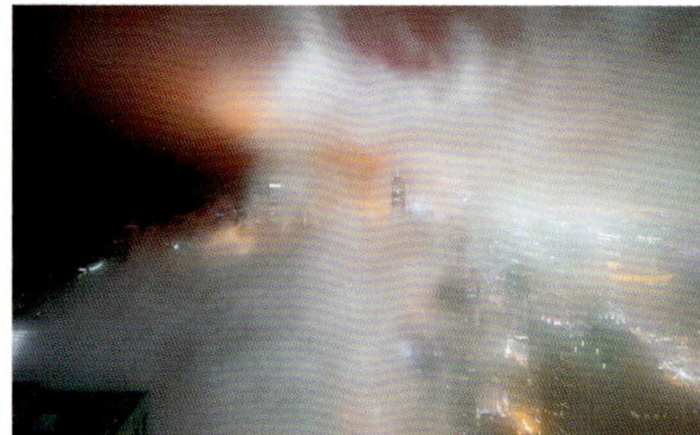

106-107 David Sowa
Above downtown Chicago

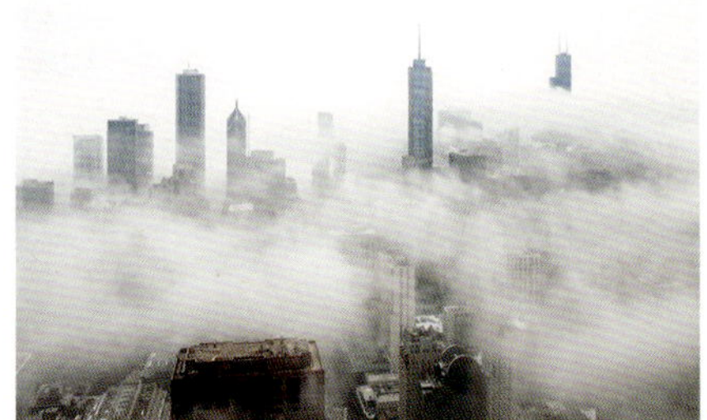

108-109 David Sowa
View of downtown Chicago

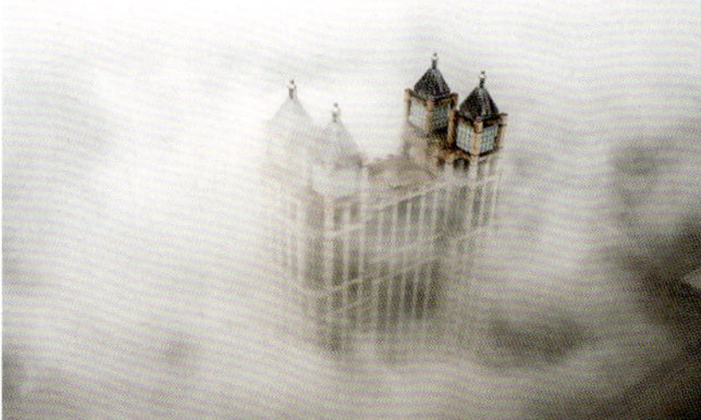

110-111 David Sowa
Above 900 North Michigan

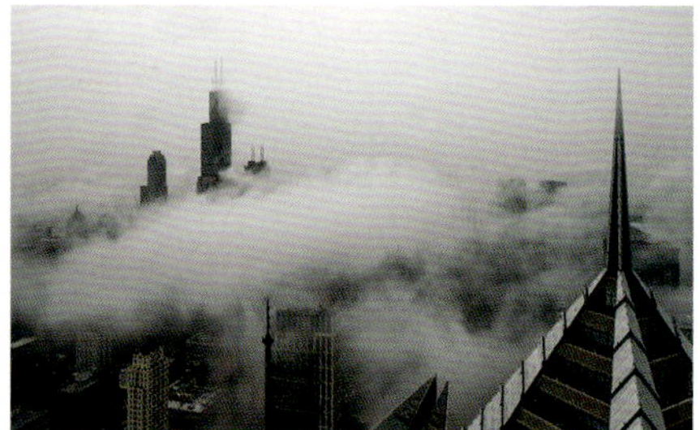

112-113 Kwe Bentum
Above downtown Chicago

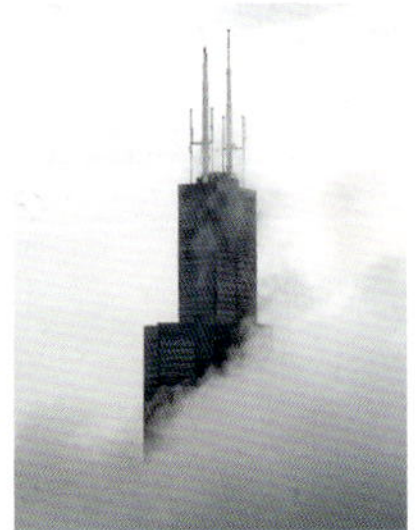

114 Kwe Bentum
View of Willis Tower

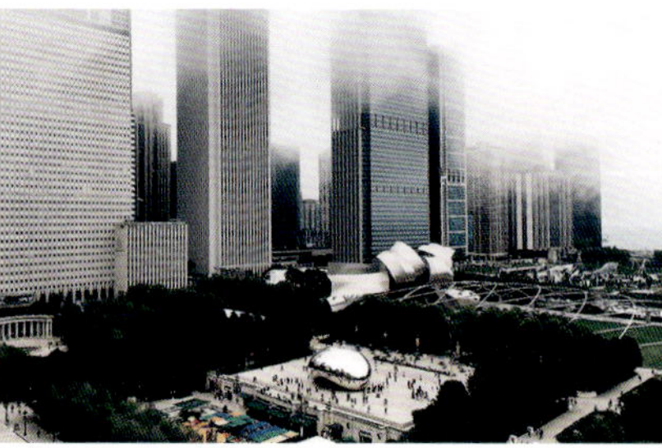

115 Cocu Liu
View of Cloud Gate and Millennium Park

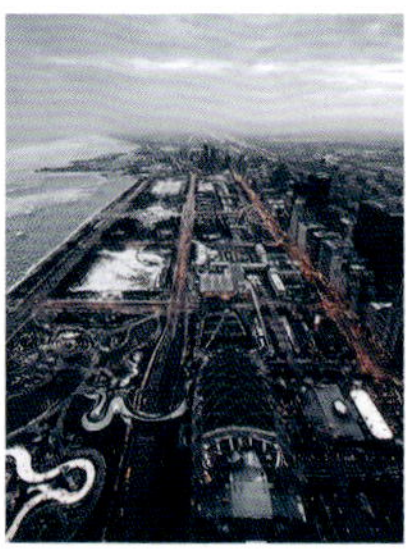

116 Max Leitner
Above Millennium Park and
Grant Park

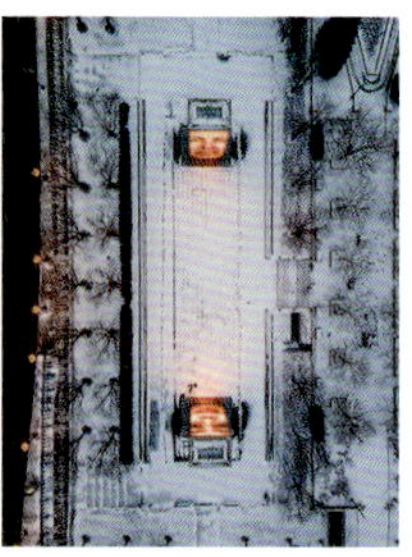

117 Daniel Moreno
Above Crown Fountain,
Millennium Park

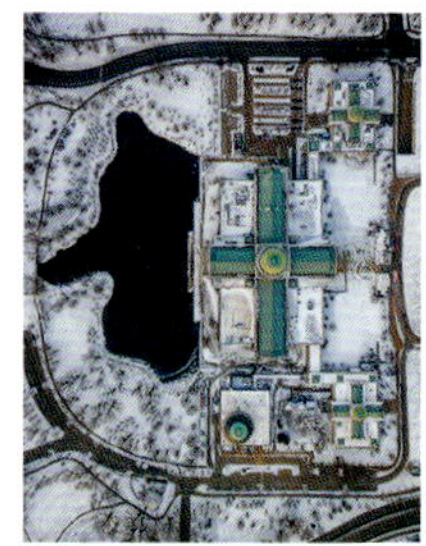

118 Daniel Moreno
Above the Griffin Museum of
Science and Industry

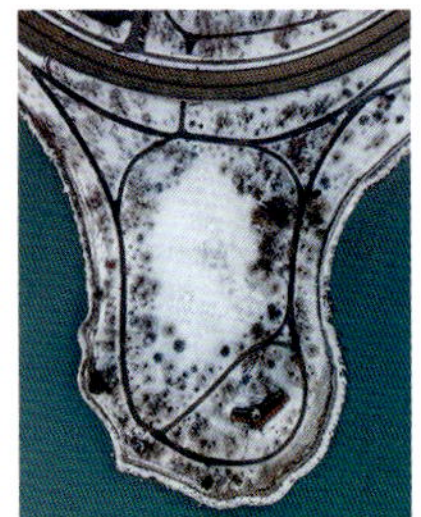

119 Daniel Moreno
Above Burnham Park
Promontory Point

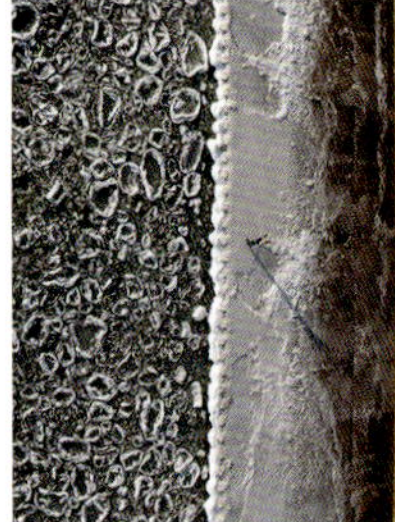

120 Dominika Brzykcy
Above Lake Michigan

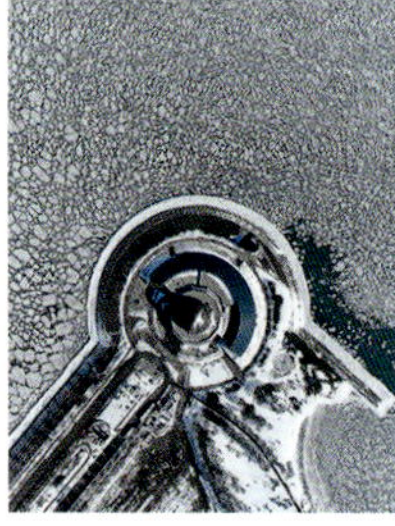

121 David Sowa
Above the Adler Planetarium

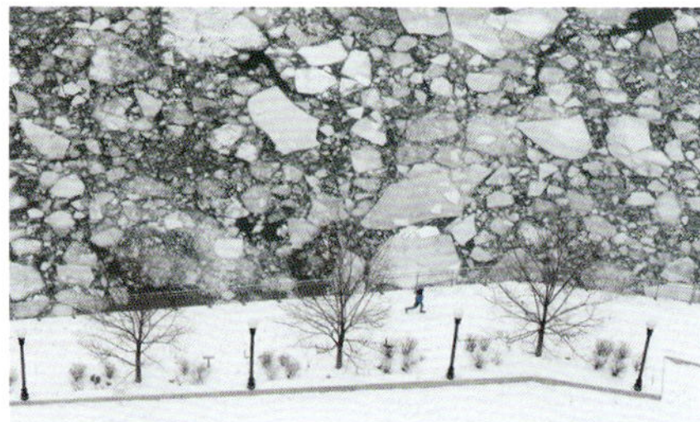

122-123 David Sowa
Above Lake Michigan

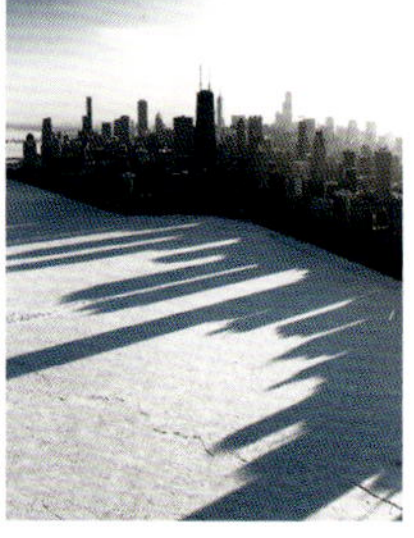

124 Jason Lumsden
View of the Chicago skyline

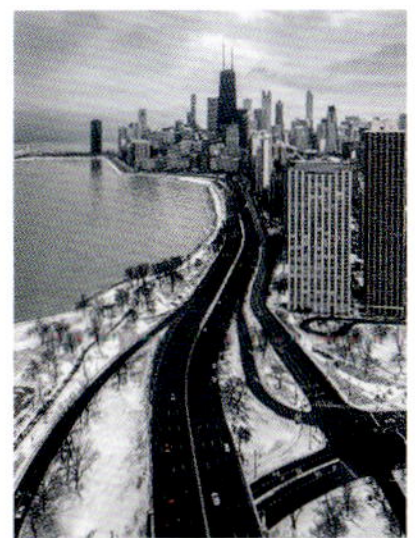
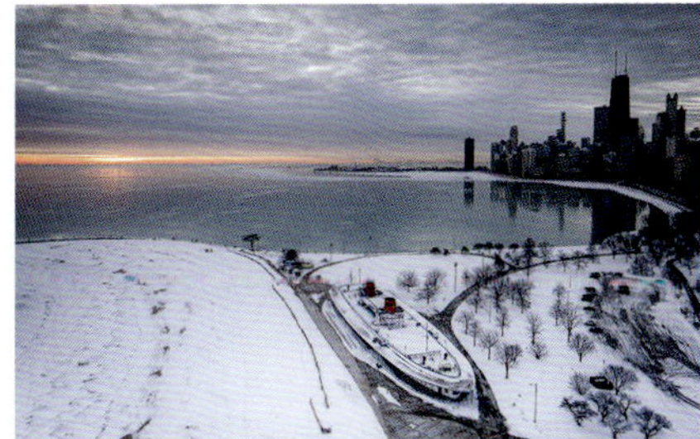
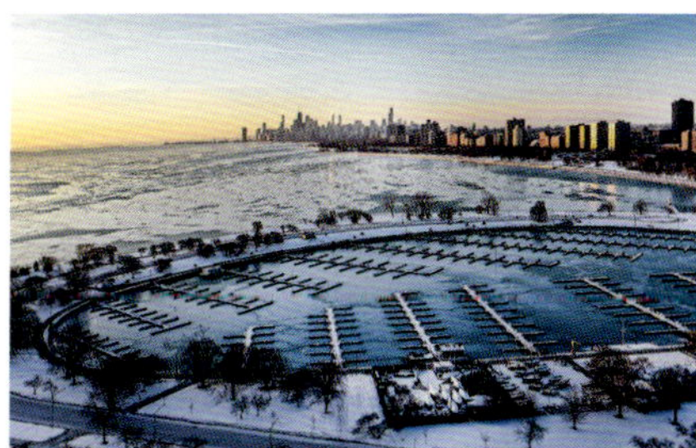

125 Jason Lumsden
View of North DuSable Lake Shore Drive

126-127 Dominika Brzykcy
View of North Avenue Beach and Lake Michigan

128-129 Lichao Liu
View of Montrose Harbor

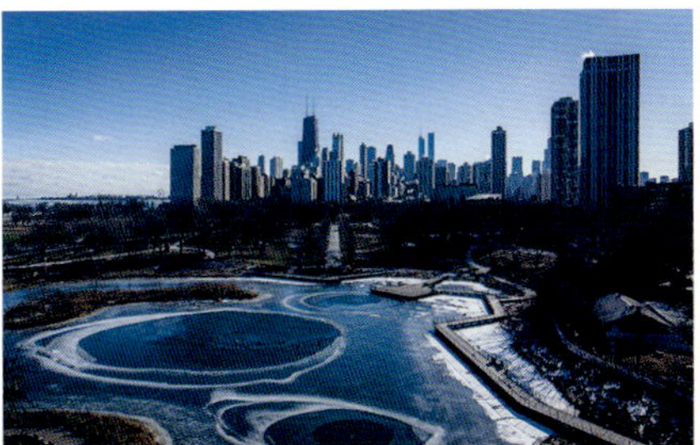
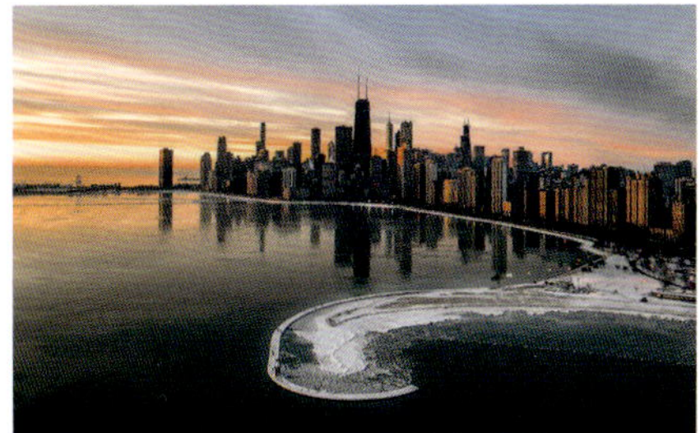
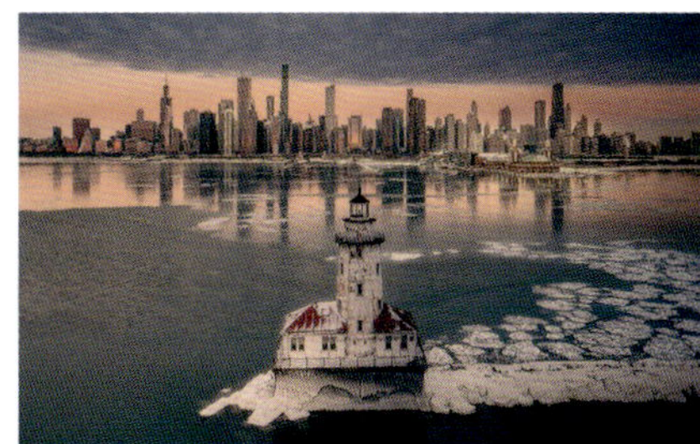

130-131 Dominika Brzykcy
View of the Lincoln Park Zoo South Pond

132-133 Jason Lumsden
View of North Avenue Beach and the Chicago skyline

134-135 Adam Pearson
View of the Chicago Harbor Lighthouse

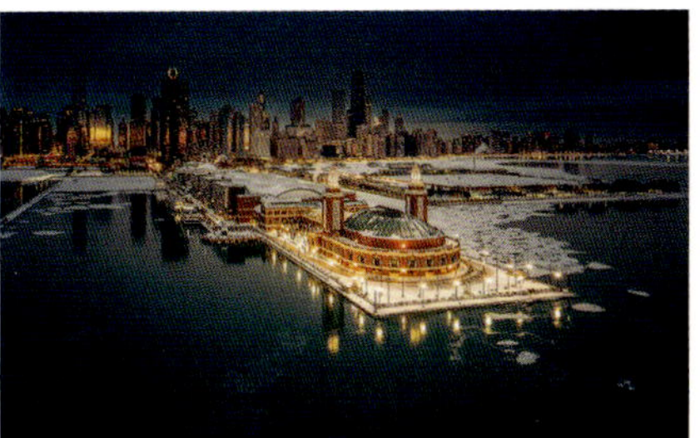
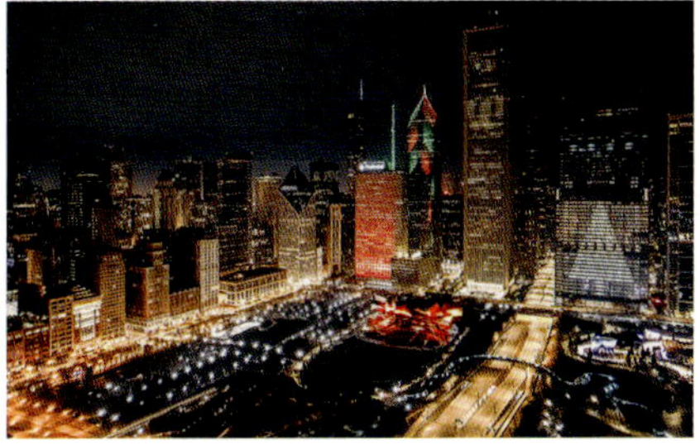
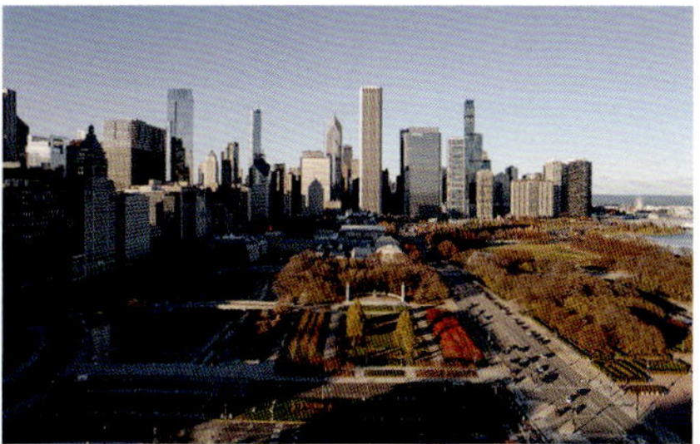

136-137 Adam Pearson
View of Navy Pier

138-139 Dominika Brzykcy
View of Millennium Park

140-141 Dominika Brzykcy
View of The Art Institute of Chicago and Grant Park

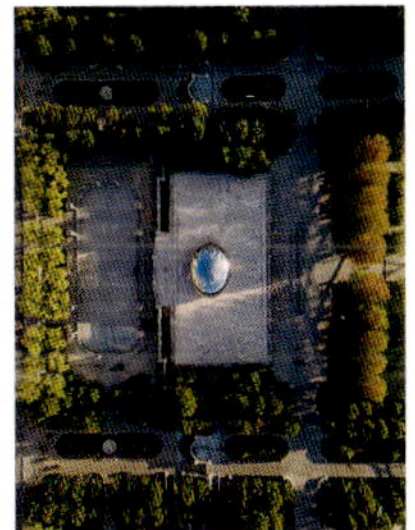
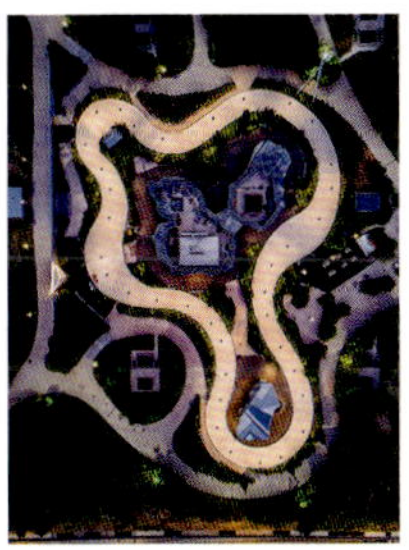
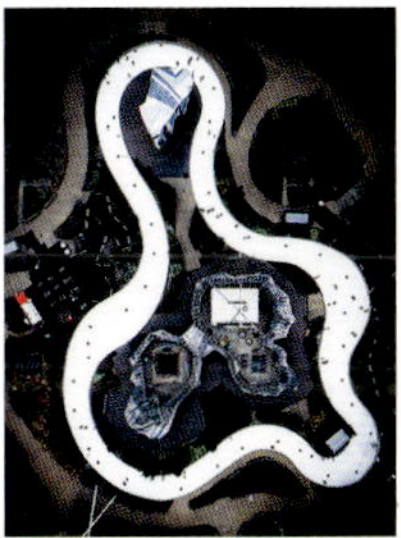
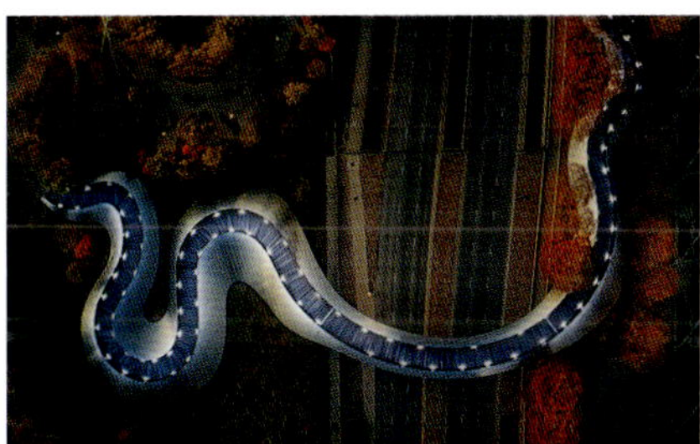
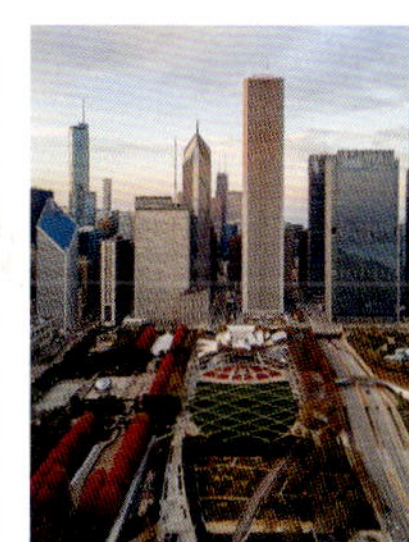

142 Daniel Moreno
Above Cloud Gate

144 Daniel Moreno
Above the Maggie Daley Park Ice Skating Ribbon

145 Dominika Brzykcy
Above the Maggie Daley Park Ice Skating Ribbon

146-147 Adam Pearson
Above the BP Pedestrian Bridge

148 Daniel Moreno
View of Millennium Park

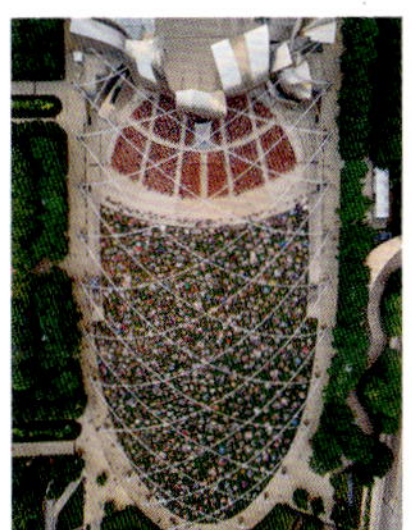
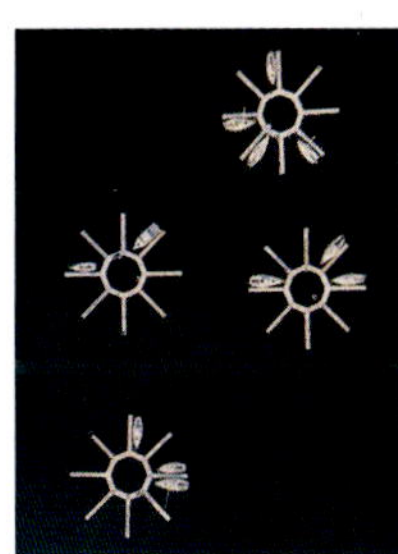
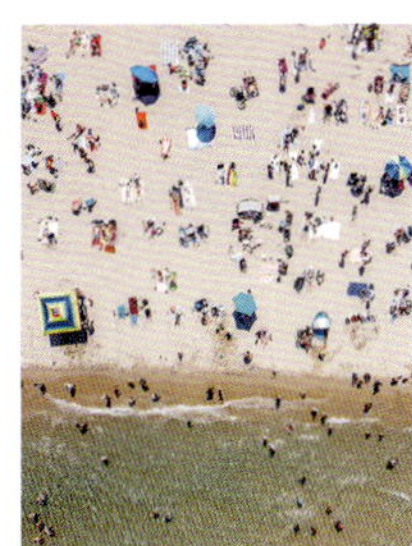
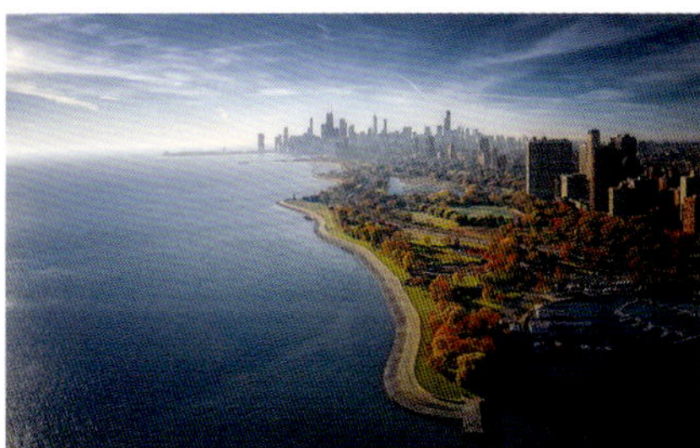

149 Daniel Moreno
Above the Jay Pritzker Pavilion

150 Daniel Moreno
Above Montrose Harbor

151 Daniel Schindler
Above North Avenue Beach

152-153 Adam Pearson
View of the Chicago Yacht Club and Diversey Harbor

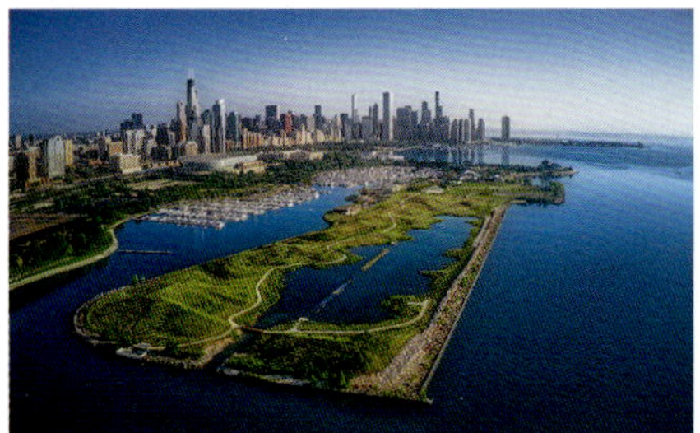

154-155 Adam Pearson
View of Northerly Island Park and downtown Chicago

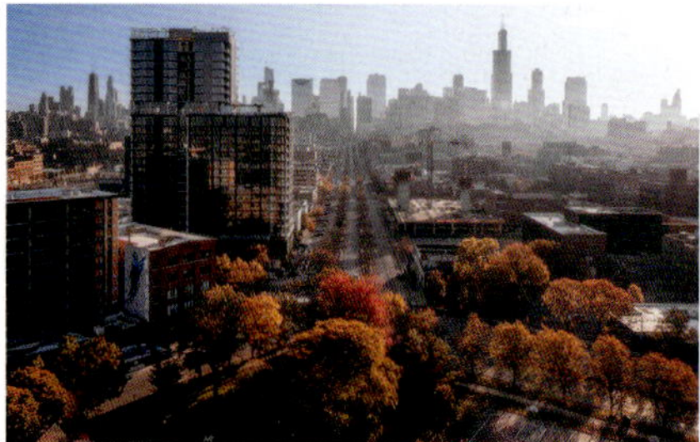

156-157 Adam Pearson
View of West Randolph Street

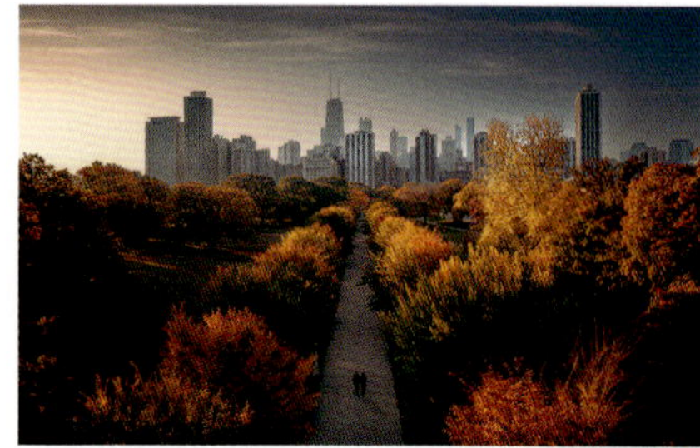

158-159 Adam Pearson
View of Lincoln Park

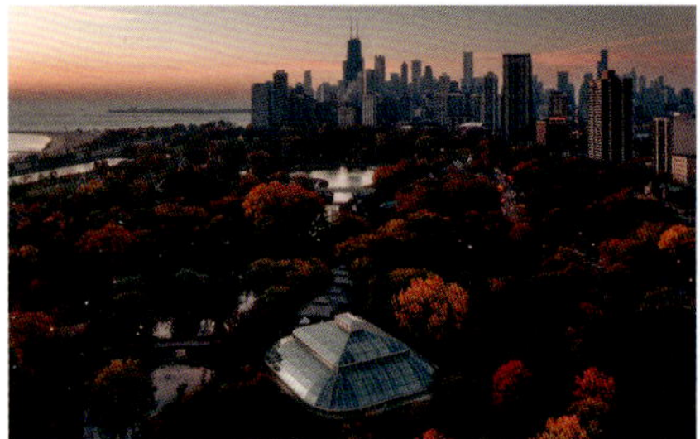

160-161 Adam Pearson
View of Lincoln Park Zoo

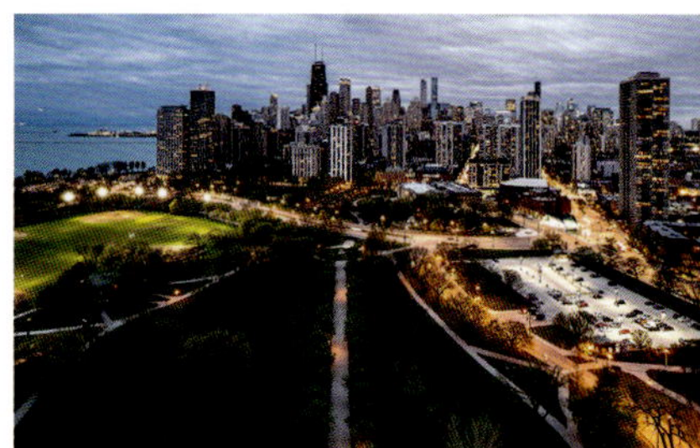

162-163 Dominika Brzykcy
View of Lincoln Park and Streeterville

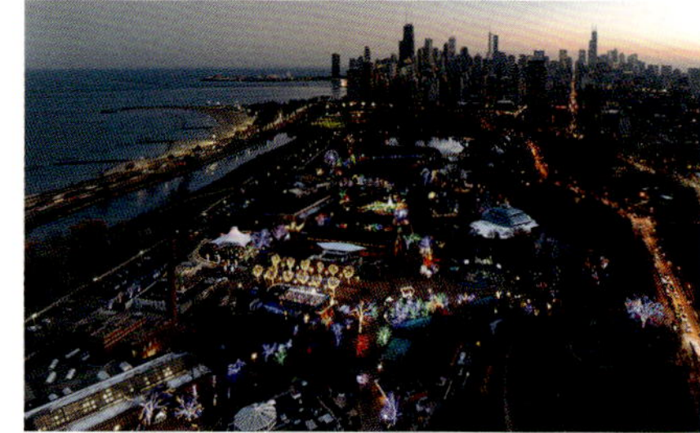

164-165 Terry Maday
View of Lincoln Park Zoo

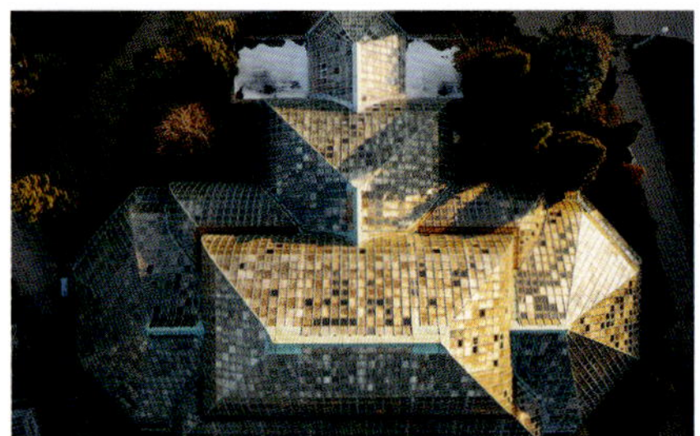

166-167 Terry Maday
Above Lincoln Park Conservatory

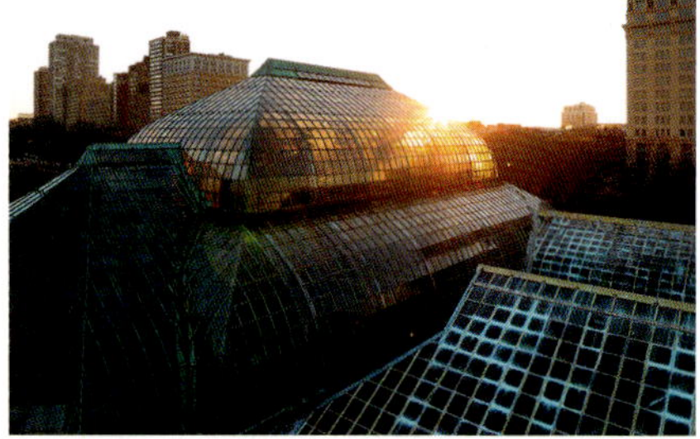

168-169 Terry Maday
View of Lincoln Park Conservatory

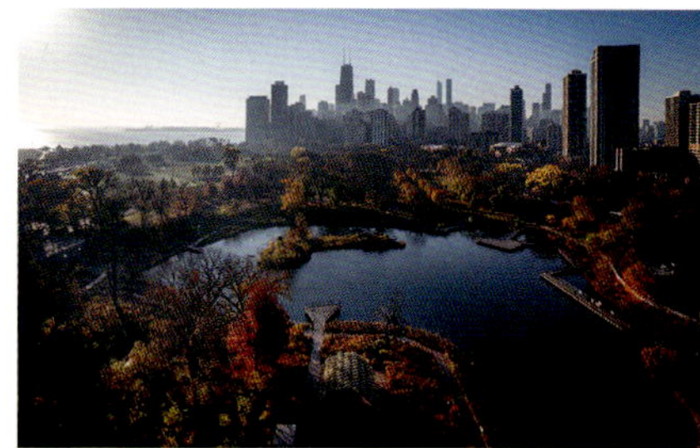

170-171 Dominika Brzykcy
View of Lincoln Park South Pond

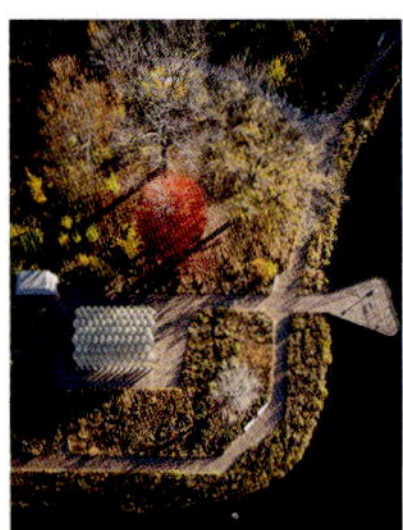

172 Dominika Brzykcy
Above Peoples Gas Pavilion

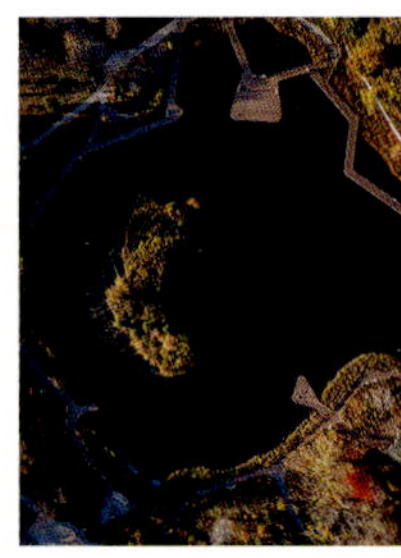

173 Dominika Brzykcy
Above Lincoln Park South Pond

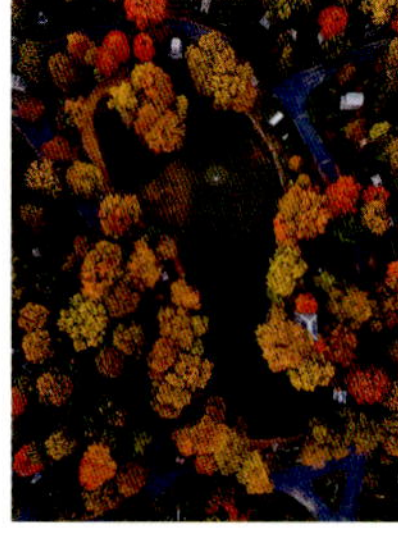

174 Daniel Morneo
Above Graceland Cemetery

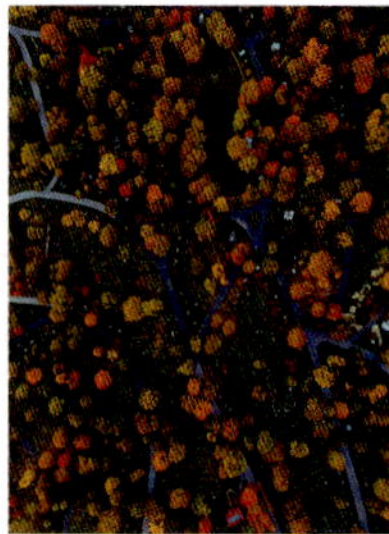

175 Daniel Morneo
Above Graceland Cemetery

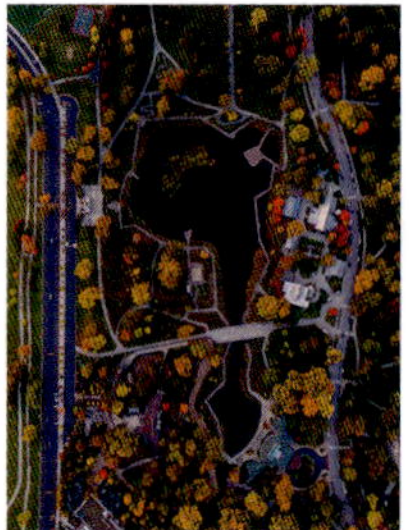

176 Daniel Morneo
Above Lincoln Park South Pond

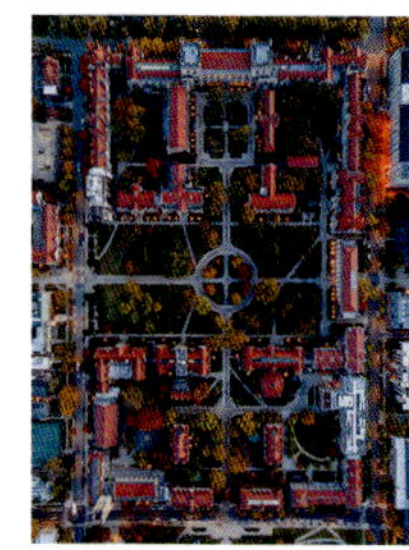

177 Daniel Morneo
Above the University of Chicago

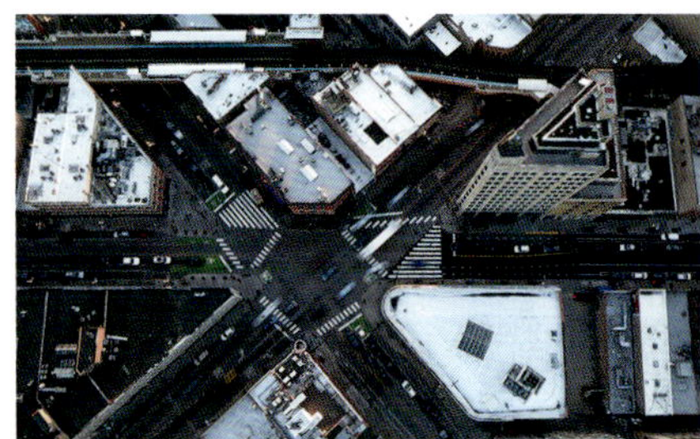

178-179 Terry Maday
Above Wicker Park Six Corners

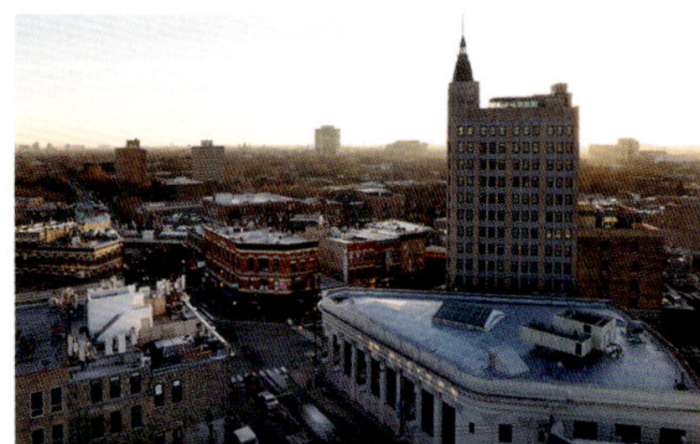

180-181 Terry Maday
View of Wicker Park Six Corners

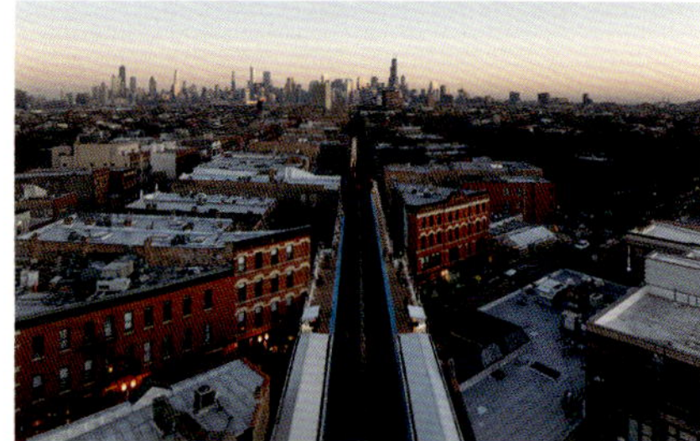

182-183 Terry Maday
View of the Damen CTA station

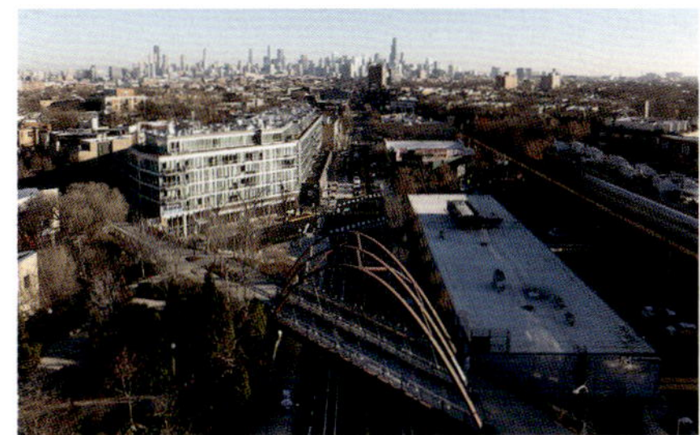

184 Terry Maday
View of North Milwaukee Avenue and the Bloomingdale Trail

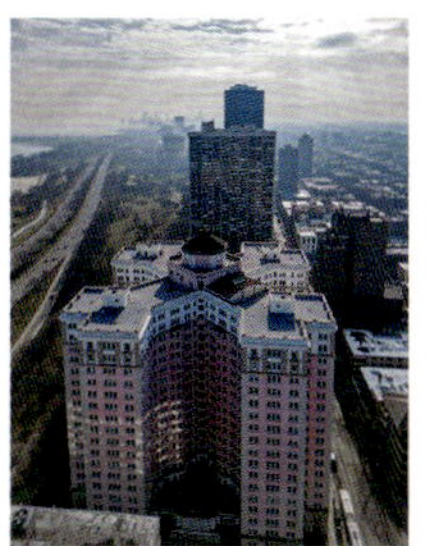

185 Daniel Schindler
View of 5555 North Sheridan Road

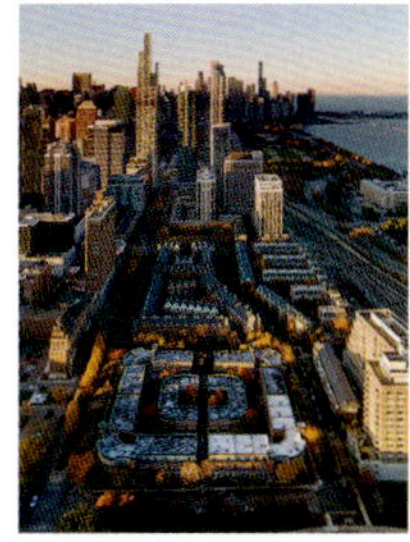

186 Daniel Moreno
Above South Prairie Avenue

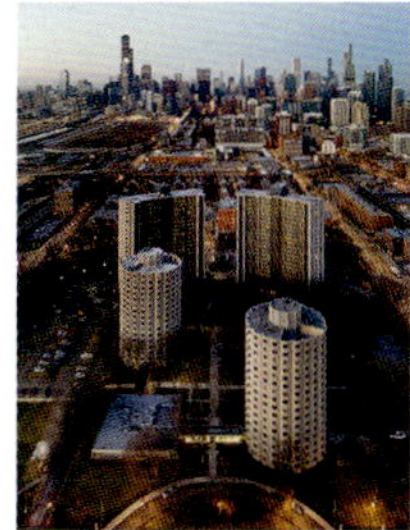

187 Daniel Moreno
View of the Hilliard Apartments

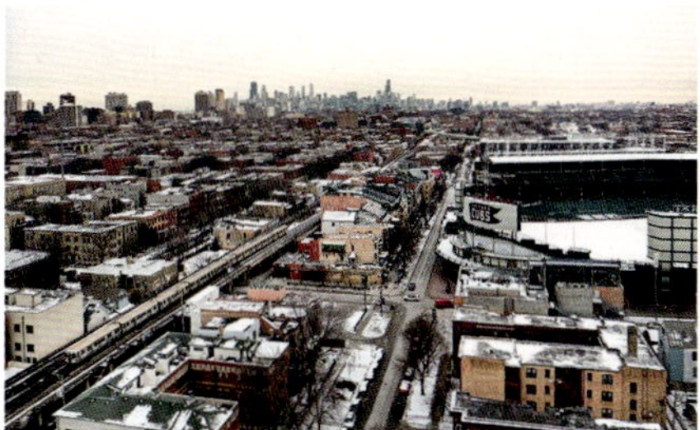

188-189 Lichao Liu
View of Wrigleyville

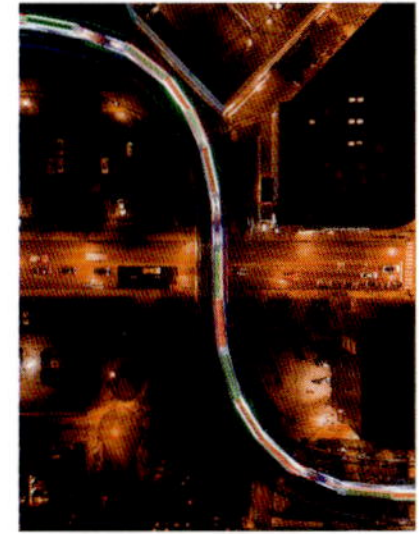

190 Daniel Moreno
Above the CTA train

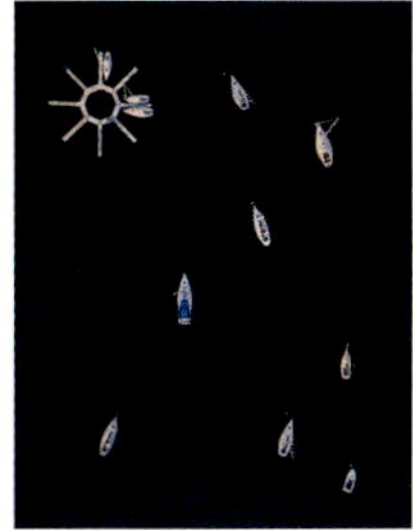

192 Daniel Moreno
Above Montrose Harbor

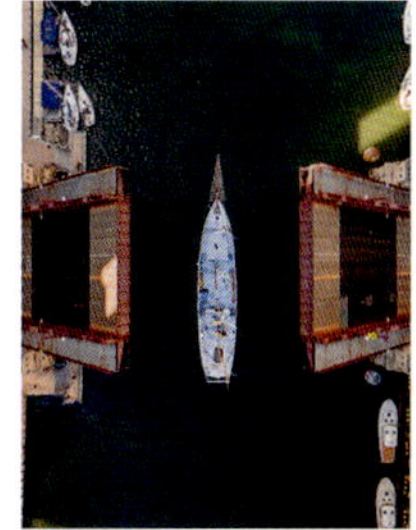

200 Daniel Moreno
Above the Chicago River

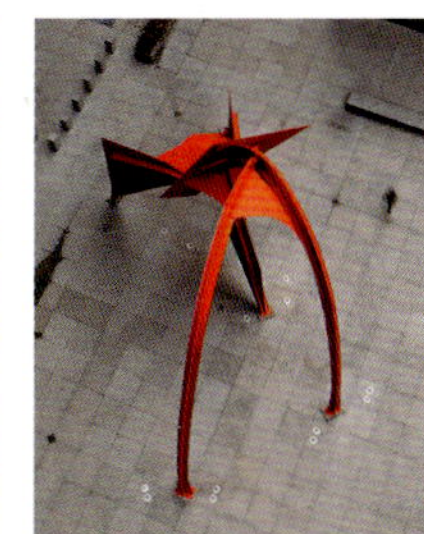

202 Terry Maday
View of Calder's Flamingo

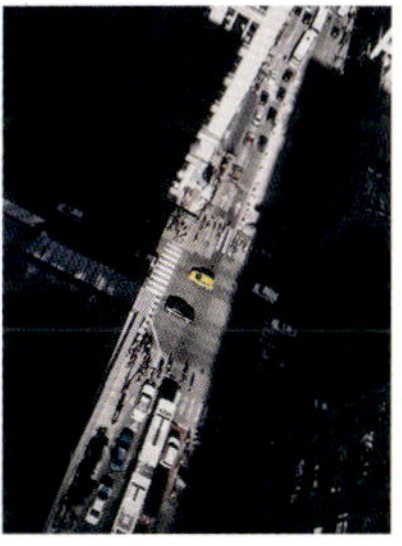

204 Cocu Liu
Above North State Street and East Washington Street

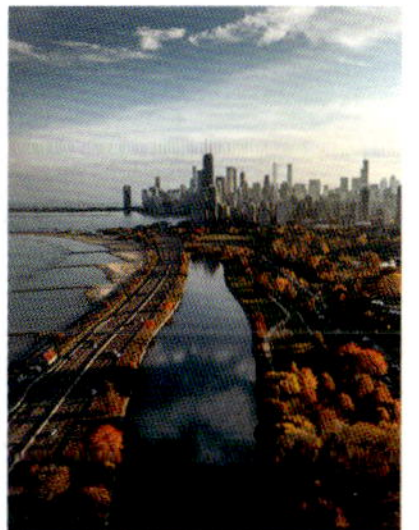

Back Cover Jason Lumsden
View of Lincoln Park South Lagoon and the Chicago skyline

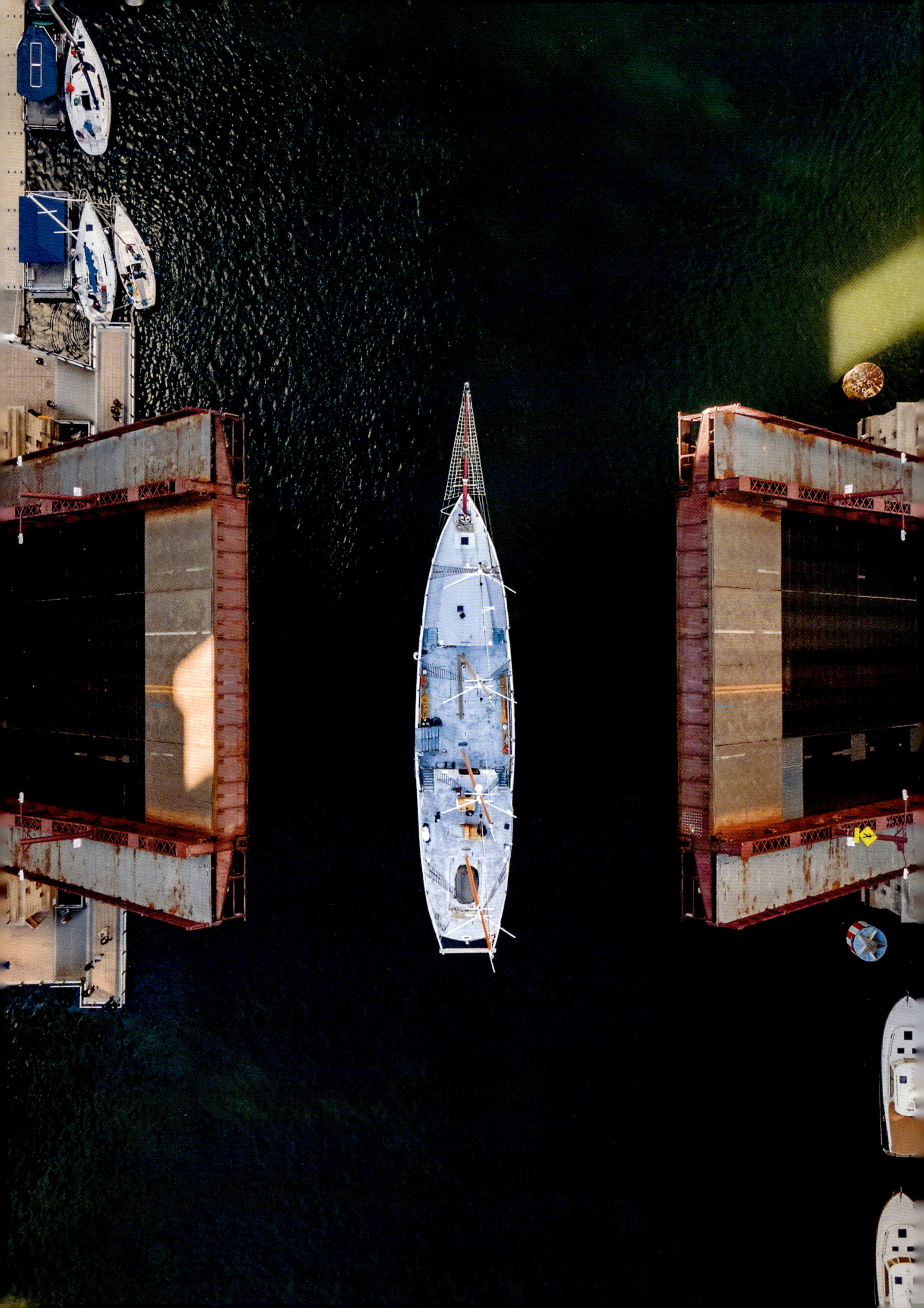

PHOTOGRAPHERS

+ ADAM PEARSON
Born and raised in the Chicago area, Adam Pearson is an aerial and ground photographer capturing all of the beauty Chicagoland has to offer. @a_e_rialp

+ ALBERTO SANTIAGO
Alberto Santiago is a Chicago street photographer and musician who studied at Illinois Institute of Art Chicago. @solaphotos

+ ALEX SHEYN
Alex Sheyn is a designer, illustrator, typographer, and photographer based in San Francisco. @theonlygoodalex

+ COCU LIU
Cocu Liu is an award-winning mobile photographer and product designer based in San Francisco. @cocu_liu

+ DANIEL MORENO
Daniel Moreno is a Chicago-based photographer whose fascination with film and audiovisual media helped him discover his love for photography. @daedmorgon

+ DANIEL SCHINDLER
Daniel Schindler uses his photography to explore Chicago and as a platform to share his passion and knowledge of the city he calls home in a fun and approachable way. @chidrone

+ DAVID SOWA
David Sowa's transition from architectural design to photography has changed his view of the world and taught him to find beauty in everyday life. @david.sowa

+ DOMINIKA BRZYKCY
Dominika Brzykcy is a Chicago-based photographer enthusiastic about showcasing the beauty of the city through her lens. @_b_dominika_

+ JASON LUMSDEN
Jason Lumsden hopes his love for Chicago, as seen through his work, will inspire people to visit the great city he fell in love with as a child. @waywelling

+ KWE BENTUM
Chicago-based Kwe Bentum is a photographer whose style focuses on urban lifestyle and architecture. @quake18

+ LICHAO LIU
Lichao Liu is an architect who views photography as a form of frozen art that turns any fleeting moment into a tangible and lasting memory. @jennylichao

+ MAX LEITNER
Growing up in Germany, Max Leitner developed a love for photography early on which took him across the globe in pursuit of his art and then home again. @maxleitner

+ NICK CRAWFORD
Nick Crawford finds inspiration from peers, contemporary artists, and famed photographers from the past. @nickcrvwford

+ SONJA WEISS
Scientist by day, photographer by night (and weekends), Sonja Weiss started shooting after a move to Chicago from Atlanta. @badluckbae

+ TERRY MADAY
Terry Maday is a Chicago-based global storyteller working as a Director and Director of Photography. @madayproductions

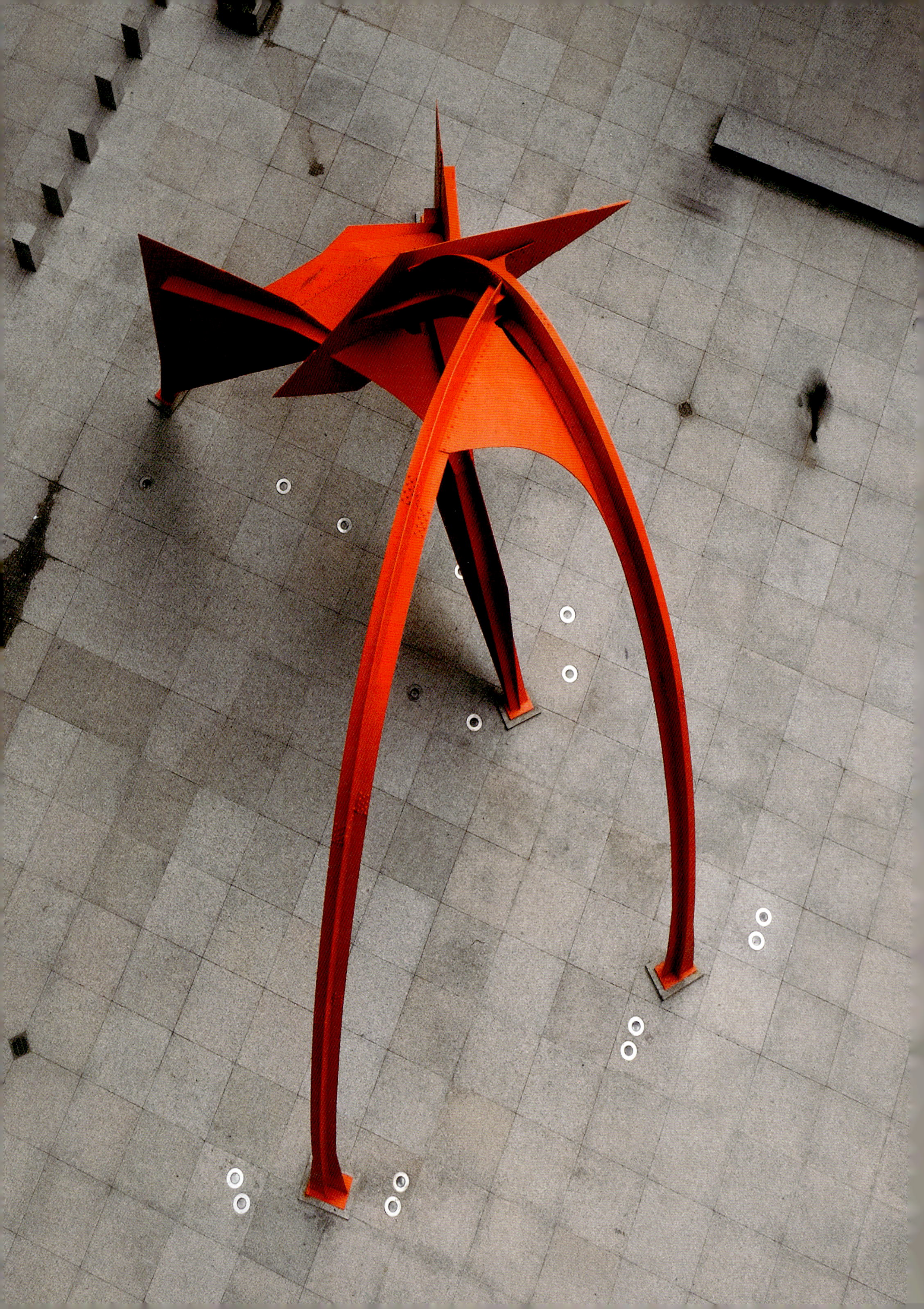

ACKNOWLEDGEMENTS

SPECIAL THANKS

+ We would like to thank all of the photographers who have generously donated their time and allowed us to use their images to create *Above & Across Chicago*.

Additionally, we thank the following individuals who worked tirelessly through the production of *Above & Across Chicago*.

+ ADAM RUBIN

+ JOHN SLIVKA

+ TERRY MADAY

+ KATHY RODERICK

ABOUT THE EDITORS

+ SAM LANDERS
Sam Landers is the Publisher and Editor at Trope Publishing Co. and has edited *Chicago*, *London*, *Hong Kong*, and *Tokyo*, all titles in Trope's City Edition series. Prior to launching Trope, Sam spent over two decades working in digital marketing. An avid photographer, Sam enjoys traveling, always taking his camera and notebook.

+ MICHELLE FITZGERALD
Michelle Fitzgerald is a fierce advocate for books and is passionate about sharing them with the widest audience possible. A veteran of the book publishing industry, she is the Associate Publisher at Trope Publishing Co. and served as editor on *New York*, part of Trope's City Edition series.

LCCN: 2023924401
ISBN: 978-1-951963-23-1

Printed and bound in China
Second printing, 2025

The photographs from *Above & Across Chicago* are available for purchase. For inquiries, email the gallery at info@trope.com

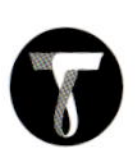

+ **INFORMATION:**
For additional information on our books and prints, visit WWW.TROPE.COM

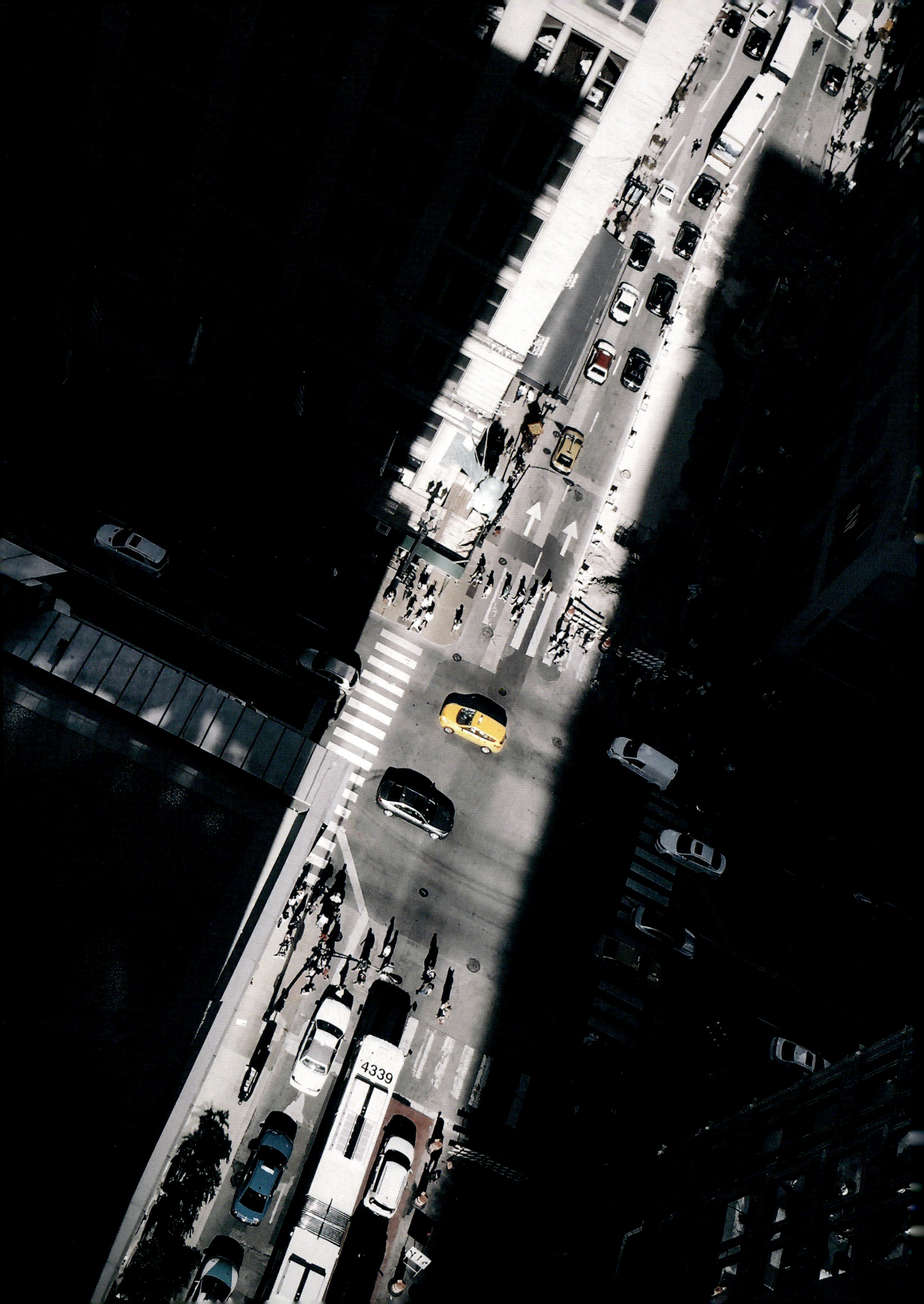